Celebrating 250 Years of Hodges Figgis

shopfront, 56–58 Dawson Street, c. 1990s

Alan Hayes
EDITOR

READING THE FUTURE
New Writing from Ireland

ARLEN
HOUSE

Reading the Future:
New Writing from Ireland

is published on 26 April 2018 by

ARLEN HOUSE
Dublin : Limerick : Syracuse, NY

in association with

HODGES FIGGIS
56–58 Dawson Street
Dublin 2

978–1–85132–201–5, paperback

978–1–85132–200–8, proof (1 January 2018)

Typesetting by Arlen House

back cover image 'The Bookshop' by Aileen Johnston
43cm x 30cm, stitching, 1995
reproduced courtesy of the artist

front cover painting by Pauline Bewick
'Letter to Eckhart Tolle'
44" x 31.5", acrylic and watercolour on handmade paper
reproduced courtesy of the artist
www.paulinebewick.ie

Contents

13

RICHARD MILLIKEN
Bookseller
Grafton St., Dublin.

Richard Milliken, Bookseller, Grafton St, Dublin. This portrait was acquired by the NLI along with an original manuscript deed appointing Richard Milliken as bookseller to the Duke of Clarence, in Ireland and another deed by which the assignees-in-bankruptcy of Andrew Milliken, transferred all the Milliken bookselling interests to John Hodges & George Smith (1844) (NLI)

HOUSE OF COMMONS,

THURSDAY APRIL 11th, 1799.

———•ɵ❀❂❁❀❂•———

REGENCY BILL.

T H E Order for the Houſe going into Committee
on the Regency Bill being read,

Lord CASTLEREAGH roſe. His Lordſhip
ſaid, that when this Bill had been originally pro-
poſed by the Right Hon. Member who introduced
it, he had declared his intention not to oppoſe the
meaſure, provided it ſtrictly followed the prin-
ciple of the Act of Annexation, and if it reme-
died all the evils, which the principles adopted by
the Houſe in 1789 had produced. On the ſe-
cond reading of the Bill he had ſtated ſeveral of
the inconveniencies which aroſe from our preſent
ſituation, which would not only be continued, but

B   increaſed

first page of a pamphlet published by John Milliken in 1799

REPORT

OF TWO

SPEECHES

DELIVERED BY THE

RT. HON. LORD VISCOUNT CASTLEREAGH,

IN THE DEBATE ON THE

REGENCY BILL,

ON APRIL 11th, 1799.

Dublin.

(*Skee*)

PRINTED BY *GRAISBERRY & CAMPBELL,*

FOR J. MILLIKEN, No. 32, GRAFTON-STREET.

1799.

title page of a pamphlet published by John Milliken in 1799

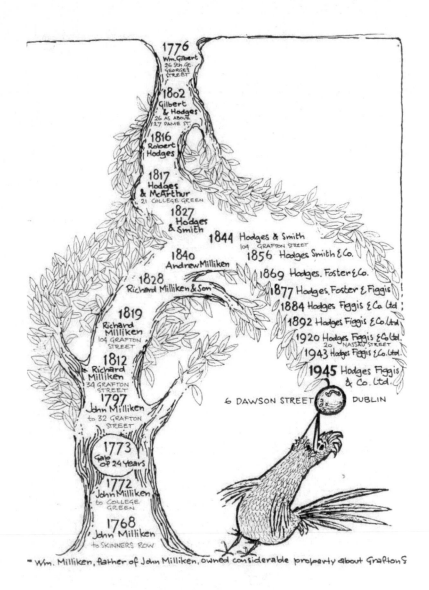

Hodges Figgis family tree, 1768–1945

Hodges Figgis 250
Celebrating and Supporting Irish Writing

Alan Hayes

Early in the summer of 2017 a chance encounter with Gina O'Donnell, manager of Hodges Figgis, resulted in a brainstorming session with Tony Hayes, Liam Donnelly and Sinéad McCorry on how best to commemorate HF's 250th birthday in 2018.

The shop has sold millions of books over the centuries, and promoted and hosted many thousands of Irish writers. Also, for almost 200 years, HF was a very distinguished publisher of books and journals, publishing many Irish literary and cultural writers, and acting as official publisher and bookseller to Trinity College, the Royal Irish Academy, the Royal Society of Antiquaries and the Royal Dublin Society. Indeed, from the 1840s onwards, it made a significant contribution to the emergence and growth of the Irish literary renaissance, and to Irish language publishing.

Therefore the best way to celebrate HF's contribution to Irish life was, I felt, to publish a book of new Irish writing in 2018 – namely *Reading the Future: New Writing from Ireland*. The original intention was to invite 50 writers to contribute from work in progress. However I realised we would need 250 writers in order to represent the widest range of Irish writing. Thus, for the first time ever, fiction, poetry, drama, Irish language, crime, young adult and children's writing are all included together. This anthology contains a representative selection from all of these different forms. I endeavoured to find Irish writers from all corners of the island and from overseas (including the US, UK, Italy and Singapore). The age range stretches from 23 to 93.* All writers included in the anthology have published at least one book, many have published dozens.

Combined, these writers have sold millions of books and have won many awards, including the Oscar, Booker, BAFTA, Kavanagh, Costa and the Dublin Literary Award. While there has long been a debate on the poor representation of women writers in Irish literature, it is a particular pleasure that in this anthology 55% of the contributors are women – the first time this has ever happened in Irish writing.

As no funding was available, it was agreed from the outset that it would be a non-profit project. All the contributors, the editor, the cover artist and HF staff gave of their work, time and skills for free. Hodges Figgis and Waterstones decided that they would donate the profit from sales into a fund to support the literary community. We are setting up a panel of independent judges to decide where this funding will be distributed. Thus this anthology fulfils a dual mission: celebrating an extraordinary anniversary of a much-loved institution, while at the same time generating some much-needed funding for Irish literature.

The initial invites went out on 19 June. Donal Ryan was the first to sign up, and the first submission came from Medbh McGuckian, setting a very high standard that all writers have met. Pauline Bewick offered a stunning new painting for the cover – this was fitting since Pauline first worked with Hodges Figgis in 1956. Many writers had no work in progress available, while many others wanted to be part of the project, but unfortunately it was not possible to accommodate everybody. We are extremely grateful to all the writers and artists who have supported this project.

Literature is widely regarded as Ireland's greatest artform. We have a literary history and reputation that is unparalleled worldwide, and indeed Dublin was only the fourth city in the world to be honoured with the prestigious title of UNESCO City of Literature. To engage with contemporary Irish writing is to realise that Irish writers represent the 'new Ireland' now. In this anthology, I have attempted to publish writing that crosses geographical, religious, sexual, cultural, racial, gender and political borders.

In addition to new work from 250 contemporary writers, we are honoured to publish, for the first time, work from two of the most successful Irish writers ever. Shortly before he died this autumn, J.P. Donleavy offered us a chapter from his final novel, *A Letter Marked Personal*, which The Lilliput Press will publish in 2018. And we present ground-breaking drama from the legendary Maeve Binchy, who addressed the issue of abortion in her Israeli play, *Half-Promised Land*, staged in 1979 by the Abbey Theatre; this play will be published in 2018 by Arlen House.

Interspersed throughout *Reading the Future: New Writing from Ireland* are images from HF publications from the eighteenth to the twentieth century. A short history of Hodges Figgis is given, and the anthology ends with recommended reading by all of our contributors. We hope you read their work and spread the news that Irish writing is undergoing another renaissance.

Dublin,
1 December 2017

* *Contributor Val Mulkerns sadly passed away on 10 March 2018, age 93.*

Many hundreds of people helped to make this book happen, and we thank each and every one of you wholeheartedly.

Tony Hayes, manager of the 250th celebrations at HF

Gina O'Donnell, Liam Donnelly, Sinéad McCorry, Paul McGrath, MaryBrigid Turner, Alyson Wilson and Fiona McCorry at Hodges Figgis and Waterstones

Pauline Bewick

Aileen Johnston

Mary Esther Judy, Charlie Byrne's Bookshop

Antony Farrell, The Lilliput Press and the Donleavy family

Niamh Brennan

Lian Bell, Waking the Feminists

Sinéad Gleeson

Donal Ryan

Martin Dyar

An tOllamh Nollaig Mac Congáil

Phyl Herbert, *former PA to Allen Figgis*

Neville Figgis

Christine Green

David Parsons, Imprint Digital

Arlen House collection

Katherine McSharry, National Library of Ireland

Dean, Laura and Shane at Kennys Bookshop, Galway

Alison Lyons, Margaret Hayes, Jackie Lynam, Dublin UNESCO City of Literature

Jane Alger, former Director, Dublin UNESCO City of Literature

Dr Enda Leaney, Dublin City Library and Archive

104 Grafton Street.

Dublin 5th September, 1918.

Rev.S.J.Brown, S.J.

Dear Sir,

It is with considerable regret that
we have to make a very unfavourable report
as to the sales of your book. All through
the summer we have not received any orders,
nor have we received any further orders
from Messrs. Longman beyond their original
supply as reported to you. We were in
fact intending to write to you to see if
you could suggest any method by which we
could secure a market.

We can only hope that with the Autumn
season a revival may set in.

Yours faithfully,

Hodges Figgis & Co

Hodges, Figgis, & Co., Limited,
104, Grafton Street, Dublin.

READING THE FUTURE
New Writing from Ireland

Chris Agee

AFTER RAINS

A large seed-parachute from a plant's pod
floated up from the night yard
and rose into the door's lampshine
on fresh air's slightest breath
like thistledown in slow motion,
a snow-crystal, or some sea creature
out of the abysmal depths. I knew before I tried

I would never find it.
It was so linty and delicate, so immaterial,
it would vanish as spider's web
on the wet Earth's solidities.
It reminded me instantly of that first May
thistledown after apocalypse.
When I moved forward, it moved off and down

towards the dark beyond the table legs.
When I searched the verandah flagstones, half-lit
in penumbra, it was nowhere
to be found. When I shone a flashlight
close-up on the stone, there was still no trace
of its image, a trout-fly reeled in.
Some low undercurrent

probably took it from my ken.
It felt like a last omen,
approached and touched me,
and returned to the night.

John Banville

CHARACTERS

I shall begin with a couple of quotations. Here are the closing stanzas of Wallace Stevens's great poem, 'Credences of Summer':

> The personae of summer play the characters
> Of an inhuman author, who meditates
> With the gold bugs, in blue meadows, late at night.
> He does not hear his characters talk. He sees
> Them mottled, in the moodiest costumes,
>
> Of blue and yellow, sky and sun, belted
> And knotted, sashed and seamed, half pales of red,
> Half pales of green, appropriate habit for
> The huge decorum, the manner of the time,
> Part of the mottled mood of summer's whole,
>
> In which the characters speak because they want
> To speak, the fat, the roseate characters,
> Free, for a moment, from malice and sudden cry,
> Complete in a completed scene, speaking
> Their parts as in a youthful happiness.

And here, in all modesty, I assure you, is a paragraph from the final pages of my novel *Ghosts*. The narrator has been considering a painting by one Jean Vaublin, an invented artist – invented by me – who is not entirely dissimilar to the great Jean Antoine Watteau:

> What happens does not matter; the moment is all. This is the golden world. The painter has gathered his little group and set them down in this wind-tossed glade, in this delicate, artificial light, and painted them as angels and as clowns. It is a world where nothing is lost, where all is accounted for while yet the mystery of things is preserved; a world where they may live, however briefly, however tenuously, in the failing evening of the self, solitary and at the same time together somehow here in this place, dying as they may be and yet fixed forever in a luminous, unending instant.

Who and what are a novelist's characters? What are they to him, and what are they for him? Or, stepping down from the grand generalities so as to preserve my assumed state of modesty, let me rather ask, who and what are *my* characters, and what are they to *me*, what are they for *me*? I distrust authors who claim that at some point or other in the course of a novel their characters 'developed a life of their own' and 'took over the story'. I always think that such authors are either liars or fools. In the particular lunatic asylum wherein we novelists work, our little manufactured madmen are never allowed to wrest the pen out of our hands and assume command.

However, we keepers of the padded cells are not entirely free, either.

When I was a young man, beginning to publish fiction, I believed that I was wholly in control of what I wrote. To Beckett's famous question, which was famously taken up by Michel Foucault, 'What does it matter who speaks?', the resounding answer for me was, 'It matters everything'. In my novel *Kepler*, for instance, published in 1981, I devised a fiendishly complicated work-scheme, based on Kepler's theory of the five perfect solids – don't worry, I'm not going to attempt to expound that theory here – the characters were forced to move and congregate according to a strict formula of my making. At the time I was much taken with numerology, and tried to follow artists such as Béla Bartok, who frequently composed according to the rule of golden section, and imposed forms on his works that sometimes involved counting the very notes in order to make the parts accord with esoteric rules that were more magical than mathematical.

Then something happened. In the mid-1980s I broke with my own rules of engagement, and began to work in a far more instinctive way than I had heretofore. I am not sure what caused this shift, although I do remember the precise moment when it occurred, or at least I remember the precise moment when I noticed that it had occurred. My parents had died, and I suspect I was in deep, subconscious mourning for them, and in *Mefisto*, the novel I was writing at the time, I arrived at a section in which the narrator, wandering erratically in the wake of Goethe's Faust, paid a visit to a priestess of the Eternal Motherhood. Suddenly I realised that I no longer knew what I was doing. That's to say, I was writing in a new way, unrestricted by any rational plan. Obviously, in describing my narrator's encounter with the strange, unreal, monumental Woman I was in some way writing about my mother, who in death had become strange, and unreal, and monumental. It was a revelatory experience, and after it, I knew, nothing for me – for my writing, I mean – would ever be the same again.

Both Kafka and Beckett had similar experiences – perhaps all artists have such moments of revelation, of clarification. For Kafka, the long night from evening to dawn during which, in a transport of composition, he wrote in its entirety the story 'The Judgement', was the occasion of his coming-of-age as an artist. Beckett's transformative insight, fragmentarily described in *Krapp's Last Tape*, came to him on Dún Laoghaire pier one stormy night at the end of the war – in fact, as Beckett told his biographer James Knowlson, it was not at Dún Laoghaire but in his mother's room that he experienced his 'revelation' – when he at last began 'to write the things I feel'. As against Joyce's method of 'always *adding* … I realised that my own way was in impoverishment, in lack of knowledge and in taking away, in subtracting rather than adding'.

What I had found – again, in my humble fashion – was a new way, for me, of presenting human experience in fictional form. The thing to do, I saw, was to move away from the realism of novels such as *Kepler* and its predecessor, *Doctor Copernicus*, and into a new realm in which I would think less and dream more – I would subtract *and* add – and in which my characters would have at least a certain autonomy.

Yet what does it mean to say that a 'character' will have 'autonomy'? The marionettes who populate my novels are all aspects of me, necessarily, since I am the only raw material that I have, that is, since I am the only human being I know from the inside, as it were – though what 'knowing' means in this context is a knotty philosophical question we shall not try to unravel here. My fictional characters are like the figures I encounter in my dreams, all generated out of my dormant consciousness. They take the forms of others, of loved ones and strangers, friends and relations, objects of desire and harbingers of terror, but in the end they are *me*, the fragments of a self, *my*self, that has been temporarily disassembled by the mysterious agency of sleep.

To write fiction is to be made myriad. There is a theory in physics, the 'many worlds syndrome', which posits that reality is at every instant splitting into billions upon trillions of alternatives of itself, other worlds in which each singular probability becomes a certainty. In our small and all too finite way, we novelists present ourselves with other realities in which to live out other lives. The languishing protagonist of Huysmans' *À rebours* recommended that we should let our servants do the living for us; I can have my characters do that, and much more colourfully.

I recognise the solipsism implicit in my version of what the novelist – Stevens's 'inhuman author' – does. The novel is regarded as the most democratic, the most demotic, of the art forms. Henry James deplored George Eliot's *Middlemarch* for the 'loose, baggy monster' he judged it to be, yet there are many critics, and many readers, who prize the novel form precisely for its accommodating looseness, its glorious bagginess, in which the 'roseate characters' will have room to wander at will.

People insist on believing in the reality of fictional characters. Don Quixote, Emma Bovary, Leopold Bloom can seem more vividly real to us than the person sleeping in bed beside us while we sit turning the pages and biting our nails in suspense as, say, poor Anna Karenina walks towards the railway line. The pact the reader makes with the fictional text is a fascinating one. No matter how hard one presses upon the reader's credulity and willingness to suspend disbelief, the contract holds: Lemuel Gulliver, however improbably pinned to the sand by a multitude of tiny people or quizzed by talking horses, is for us alive in one of the multiple worlds of fiction.

How is this magic trick brought off? By the power of the imagination, working in its dreamlike fashion. The imagination, that 'inhuman author', makes worlds and populates them. It is a kind of transcendent playing. Our little, lifelike figures are made, in Auden's phrase, 'out of Eros and of dust'. Who on earth are they? And are they on earth? They are real, and yet how can they be? But if unreal, what a clamour they make:

... the characters speak because they want
To speak ...

published by Hodges Figgis in 1937

THE
WAY
THAT
I
WENT

R. LL. PRAEGER

Kevin Barry

from AUTUMN ROYAL

[May and Timmy, sister and brother, in their 30s, are living at home still, in Cork city, with their deranged father confined to the bed upstairs. Have they any way out? Have they a future? What can they do to escape?]

May, with a belligerent head on her, takes an 021 area Yellow Pages *from a shopping bag and fucks it across the table towards Timmy. Timmy looks at it, looks worried, and almost collapses into a chair. Timmy stares at the* Yellow Pages *as if it's a loaded gun.*

TIMMY: Are we doin' this so, are we?

She doesn't reply – they exchange a long, worried look. Timmy pulls the phone book towards him with a heavy sighing. Opens it, speaks very quietly.

TIMMY: What do we look under, May?

MAY: 'O,' I'd say, Tim.

TIMMY: 'O?'

MAY: For 'old people farms.'

TIMMY: Hah?

MAY: Fucksake, Timmy, 'N!' For nursin' homes!

TIMMY: Right so.

He flicks through the directory, comes to the right section. Now May looks very anxious as he reads down the page – she lays a hand flat on her belly and tries to take some deep breaths.

TIMMY: There's rakes of 'em.

MAY: Sure this is the whole problem *(She looks darkly upwards)* ... the aul' fuckers aren't dyin' off on us no more.

TIMMY: 'Seaview Lodge' ... Sounds nice enough, don't it?

MAY: Our father isn't gone on the sea, Timmy.

TIMMY: There is that, I suppose. Ever since that day at Myrtleville ...

MAY: Garretstown! ... We'd only be tauntin' him with the sea, Tim.

TIMMY: There's, am ... the Heron's Rest? ... Out near Bandon someplace.

MAY: Timmy, are these nursin' homes or B&Bs?

TIMMY: Nursin' homes! There's St Ita's ... there's the St Philomena ... there's St ...

MAY: Get past the saints.

TIMMY: No saints?

MAY: Saints gimme the gawks. Get past the saints.

TIMMY: There's a place called ... Whispering Groves?

MAY: That sounds, kinda ... lovely.

TIMMY: Don't it?

MAY: I suppose it's by a woods, kinda thing, is it?

TIMMY: I'll check it on Maps.

He fishes out the iPhone and noodles at it. May, meanwhile, goes to a dreamy place.

TIMMY: (*typing*) – 'Whispering ... Groves' ...

MAY: Must be by a woods ... Bluebells, kinda thing ... Little rabbits ... Deers, what's it small deers are called? ... Fawns ... Little fawns ... And the breeze in the leaves ...

TIMMY: It's out by the Ballincollig roundabout.

May sharply comes out of her dream.

MAY: Handy enough, I s'pose.

Timmy continues his search of the Yellow Pages.

TIMMY: There's ... the Winter Roses Retirement Village.

MAY: Sounds gorgeous!

TIMMY: Big display ad and all, watch?

MAY: What's it say 'bout it?

TIMMY: 'Max, 32 residents.'

MAY: Lovely. The place isn't crawlin' with 'em, like.

TIMMY: 'Constant entertainment and activities ... 'Hairdressin' salon' ... Poor man would have no great need at this time of his life ... 'Lounge bar' ...

MAY: Lounge bar? Is this a nursin' home or a knockin' shop?

TIMMY: I'm only sayin' what it's sayin', May ... 'Lounge bar with regular singsongs'.

MAY: Singsongs? Timmy, our poor father have a singin' voice like a tormented crow.

TIMMY: He could say his poem.

MAY: 'A duck walk across a puddle'? Standin' room only, I'd say.

TIMMY: This could be the one though, girl ... Winter Roses ... Lovely, isn't it? ... Roses, like ... Means they're all still bloomin' even though ...

MAY: Yeah but it's a bit, kinda ... Final ... Winter, like ...

TIMMY: I know what you're sayin' ... Winter ... It's kinda sayin', lads, we're in extra time here.

May reaches over and takes the Yellow Pages *and starts to read through it herself.*

MAY: Nursin' homes ... They're not for the old people at all, really.

TIMMY: How'd you mean?

MAY: They're for us.

But now May shrugs – fuck it – and she starts to look down through the list again, and she suddenly brightens.

MAY: What about this one?

TIMMY: Which?

MAY: The Autumn Royal.

At the very mention of the place, there are noises off – ructions and shuffling from upstairs, a sense of noisy consternation.

published by Allen Figgis in 1969

Respectfully dedicated to the part-time soldiers of Ireland, Great Britain, Cuba, France, China . . . and everywhere else, this startling sequence of hilarious happenings could only involve the unpredictable members of the F.C.A., Ireland's volunteer reserve—or could it? Join Patsy Flynn and his friends and find out.

riverrun

Eamon Francis **the**
Ballydoolin
privates

ÚIRT AN MEADON OIĊE, BRYAN MERRYMAN's famous masterpiece, which has been so long inaccessible to the public.

This most readable edition, running to almost 200 pages, has been brought out under the editorship of MR. R. A. FOLEY ("Fiachra Éilgeach"), who has been engaged on the work for many years. It contains the text of the "Midnight Court" (1026 lines) in fine Gaelic type; Life-sketch of the Author; Variant Readings; Notes, Glossary, and full Vocabulary, as well as an exhaustive critical interpretation in English by MR. PIERCE BEAZLEY.

The reading of R.I.A. MS. 23 L 31, made by JOHN MACSHARRY in November, 1792 (twelve years after composition, and some thirteen before MERRYMAN's death), has been adopted as a basis, and collation has been made with the most reliable known texts in National Library, Royal Irish Academy, British Museum, &c., &c. Two shorter poems by the author are also given.

A mass of information concerning MERRYMAN, who died in Limerick, 27th July, 1805, is recorded for the first time, affording details as complete as will probably ever be forthcoming of the career of this very interesting personality.

Price 10s. 6d. net.

Inland Postage 4d.; foreign 6d.

HE POETS OF IRELAND.—This is one of the most important books issued in Dublin for many years. It is a monument to the indomitable patience and research of the Librarian, University College, Dublin, MR. D. J. O'DONOGHUE.

It covers the whole field of Anglo-Irish Literature and Biography. Irish writers of America, Canada, and Australia, no less than those of Ireland and England, are now for the first time fully represented in a Biographical Dictionary.

Altogether nearly five thousand Irish writers are catalogued, and over twenty thousand of their books dealt with.

Royal 8vo, over 500 pages. Price, cloth 21s. net. Half Morocco, with added pages for notes, 27s. 6d. net. Inland Postage 6d. Foreign 1s.

Hodges, Figgis, & Co. have a large stock of books on Ireland, including many that are scarce and out of print.

Eileen Battersby

from HARMONY

More of that flat heat; just humming away, causing his head to throb real bad. Making watery shapes shimmy before his eyes, wavery lines and shadows, tricksy spirals that weren't there at all ... No air, not a breath of it. Arid. No pity for the living or the dead – not that the dead needed it none. His mouth parched and dried out was feeling stuffed full of cotton ticking or just badness ... he feared his throat would seize and if he tried to cough, well who knew what would happen, might choke to death. Pity and sorrow; not a sinner looking for to find him. That thought made him laugh, sudden and harsh ... sounding like a hyena, out there in the empty, wide open.

Most like though there was somebody busy tracking him down ... reading tea leaves, sniffing for clues. Maybe even shouting his name, 'we're coming to git ya,' long and low on the breeze, except there weren't none, no signs – no, not a track. He'd left no traces; was sure not to; smart, real careful like an injun. He'd moved along, over miles and weeks as if the surface underfoot was made of glass. Hitched some rides on supply wagons but not too many, stole a horse from a fool dumb enough to trust him but that ended badly, no denying.

Was he going crazy? Could be he already was certain crazy ... didn't much mind ... nobody's business ... His hide smelling like charred paper; hands already blistered something painful. Born a town boy, the laboring life is hard and mean ... make no mistake. Memories of seeing men spit on their palms ... before bending their backs low, their knees too ... he'd always thought it was some kind of pointless ritual. But the recollecting of it now made him think to try it ... couldn't hurt more than it already did ... but no, his raw, cracked palms were already criss-crossed in blood, dirt and sweat ... with the sun getting hotter, maybe burning a hole in his back, clean through his shirt, sending him straight to Hell ... could the sweaty cloth take fire, whoosh up into flames? Wager he'd find a scorch mark on the middle, running along his spine ... the Lord's image had imprinted itself on a linen back in Bible times, or so the old jackass preacher used to tell the Sunday school class he'd attended as a small boy in knee britches handed down from some boy dead of a fever.

'Your face is as clean as your young soul,' his poor mother often sang out, pleased and right happy, as he set off, if only she knew. Nothing to do with salvation as he hurried along, all eager, seeking only his fill of milk and apple fritter, without having to worry none about arithmetic or trying to spell words that sure looked different from the way they sounded.

Thinking of his Mama watching from Heaven made him uneasy. Could she see how he turned out; what he'd done, all of it? Nothing planned, though; it always seemed to happen without him thinking anything bad, never intended it. He felt maybe that made it not so wrong ... the Devil getcha, but only if you was slow and stupid and too darn lazy to deserve to live.

Pesky fly made him swat blind at it but turned out to be oily sweat bubbling and slipping down his face ... sure hated feeling his hair sorta stuck together, all itchy and disgusting, although he could go days without washing his feet or any other place you'd care to mention. Easy to sleep in your clothes, get used to the familiar but dang it, always wash your hair, clear your head even if bugs were hatching battalions in your armpits. A body could die of thirst; he knew that, lack of water kills you faster than no food, any dunderhead learn that as soon as he could walk.

Only before thirst struck you down, your tongue had to first swell up like a thick snake filling your throat, only you kind of expected to be stuck in the middle of some godforsaken desert, miles of nothing and buzzards circling, not like he was – a couple of hundred yards from a barn where some animal, sounded big, a cow, he guessed, too lucky for him to be another horse, handy and willing. It had to be a skinny old milker; or as like a ram gone loco, rearing to kick his brains sky high, busting to get out and enjoy the merciless brightness of the day's relentless light. Whatever it was – would be welcome to the furnace; he wanted to finish up and find some shade and water, fresh cold water – wherever they kept it, there had to be some. There'd be a well for certain, bucket nearby and not rusty-tasting, waiting to do its job. It only stood to reason; he had to smile at that. His old man prefaced every comment he made – and he made plenty – with a slow and serious: 'Only stood to reason' as if he was laying down some case in the county court of law, hoping to sway the jury with his serious talk. Never lost an argument, his old man, could talk as if he knew what he was yakking on about, making up a bunch of random facts as if the Lord himself come and wrote them down especially for Pa to spew out stern and deliberate, a prophet of old ... Moses returned to lead his people towards the promised land that never was.

Time was passing. No it wasn't – it dragged slow enough to believe that maybe it had stopped altogether. Not an inch of give in the soil harder than mountain rock; probably was rock, genuine granite ... why there weren't even a weed to be seen aside from those yucca things and trees suffering from drought and the mighty effort of standing for no good reason that he could see ... The sun was high now in a sky that seemed more white than blue. Thinking of blue made him stop and peer back down towards the little house, he knew there was something unsettling, bothering him. It had touched some long-dead part of him, a dull hankering. A nicety as Mama would say, smiling her broken-hearted smile. Was his mind playing tricks? Oh yeah, somewhere down there, near the back door, the one he'd come in was a gate, not much of one, made crude with no skill, not like where he'd come from, the simplest wooden objects, finished balanced and crafted, handsome pieces shaped to last. But that mingy little gate, sort of crooked and hanging loose, he'd had to lift it, out here in the middle of no place much. That gate had once been painted the blue you'd find on an infant's rocking cradle. It was faded by the weather, as dried out as pretty much everything else, including him, but blue it had been and painted with a care that near concealed the clumsy handiwork.

Why was he pondering about the color of some fool gate? Mama used to tell him he was sensitive; taking comfort from believing that she'd raised him good. That was then. Now, this was where his running and all the lies and ... rage ... his righteous anger ... had gotten him. He would atone and see the error of his ways. Scalding pain, the salt of his sweat inching across his seared flesh. His shoulders were burning beneath his damp shirt, maybe full of blisters ready to pop, full of puss and blood ... and as he fumbled with his trouser buttons he watched the feeble stream trickling, struggling to begin, barely there ... could be he was too thirsty to even piss. Then concluding with a burst of urine making the red earth appear that bit darker. Wishing for rain, a wild storm to revive his surroundings, he hoisted up the shovel one more time. Nothing, the ground was too hard and his hands pained something awful, his joints all screamed ... enough ... and his aching back about to seize.

Claire-Louise Bennett

WAITING FOR THE DEVIL

I'm waiting for the devil to come and while I am waiting for the devil to come I write down I'm waiting for him to come. I don't know you. You on the bridge. You in the ditch. You reaching into the scribbled branches of a tree. I don't know you. Your back towards me. Your fingers towards me. Your dark looks towards me. I'm waiting for the devil to come and while I wait I write it down you see. On the glass table there is the window so clear and through the window on the glass table I see the trees, the tops of the trees nearest the window, and the tops of the trees nearest the window tip back and forth because of the wind yet when I look at the trees through the window on the glass table it is not the wind that tips them back and forth, it is something beneath the table surging and that sound I hear, that is not the wind, it is the sea or it is lava, or it is a petticoat, or it is my hair. I am waiting for the devil to come and while I sit here and wait still I write down I am waiting – waiting – waiting for the devil to come and all the while the door bangs so hard I think can't anyone hear that, why can't anyone hear that, is it because there isn't anyone here to hear and I am all alone at last? On the table next to me the clouds go by, but are they really, moving so fast, like that, across a glass table – I can't look for very long when they really move so fast and all the while the door slams, back and forth it goes, bringing to mind that pining Frenchman who sprang up from the kitchen table over and over and flung open the front door wide. Surely a gesture repeated cannot he thought go unmet. I don't know you. You with your hat. You with your feet in the dirt and in the stream and going by, up and down, every day all day long. I'm waiting you see. Staying here behind the window, staying here, behind the screen where I can see you, if I want to, where I can hear you, regardless, just as if it were the very first day. You with your shovel and your stones and your hands taking hold of the wheelbarrow and its vortex of thorns. I am waiting for the devil and when the devil comes I'm going to show him everything I've been saving up and I'm going to keep my eyes open tight and I'm going to enjoy myself very much until the walls change colour, until the stream reverses, until the tiny donkeys fall open like knackered pomegranates, until the scudding glass plunges right the way through me, until I have once again been wrenched asunder by the break of day.

Where was the hand today? How was it when it moved?

Not being quite so tender I felt not a thing neither am I one given to reflection so the questions shall not linger, and spared am I from squandering a voluptuous drop.

published by Hodges Figgis in 1956

cover design by Pauline Bewick
edition of 300 copies

Pauline Bewick

Maeve Binchy

from HALF-PROMISED LAND

JILL: Sheila, would you do me a great favour?

SHEILA: Sure.

JILL: Will you come with me to Tel Aviv on Tuesday for the day?

SHEILA: For the day?

JILL: Yes, up on the early bus and back again that night.

SHEILA: Oh Jill, Jill, I'm sorry, I can't really. I mean we promised we'd work here for the whole summer. I can't be asking for days off.

JILL: They won't mind. I'll ask them.

SHEILA: What do you want in Tel Aviv?

JILL: I have to see a doctor.

SHEILA: But what about the man here on the kibbutz, the Scottish doctor?

JILL: Yes, Dr Levy, I've seen him. I need a special doctor in Tel Aviv. You see I have to have an abortion.

SHEILA: (*Shocked*). An abortion. Oh Jill, Jill. No, you don't. Why on earth do you have to have an abortion?

JILL: Because I'm pregnant. It's just been confirmed.

SHEILA: But it's lovely to be pregnant ... you're married ... you can have a baby here. I mean Nicky and Daisy are gorgeous. Wouldn't you love to have another baby like them?

JILL: That's not the point. It's the rule you see.

SHEILA: (*Still stunned*). The rule, that you have to have an abortion?

JILL: No, no, you don't understand. Let me explain. You see. Everyone has two children here, that's the agreement.

SHEILA: Well, one more won't make any difference. This place is built for children.

JILL: (*Gritted teeth*). But two per family.

SHEILA: You can't make me believe that you have to go and have an abortion because of a rule. They're not like that here ...

JILL: Listen.

SHEILA: Are you absolutely certain that that's the rule?

JILL: Yes. There are no misunderstandings ... everything was made clear right from the start. Other places don't have this particular rule. But we do.

SHEILA: Well, I think it's ridiculous.

JILL: But it has to be done. Please believe me, I've been thinking about it since Tuesday. Since Dr Levy's visit. We've arranged a termination for me in Tel Aviv.

SHEILA: But you can't, Jill, you can't get rid of a child. It's destroying it. Jill, it's wrong.

JILL: Sheila, my mind is made up.

SHEILA: Well, what about Johnny?

JILL: Oh, I told him. Last night.

SHEILA: Does he want you to get rid of it? Does he think it's the right thing to do?

JILL: Oh yes. It's the only thing to do.

SHEILA: Well, why doesn't he go with you? I mean it makes more sense. It's his baby. It's his problem as well as yours.

JILL: No, I don't want him to come.

SHEILA: Why not, if you both agree.

JILL: No, he said he would, but I said I wanted to go by myself. You see, it's my fault. I didn't take the pill because it made me fat. And I didn't get anything else. Properly you know.

SHEILA: Yes, yes, I see.

JILL: And, anyway I don't want Johnny to know how ... nervous I am. I was very nervous having Nicky and Daisy, but I didn't let him know.

SHEILA: Jill, they wouldn't expect you to get rid of it. Maybe if you asked?

JILL: No, it's a decision ... it's a group arrangement. I want to be part of that group.

SHEILA: I can't believe all this. Jews don't approve of abortion. Jewish religion doesn't allow you to go around having abortions just like that.

JILL: And I suppose Roman Catholic religion is all in favour of Una as a good little Irish Catholic being screwed silly night and day by Perez?

SHEILA: No, no, of course not, but that's got absolutely nothing to do with it.

JILL Right and Jewish religion has nothing to do with this.

SHEILA: Yes, you're right, of course, it hasn't.

JILL: Look, Sheila, do try to understand a bit.

SHEILA: But that rule, it doesn't respect life. It doesn't take human relationships, people, into consideration ...

JILL: It was a decision made out of consideration for people ... from time to time someone might like a third baby but in this family, our kibbutz family ... we have to have rules.

SHEILA: Well, yes, I know.

JILL: I mean once your baby is born here you never have to worry about whether you can afford him or not, all his food, clothes, education are free for life, or until he's grown up. Nobody abuses this.

SHEILA: Can it be abusing a system to have a baby?

JILL: No, but don't you see, if I were to have this baby, Ruthie or Miriam might say, oh, that's nice for Jill, she doesn't bother to use birth control, she has a third baby, she spends quite a lot of her pregnancy being unable to work as hard as the rest of us. Why her, why not me?

SHEILA: (*Sighing*). I see what you mean.

JILL: But, of course, it's much worse for me.

SHEILA: Why?

JILL: Because ... we're not members yet. We haven't been accepted. If I have the baby, that's handing them a real excuse if they don't want us.

SHEILA: Yes, I see.

JILL: And if I start going around the place talking about how brave I am, then they're going to feel guilty. Do you see how complicated it all is?

SHEILA: Yes, it's an awful situation to be in. No wonder you're upset.

JILL: Sheila, please come with me.

SHEILA: Jill, I'd be useless. I don't know anything about abortions.

JILL: Please.

SHEILA: Look, why don't you ask Ruth.

JILL: No.

SHEILA: Or else one of the women who's already had an abortion to go with you.

JILL: No, no.

SHEILA: They would say all the right things, like it doesn't hurt, and there's nothing to it.

JILL: I don't want anyone else, I want you.

SHEILA: I'm hopeless in a crisis.

JILL: It's not a crisis.

SHEILA: Jill, anyone would be better.

JILL: I don't want any of the *haverim*. I don't want any of them feeling sorry for me when she comes to vote.

SHEILA: Will it be awful?

JILL: I don't think so. I hope not.

SHEILA: Ok.

JILL: You're coming with me?

SHEILA: Yes, yes, I'm coming with you.

[...] The waiting room of a doctor's surgery. There are a few medical type certificates on the wall. Possibly the Red Star of David – the equivalent of the Red Cross for us. Enter DOCTOR with JILL. JILL looks frail and holds her head on one side.

DOCTOR: *Achot, tomri la chavera shaila Ie likeness. B'saida? Nakon?* (*Ok? Right*).

JILL: (*Weakly*). *Ken, ken. B'saida.* (*Yes, yes. I'm ok*).

DOCTOR: You feel fine, do you?

JILL: Yes.

DOCTOR: You can stay here for a while. No one will disturb you for about an hour. It's alright, you can come in now. You can stay with her here for a while.

SHEILA: Is she ... is it over?

DOCTOR: Yes, Yes. You can stay for about an hour. Don't let her get up, tell her to rest for a while.

SHEILA: Is she asleep?

DOCTOR: No, she's just a little weak from the anaesthetic. (*Softening a bit*). No need to look so worried. It's all purely routine. No complications. There's a coffee machine in the corridor ... Ok. (*Exit DOCTOR*).

SHEILA: Thank you. Jill, Jill it's me, Sheila.

JILL: (*Low voice*). Hello Sheila.

SHEILA: Oh Jill, how are you, are you alright?

JILL: Fine.

SHEILA: Was it awful? It's over now anyway.

JILL: Yes.

SHEILA: You look very well, there's a bit of colour coming back to your face.

JILL: Good.

SHEILA: You sound a bit tired. Maybe you shouldn't talk.

JILL: I just feel a bit ... woozy.

SHEILA: Is it sore ... was she nice to you, I mean was she kind to you?

JILL: Yes, very kind.

SHEILA: I would have stayed. I told them when I went in with you that I promised you I'd stay and hold your hand. But they wouldn't let me ...

JILL: I thought you were there behind the chair thing ...

SHEILA: Yes. I was for a bit, and then they said I was to go away. They said you wouldn't notice ... I wanted to stay. I didn't chicken out.

JILL: (*Smiling weakly*). Don't get upset, Sheila. I understand.

SHEILA: (*Moved, goes over closer and holds her hand*). Well maybe it's not such a big thing really to have done. After all if it's all done in a chair, it is less major than an operating table, you know.

JILL: Oh yes, I'm sure you're right. (*She tries to stand up but falls back. SHEILA is alarmed and settles her back into the chair*).

SHEILA: No, she said you had to rest, she said you had to rest for an hour. Jill, don't get up, it might be dangerous. You might start to bleed or something.

JILL: No, no, I have tablets for that.

SHEILA: Jill, please sit down. I've been thinking. I'm going to ring the kibbutz and tell them we're staying here the night.

JILL: (*Weak and distressed*). No please don't.

SHEILA: But you can't go 50 miles on a bumpity bus in your condition. It would be madness.

JILL: Please don't ask them ...

SHEILA: No, I'll tell them. That's what I'll do. I'll wait till the bus has gone and I'll ring and tell them we've missed it. And I'll find us a nice hotel and we'll have a meal. Sure we'll have a great time.

JILL: Well, if you think it's alright.

SHEILA: (*Gets her guide book*). Now, the Tel Aviv Hilton is a bit out of our price range. The Young Men's Christian Association mighn't see us as their kind of people.

JILL: (*Making an effort*). You have a guide book.

SHEILA: Well I thought I'd be doing a bit of sightseeing in Tel Aviv, but ...

JILL: Oh dear, it did turn out a bit differently didn't it ...

SHEILA: (*Pleased to see Jill becoming a bit more alert*). Oh, but think of the wonderful stories I'll have when I get home. For Reverend Mother in particular ...

'Miss O'Connor and how did you enjoy your visit to the Holy Land?'

'Well Reverend Mother it was fine, but tiring'.

'How do you mean tiring, Miss O'Connor?'

'Well Reverend Mother you see Miss Murray and this soldier were at it every afternoon in the bedroom, so I couldn't have my siesta ... and that wasn't only the half of it, Reverend Mother, the soldier didn't know two words of my language ... so I had to keep interpreting for them ...

JILL (*Beginning to laugh almost uncontrollably*): Oh stop, stop ...

SHEILA: Then there was this other friend of mine. A Mrs Kent and you see she had to have an abortion, so I went to Tel Aviv with her, Reverend Mother, and sat through all that very instructive pilgrimage, all right, Reverend Mother ...

JILL'S laughter has now got to fever pitch and has become sobs and tears. SHEILA puts her arms around her and comforts her. JILL is standing in her slip with the blanket on the floor and SHEILA has her arms around her, soothing her like a child.

published by Allen Figgis in 1973
cover painting by Louis LeBrocquy

CARLOS

Francis Tredinnick

Sam Blake

from NO TURNING BACK

The bullet passed her like a clandestine kiss, hot and fleeting, its path seared across her cheek. She heard a dull thud as it embedded in the chest of the man standing behind her; and something hit her cheek; sticky, cloying.

But Anna Lockharte wasn't about to turn around. She was mid-dive, her arm wrapped around her fourteen-year-old niece, their auburn curls mingling as they hit the black and white tiled floor of the Banque Nationale de Paris. Hope was rigid, paralysed by fear; Anna pulled the teenager to her, covering her with her body. Her senses on full alert, heart pounding, every sound, every scent was magnified; the clock ticking on wall, beeswax floor polish and expensive aftershave, the bitter odour of urine.

Garbed completely in black, only his dark eyes visible through his balaclava, the gunman was holding a Heckler & Koch MP5, a weapon that Anna saw every day in the photos she used in her class on political extremism. Photos taken in the Syrian desert, from training camps at Al Farouq near Kandahar, and in Southern Yemen; photos of boys not much older than Hope. Anna could see sweat staining his t-shirt, his knuckles white as he gripped the gun, surveying the banking hall again. He would have exercised this a thousand times, but now adrenaline would be pumping like an electric charge. Making him jumpy, unpredictable.

He sent out another spray of bullets at those who had been standing in the queue, business people and tourists. Old and young. Suits, pencil skirts, stiletto heels, backpacks and Birkenstocks.

Anna moved a hair's breadth, her cheek pressed to the back of Hope's head. The girl was beginning to shake. *Where was Jen?* Moments earlier, Anna, her sister Jennifer, and Hope, had entered the bank to conduct a perfectly normal transaction. *How could something so mundane turn into this?* Anna was over from Dublin for the weekend – it was only May but the sun was hot, creating shadows on the broad pavements between Jen and Hope's home at the US Ambassador's residence on rue du Faubourg Saint-Honoré, and Paris' main shopping areas. The three of them out on the town. Together. Simple. But now, not so.

The next spray of bullets ricocheted off marble pillars, embedded in the dark mahogany of the tellers' counters. A whimper behind them, a half gasp. In the monastic silence of the bank it drew the gunman's attention. Another burst of automatic fire and Anna heard an unearthly bubbling sound and a sob, quickly muffled.

Oh holy God, lecturing at Trinity College wasn't exactly fast paced, and she was getting to an age when she needed a bit of excitement in her life. But this wasn't it.

Where *was* Jennifer? As they'd entered the bank, someone had proudly introduced the Ambassador's wife to her wheelchair-bound mother. Anna had slipped around them urging Hope into the queue before it got any longer.

And then behind them a heavily-accented voice had announced that the Islamic State was all powerful.

Anna moved a fraction, peering through Hope's curls. She could see two of them now, both in black military combats, their weapons trained on the queue of people who had been going about their business on a normal day, but who now lay injured and dying on the floor of one of Paris' central banks. The whole episode had taken less than a few minutes. A few minutes that had lasted a lifetime.

Another round of gunfire. This time aimed at the tellers' counters, the bulletproof spidering under the high velocity automatic fire.

Anna lay still. She knew the men were likely to be on a suicide mission; the most dangerous sort of terrorist. This was the ultimate expression of faith, the men were *šuhadā,* witnesses, martyrs. If they got out they would be back in Algeria within twenty-four hours, if they didn't, seventy-two dark eyed virgins were waiting for them in heaven. Or so they thought.

For the first time in her life Anna wished she knew a bit less about international terrorism, about what drove young men to political extremism. Living her PhD really hadn't been part of the master plan for this trip. For life.

'Play dead,' her words were whispered into Hope's hair, so quietly Anna wondered if she could hear. But Anna felt Hope relax, her breathing slow. Having something to focus on would help get them through this.

If getting through was an option.

Her mouth dry, Anna caught the sound of advancing sirens. The authorities were starting to react. Anna wasn't sure if that was good or bad. A siege couldn't end well – would the men blow themselves up? If they were valuable operatives perhaps they had been instructed to cause maximum damage and get out?

From where she was lying she couldn't see properly if they were bulked out, padded with explosives. Human bombs.

The ornate hand on the huge clock face at the end of the banking hall moved on one more minute.

And suddenly the men were shouting; another hail of bullets sprayed across the hall. Anna lay frozen. The sound of a door banging shut.

And then the dull thud of an explosion. Shockwaves that made the ground they were lying on shake; glass and plaster dust showering over them from the windows facing the street, the sound reverberating inside Anna's head.

And then silence.

Silence that was almost as loud as the echo of automatic gunfire.

Eavan Boland's debut collection published by Figgis in 1967 (rep 1968)

Gerry Boland

from UNLOCKING TIME

'Dad, I don't think …'

I don't get to finish my sentence because just then the terrified stag breaks from the trees to our right and, panting and sweating, stops in front of the jeep. Dad jams on the brakes and we shudder to an abrupt stop. The front bumper is only inches from the stag, who is staring in through the windscreen, his eyes locking with Dad's. The two of them stare at each other like this for what seems like a couple of minutes but which can only be five or six seconds. Dad is muttering under his breath. It's as if he's trying to tell the stag something desperately important.

'It will be alright,' I hear him say. 'Follow us down the hill.'

He puts the jeep into reverse and backs down the track we've just come up. To my amazement, the stag follows. I can see where the bullet has entered and where it's exited. It's a stomach wound, and it looks worse than it probably is. I have a good feeling about this stag. I think it's going to live.

As we descend, Dad's eyes switch constantly from the wing mirrors to the stag and back to the mirrors. The stag is concentrating as if his life depends on it, which I'm guessing it does. He's keeping his eyes on Dad all the time. Dad is leading him out of danger and somehow the stag understands this. We have reached the junction we were at a few minutes ago and Dad is swinging the jeep around so he can continue the descent with the jeep facing forward. There's a few seconds when the jeep is turning that eye contact is broken, and it's during this brief separation that a second shot rings out. The stag's head jolts upwards, his legs buckle and he goes down like a sack of potatoes falling off a trailer. Without thinking about the consequences, Dad turns off the engine, reaches back and grabs his rifle, and clambers out of the jeep.

'Don't leave the jeep!' he shouts in through the open driver's window, then he heads off into the forest.

This is crazy. The poacher must be close by, he's a good shot, and because of the look in his eyes – which I saw and Dad didn't – I am convinced he will shoot Dad if he has to. Dad going after him is madness. There is no way I'm sitting here in the jeep, waiting for the sound of a third shot, and not knowing if Dad has been killed. He's acting as if he's a soldier in the middle of a battle, not someone who spends six days a week running a café and who in his spare time drives into the hills to look for wounded deer.

I get out of the jeep and I shout as loud as I can.

'Dad! Dad! Come back.'

What happens next is hazy. Every time I try to bring my mind back there, it refuses to go, or if it does, my mind arrives back in the forest in the heart of a heavy mist or fog. Yet there was no mist and no fog that morning.

The only clear memory I have of the next hour or two is of a little brown dog appearing from behind a tree. A dog I have seen before, not so long ago, in a place that was both real and unreal. It is nothing short of bizarre to find him here, in the middle of a forest on House Mountain. He is looking straight at me, as he was a few weeks ago. He is giving me a signal to follow him. I don't know how the signal arrives in my brain, but there is no doubt about it: he sends and I receive the signal to follow him.

I should mention that, at the time when I see the dog, I am utterly lost. The forest is enormous and is densely planted. It is a bright morning, but because the trees are planted so close together, very little light gets through to the ground. It's not dark, like night time is dark, but it is very gloomy. And quiet. And lonely. I have no idea where I am when the dog makes his appearance from behind a tree. I've been wandering around aimlessly for what must be an hour, maybe more, constantly calling 'Dad! Dad!' I haven't come upon any tracks or trails. I seem to have wandered into the densest and scariest section of the plantation. I never would have guessed it was this vast. I am worried about Dad, but I am even more worried about my own safety, and whether I will ever find my way out of here. I haven't heard any shots. That's the only good news there is.

I follow the dog. He leads me from one tree to another, stopping often to turn and look at me, before proceeding. There is something very unusual about him. It feels like he is there and he is not there. I know that makes no sense, but that is what is going through my mind as I follow him.

We come upon a well-trodden track. The dog leads me along this track until we reach a fork. This feels familiar. We take the right fork and ten minutes later I see the jeep straight ahead. I immediately start to run towards it, overtaking the dog, who in any case has stopped now that I am back where I belong. I do not see the dog again, because when I go to look for him – after I've looked into the empty jeep, with the keys still in the ignition, and Dad's phone on the dash, and after I've phoned Mum and told her what has happened – he is no longer there. Like Dad, like the poacher, like the stag, who is no longer lying on the ground in front of the jeep in a pool of blood, the dog, too, has vanished.

Twenty minutes later, a jeep comes speeding up the track. It's a mountain ranger jeep, and it's me they are looking for.

'Your mother is on her way,' one of the rangers says to reassure me, but I am beyond reassuring. Dad is missing. There's an evil man out there somewhere and he has a high velocity rifle and he knows how to use it. The dead stag has been removed.

Rosita Boland

THE DAY 'A IS FOR APPLE' PUNCHED ME IN THE EYE

I grew up in a house full of books and newspapers I could not read. Books filled my father's study, they spilled from shelves in bedrooms, they were to be found abandoned all over the house; on the bathroom floor, the living-room rug, the kitchen table. Those were just the books. Each day, we took *The Irish Times* and *The Irish Press*. Each week, we took *The Clare Champion, The Limerick Leader* and, sometimes, *The Kerryman*. On Sundays, we took *The Sunday Press, The Observer* and *The Sunday Times*.

Everyone was an enthralled reader in my house; my parents and three older siblings. I was three, and could not read. I looked at the cartoons in the back of the newspapers, and gingerly picked up the slabs of bound paper that lay around the house and peered inside, mystified. I had no idea what my family saw inside those books.

Sometimes they laughed as they read, although nobody was talking. Sometimes, my siblings were permitted to read at the table, although usually not during dinner. I learned early on that my father in particular greeted the arrival of each newspaper with joy and anticipation, and could not be budged from his armchair until it had been read. There were almost fights over who got to read the paper first. My mother pilfered sheets from whatever newspaper he was reading, and then they swapped over pages when they reached the middle. There were cracks of light under bedroom doors at night as my siblings continued to read, which I saw on visits to the bathroom.

I knew I was missing out on something huge. I had no idea what it was, but I knew I was outside some inaccessible, arcane world. I had my own books, with pictures in them. Some of them had fractured black lines under them, which I did not understand. They were unsatisfying and frustrating, although I didn't have the language then to identify what I felt when I turned their pages.

At three, I went to a little primary school in a hall beside the local Franciscan church. It was for children between three and five, and we were all taught in the same room, at trestle tables organised in a U. Our enlightened teacher had a simple modus operandi. When you learned something, you taught it to another child.

My life became a series of alphabet letters in bold fonts, that I copied over and over again. The book of letters had pictures. 'A is for apple,' the child on my right said, over and over again each morning, pointing at a fairytale-red apple. He could read and write. He was my tutor. He was five at the most, as that was the age we left and went on to Big School. On and on we went through the pages. H is for hat. U is for umbrella. Every time we started, on the 'A is for apple' page, I felt a sensation of vertigo, as if maybe this time, I would understand. That maybe this time, what I now knew was a word, made of letters, under the picture, would unscramble itself and make sense to me. But it never did.

At home, we were members of the local library. My sister chose my books for me; more thin books with pictures. One summer's day, when the heat was making the town's river smell, and the mown grass turn brown, we walked inside the library, which was housed in the front room of an old Georgian house. Through the fanlight over the door, the sun cast shadows like orange segments on the wooden floor. My sister searched through the shelves, and so did I.

I took down a book with a picture on the cover of a boy holding a white mouse in his hand, cranes in the background. It had a few black and white illustrations scattered through the pages inside, but mostly it was a proper storybook full of words, not a picture book.

'*One White Mouse,*' my sister said, reading out the title for me. She looked through it, and put it back on the shelf again. 'You can't read this.'

I took it down again. 'I want it,' I said, stubbornly.

My sister was right. I could not read *One White Mouse.* There were too few pictures to follow the story. I turned the pages at home, over and over again. I wanted to cry. The world was too complicated. I would always be the youngest. I would never know what everyone else knew.

As I turned the pages in resignation, my eye caught on something. Apple. *A is for apple.* The word punched me in the eye. Startled, I turned back to the first page; a whole unbroken page of text. And then, unforgettably, it happened. Word by word, sentence by sentence, the page slowly came into focus, like a puzzle being solved. Magically, thrillingly, heart-stoppingly, the printed words finally revealed themselves.

'Chapter One. Brian took a biscuit and broke it into half a dozen small pieces on his plate. When no one was looking he took one of the smallest pieces and dropped it into his pocket for the mouse ...'

'I can read!' I roared. 'I can read!'

undated newspaper article, c 1980s

TWO HODGES FIGGIS SHOPS ARE LOOKING FOR BUYERS

THE TWO Hodges Figgis bookshops in Dublin are up for sale following the collapse of British parent company Dillons, which is owned by Pentos, now in receivership.

Staff at the shops in Dawson Street and at DCU continued working yesterday as the news came through of the collapse of Pentos with debts of about £50m.

A spokesman for Pentos, Mr Jonathan Benda, said that the receiver was seeking buyers for the three businesses owned by the company, Dillons, Rymans Stationers, and Pentos Office Furniture. The company could be sold as a single entity or as three separate businesses, he said.

It would be "possible" that the Hodges Figgis bookshops could be sold off separately if a buyer came forward who was only interested in the Irish shops, he added. At this point no redundancies were planned or expected, but if a buyer was not found "then it doesn't look so good," he warned.

Pat Boran

On the Ben of Howth

The small stone circle on the Ben of Howth
is the perfect setting for a signal fire
or pagan offering. Half a dozen times of late
I've climbed it with my dog and found a flower,

a neat pyramid of stones, or some such treasure
left there to appease the local gods.
The city down below is a modern elsewhere;
up there the old beliefs live on.

This morning, for example, first of July,
out since early, grateful for our luck,
we reached the high point of our day to find
the charred remains of someone's schoolbooks –

a history primer, an essay on 'liquidity and trade' –
the ashes restless in the breeze, keen to be away.

published by Allen Figgis in 1970

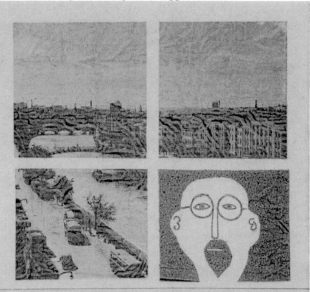

When Myles Keating returns from Oxford to take up a post at the Dublin Institute for Historical Studies, his magnetic, irresponsible personality and his beautiful Polish wife Katherine set up diverse reactions, some disastrous, some richly comic. Jack White analyses them with flair and a ruthless satirical style.

riverrun

Jack White **the devil you know**

Eva Bourke

CATCH OF THE DAY

At nightfall in the calm city the crab fishers bring
their catch, solemnly bedded on ice to the restaurants
where starred cooks with fast practiced hands
wreathe plates with dill and bay leaves as if for a
funeral or a poetry prize. I am told that
if you sit by the water in the old harbour
with the seafarers and exiles from Genoa, Venice
Phoenicia, a sea otter might pay you a visit,
sleek robber, native of distant kelp forests,
slowly padding up the stone steps out of the estuary's
black stinking sludge, his inquisitive
demi-god's face turning to peer in puzzlement
at the alien upper world, where all is air
and movements have little weight, looking as if
he had stepped out of some aquatic fairy tale,
the water rolling off his grey pelt
in silvered drops, his whiskers abristle in the moon light.
If the moon nets him out at sea in its trembling mesh
of beams it will release him with the other
species of misfits, those dreamers who drift in the water
with their hands folded and their eyes on the stars.
He will send them back into the dark depths.
He will move on to find other fish to ensnare.

Conor Bowman

PINBALL PRINCESS

I could never get the hang of pinball when I was a kid. Every time I played, on one of those Jailhouse Rock or Space Ship themed models, in dusty whitewashed games-rooms on French campsites, I got hammered by the technology. My daily allowance, of a franc from my folks, was invariably swallowed in jig time by the mad clunking of the insides of the machine as it refused to disgorge that 'Extra' ball which was always available, but never availed of by me. I tried my best, watching and learning, as boys in bomber jackets with Johnny Hallyday grinning on the back, tilted and tipped their ways to seven figures on the scoreboard while unfiltered Gauloise cigarettes burned brown stains in the glass as they shrunk to fit the inadequate tin ashtray just above the slot which gobbled my daily allowance. I watched and waited and wilted as my turn came around in the lulls between the locals, who would turn their hand to snogging babes to refuel themselves for another crack at the record score.

This was an ethereal number for me, as close to my own experience as a gardening weekend on the moon. It was an oppressive presence, written in chalk on the small square blackboard nailed to the wall above the machine itself. This number was sacred among the pinball fraternity, but of even more significance was the name of the current champion, which rested inside brackets which had been fashioned from Tippex into permanence below the space in which the score resided. In the summer of 1975 I was 10 years old and the top score in the games room at Camping La Madonne was more than a million times my age. The Mediterranean lay only yards away, out the door, left, and down a set of sandy steps to where African men sold handbags and topless women fulfilled the fantasies I might have had if I had been bothered to be bothered about the beach. Instead, I watched the King of Rock and Roll flipper his way to higher scores than his own calorie count underneath the glass-topped electric-powered Valhalla of competition with the laser-gun sound effects and the promise of chalky immortality!

On the day before our holiday ended, the campsite organised a boules tournament. As a result, the games room was deserted. I walked up and down the room rolling my one franc coin in my hand and knew for the first and only time that summer I was somehow in control. I could play, or not, and if I didn't or if I did and I failed again, no one would know. There was no audience, no coterie of Teddy Boys to laugh at me and to turn to their molls to share the joke. I stared Elvis out for a couple of minutes and then fed the electronic beast my last franc.

Ball number one made little enough impression but somehow the next two seemed determined to stay in play and to do the King as much damage as possible. They paraded through the body of the game under the glass as if they were performers who could not countenance retiring to their dressing rooms until the whole world had seen them. My hands were like independent limbs lent to me for a period of minutes while my real hands took a rest. They acted against my will, my command and my better judgment. The flippers flipped and the rubber bands catapulted the miniature steel boules over and across and up and down the empire below the inadequate ashtray. From the relative comfort of the County Jail, the bombardment of the abdomen, legs and guitar of Elvis-Himselvis continued unabated for an eternity of whings, clatters, clunks, zings and whizzes. All the while the meter clicked on and nines became zeroes and numbers began to appear where I had always believed the electronic display ceased to exist.

On and on it went, through an unbelievable and undeserved series of replays, extras, commendations, racing lights and cascading prison uniforms, as the score mounted with the building excitement of the pinball machine itself. Fingertip saves by the flippers transformed the cavalcade of lights around the edge of the playing surface into the changing colours of success as the credits and the balance zoomed up and up and up. When it finally ended I was a sponge of sweat. However, even in my wildest excesses of untrammelled fantastickness and skill, I was still short of the record and wide of the target. My money gone, I turned to leave the games room.

As I retreated, I encountered a girl of about the same age as myself. She spoke in French and began pointing excitedly at the end of the room where the pinball machine was now at rest. Something in her voice and her demeanour made me look back. My score sat across the top of the machine like a headband and, while I initially felt deflated at just missing the record, I suddenly realized that my score was not short of the mark but in fact was better than it by a multiple of almost my own age!

I walked to the blackboard and wiped out the now deposed high score with an insolent movement of the duster which hung beneath it by a string. I wrote down the new score and then erased the name of the defeated champion who had lived inside the brackets for more than a week. I remembered my saviour and then turned to her and through a routine of pointing and explaining told her my name and asked her for hers.

'*Je m'appelle* Colette,' she said.

As the Hells Angels began to return to the games room after the boules tournament, I wrote the girl's name with chalk in the space provided. I left, leaving them to contemplate an impossible future without me.

Niamh Boyce

from HER KIND

Ledrede appeared with a clutch of monks, the hem of his embroidered robe sluiced in muck. When last we'd met, I'd knelt at the foot of his throne and he had seemed as solid and powerful as a statue. Standing outside my cell, he was shorter than I and swamped by his robes. I thought of a servant trying on costumes while his master was away. It was a mistake not to be afraid of the bishop, I reminded myself; he had taken my liberty. He blessed himself and began to recite. *Ave Maria, gratia plena Dominus tecum benedicta tu in mulierbus et benedictus fructus ventris tui* ... It would become his habit not to speak until he had recited a prayer. I didn't know it then, but it was his means of protecting himself, from me – the woman he kept caged, whose skin he would break.

He cleared his throat and took a step forward, gripping the bars. I stared at his white knuckles, the large ring with a purple stone, the fingers as ink stained as my mistress's.

'Where are Kyteler and your daughter? Traitors to God and all holiness, how did they conjure their escape?'

Conjure. If I knew how to conjure, would I be here?

'I don't know where they are. Have mercy on my daughter, Liadan is an innocent girl ...'

The bishop pounded his crosier.

'Innocent? She and your mistress have transformed and fled. A practitioner of evil alchemy cannot be innocent.'

There were easier ways to gain release; for a woman like Alice, everything could be bought. The Bishop must know that, yet he ranted on, insisting there was magick to it. He claimed that I too possessed powers.

'Confess,' he insisted, 'to your magical crimes.'

'I've nothing to confess.'

'The rest of your household had plenty; ignorant heretics that they are. You though, you're more cunning, aren't you?'

What had the women confessed to, what had they said? The bishop left and all followed except one; a monk who tied a sign to the gate. A length of parchment crammed with lines. His hands were big, his fingers thick and chilblained. He worked in haste and avoided my gaze. The paper curled up after he'd left. I wondered what it said. Whatever it declared, it wasn't the truth. 'Let me see the mouth moving from whence the words come.' My voice echoed over my head, I looked up; there were fathoms between me and the roof. 'Who do I speak to, when I talk to myself?' My voice carried upwards, the sound hollowing out.

When it was dark, a figure approached, one of the gaolers. He knelt and without a word, began to push something under the gate. A parcel of some sort. I crept forward and grabbed his wrist, he could've pulled away, but he didn't.

'Please,' I whispered, 'release me, like you did the others.'

'I didn't aid them. I'm locked in too, at least till morning when the constable opens the outer door.'

He nudged the package forward. It was warm, a stone from his fire wrapped in rags. 'Thank you,' I said, but he had already gone.

The wind whistled through the window and soft blasts of snow floated down. It dusted the floor, my shoulders and arms. If the gaoler did not release Liadan and Alice, how did they escape? Stupid with tiredness, I knelt there, crystals melting on my gown. I held the warm stone close; my fingers aching as they thawed. The snow blew in, over and over. I might die a woman of ice, frozen in prayer. Would they call me witch then? Yes, they would call me witch no matter what.

After some time, I heard the gaoler snore, smelt the spice of wood smoke from his fire. What was the noise I had heard last night? A gate opening? The wind? Maybe it was nothing. Yet, at some time during the night my daughter and Alice Kyteler had escaped. I had presumed a simple bribe, the night gaoler turning the key, guiding them through the passage, releasing them into Hightown, but I was wrong.

I imagined my mistress and my daughter in their cell – Alice with her hands clasped, praying. My girl leaning close, her lips in silent movement. As if by unspoken agreement, they begin to softly chant, chant words that are strange yet familiar, as if all the tongues of Hightown – Welsh, Irish, English and French, are mixed together into a gentle gibberish. My girl pulls down her hood, unties her plaits and releases her hair. Alice does the same with hers. Their hair flows down, covering their bodies, darkening their shape. The vision ripples then as if water flows through it. Shards of colour, the blue of Alice's cloak, the red of my daughter's hair, the black of their skirts, rush towards and away from each other. Then it stills, rinses clear, and the cell is dark and empty.

That couldn't be what happened, could it?

Morning came, and women began to bicker nearby. I recognised Cristine, Beatrice, and Esme. I heard Helene too. The voices came from another cell. They fought, tried to make sense, to apportion blame. Often, I heard my name. Then, the noise ceased. I looked up at the high window. No guard. No taunting faces. Snow was still falling. I squinted till the bars looked like distant trees. I thought of the woods of my childhood, and suddenly longed to return there. Skirts rustled, someone let a soft sob, then, one by one, they moved like ghosts past my cell, Helene, Cristine, Beatrice and Esme. Each had a large yellow cross, roughly cut and stitched to their fronts, each looked at the ground. Then they were gone. A gate clanged, a heavy door ground shut. They were gone. I was now the only one of the accused left in Kilkennie gaol. I leaned against the bars. I was imperfect, flawed, but not this thing they keep calling me, not that.

published by Allen Figgis in 1969

Swift's Dublin—and the way it was to develop into the Dublin of Bloomsday—is described in the beautifully illustrated account of the builders, the buildings, and the social life of this 'Augustan Capital of a Gaelic Nation,' the focus of all the vital traditions of Ireland.

riverrun

DUBLIN 1660–1860
MAURICE CRAIG

Maureen Boyle

So Lightly Here

So come, my friends, be not afraid
We are so lightly here
                    – Leonard Cohen

At Kilmainham, Leonard Cohen's
face enlarged on the screen becomes yours
in your thin, aged frailty singing over us
in the pale early summer sky.

Later, I wonder how it was for you that night.
My mother says you spoke of flowers
and stumbled to the bathroom. What is it like
to wake for the last time? Did you know
that your heart was going to stop?

And for days when I'm alone,
I pick up the phone saying 'Daddy'
in all the tones I'll never need again,
as if the redundant word could reach you,
could travel down the dead line.

John Boyne

PORTRAIT OF GINEVRA DE' BENCI
from the painting by Leonardo da Vinci (1474)

The morning after her wedding, she wakes alone with a plan for happiness.

Twenty-four hours earlier, she opened her eyes to find four servant girls standing around the bed, whispering together, tittering like fools. She ordered them to leave but they only laughed, cackling as her fury grew. You are just a maid, the woman who had married her father told her once. And maids have no voice.

But she was no maid, that was the truth of the matter. There was a boy, his name Carlo, who had come and gone from her bedchamber many times and they had lain together like husband and wife. He was beautiful, this boy, with fine dark hair and an expression that suggested intelligence although she knew he had none. His family came from Turin, he told her. His father was a shoemaker, his mother a whore. He had come to Florence to make his fortune. Every night, after their play, she would trace a map of Italy along the contours of his chest, making him sigh at Bologna, gasp at Rome. When her fingers touched Cantanzaro his back would arch and he would turn her over in one quick movement. Afterwards, he would leave, unseen by anyone.

– You will marry Luigi, her father told her. His family have proposed the match and I have agreed to it.

– Luigi. The Niccolini boy, you mean?

– Of course.

– Must I? she asked, although she knew she must for she could have no say over her alliances. Her father returned to his ledgers, dismissed her. Isn't the Niccolini boy a strange one, she thought to herself. There had been talk about him, after all. About his affection for Pietro di Castilleto. The two boys had painted portraits of each other. Nudes. They had presented them, side by side, and the Fiorentini had stared and said nothing; the boys were fine artists, but there was indecency here. The Archbishop visited Niccolini at his palace on the banks of the Arno. Your son, he said. He has the devil in him. He called on di Castilleto at his place of business and spoke of the boy's shame. The paintings were taken away and destroyed, the boys separated, one sent to Venice to marry a cousin, the other allowed to remain, his punishment Ginevra.

– I will be married tomorrow, she told Carlo as he lay beside her that last night. And you can come to me no more. Will you be lonely without me?

– There are others.

– And if I asked you to forsake them?

– He considered it. I would not.

And so she married the Niccolini boy, despite his devil. Her father stood next to her as the vows were exchanged, his mind elsewhere, lost in matters concerning money. The boy, Luigi, turned to examine his bride with a shy expression, hoping for something that would attract him. Other boys had called her a beauty, they had made coarse remarks about horses and she-wolves, rutting and snorting like pigs in the yard when they spoke the name of Ginevra de' Benci. He smiled at her now for politeness's sake and she ignored him, for modesty's. He held her hand as they paraded their disinterest along the nave. It was clammy to the touch. It repulsed her.

In her new chamber the bed was blessed with holy water and a prayer invoked that the union between the two children would be blessed with a third. They found conversation when others were present; alone they fell to silence and consideration of the boys for whom they longed.

She lay in her nightgown, bare beneath it, hoping that Luigi's fingers would find her with Carlo's greedy need but the boy seemed uncertain of what to do. He reached between her legs, found nothing of interest there, and a sound of dismay issued from his throat. He turned from her and said that she was a good wife who pleased him greatly before lying on the stone floor, fully dressed, placing a hand beneath his head as he fell asleep.

He snored loudly. He was only young but he snored like an old man, stuffed full of food and wine. He snored like a tame boar.

She wakes now to an empty room. It is the custom that the bridegroom rises early on this morning and eats with his closest friends. They will fill plates for him for he is sure to be hungry. They will pour wine down his throat for his thirst will be legend. They will make bawdy jokes and talk respectfully of his wife while at the same time speaking of her as if she is a common jezebel.

Her mood of anticipation has turned to disappointment. It is not that she dislikes Luigi – he is too stupid to dislike, after all – but he will never lay with her, she knows that now, and a child will be required, it is the natural way. Niccolini needs an heir and she has been employed for this purpose. Her plan hatches. There is still Carlo, after all. She has exiled him but he may be recalled. Luigi will like the boy, certainly. He might allow him his wife if he can observe the union. Perhaps he will paint him, like he painted Pietro di Castilleto. Carlo would surely disrobe for an easel. He may even permit Luigi to share their bed. She will wait until her husband returns and propose the idea. He will see that it is the only way.

They may be happy yet. They are married now and only sixteen years of age, after all. There is endless time ahead. They must find a way to live together.

She considers it, the scent of juniper drifting into the room from an open window. Her eyes drift, remain unfocussed. Outside, the horses whinny, the dogs in the street approach one another, awaiting the moment when leave might be granted to pounce.

Deirdre Brennan

CUAIRT Ó MHÓRMHÁTHAIR NA CRUINNE

Ní liomsa an lá samhraidh seo.
Tá bagairt i gciúnas critheaglach na n-éan,
cuaifeach gaoithe measc dhuilliúr an labhrais
seachas an monabhar mar a bhíodh,
is gan fiú plimp toirní ar a teacht, airím í
mar shiosamar as raon cloiste sna craobhacha
a mhéadaíonn is a dhianaíonn ina guth ardghlórach
ag caitheamh diabhlaíocht cainte im' threo.

'An carn aoiligh duitse, a iníon ó!
Níl fríd fiúntais fanta ionat domsa.
Nílir uaim a thuilleadh,
tá do phort seinnte; idir chorp
cleití is sciathán táir thart,
scafaí do chraicinn ag titim
mar sheanachearc ag foladh,
gan i do chonablach ach brosna,
díoscadh chnámh do chromáin
chomh meirgeach le guth an traonaigh,
fachailí is fionna ar do shúile agat,
fadharcáin is pachaillí ag bacadradh na gcos,
d'fhuil mhíosta dulta i ndísc le fada,
do bhroinn caite i mias dhríodair
ag an máinlia úd i gCill Chainnigh.
An carn aoiligh duitse, a iníon ó!'

Ise gan chuma gan déanamh,
guth díchollaithe ag tabhairt an tsaic dom,
is mise gan argóint ina coinne
ar chuma péist talún hiopnóisithe
a ardaíonn ón bhfód go gob éin ag damhsa;

samhradh na meala, is droim díbeartha curtha orm
go geimhreadh síoraí, práta seaca
caite ón mbanrach nach ndéanfadh pórú choíche.

first published by Allen Figgis in 1968

Encyclopaedia of Ireland (1968, reprinted 1971, 463pp), editor: Victor
Meally: assistant editors include Eavan Boland, Anthony Glavin and
Eoghan Ó Tuairisc

Olive Broderick

MARK-MAKING
for Sarah Warsop

Dreamer in a black dress: moves among
the book stacks. They are tightly packed
and their blank spines make her seem
trapped within their barricades. She never
even looks to ford the gap – Eve before
the apple – she carries her own core
material: staccato words which she draws
out to complete lines with her body.
Somehow it's the half-light greys that mark
the dance out from the darkness.

This book gives a gripping picture of life in a provincial Asylum, the kind of institution that preceded the mental hospital of today. It is the story of a young woman's courage, fortitude and faith before the most sinister kind of imprisonment.

riverrun

birds' nest
hanna greally soup

Ken Bruen

In the Galway Silence

Jean and Claude Renaud were twins.

Terrible twins.

Truly.

'L'Enfant's terrible.'

Their father was French and the mother from Galway.

On their 18th birthday, they were given matching sports cars. That neither could drive was neither here nor there. The father had made a greedy fortune from one of the first hedge funds in Ireland, and was cute enough to get out before the axe fell, he then invested in property and made more.

Instead of jail, he was made a Freeman of the city.

The twins on the said birthday went on a massive pub crawl.

Ingested

Ecstasy

Speed

Coke

Jack Daniels

And did it bring them any joy?

Nope.

Just added to their sense of entitlement. Barred from the clubs along Quay St, they headed for Spanish Arch, seeking aggravation. Saw a man huddled in a wheelchair, on the edge of the pier. Jean said:

'Let's fuck with the retard.'

Claude shouted:

'Hey spastic.'

Jean came up behind the chair as Claude came from the front. There was a moment of utter quiet then the man lashed out and caught Claude in the groin, then he was out of the chair and hit Jean with the flat of his hand in the throat. Moving quickly, he bundled them forcibly into the chair and secured them with duct tape, he then grabbed Jean's mouth and applied a liberal dose of superglue to his lips, then the same to Claude.

Finally, he took a sign wrapped in cellophane, attached it to the back of the twins, stood back, then with a firm push, sent them into the water.

He waited as the water settled over their frenzied thrashing and satisfied that he could read the sign, he turned on his heel, strolled away.

published by Hodges and Smith, 1848

annala rioghachta eireann.

ANNALS

OF

THE KINGDOM OF IRELAND,

BY THE FOUR MASTERS,

FROM

THE EARLIEST PERIOD TO THE YEAR 1616.

EDITED FROM THE AUTOGRAPH MANUSCRIPT, WITH A TRANSLATION, AND
COPIOUS NOTES,

BY JOHN O'DONOVAN, ESQ., M.R.I.A.,
BARRISTER AT LAW.

" Olim Regibus parebant, nunc per Principes factionibus et studiis trahuntur: nec aliud adversus validissimas gentes pro nobis utilius, quam quod in commune non consulunt. Rarus duabus tribusve civitatibus ad propulsandum commune periculum conventus: ita dum singuli pugnant universi vincuntur."—TACITUS, AGRICOLA, c. 12.

VOL. II.

DUBLIN:
HODGES AND SMITH, GRAFTON-STREET,
BOOKSELLERS TO THE UNIVERSITY.
1848.

published by Allen Figgis in 1970

'There were times when I did not hate my father at all'—
his ambivalent relationship with his father dominates
young John's life. How he comes to terms with it, with
life in a small Irish townland and at boarding school,
is the difficult theme of this strong, compassionate and
perceptive novel.

riverrun

HONOUR THY FATHER

Eamon
McGrath

Declan Burke

from THE BIG KNOCKOVER

Alas! The best laid plans o' mice, men and the serious dramatist *gang aft a-gley*, if we may paraphrase the immortal Burns, and rarely has said philosophical proposition been put so sorely to the test, before passing with flying colours, as when your humble n. came *brum-a-brum-brumming* up Main Street in the nifty two-seater aforementioned only to discover a sizeable crowd gathered before the Blue Parakeet and plumes of smoke issuing thereof, which smoky issue the attentive reader will no doubt suspect is in some way connected with the *far-off boom* and *dull crump* previously advertised in chapter the last.

More pertinently, said attentive reader will no doubt further recall that said Blue Parakeet was the venue to which Twombley Bumppo had recently repaired in the company of RJ 'Lefty' Fotheringay II and his Wilde Bunch in quest of the true and blushful Hippocrene, said blushful H. being not, as might be supposed, Adele Fitzhalligon, aka 'Blavatsky', but, *pace* the immortal Keats, a beaker full of the warm South with beaded bubbles winking at the brim, it being truer to suggest that Adele, being a woman as opposed to a mythical spring on Mount Helicon in Greece, was more akin to blushful Hippolyta, if Hippolyta might be said to blush, Hippolyta being an Amazonian queen allegedly much given to the displaying of bare breast, this despite being in possession of a magic girdle, of which contention, or allegation, your humble n. has no opinion, it being the case, according to legend, that Amazonian warriors bared the right breast in order to free up the right arm for the serious business of javelin-tossing, arrow-pinging and the wreaking of generalised mayhem once the spine had been cracked on war's purple testament (*cf.* the Bard), the rights and wrongs of which we lay aside for the nonce in order to state that any woman regularly engaged in the laying waste of (largely male) opponents on the field of battle is highly unlikely to be so concerned with (largely male) prudish sniffery as to blush.

Thus – i.e., the smoke-issuing Blue Parakeet being the venue previously sketched in as the preferred destination of the Bumppo-Fotheringay II party, with the strong possibility of Adele Fitzhalligon being discovered on the premises – I say, thus we hasten driftingly to the side of Redser McGrew where he stands with hands on hips before the aforementioned sizeable crowd, Redser having recently returned from the low hill o'erlooking the vast plain east-sou'-east of Tropico Springs to take command of the situation in his role as newly-appointed Chief of Police with the Tropico Springs Police Department (TSPD).

There followed a brief hiatus, in which the Blue Parakeet's occasional pianist Dulcie McGonigle insisted in no uncertain terms, but terms that were both certain and piquantly Anglo-Saxon, that Redser McGrew remove his hands from her hips forthwith lest she be obliged to land him a facer, upon which, acknowledging the error, Redser withdrew said offending hands from Dulcie's hips, in the process suggesting that said hips were so shapely as to prove, *pace* the immortal Marlowe, strong enchantments to tice his yielding soul, whereupon Dulcie, being of the opinion that an apology masquerading as a compliment was no apology at all, nor compliment, as far as that goes, which distance may be measured in parasangs, and not least because it placed the blame for Redser's knavery as squarely upon her hips as his offending hands had been, and, further, that the one cancelled out the other – I say, Dulcie found herself with no option but to follow through on her promise and pop Redser a straight right to the old beezer.

There then followed a further hiatus, whilst Redser reeled about somewhat tending to his snoot whilst echoing the imperishable Wilkins Micawber, Esq. in declaring himself the very sport and toy of debasing circumstances, at which point one of the Tropico Springs gendarmes, Ambrose O'Flaherty, stepped in to propose that Redser interview the Blue Parakeet barman with a view to ascertaining the whys and wherefores of said Blue Parakeet finding itself in an advanced state of issuing sufficient smoke such as to cause e'en the least suspicious of onlookers to wonder if perhaps there might not be a fire responsible, and preferably before said apron-wearing worthy expired from old age.

This being sage advice, as is generally offered by gendarmes, Redser now snapped to and commenced the old *pourparlers* with said apron-wearing worthy, having first ascertained that his name was Bob.

'Fine day, Bob,' quoth Redser.

'Not sure I'd agree one hundred per cent with you there, Chief,' quoth Bob. 'The humidity has been playing havoc with my starched shirt-points all afternoon.'

Redser, now realising that he was dealing with a hostile witness, swiftly changed tack.

'I put it to *you*, sir,' quoth he, 'that *you*, in fact, are responsible for the wanton slaughter perpetrated here today.'

'Wasn't me,' quoth Bob.

'No?'

'Not I.'

'Ah.'

'The man you're after,' quoth Bob, 'is about yea high, with a big bushy head of curly red hair.'

'I see.'

'Ran in off the street, he did, and tossed a pineapple into the booth wherein a party of eight was at revels, said party being composed of the notoriously dapper gent RJ 'Lefty' Fotheringay II, if the Wanted posters are any guide, a further trio I assume to be his gang, aka the Wilde Bunch, another guy who signed his checks Twombley Bumppo, and Adele Fitzhalligon from the Blue Cockatoo up the road, who earlier assured Muriel the cigarette girl she was glomming on to the Anglo-Irish aristocrat Sir Archibald l'Estrange-B'stard not for his mazooma, but only for love.'

'I make that a party of seven, Bob. Are you holding out on me?'

'Well, the eighth guy was Sir Archie's gentlemen's gentleman, which is to say a factotum of the lower classes, so I didn't think you'd be interested in him.'

published by Allen Figgis in 1969

Heather
goes
hunting

Anne MacMillan

Paddy Bushe

In a Walled Garden

There are street noises. Church bells overhead
Reassure me. With things as normal as they seem,
I cannot believe what is now being said.

Officials have warned against being misled
Into outdated loyalties, to beware of extreme
Threats in our streets to church bells overhead.

People have disappeared. Officials say they've fled –
Clear evidence of a plot against the regime.
It's hard to believe what I sometimes hear said.

At night I hear sirens fill the air with dread,
Then urgent steps, warnings. Sometimes a scream
Muffled by street noise, church bells overhead.

Outside my wall's barred window, sullen as lead,
The river crawls by, inexorably. Downstream,
The sewers overflow with what's being said.

But here there is calm, order. A wall, a hedge,
Shelter me. In the sunlight, I can sit and dream
Of ordinary street noise, church bells overhead.
I must not begin to believe what's being said.

David Butler

WINTERSCAPE

Raw morning, breath
nebulous. Bray Head
frosted to quartz. High up,
the tiny nib of a jet
inscribes the scoured ozone:
intimations of a homecoming.
It draws the mind back
to the prodigal returns,
the bustle of preparation:
the crib, the pine-scent,
a low sun caught in a hedgerow
white and senescent.
Somewhere, a church-bell.
Somewhere, an ass working
the stiff hinge of its larynx
back-forth, back-forth.

published by Allen Figgis in 1963

poems of Katherine Tynan

Edited with an Introduction by Monk Gibbon

June Caldwell

LETTER TO MY MURDERER

The Irish countryside is dark countryside, potted with grubby fields and grimy ditches, mucky mountains and lonely out-of-the-way places good for trapping animals and smashing up stones. You offered me chips, piping hot, loaded with vinegar. Sleet nicked at the night hairs. With each minute that crawled off away from itself, citron bulbs on the lower decks of retreating city snuffed themselves out.

We always hitched. In the countryside of then this is what you did to get through, to get to anywhere else at all. You wore a council uniform: yellow, orange and black. The ones hedge cutters and odd-job men wear until they're old.

'Seamus,' you said, reaching a warm hand across to the passenger door. 'I can take you ten miles as far as Castledermot if that's any use? Hop in'.

'That's perfect,' I said.

I want you to know you have a nice smile. You smelled homely, of roast chicken. Sandy hair, roughly ruffled. Pale freckled face. Dark green eyes, lit up gentle under the oblong roof light, even after the car door slammed us in.

'Did ye ever feel a night as cold ... as utterly bitter as this?' you said.

'Temperature drops like nothing else as soon as you're out on these roads'.

You'd been paid to remove rubbish from the side of the road, a glut of giant oak trees damaged from falling branches.

'Where exactly are you from?' you asked.

'A few different places. We moved around a lot in the early days. We're in Moone now'.

You are the painter up the road. The postman warbling about scammers opening and stealing bank statements. Oh God, that pink-faced ham slicer in the shop resembles his own produce. The one who always said: 'I bet I can guess what you're going to make for dinner'. You are uncle Mike. The local counsellor. A smart arse Guard.

Sickly smell of tobacco and beeswax. Box of tomatoes on the back seat (weirdest thing to see at midnight). Empty packets of things. Fishing tackle. The awful way you laughed, rasping your hands as you drove.

'Do you go out around Moone at all?' you said.

'Fletchers, sometimes,' I said. 'The karaoke is proper dreadful.'

'Does your boyfriend bring you there?'

'I don't have one.'

'Ah now, that is surprising.'

'Is it? I think it's harder to meet people than most will let on.'

'Does your old man know you take lifts from strangers?'

Dad picked up young girls on the roads all the time, teasing my mother about it. You'd want to have seen the gettup of her, legs longer than a giraffe's. Would you listen to him, would you, ye'd swear he was a swash-buckling Gregory Peck, not a middle-aged man with a wonky knee and only half a head of hair if the sunlight hits a certain way.

'So where were you earlier?' you asked, scanning my knees. 'I suppose you were supping with friends in the city, throwing a bit of fancy swagger ...'

I explained about moving, heading back to Dublin to clean the flat I'd rented with friends.

'It's late,' you said. 'Late to be out on the roads for a girl like you.'

Your breath visible in the chrome dash of mirror.

'You're very good to stop and give me a lift. Really, I can't thank you enough'.

We'd been to at least six bars. The one with the rugger buggers and craft beers off Grafton Street. The tiny 8X8 foot crypt with barrister wigs and stuffed stiff dolls on the lumpy plaster walls. A basement cocktail spot that only served blue drinks. Dark musty old man's bar with more Jack Russell paraphernalia than the cat and dogs' home.

You turned to sigh out the window into a passing slab of black. Small green lights squinched on the dashboard. A single slash on the roof lining opened and closed like a fish mouth spilling threads onto my hair. The moon jittered in her satiny skin. I travelled these roads with my pigtails flapping out the car window on Sunday drives at nine years old. I travelled these roads to teen dances and sleepovers. On a school trip to Kells to the passage tombs of Loughcrew, eight hundred years older than Newgrange. I travelled these roads to be dropped off at friends' houses, to work part-time in a cattery, to claw at independence.

'It's late alright,' I said, 'But there's little choice when the bus sprints off early.'

Thistles scratched the car windows too fast. Electricity wires hammock the dent between the city and here, dancing a dull disco in the gash of things.

'I suppose you think you're the type that's quite clever behind it all,' you said.

'If it's any trouble at all I can get out just about anywhere.'

'Everything's hunky dory with me. And sure, if it's not, what difference does it make now. You're in for the long haul, aren't you, Miss Smarty Pants?'

Asphyxiation is a horrible dance of twitching and spluttering, followed by convulsions and a sluggish coma that's truly shocking when it's happening to you. Even in the closing seconds when the brain is fizzing, popping, fading, I knew not to make sense of it. In between there is of course: vomiting, struggle, scratching, wheeling, rolling, shitting yourself. Finally, there's death, which, ironically, doesn't feel that bad when you give way to it. You just stand with your arms out and take it in, like you do when perched on a cliff-top alone or lean over a motorway bridge with the bare guts just to listen. When shock and disbelief eventually come to pass, there's nothing for it but to stare. Though this delicious despair makes you come in your pants every time.

'You're nothing but a dirty fucking cunt,' you said.

Dreary farms and dead-goose ditches; forests speckled with umbrellas of wych elm and lemony-yellow broom as far as the eye can take in. So many quarries that when it came to a government survey some years ago now: the GPS antenna had to be mounted to the tail end of a bird. There is nowhere more hideously beautiful on the planet. You have a wife and three boys. One of them, Hugh, has a club foot, and you sit up at all hours of the grimy night worrying how he'll be bullied in school.

undated ad, late 1970s

hodges, figgis and Co., Ltd.

BOOKSELLERS TO THE UNIVERSITY.

Agents for the sale of Ordnance Survey Maps.
Large stock of Bartholomew's Maps. Guide Books,
General Literature. ❧ *The Literature of Ireland.*

104 GRAFTON ST., DUBLIN. DESERVES A VISIT FROM THE TOURIST

Books which the traveller in Ireland should certainly possess—

Murray's Handbook to Ireland	0	7	6
Wakeman's Handbook of Irish Antiquities	0	6	0
The Dublin Book of Irish Verse	0	7	6
Coffey's Bronze Age in Ireland	0	6	0
Coffey's New Grange	0	6	0
Scott's The Stones of Bray	0	5	0
Praeger's Flora of the West of Ireland	0	3	6

A few that he should bring home with him—

Robinson's Celtic Illuminative Arts	2	2	0
Brown's Guide to Books on Ireland	0	6	0
Champney's Ecclesiastical Architecture	1	11	6
Joyce's Social History of Ancient Ireland	1	1	0
Walpole's Kingdom of Ireland. 5th ed.	0	5	0

CATALOGUE OF BOOKS ON IRELAND GRATIS.

HODGES, FIGGIS & CO., 104 GRAFTON STREET. DUBLIN.

Undated circular, c 1910

Siobhán Campbell

EVE

The fields and the walls, the walls and the fields
the walk down to the strand following tracks of cows
　　　who know where the stream flows in
　　　　　who drink from the tribute stream.

No-one told you that you are made of this but you know
tuft and hallow, cowpat and thistle, the spiked and the soft,
what gives and what resists, wind-rushed dust fiends
twirled in small tornados, reminders of other powers
unnamed but acknowledged.

　　　　　You are this. If you had to recompose,
these would appear: landline bleached to a westerly sun,
hedges leaning into shadow, the threat
of hawthorn casting a curse for later, shucked peas
in a green popped mouth, stooks of turf footed to dry
so they will burn heat into the winter.

　　　　　And the horses –
fen wide they breed horizon, flattening the walls and the
　　fields.
You, tucked into a ridge, maybe a lazy bed, abandoned in
famine. The horses' arrival; snort-still they halt out of speed,
half-turn, a rearing eye roll, seeing what you cannot,
manes wet, tails high and then the shift –
they decide against all odds to graze, while your heart
stores the flown proofs, the hinge between theirs
and yours. You are not disturbed but date this down
　　　　　as if a new year is not illusion.

Moya Cannon

MAL'TA BOY, 22,000 B.C.

The Palaces of the czars rise up again
newly gilded and painted, along the Neva.

Curled up in a dusty display case
in a dusty corner of their great palace
is the rickle of a small child's bones,
found under a stone slab
by a lake in eastern Siberia.

Half of his skull painted red,
he was buried with his necklet and bracelet,
his arrowheads and swan amulet.

Little nomad, buried as your people
moved on their seasonal rounds, tracking herds
of reindeer and mammoth, flocks of waterbirds,
a slice of your arm bone is pored over
by tribes of scientists in laboratories.

On bright screens,
they unravel the complex
code of your cells,
shoot images around the globe
to track skeins of our human journeys
eastwards and westwards,
across three continents –
footfalls on rock, on snow, on grass
in sandy river fords.

Fallen sparrow,
improbable kinsman,
buried with a baby sibling,
what are the filaments

that join us?
Used you pull flowers
when the snows melted?
Used you run after flapping birds?
Did you die in affliction
or in your sleep?
For how many moons
did your mother weep?

published by Allen Figgis in 1970

The story of the tempestuous Gráinne O'Malley, sixteenth-century sea-captain and rebel leader, and one of the great legendary figures of Ireland's past, eloquently set against the background of political intrigue, feud and counterfeud which led ultimately to the Flight of the Earls.

the
Eleanor Fairburn **white**
seahorse

Ruth Carr

READING THE FUTURE

Once upon a time there was the turning
of pages, in libraries and bookshops where
you could browse through books and take their pulse,

hold in your hands the stilled communication
of someone else's life, not lightly felt.
And then *voilà*, the virtual treasure store –

the cloud's the limit, more and more to scan.
Somehow that physical tie to place and
touch allowed a concentration that was true.

And yes, we still messed up. I don't know how
to save us from ourselves but I know this:
it takes time and experience to read things

deep – but what you reap: distilled thought, tender
brutal words can ignite imagination,
transfigure how you live. Whoever you are,

maintain the right to think, to read and write.
Whatever your lot, practise this human art
and read to your children – promise!

Once upon a time there was the turning of pages ...

Alvy Carragher

POETRY BOOKS AND BAGGAGE ALLOWANCE

I pack with such deliberate care
books, ones I read over and over,
full of poems about death and sadness,
love and the way words don't always fit.

I carry them across continents,
sit them on the shelf,
here in a land full of fans whirring and cicadas,
the air, a smell they're unaccustomed to.

And in a year
will their pages taste of kimchi?
Will they wake one day
with Korean tripping over my beloved English?

The Nation, 14 December 1844

PUBLICATIONS

NOTICE OF REMOVAL.

HODGES AND SMITH,

*Booksellers to the University, and Agents for the Sale of
the Maps of the Ordnance Survey of Ireland,*

RESPECTFULLY inform their Friends and
the Public, that they have removed their Business to
104, GRAFTON-STREET,
OPPOSITE NASSAU-STREET,

having purchased that Establishment and *good will thereof*
from *Mr. Andrew Milliken.* Their arrangements of the
several branches of Professional, Scientific, and General
Literature, having been completed, they are enabled to announce that all the new Publications, HOME and FOREIGN,
can be had at their House immediately after their announcement.

HODGES and SMITH beg to assure the Nobility and Gentry
that they feel under increased obligations to continue that
prompt and careful attention to their commands which had
hitherto secured for them so large a portion of public pa-
tronage.

December 10th, 1844.   m 14

Jan Carson

from AMUSEMENTS

She rests her head against the glass, for balance and support, leaving a second make-up stain just inches from the first. Part of her is stuck to the claw machine now, like fingerprints but less romantic. She doesn't even try to remove it with her tissue. It's just another mark to ignore. She lets her eye fall loose. All she can see is heaped yellow. She doesn't care about any of the marks she's leaving behind.

When they're trying, as they were last night, she often tears at him: letting something in, clawing another thing out. She can't keep her hands from saying how much she wants this. This is the thing which will make them proper, (proper couple, proper family, proper Christmas, as it is in the movies). It never quite catches but they keep trying. The marks remind her how hard they've tried. When she sees them lining down his back she thinks of prisoners crossing the days off their walls. This is not a bad feeling for her. It is similar to the feeling of tiredness after exercise, after putting the effort in. She has put the effort in. She is not the one who wants to stop. She has marks too. They can't be covered with a t-shirt.

The machine clink-clunks into life and the claw slides sideways with greedy intent. It is fashioned from four prongs of cheap chrome, the kind of metal used for clasps on ladies' handbags. It looks vicious. It will not go where she wants it to go. The sticks are overly sensitive in her hands: an eyelash of a nudge translates as ten lurched inches inside the tank. The claw shudders and swings like an Alpine cable car. It stops. It starts. It moves along its tracks with arthritic determination and ploughs into the stuffed creatures, causing the topmost to tumble from its perch.

'Like a burst yoke,' she thinks as she watches the yellow run. Her stomach heaves. She no longer eats eggs. The idea of cooking one disgusts her. Even scrambled she can still see what it could have been and horrors herself on the thought of half-formed wings, of beaks and thready legs sizzling as they hit the frying pan. She hasn't eaten an egg in years. She won't even let his mouth near hers after a cooked breakfast.

Now, there is a hole in the yellow. Behind the yellow there is pink. Her eye catches on it. He sees it too and leans in for a closer look. Pink is not the right way of saying this colour. It is more like peach or pale, mottled cream: the colour of raw sausage. Or flesh.

'What's that?' he asks.

'I don't know,' she says.

She knows exactly what it is.

She can feel the urgent pull of it singing its way up the claw and into the various wires, all through the machine's electrics and down her own arms, into the pit of her belly where she has, for so many years, been waiting to sing. She feels three full months of morning sickness go rising up her throat in one brief swallow. She wonders if the water will come rushing out of her, forming a puddle on the Arcade floor. People will think she's pissed herself. The cleaner will come and mop her waters up as if it is ordinary water or spilt 7UP. They won't understand the miracle of it. How could they?

'Is it a baby?' he asks, and she doesn't even have time to say, 'yes, yes it is. It's the smallest, most unlikely looking baby I've ever seen, but I'm going to have it anyway,' because her thumb has run ahead of her and pushed the red button and the claw is already descending and here comes the baby, dangling for a moment like the Christ child, cloud-suspended in medieval paintings. The claw has it by the waist, its head turned towards the glass so she can see its furious little face, its fists like two curled walnuts, its eyes which are maybe, possibly – she chooses to say definitely –

her father's eyes peering through the glass. Then the baby drops and it is pure luck or some sort of instinct which bids her bend to catch it just before it hits the floor. She holds it in both hands like water cupped from the sink. It is beautiful. It is the luckiest thing she has ever touched.

'We have to put it back,' he says, 'we can't keep it.'

'But it's everything we've ever wanted,' she says.

She is careful to say 'we' and not 'I' though she isn't – in the moment – thinking of anyone but herself and the baby, who she's planning to call Mary, after her just-dead aunt and also the Virgin Mary, because of the association with miracles.

'I do want it,' he says. 'But not like this.'

Eventually he'll come round to the idea of it, she thinks. In the same way he warmed to the wallpaper in the downstairs bathroom. Eventually he'll admit that those blue water eyes are her father's eyes blessing up at them. And he will be happy to say 'yours,' and then, 'ours,' and one day, possibly, 'mine,' which will be the end of everything she wants.

Standing next to her, he thinks, how different it would have been, how much more bearable, if I'd been operating the machine.

'Blinketty, clinketty, beep, beep, beep,' sings the claw machine. This is the first sound the world gives the baby. It is not a particularly pleasant sound, something classical would have been better, but the baby doesn't even cry. It is just relieved to be here in the ordinary air.

High above them the lights flash red, yellow and blue, all the colours of the disco spectrum. Here is the noise of young people living. Here is the glory and all the shame. Any minute now someone will break into song.

Andrea Carter

from LADYBIRD, LADYBIRD

Past the offices he walked, through the stream of crumpled suits, envying their sense of release, the Friday afternoon spring in their step. What Ian felt was the opposite, the dread of what lay ahead. A voice in his head said to run, return to where he had come from and not come back.

He crossed at Earlsfort Terrace and cut through Stephen's Green, the early evening sunshine bleeding through the trees and dappling the grass; a patchwork quilt of people. Every spare metre was occupied: families with children and picnics and push chairs, couples with ice-creams. He walked by the lake, past the bench where he used to read in winter when the Green was quiet, bundled up with coat and scarf and takeaway coffee, watching the ducks fight viciously over the remains of his sandwich. The bench was free, but he didn't feel much like sitting. Not today. Maybe he would again. Maybe things wouldn't be as bad as he expected. Maybe this time he could handle it, do the right thing.

He checked his watch. His train was at seven – two hours to kill.

On Grafton Street, he stopped to listen to a band of buskers belting out a song he didn't recognise. Watching the guitar player jump up and down on his skinny black legs, he envied him his energy, his youth, the optimism in his face, the absolute certainty that stardom awaited just around the corner. He waited until they had finished their song, threw some coins into the open guitar case and walked on, cutting across to Dawson Street.

He made his way to the window of Hodges Figgis, crossing people's paths, provoking irritated looks and sighs. The display seemed comprised entirely of crime fiction and cookbooks; an odd combination, he thought, smiling to himself. He hadn't felt very much like smiling the past week.

His gaze was drawn towards the door. A woman crossed the shop floor, walking towards the shelves on the left. It was, he thought, nineteen years since he had last seen her. But there was no doubt it was her.

He hovered inside the doorway, pretending to look at a display of moleskin notebooks, casting a glance in her direction every few seconds. Her hair was short, still black, cut now in a sharp bob with a straight fringe that stopped an inch above her eyes, and she was wearing some sort of black dress, or a skirt and top, he wasn't sure. He tried to angle himself so that he could get a clearer look at her shape.

As he did, she turned slightly in his direction and he averted his eyes. But not before he caught a glimpse of her face. She looked older, but not significantly; wearing a little make-up, he thought, around her eyes. Her mouth was the way he remembered it, the skin on her neck still white. His breath caught.

A customer walked in front of him, blocking his view. Frustrated, he left the notebook display and walked a little way past where she was standing, stopping at the next shelf. A man in Hawaiian shorts stood between them but far enough back from the bookshelf to leave Ian a clear view. It was odd how seeing her again made him feel. He knew, now that he was mere feet away from her, that he hadn't ever expected to.

She took a book from the shelf, her brow furrowed as she examined the cover; her fingers gripped the edges like a photograph, holding the book with a reverence, a delicacy you never saw anymore. Ian was mesmerised. There was such intimacy in that moment – intimacy *he* was a part of – that when she turned her back to replace the book and take down another, he felt almost hurt.

But then the man in the Hawaiian shorts moved away, and without hesitation Ian crossed the few remaining feet towards her, closing the gap.

He leaned in, his voice low. 'Your glasses are gone.'

She looked at him and for a second he wasn't sure. There was something in her expression that hadn't been there before, something guarded, wary. Her eyes widened and then narrowed. She reached out to touch the bookshelf as if for balance.

'It *is* Eve, isn't it?' he said smiling, although the doubt had vanished as quickly as it had appeared. He knew it was her.

She nodded. 'Yes.'

'I wasn't sure I should speak to you, wasn't sure you'd recognise me without your glasses.'

'I wear contact lenses.'

'You have green eyes.' He gazed at her. They were very green. Liquid green, the pupils a dark brown rather than black. Feline.

She looked away. 'Yes.'

'And you've cut your hair. It suits you. It's kind of ...' he hesitated, searching for the right word. '... funky.'

'Thanks.' She turned her attention towards the shelves again, as if searching for a book, although she still had one in her hand.

There was a short silence. Ian rocked back and forth on his feet. 'You're not going to make this easy for me, are you?'

She turned to face him again, clasping the book she was holding to her chest like some kind of shield. 'What are you doing here?'

'Buying a book.'

She raised an eyebrow.

'Sorry, I'm being facetious. I've been away. I'm just back, well, a week or so.'

'Where have you been?'

He felt his expression soften. 'Uganda. Teaching. Ten years.'

'Oh.'

He looked around him. 'Although I suspect I'm going to be spending a lot of time in here from now on. Or somewhere like this.'

'Why?'

He smiled again. 'Have you never heard that bookshops are full of people who hate their jobs?'

'You hate your job?'

'I do now. First week. I'm teaching the greatest little tribe of over-privileged brats I've ever come across. What the hell happened to this country in the last ten years? When did we start producing such unpleasant kids?'

Eve smiled. It was more of a half-smile; a flicker of amusement that caused her mouth to quiver.

Ian made a face. 'Sorry. You don't have kids, do you?'

The flicker disappeared. She shook her head. 'No.'

She looked down, and then back at the shelf, as if she wanted to return to what she had been doing.

Ian lifted the book he had in his hand – the latest by Jo Nesbo – the first one he had picked up. 'Anyway, I'd better go and pay for this. It was nice to see you.'

'Yes.'

He looked into her eyes again briefly before he turned. 'You don't seem very pleased to see me. I feel a little sad about that.'

She looked away.

Deirdre Cartmill

BLOSSOM

Lying lost and crying
under the apple blossom,
when the wind lifts
and blossoms fall down on me

and I know love as a miracle,
focused in a petal
that zig zags down on the breeze,
is caught in my palm,

skin thin
yet holding infinity.

Eileen Casey

SUBJUNCTIVE

There is no warning, no funeral in my brain.

Morning's mirror unveils my left eye, drenched
in a crimson flood, shaped more exotic bloom
than floating lily.

The doctor calls such sudden detonation
a Subjunctive Haemorrhage
(Sub H in layman's language), citing causes
for such violent explosions as:
Increase in blood pressure, constipation, coughing,
sneezing, lifting heavy objects, advancing age.

This sudden *apparition* – his word –
(I do not claim it has the face of Jesus
or any of the saints)
could surely just as well result from:
Laughter (the belly wobbling kind),
sex (strenuous), dance (hip hop, salsa)
yet, these remain unlisted.
He suggests I wear an eye patch.

No doubt I could. Become
an older New Romantic (my words)
like Boy George or Adam Ant.

Yet, as it fades, lighter shades drop
paler berries into this subjunctive stream;

more silver apples of the moon,
than golden apples of the sun.

Paul Casey

SOMETHING TO GIVE

I'm an unseen red dari seed
an unbroken sunflower seed
around a big healthy heart pumping
vulnerable beats into corrupted atmosphere.

The gold I spin and cast away
the art I build from air,
and a full belly, is hardly privileged –
is it a privilege to eat?

An untouched horse chestnut seed
I hand out leaves in the street, the last
of the year's green before life proclaims its end.
I gift unearthed weeds to well-suited unhappiness

sprinkle wildflower seeds for my mother
into grooves between the edges
where narrow beds keep grass from concrete
where the lawnmower man won't go.

Evenly spread along the haphazard craters
the remnants of thistle and groundsel,
chickweed, ragwort and dock,
I gently cover them over.

'We can't let the place go to the dogs'
the landlady told her, she says, as her left knee,
the one on the polio side, retreats forty-five degrees
backwards, left knuckles whitening over the shillelagh

We'll sort that out mom, have you fed the birds today?
We don't want them gobbling down all tomorrow's colours.

Patrick Chapman

AN ORANGEWOMAN IN NEW YORK
July 12ᵗʰ, 1991

Over café bustelo in a broiling
Village apartment – its fan
immobile, A.C. busted, your

patchouli incense smouldering –
you consider the women
of Little Phnom Penh, whose

autoblindness tried to shut away
the memories of napalm
branded on their wattle walls.
Ophthalmologists had found their eyes
to be in perfect working order yet
the women had en masse

relinquished sight and gone
to live in the OC. Oh well, you think,
at least they said no.

Sarah Clancy

SEDENTERISM

This morning below me as I hang out the laundry a striped Circus big top is hovering and almost extra-terrestrial down on the thinly grassed dunes with their grey sea behind them, yesterday evening the queue was desultory and from the flurry of people I see down there moving it looks like they're about to break camp and get going out on the February roads.

A flock of Brent geese sit between them and the water dreaming of March and of Canada and over at the harbour where the sea is deepest the noise of truck engines straining uphill signals that a ship has come in and unloaded its cargo, any moment now a swarm of merchant seamen will converge on an early house to strut about lightly like mosquitos on water. They'll drink their fill as if looking for ballast as if looking for lifespan but soon they'll be off too leaving nothing behind except a wake of mirror like oil spill and a fair weather yacht, dancing at anchor.

And I hang the stark white sheets on the clothes line where they twist and try to break free of their pegs, and you are remote in the kitchen already writing your coffee is cold beside you and your fingers swoop on the keyboard, expertly typing and like many such nomads who've found themselves washed up on this coastline I think we could perch here without realising we've settled just so long as everything around us keeps moving.

Jane Clarke

ALGEBRA
i.m. Nancy Mackenzie 1934–2017

Algebra's for the young, the pleasure
of searching for answers, values
to balance known with unknowns.

Later, your mind takes you back
through the patchwork you've made
from fragments and scraps –

a baby confined to an iron lung
for months without visitation; a little girl
standing on the quay at Southampton,

a brown leather suitcase by her side;
a woman learning to heal wounds
under matron's critical eye.

What's constant is the unsolvable –

feeling your way through unlit rooms.

Harry Clifton

ANABASIS
Saint-John Perse, Peking 1917

Forbidden to the city, looking out
Beyond Mongolia, lies the hinterland
Of imagination. Watchtower and redoubt,
The lost Qing dynasties, are grass in the wind.
Gone the binary world of time and place,
The Occident, the Orient, interchangeable –
Pieces in a chessgame ... On he plays
With Liang Kichao, with Liu. Already the Stranger

Forms inside him, like a pure idea –
He who writes the book of yellow dust,
Who contemplates the ends of civilisations,
The beginnings ... Of all hours, these the happiest
While the stable-boy from the Legation
Currycombs his desert horse, tamed before the Fall,
And tree frogs, a mosquito off the wall
Perch at his plate, a woman pours green tea

And the epic goes on forming. *Anabase* –
The movement of peoples, after Xenophon,
To and from the ocean ...
                              Here inland
The north-west wind. She lights the Russian stove
In the winter garden, where a lizard plays
At killing insects, and the War goes on.
Liang Kichao has moved. A counter-move
From Liu Tsiang-tsen. Outside, blown sands

Of plague, oblivion, warlords at the gate.
Tomorrow to set up a quarantine.
Tomorrow Li and his hundred concubines
To be sheltered here, in this state within a state,

The diplomatic zone ... Minutiae,
Duties. Let the real thing grow
Inside, where no man sees it. Lei Hi-Gnai
His chessmates call him. Thunder beneath the Snow.

And some day, come the summer, he will go
Behind the veil of time and history
Where the gods lie around, in smashed theogonies
Of stone, to sleep in the ruins of Tao-Yu
And wake to the human caravan setting out
All over again, forever going west –
The wild geese flying, absence of whereabouts,
Mountain cold, a mythic space as vast

As Inner Mongolia, setting itself free.
By the roads of all the earth, the Stranger to his ways ...
The child of an island race, in the Gulf Stream,
Who sees it all already in a dream
(Gone the binary world of time and place).
The horse on the desert route, who scents the sea
And dies inland. The son without a mother
Grown into a man eternally other

Sleeping under the stars, in high Xinchan
Tonight, Beijing in the distance, incoming flights,
Thalassal surge of traffic, avenues of lights ...
Here comes the boy, from the other side of time,
With eggs, a pullet, legends of Verdun,
A child of the future, beating a little stone drum
Below by the river, for the ferry across
From the city forbidden, to Xenophon's wilderness.

Michael Coady

WOMAN AT WEST GATE

When I ask in passing
how are things with her,
a woman by the West Gate
shares with me her world –
night and day minding the man
who was her only love
but has these last
few years forgotten
his own name
and hers.

I struggle to find words
above the traffic. She lets me
off the hook, explaining
she must hurry to get
something for the dinner.
Turning to go on
she leaves me with
a saying she remembers from
old people who've long passed:
Nothing bad but could be worse.

Mary Coll

from EXCESS BAGGAGE

Present day. The bleak area around a departure gate in the furthest reaches of Stanstead Airport.

ALICE: Over for work, were you?

RUTH: Just a quick in and out, well that was the plan anyway.

ALICE: I knew it! I can read people's faces. It's a gift. I took one look at you and I said to myself, she's the professional type. And you're engaged too, I see. That your fella ringing to see if you're alright?

RUTH: A colleague.

ALICE: Here, give us a look at the ring. (*Alice reaches over, grabs Ruth's left hand and lifts it up to within an inch of her face*). Ah, it's lovely!

RUTH: Thank you. (*Obviously uncomfortable and trying to take her hand back, but Alice grabs it again and holds on to it firmly*).

ALICE: Asscher cut, 3.5 carats on 18k white gold with Palladium, excellent clarity too, although there is a very slight inclusion if you look closely, but nothing worth worrying about …

RUTH: Sorry?

ALICE: There at the top right, maybe it's just from this angle, sure the light in here is rubbish anyway.

RUTH: Are you in the trade or something?

ALICE: The trade?

RUTH: Jewellery, do you work in the jewellery business?

ALICE: No pet, I'm just really good on rings. Make sure and get a decent one up front, I always say, but you just can't tell some people, can you? My niece, for instance, it was her wedding I was over for, her first. 18ct … yellow … three stone bar, set with about .33 carats. I took one look at it and thought, Argos! Could have told her there and then what nobody wants to hear, but deep down she already knows. Girls always know, don't we? You have to put a price on yourself, and make it high, but sure she'll work it out eventually.

RUTH: I think there's a bit more to a relationship than a ring.

ALICE: Easy for you to say, with that big rock on your finger! Tell me what she'll do for running away money if she needs it? Where can she go on less than five hundred quid?

RUTH: Well if that's the way she was thinking she wouldn't have married him in the first place, now would she? (*Returning to her paper satisfied that she has concluded this discussion*).

Alice fiddles around with her bags again for a little bit, rearranging them carefully but for no apparent reason.

Gate Announcement: *Attention please, passengers waiting to board FairAir flight 136 for Shannon are advised that this flight will continue to be delayed due to ongoing rotation difficulties. You are requested to please remain at Departure Gate 44C until futher notice.*

ALICE: Look! There she goes, told you so! Gone like a bullet before the riot starts. It'll be every man for himself now, Ruth. Aren't we lucky all the same we teamed up.

RUTH: I'm sure they'll have us on the move in no time.

ALICE: Sagittarius?

RUTH: Pardon?

ALICE: The optimists of the zodiac!

RUTH: Taurus actually …

ALICE: You probably don't think our plane's going to crash either?

RUTH: What?

ALICE: I'm just asking if you think it's going to crash?

RUTH: Of course, I don't think it's going to crash! Are you nervous or something?

ALICE: No, but we'll still pay attention to the safety thingy, won't we? A marriage on the rocks is like losing cabin pressure at 35,000 feet. You'll be rightly Shanghied without an oxygen mask!

RUTH: More people are killed driving their cars than in plane crashes!

ALICE: And more wives are killed by their husbands than passing strangers! All I was saying is that marriage is a big step and a girl needs to be well prepared. Am I right or what?

RUTH: Well I'm sure your niece will be fine. (*Trying to finally conclude the discussion*).

ALICE: Fine? She will in her eye be fine! (*Takes a mobile phone out of her bag and starts searching through the menu options looking for a photograph*). I wouldn't mind but she could have had her pick of fellas, look at her there, isn't she one lovely girl. He looks kind of nice too, I suppose, (*almost in spite of herself*), but then they all look nice in a suit. Never met him before the reception, but I could see it's going to be all about him, loves himself, thinks he's only gorgeous, and so does she, for now, but she'll get tired of that, and then he'll get tired of her. Still, at least she's young, only twenty.

RUTH: That is young.

ALICE: I was two years married at her age.

RUTH: Eighteen? God!

ALICE: I was old enough to know what I wanted.

RUTH: Did it work out?

ALICE: Mostly.

RUTH: You're still together?

ALICE: No, lovey, we're not.

RUTH: Oh, sorry.

ALICE: Nothing to be sorry for, sure you have to keep going, don't you, and I had the little ones to distract me.

RUTH: You've children?

ALICE: My babies! Wait till I show you, you'll be mad about them. (*Taking out a wallet with a picture section and opening it like an accordian for Ruth).* That's Mindy there, and Daisy and Chico, she's their mammy, and that little angel is Smuts, he won best of breed last year, he could go all the way at Crufts, you know.

RUTH: They're poodles?

ALICE: Bichon Friese! (*Clearly offended*).

RUTH: Sorry, it's just that they look a lot like poodles, don't they?

ALICE: How do you mean? (*Turning the photos to different angles and shaking her head as if puzzled, before putting them away again*).

RUTH: Well the little curls, and they're small, and white, and kind of ...

ALICE: Sure that's like saying a Shih Tzu is the same as a Maltese.

RUTH: No, I'd recognise a Shih Tzu, my aunt had one of them. He bit my hand once when I went to rub him, look you can still see the white marks near my knuckle, just there and there. (*Holding her fingers up so that Alice can see*).

ALICE: What did you do to upset him?

RUTH: Upset him! I was just trying to be nice.

ALICE: Well you must have done something because a dog doesn't just bite you all of a sudden for the craic!

RUTH: That's exactly what my aunt said! Accused me of teasing him, so she did. My mother was raging with her, they didn't speak for years after it.

ALICE: Well she knew her own dog didn't she, your aunt.

RUTH: Put me right off them for good anyway.

ALICE: Dogs? Pity that, cause you always know where you stand with a dog.

RUTH: Well I just don't like them as pets! (*Emphatically*).

ALICE: Dogs are family (*putting Ruth firmly in her place*). You'd like one I suppose, a family?

RUTH: One step at a time.

ALICE: You're probably still in with a chance, anyway.

sɣéalaıɣeaċt ċéıtınn.

STORIES

FROM

KEATING'S

HISTORY OF IRELAND

EDITED WITH NOTES AND GLOSSARY

BY

OSBORN BERGIN, Ph.D.

𝔇𝔲𝔟𝔩𝔦𝔫

SCHOOL OF IRISH LEARNING, 122a ST. STEPHEN'S GREEN

HODGES, FIGGIS & Co., LTD., 104 GRAFTON STREET

1912

'The Bookshop' by Aileen Johnston

Evelyn Conlon

from CHALK IN THEIR HANDS

Henri Gaudier and Sophie Suzanne Brzeska met for the first time at the St Genevieve Library in Paris during the early part of 1910. It was the strange meeting of two people with violent temperaments. They had what is called a wide difference in age, although what that adjective means to that noun is a mystery to me. They were utterly unsuited to each other – well that's one way of looking at it. It could also be said that their temperaments were those of people who wanted to do something more with the day than live it, people who had chalk in their hands, endlessly looking for places to make a mark. They were lonely, she a writer he a sculptor, neither yet seen by the public, living in the limbo place of pre-natality. She had written many stories, he had been drawing since he was six years old. Henri was poor, a little ill, and his wish to be an artist consumed him even while asleep. He was afraid too, but didn't know how to be properly fearful so could therefore be wild and excessive.

Miss Brzeska, a Polish woman, fluent in several languages, was working to learn German here in this library. She was highly strung, as they say, which means she had not learned how to fit in with what had happened to her so far. She was widely read and much travelled, if not always in the happiest of circumstances. She had in fact come to Paris to kill herself, having good reason to do so. A daughter among sons given free rein to abuse her at will, she had a mother whom she hated for leaving her unprotected and a father who did not notice, his main interest being in entertaining women; all women, provided they were not his wife or daughter. But Paris had turned out to be a bad choice of place in which to execute herself, she had got wakened up there and even felt the remote sound of happiness.

In Paris in 1910 many things were being discussed, as is the way in cities always. That time a lot was being exhaustively said about the possibilities of dangerous things, how new weapons have a way of needing to be tested, how man cannot be trusted not to push war to further limits, not to devour his young. Also being discussed was how the sea plane could possibly have taken off from water, the new tango dance and neon lights. But mostly in cafés people wondered if Halley's comet meant anything. Henri and Sophie talked about how he might be able to work, about what it was he wanted to do, about where might be the best place to do it, about how Sophie's face became unexpectedly playful, about what her smiles to the Russian meant, about what beauty meant, about Shakespeare's sonnets, about stories, about the shape of their wrists and about visiting Henri's parents in the south of France. And indeed about the possibility of living and working there, where the air and the sun and the colour would be benevolent.

The visit went well enough, considering. The marginal success of it was helped by the fact that Sophie had separate lodgings and did not hear what his parents actually thought. Then, strangely, the landlady arrived at the lodgings just as Henri and she were tracing the bones on their faces. An eviction had to occur because at that time in that place such a tracing was not acceptable. And so it was back to Paris, where they secured lodgings, where Henri drew birds and other things and began to get the proportions of longing, elation, despair and threadlike lines just exactly right. Sophie made sure that they ate in the evenings, which was a help to their health. Henri made sure that they walked the streets and looked at the colour of the sky fanned out over the glorious bricks of the city. He now understood that he needed this noise and this edge of chaos, that although the country and its spaces afforded the perfect symmetry, walking in the fields also dissipated the need for his work, but in the middle of the sweat and occasional filth and history he could be the anarchic soul that he had to be. And could, in the evenings, learn from Sophie's stories of strange survivals, and from her knowledge of other places, Cracow, Philadelphia, New York, and learn too from her how to make a city a village when you were uneasy and a galaxy when you were not.

Henri thought it was now time to go. And time to tell Sophie. And no matter what she said about war and death and destruction and bad dreams he would go. He would answer her with Vorticism, Machinery, Virility, Men. It didn't sound right, coming from him, but it would have to do. In Calais they arrested him for having failed to answer his National Service call.

'But I'm here now.'

'That does not absolve what you have done.'

Henri scaled the wall and got the boat back to Dover. On the next night Sophie and he created their own tableau, with the curtains drawn and the bath on the floor in front of the fire.

More art was made and scattered and given away free. And more joy was had in pieces made perfect. And more rain fell.

'The next time I go I will do it right. The war is expected to last another month at the most. See the headlines.'

'You are only going because you want France again. Wait until the war is over. Look what the poets have said.'

But Henri would sign up this time with no trouble, men were more needed now for the trenches, you could run out of men of a certain age.

Ezra Pound said that if they killed him it would be the worst they would have done. Sophie scoffed that that was likely to keep him safe.

In the muck and blood Henri found wood or metal bits

from which to file things. Those things are in the ground maybe.

Dearest Love,
Mamuskin, I cannot tell you what horror this is, you were right. But send me letters and I will learn them by heart and I sometimes get things carved, and once in a blue moon I feel something soaring in my chest and I try to remember it for as long as possible.

Dearest Henri, here are the pieces that I cut out of the paper. And I will answer you properly about getting married when you are before me, where I can put my hands on you.

The noise of the shot woke Sophie, the pain went right through her, that's the way it happens they say. Over and over again that's the way it happens.

Sophie walked the streets. The rain poured on her. She walked more. She was seen pulling hair out. She cried out in the rain. She spun into a loud scream. People stayed away from her. There was no need to go to her, Henri was dead. But Horace came.

'You know that we are not brother and sister.'

'Of course.'

He even laughed and Sophie smiled.

'What will you do now?' he asked.

'I will find as much of his work as I can, I will round it up and beg it back so that it will be there in the future. And I will stay alive until I have that done.'

You may wonder how I know these things. I am the person who left her papers with Cambridge Library. I left them in a brown box, it was all I could find at the time. The top page has a footmark on it, the accidental trod of a shoe I suppose. I think it might be Henri's.

Stephanie Conn

ECTOPIC BEAT

Meet me on the beach at midnight.
I'll bring a bottle of red, a chequered blanket.
You bring yourself, and if you don't mind,
wear a suit but please keep the collar buttoned.

I've checked the forecast; the sky will be clear,
the stars bright, a gibbous moon will light
your path across the dunes. When you greet me,
let me graze your bottom lip with my thumb.

Let me slip my hand inside your jacket,
press my palm against your chest, feel
the cotton's warmth, the pocket stitched
in place, its gentle rise and fall, quickening.

I'd like to offer up my skin to your fingertips;
I'm told it's soft as feathers, smooth as amber –
but I will layer it, though the night's heat
is sticky and tight around my throat.

Let me hold your hand, interlace my fingers with yours,
remember touch, its electric current licking at my ribs.
Let me hold your gaze. See in my damp eyes
all that the mainland keeps silent.

Know this, below these linen folds
I am stripped bare – naked in the moonlight,
nipples erect, despite the record temperatures,
longing to cool themselves in your mouth.

Enough. There is nothing I can offer –
but I will hold you long after tonight,
the memory of the moon turning the sea luminous
branded on my thumping heart, making my pulse irregular.

John Connolly

from THE WOMAN IN THE WOODS

Louis sat by Angel's bedside. Some colour had returned to
his partner's cheeks, or perhaps this was simply wishful
thinking on the part of Louis: Angel was still pumped full
of the kind of medication that left the world a blur, and
made arduous all but the simplest and shortest of
conversations. Now Angel was sleeping while darkness
laid claim to the world beyond his window.

Two hours went by, during which Louis read. Reading
was not an occupation that had previously consumed
much of his time, but here, in this hospital room, he had
begun to find in books both an escape from his cares and a
source of solace when their avoidance proved impossible.
Uncertain where to start, he'd discovered on the internet a
number of lists of the hundred greatest novels ever
written, which he combined to create his own guide. So
far, in the course of Angel's illness, Louis had read *The Call
of the Wild*, *Lord of the Flies*, and *Invisible Man* – both the
Ellison and Wells titles, due to a mix-up at the bookstore,
but Louis didn't mind as both had been interesting in their
different ways. He was currently on *The Wind in the
Willows*, the inclusion of which initially appeared to
represent some form of cataloging error, but it had grown
pleasantly strange as his explorations of it progressed.

'Why are you still here?' asked a voice from the bed.

'I'm trying to finish a chapter.'

Angel sounded hoarse. Louis put down the novel, and
fetched the no-spill water cup with its flexible straw. He
held it until Angel waved a hand to signal he was done.
Angel's eyes seemed clearer than they had been since
before the operation, like those of a man who has just
woken after an undisturbed rest.

'What are you reading now?' Angel asked.

'*The Wind in the Willows*.'

'Isn't that for kids?'

'Maybe. Who cares?'

'What are you planning to read next?'

Louis reached for his coat and removed a folded sheet of paper. He examined the contents of the list.

'I might try something older. You ever read Dickens?'

'Yeah, I read Dickens.'

'Which one?'

'All of them.'

'Seriously? I never knew that about you.'

'I read a lot when I was younger, and when I was in jail. Big books. I even read *Ulysses*.'

'Nobody's read *Ulysses*, or nobody we know.'

'I have.'

'Did you understand it?'

'I don't think so. Finished it though, which counts for something.'

'You still read now. You always got a book by the bed.'

'I don't read like I used to. Not like that.'

'You ought to start again.' Louis waved his papers. 'I got a list you can use.'

'*The Wind in the Willows*, huh?'

'That's right.'

'So read me something from it.'

'You mean out loud?'

'You think I'm psychic, or I'm gonna guess the words?'

Louis glanced at the half-open door. He had never read aloud to anyone in his life, nor had he been read aloud to. He could recall his mother singing to him as a child, but never reading, or not unless it was from the bible. He thought of Angel's bodyguards. Their shifts had crossed just as Louis arrived, and he had instructed them to go eat.

He didn't want them to return and find him voicing toads and weasels.

'You too embarrassed to read to me?' asked Angel. 'If I die, you'll be –'

'Ok!' said Louis. 'Man, not the dying again. You want me to go back to the beginning?'

'No, just from wherever you're at.'

With one final check of the door, Louis began.

'The line of the horizon was clear and hard against the sky,' he read, *'and in one particular quarter it showed black against a silvery climbing phosphorescence that grew and grew. At last, over the rim of the waiting earth the moon lifted with slow majesty till it swung clear of the horizon and rode off, free of moorings; and once more they began to see surfaces – meadows wide-spread, and quiet gardens, and the river itself from bank to bank, all softly disclosed, all washed clean of mystery and terror, all radiant again as by day, but with a difference that was tremendous. Their old haunts greeted them again in other raiment, as if they had slipped away and put on this pure new apparel and come quietly back, smiling as they shyly waited to see if they would be recognized again under it ...'*

All was dark now.

Angel was once again asleep. Louis stopped reading.

'That,' said Tony Fulci, from his seat on the floor, 'was fucking beautiful.'

Beside him, his brother Paulie – fellow bodyguard and now, it appeared, literary critic – nodded in agreement.

'Yeah, fucking beautiful.'

Louis sighed, and prayed for patience.

Gavin Corbett

WATER AND ELECTRICITY

'Mrs Finan,' said the man in the suit at the door. 'My name is Paul Wilders. I'm the chief executive of Slee Electrics. Ararat Showers is part of our family of companies. I wanted to come here to you, in person, to say how sorry I am, and we are, for what happened to your husband, Donald.'

There was a young woman with him. Mrs Finan looked past them, at the toile curtains of the house across the street. Then she looked at the Mercedes double-parked at next door's house. The driver was on his phone.

'Would you like to come in?' she said.

The front door opened straight into the living room. A neat little stairs led away at one end, and a leather two-seater was tucked into the eaves-like space underneath.

'Open plan,' said the man. He was huge.

Mrs Finan invited him and the woman to take the two-seater, while she sat in a matching armchair by the window that looked to the street. 'Are you American?' she asked.

'No, Mrs Finan. I'm Dutch.'

'From Holland. Did you only just come over?'

'Did I only …?'

'Just come over?'

'We flew over last night,' said the woman. 'From Stuttgart. We're staying at the Marker Hotel, in Misery Hill.'

'In where?'

'Yes,' said the man, him and the woman laughing.

'Is she from Holland?' said Mrs Finan, indicating the woman.

The man turned to his companion.

'This is Annabel, my assistant.'

'I'm from Australia,' said the woman.

'I've many cousins in Australia,' said Mrs Finan. 'Most of them live in Sydney, although some of them moved to Western Australia. Where are you from?'

'I'm from close enough to Brisbane,' said the woman.

'You're very beautiful,' said Mrs Finan.

The man turned to the woman again.

'You have Malaysian ancestry, don't you, Annabel?'

'Yes, my mother is Malaysian.'

A fly had got into the house from the open door. It embarrassed Mrs Finan.

'Now,' she said, pushing herself to her feet. 'Would you like tea or coffee?'

'Coffee, please,' both the man and the woman said.

'Oh, do you know,' said Mrs Finan, pausing now before the step into the kitchen. 'I'm just after remembering, the jar is empty. I meant to get coffee this morning. Will you have tea, so?'

They looked at one another.

'Tea, yah, fine,' said the man, the woman smiling beautifully back at him.

'Milk?'

'Ahm, no milk for me, please, Mrs Finan.'

'I'll have milk, please,' said the woman.

'Good girl.'

'I spent six years in England.'

'I'd the kettle just boiled before you came in anyhow,' said Mrs Finan, disappearing into the kitchen.

'What brand of kettle is it?' said the man, raising his voice and directing it into the kitchen.

There was no answer.

Mrs Finan came out some moments later with a tray of mugs. She gave the woman the tall mug of thin porcelain that widened at the top like a daffodil. She gave the man the mug shaped like a massive block of Cadbury's chocolate. Four of his fingers fit inside the handle and it looked like he was punching the mug with a fist.

'Did you get the name of the kettle?' he said.

'The kettle?'

'The brand name.'

'Oh. No.'

'Oh,' he said, smiling, his eyes dropping shyly, like a priest's. 'Never mind. I'm always looking out to see if such and such is made by one of our companies.'

They sat sipping their tea.

Mrs Finan realised she'd been rude by leaving the TV on. She'd turned the volume down so low when she'd heard the doorbell that she hadn't really noticed that it was still on. She'd been watching *Loose Women*, which she thought was a desperate programme. She turned the TV off.

'So do you know Donal?' she said.

'Do I know … "Donal", you say?' said the man.

'Yes. Donal.'

'The D is silent? It's pronounced this way?'

'No. The D isn't silent. "Duh." "Duh." Donal.'

'The second D, I mean.'

'There's no second D. Did you ever know Donal?'

'No, Mrs Finan. I never knew him.'

The woman adjusted something at the hem of her skirt. Her skirt was made of black leather, the same as the two-seater.

'He's up there now,' said Mrs Finan.

She was pointing to the stairs.

The eyes of both the man and the woman panned to their right, towards the stairs. The woman shifted her bum, making a creaking sound.

'Mrs Finan,' said the man, setting his mug down on the arm of the two-seater. 'Do you accept our apologies for what happened?'

He seemed terribly shy for such a big man. His cheeks burned up to a rhubarb and custard complexion. He'd cut himself that morning with a razor, all over his neck.

'Who did you say you were again?' said Mrs Finan.

'Paul Wilders. I'm the CEO of Slee Electrics. I've come all the way from Stuttgart, Germany, where we're headquartered, to say sorry to you on behalf of Slee, because Ararat Showers is one of our companies.'

'Ararat Showers,' repeated Mrs Finan, evenly.

'It was an Ararat power shower that was responsible for the death of your husband, Mrs Finan. You'll be getting the money soon? From the class action?'

'Yes,' she said.

'So we're sorry. Beyond words. For what happened.'

'Of course.'

'Truly,' said the young woman.

The man looked sharply at her.

Mrs Finan looked at the blank TV screen.

Beyond words.

'Mrs Finan?'

'Yes?'

'Could we take a photograph?'

Mrs Finan brightened.

'Of me?'

'Well I was thinking perhaps of you and me together.'

'No problem.'

The woman took her phone from her bag while the man got up and stood beside Mrs Finan in her armchair. He bent slightly in both knees and pressed his fist into the headrest. Mrs Finan, who stayed seated, positioned her head in a tilt and got her smile ready as the woman fiddled with her phone.

'No, it's not going to work,' said the woman. 'There's too much light behind you from the window.'

Mrs Finan heaved herself up and stood with the man at the opposite end of the room. This time he put his arm around her shoulders.

'I should go on Loose Women,' said Mrs Finan. 'Tell them a big good-looking American came into my house and had his hands all over me.'

'Ok that was perfect,' said the woman.

The man and the woman left.

The daffodil mug was on the floor at one end of the two-seater. The chocolate mug was on the arm at the other end.

catalogue published by Hodges Figgis in 1971

CELTIC STUDIES

A
LIST
OF
RECENT ACQUISITIONS
ANTIQUARIAN
OUT-OF-PRINT
NEW

SPRING, 1971

HODGES FIGGIS & CO. LTD.
Established 1768
**5 & 6 Dawson Street,
Dublin 2, Ireland.**
Telephone: Dublin 776375

Patrick Cotter

WHEN EVIL TRUMPS ALL

Had he any gift Pygmalion would be his name.
All the statues he sculpts display asymmetry.
Putatively female with breasts and hips

and *mons pubis*, but rough-hewn, rough
finished like skin dappled by pox.
He forges no faces because he prefers no faces

to the ugly travesties of features he could shape:
noses with three nostrils, puteal orifices for mouths,
mismatched ears, lips like twisted twine.

When they spasm into life, shuffle and jerk
like some notion he has of monsters, he kills them
instantly, in disgust and considers himself

no murderer. He steps in their entrails and blood
leaving unwashable bootprints. If he could hew
smooth skinned and beautiful, what he would do

in his putery would make him, in his book, no rapist.
But he can't ever make beauty – it simply isn't in him.
So he forges girlikin after girlikin he puts down without
    mercy.

Enda Coyle-Greene

A Room Without Weather

He thinks he hears it in the din
made by his worker bees
and their lone drone,

in the fricative *slip* of nylon
over sweat: someone is humming
'Joe Hill' as he rolls in.

With no windows, one door,
in a room without weather
the other bees seethe;

in the absence of a queen
she has been chosen to sing,
but he owns the floor

and the whole world
balances its cold bowl of blue
while they calculate

the hours until lunch.
When the one who hums rises –
gracile wings unfurled

at last, her coat off its hook
in the cloakroom's gloom –
she'll fly away

into elements that blaze, sip
pollen from flowers found
on Dawson Street,

pressed in the pages of a book.

Catherine Ann Cullen

A FRIEND OF THE AUTHOR

An insubstantial volume of poems
which will never be reviewed
sits incongruously among the Top Ten Bestsellers
in Hodges Figgis.

A browser,
finding the book practically invisible
due to its dearth of spine,
its cover overwhelmed
by more expansive collections,
moved it when the staff were answering queries
and took a shelfie
to send to the author,
prompting a frisson of joy
before her bitterness returned.

Irish Press, 7 December 1978

You can't beat a good book

For value and long lasting enjoyment, at Christmas and throughout the year —the thoughtful gift is a book

HODGES FIGGIS THE BOOKSELLERS

Stephens Court, Donnybrook,
Dun Laoire Shopping Centre and Belfield.

Peter Cunningham

from WORK IN PROGRESS

Worra bakes all summer long. As a child, he is brought to the middle of town, to a tall, pillar-like drinking fountain, whose copper cup is attached with a chain, and told that anyone who drinks more than a single cupful is always struck dead. He comes back alone a few days later, and when no one is looking, fills the cup a second time, brings it to his lips, but then, trembling with delicious terror, dashes the water to the ground.

Since ever he can remember there have been two of him: two Roberts: himself and Bob. They watch each other. Robert is in thrall to his majestic father, but Bob runs loose where Robert would never dare. His mother comes home one day from placing her weekly grocery order. Face as smooth and cold as porcelain. Her skirts skim the floor in feathery whispers. She is smiling as she gives his little sister a short, curved comb of tortoise-shell with a silver clasp that she has just been made a gift of in her husband's drugstore by a salesman. She pins up his sister's auburn hair with the pretty comb. They do not see Bob. Slight and pale, he fits into corners and slides in and out of the stark shadows in these white summer days of New South Wales. He remains hidden as his sister removes the new comb and her hair spills, then the women drift off, their laughter floating behind them like motes in the bars of sunlight.

As Robert watches, Bob goes to the table and palms the comb. Why? His heart is racing so fast he thinks it will pop out of his mouth. But the thing is in his pocket and he is running along the track of baked earth that winds redly down to the sluggish creek where, at dusk, cockatoos screech from the boughs of eucalyptus trees. He wants to pee but can't stop running since the panic has him, not unpleasant though, just different in a vivid way as if something new is out of its box. Pees down his bare leg anyway and knows that later his thighs will sting. At the creek, without looking at the comb, he takes it out and throws it in. Next day, a maidservant is dismissed under suspicion of theft from the employ of Mrs Henry Joby.

Robert craves Bob's intense feeling of that day. He has heard farm hands, Aboriginals who groom the horses, talk about seeing the dead rise up and walk. One night, nine years of age, he walks out into the bush where trees like skeletons stand in the moonlight, and he can imagine all the strange, untold forces of the dead and the un-dead that inhabit the earth, waiting to lay hands on him; which makes him run back home again, relishing the moment. What consumes him is the feeling that comes from going to the edge, and coming back again. Like filling a second cup from the fountain. Like stealing the comb.

Chemist Joby and his family live a quarter mile outside the town in a house built by New South Wales' finest craftsmen. The first dwelling in Worra to be roofed in slate. Salesmen arrive in the pharmacy on Broad Street, bringing their tales of Sydney and its fashions, and of the crowds thronging the Tivoli to see the new cinematographe. Henry Joby, chemist and druggist, hears them out sitting at his roll-top desk in his dispensary. The sternest man in Worra, his prematurely-white beard reaches to the top eyelet of his waistcoat and from limpid blue eyes he regards the world with the steady gaze of an evangelist. Behind his desk the wall is a blaze of framed scrolls, degrees and citations, as well as flysheet advertisements for leeches, oils and tooth enamel.

Robert's schoolteacher despairs. His pupil, the man reports, is more interested in games of pitch-and-toss than the elements of Greek or Latin.

'He disdains all written work, including the suits of algebra and geometry. His handwriting is deplorable.'

When he is twelve, a private tutor is engaged to try and salvage something. He leaves after three months. Robert's mother tells him he is breaking his father's heart, that Chemist Joby wishes to settle his entire business on his son but cannot do so if Robert will not apply himself. Up to that moment, he had never considered his father even had a heart. His own gallops when two coins leave a comb and revolve lazily in the air before falling. All his young life is compressed into the intense capsule of time between the flick of the coins and their fall.

A hotel, the Victoria, opens and serves ice with drinks – a luxury unheard of except in Sydney. Brick is becoming as common as weatherboard. The most popular laxative dispensed from Joby's Drug Store is Weston's Medical Wonder. Midway through his fifteenth year, his father summons him to the inner sanctum. One part of the room is given over to the chemist's trade: bottles and beakers, pipettes, lenses and prisms, pestle and mortar, and a high chest of tiny drawers each with the details of their *materia medica* stated in lacquered gold. Robert tries to quiet his mind in its ceaseless jumping, its straining to be elsewhere, its fretful insistence on making him see himself from a distance. As he sits before the rampart-like desk, Chemist Joby shakes his leonine head and sighs.

'I see you and I fear for the future of humanity.'

Robert finds it disconcerting not to be able to see the mouth making the voice. He wonders if his father dies will he still be able to hear him.

'I came out to this colony nearly thirty years ago because I saw the old order for what it was: a putrid mass of incoherent humanity. A succession of endless, hopeless generations. I have but one life and I will lead it, may it please Almighty God, in this new world, free from the hypocrisies of the old.'

Robert's body is changing, every day. His long limbs shine and he stands head and shoulders above his mother.

'What will you be, sir? A larrikin or a proper son to me?'
The chemist gets to his feet and, like an Old Testament
prophet, spreads his arms. 'I am giving you one last
chance. You will go down to Sydney, sir, and you will
become apprenticed there to Chemist Le Foy.'

As the train steams first east and then south, the tumbling
green vegetation glistens, the countryside widens and rises
and the sky spreads into a great embracing canopy. He
sees bush plains strewn with ancient, tar-like rocks, and
the irregular shapes of tree-ferns, and gum-trees with dark,
rubber tongues that seem to leer at him. He has an
absolute sense that he will never again return to Worra.

The first thing he notices when they get in is the noise:
hissing steam, and urgent shouting, and, far out, a great
hum, like that of a gathering storm, except that up beyond
the graceful steel arches the sky is elementary blue.
Gathering his suitcase – made of good leather with brass
angles at the corners; a gift from his father – Bob walks out
into the all-consuming, frantic life surge of Sydney.

Irish Times, 15 September 1945

The President, who paid an informal visit to the Thomas Davis Book
Fair on Wednesday, being presented with a specially-bound copy of Dr.
T. W. Moody's "Thomas Davis, 1814-45," by Mr. R. R. Figgis, of
Hodges, Figgis and Co., publishers of the book.

Judi Curtin

from NOVEL IN PROGRESS

A couple of weeks ago, my teacher, Mr Scott, had another one of his stupid ideas.

'Listen carefully, boys and girls,' he said. 'This morning I want you all to write a story.'

I smiled at my best friend, Maya, as I stopped shredding the cuff of my jumper and picked up my pen. I *love* writing stories and I already had a great idea about a girl spy who had amazing superpowers.

Then Mr Scott continued talking. 'Today we're going to do something different. I don't want just any old story. Today I want you to write a story that you could read to a small boy or girl – a fairy-tale.'

I put down my pen.

What kind of a lame idea was that?

Who wants to write fairy-tales?

Who wants to write stupid stories about stupid princesses whose idea of happy ever after was hanging out in a freezing cold castle with a prince wearing tights – a prince who used to be a frog?

Then I felt sad – I used to love telling fairy stories to Liam, the little kid who lived next door to me – but that was ages ago, when everything was different.

Maya nudged me, and I could see that Mr Scott was giving me one of his poisonous stares, so I picked up my pen again and started to write.

It didn't take long to write my story. As soon as I was finished, I closed my copy, folded my arms and waited. A few minutes later, Mr Scott looked up from his desk where he was pretending to work on his laptop.

'Why aren't you writing, Daisy?' he asked.

'Because I'm finished,' I said.

Mr Scott gave a big long sigh, like I'd really annoyed him by doing exactly what he'd asked us to. 'Bring it up to me then,' he said, quickly shutting down whatever he'd been looking at on his laptop.

I did as I was told, and stood quietly next to my teacher for the thirty seconds it took him to read my story.

This is what he read:

Once upon a time there was a darling little girl who lived with her mum and dad. They lived in a lovely little house on the edge of a lovely little town. The mum was strong and brave and loved going on adventures. The dad was clever and funny and kind (but he could be a bit annoying sometimes). The little girl … well she was just a sweet little girl who definitely didn't want to be a princess but thought she might like to be a superhero some day when she didn't have too much homework.

And they all lived happily ever after.

The End

Mr Scott took off his glasses and gave another big long sigh. I stepped backwards but I wasn't quick enough. His hot stinky breath washed over me like a toxic cloud. I used to feel sorry for Mr Scott, but now I just felt mad – everything seemed to annoy me these days.

'Daisy, do you and I need to have another talk about you putting more effort into your school work?' he asked.

Do you and I need to have a talk about you putting more effort into brushing your teeth?

I didn't say this of course. (I'm not a complete moron). I just stood there and waited for him to stop talking.

'This story is much too short, Daisy.'

So are your trousers, but I'm not giving you a hard time about them, am I?

'Are you and I going to have to visit the principal?'

How about you and I visit the barber's shop instead and you can get a haircut that doesn't make you look like your head's been mauled by a crazed dog?

'This work simply isn't acceptable, Daisy,' he said. 'What kind of a story is this meant to be?'

I could see he wasn't giving up, so I decided it was time to answer one of his pathetic questions.

'It's a true story.'

'But that's ridicul ...'

Mr Scott stopped suddenly. I could see that he'd just remembered. His cheeks went bright red like someone had been pinching them hard. He put his glasses back on, and scratched his head. A little shower of dandruff floated onto the desk.

'Very well,' he said. 'Just this once I'll let it pass. Go back to your place and read quietly until everyone else is finished.'

Maya smiled at me. I think she had a fair idea of what my story had been about – sometimes it's like that girl can read my mind.

When I got back to my desk I didn't read. I just sat there and tried not to cry as I thought about what I'd written. I didn't make it up. Once upon a time there *was* a brave mum and a funny dad and a sweet little girl who didn't want to be a princess. I should know – I was the little girl in the story.

So the whole thing *was* true – all except for the last line, the one about us living happily ever after. That's the way the story was supposed to end, but it didn't.

Maybe it's best if I go right back to the beginning – back to when my perfect life began to unravel.

Tony Curtis

BLESS

When Emily Dickinson was my age, she was dead –
she had been dead four years.
If I live long enough I'd like to visit her house –
no, her room – in Amherst, Massachusetts.

I've seen a photograph – the honeysuckle tree
by the open window with the lace curtains moving –
beneath it, there's the small square writing table
where, no doubt, her ghost now sits dressed in white.

I would then like to visit the Amherst cemetery. I imagine
there will be a creaking wooden gate, a gravel path –
and, if all is well, her small grave will be covered
in wildflowers – wild – and wilding in the wind.

published by Allen Figgis in 1963

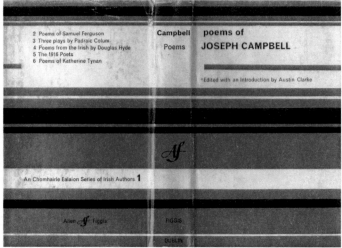

published by Allen Figgis in 1970

This is, perhaps, the most famous of Donn Byrne's
novels. Set in the Wicklow Hills, it is a nostalgic
romance of sixty years ago—yet eminently readable in
the nineteen seventies. An exiled Irish Revolutionary
wreaks vengeance on the adventurer to whom the
hangman's daughter is unwillingly married, and the
despoiled house comes deservedly to an end in flames.

riverrun

HANGMAN'S HOUSE

Donn Byrne

Gerald Dawe

LAND OF DREAMS

They passed the streams of Ocean, the White Rock, the Gates of the Sun and the Land of Dreams, and soon they came to the field of asphodel, where the souls, the phantoms of the dead, have their habitation.

In memory of Dermot Healy

JJ snatches salmon on the Salmon Weir Bridge
    or the Claddagh, then, in newspaper folds
sells for what he can the shimmering fish.

    Matty Lydon's back – 'I was schooled
in three universities but the best of the lot's
    Limerick: how are ye fixed for the rough touch?'

Render unto Caesar the things that are Caesar's
    young Matty recites as he dumps leaves over
the Bishop of Galway's palatial gates.

    The tourist guide on pony and trap
passes Moon's Corner as some kids sing
    'Oh Lord it's so hard to be humble'.

'You'd not see the likes of that in Utopia', he quips.
    One bright spring day, the shopkeeper looks both ways:
'Fucking massive' is what he says.

    Nicholas, the dapper barman of Garavan's calls
'Last Orders'; aloft, red-lipped Una Taaffe,
    whelps at her stocking-less feet, sweeps all

before her as the Patrician Brass Band, caps
    and instruments flood my room in waves
of light, sound waves, like falling asleep.

And who do you think should turn up next
    but Professor Reynolds in her black and canary yellow
Ford Capri shooting through the highways and byways

    to Eyrecourt amid the relics of colonial pewter,
the pleasure garden, the pig's foot, the rollicking wine
    as Pat Sheeran, for it is he, rises to the bait

of another unwinnable argument, a cat stirs on the sill
    and we hit out into the speckled night,
missing one turn-off after another,

    the tree line's faint light glows miles away
to the sea thrashing against cliff-face
    and the near-dark that's about to break.

Irish Times, 20 December 1876

CHRISTMAS PRESENTS.

❦ ————

HODGES, FOSTER, AND FIGGIS

Beg to announce that they have now on View their
usual choice and well-selected Stock of

ELEGANTLY BOUND GIFT BOOKS,

Comprising all the Novelties of the present Season,
both in cloth and Morocco Binding.
Also a large collection of

ILLUSTRATED JUVENILE BOOKS,

Books of Travel and Adventures.
Likewise a Choice Stock of

BAGSTER'S AND OXFORD BIBLES. PRAYER BOOKS AND CHURCH SERVICES.

In Antique, Morocco, and Ivory Bindings,
At all Prices to suit Purchasers.
To which they invite an early inspection.

HODGES, FOSTER, AND FIGGIS,

104 GRAFTON STREET, DUBLIN.

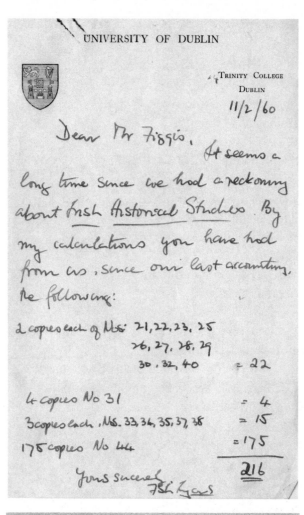

UNIVERSITY OF DUBLIN

TRINITY COLLEGE
DUBLIN

11/2/60

Dear Mr Figgis,

It seems a long time since we had a reckoning about Irish Historical Studies. By my calculations you have had from us, since our last accounting, the following:

2 copies each of Nos: 21, 22, 23, 25
26, 27, 28, 29
30, 32, 40 = 22

4 copies No 31 = 4
3 copies each, Nos. 33, 34, 35, 37, 38 = 15
175 copies No 44 = 175
—————
216

Yours sincerely
FSL Lyons

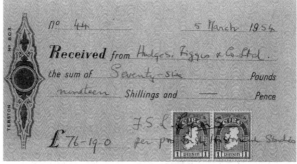

Nº 44   5 March 1954

Received from Hodges, Figgis & Co Ltd.
the sum of   Seventy-six   Pounds
nineteen   Shillings and   ————   Pence

£76-19-0   per ...

Correspondence with F.S.L. Lyons, Professor of History at Trinity

Celia de Fréine

Na Maighdeana Stuama is Místuama

Je les vois comme une ancienne estampe,
tiges sveltes et belles corolles ...

Braitheann na maighdeana místuama
barróg bhog na scáthanna
agus iad ar a mbealach trí na caolsráideanna
ach ní thuigeann siad é seo –
tá faitíos orthu roimh an dorchadas

Leanann na maighdeana stuama
sa leathsholas iad

Cinnte, tá dearmad déanta ag na maighdeana místuama
ola a bhreith leo dá lampaí
ach níor chuir a siúracha comhairle orthu faoi seo
ná ní thabharfaidís aon bhraon ar iasacht dóibh
nuair a glaodh isteach chun na feise iad

Mar seo a d'fhoghlaim na maighdeana místuama
críonnacht na comhroinnte
is a d'fhoghlaim na maighdeana stuama
mealltacht na sainte

CÚIRT AN MEADON OIDCE.

IT is proposed to issue a *limited edition* of the famous Modern Irish classic, "CÚIRT AN MEADON OIDCE" ("The Midnight Court"), composed A.D. 1780 by Brian Merriman, at Feakle, Co. Clare. The editing has been most carefully carried out, giving the full Text, with Introduction, Biographical sketch, Notes, Variant readings of the best MSS., &c., and it is intended that the form of the volume shall be in every way worthy of this great Gaelic masterpiece.

Before going to press, however, the publishers desire to have a sufficient number of subscribers to warrant its publication. The price per copy, post free, has been fixed at seven shillings and sixpence.*

If the response to this letter be satisfactory, the matter will be handed to the printers immediately, so that the book may be in the hands of subscribers on New Year's Day next, the one hundred and thirty-second anniversary of the completion of the original work.

Blank Order Forms are enclosed for yourself and any friends who may be interested. Early return of the completed form will be esteemed, but remittance should not be sent until further notice.

HODGES, FIGGIS, & CO., LTD.

September, 1911.
104, GRAFTON STREET,
DUBLIN.

* America, 2 dollars.
France, 10 francs.

Announcement by Hodges Figgis that they plan to publish a limited edition of Cúirt an Mheadhon Oídhche *by Brian Merriman, 1911* (NLI)

To

MESSRS. HODGES, FIGGIS, & CO., LTD.,

Publishers, Booksellers, &c.,

104, Grafton Street, DUBLIN.

I desire to subscribe for .... *cop*...... *of* CÚIRT AN MEADON OIDCE (**Merriman's "Midnight Court"**), *which you propose to publish.*

Name,

Address,

Kit de Waal

from TOMORROW AND TOMORROW

The tiny half-house they rented had a single room downstairs, a kitchenette in the corner and upstairs enough space for a bed and bathroom. It was a cheap conversion of a cramped Edwardian terrace in a crumbling row on a crumbling estate. The electricity metre was just inside the front door. It was Callum's job to feed it every day on his way home from work. Maria would hear his key in the door and watch him fish with pride the coins out of his pocket to appease the iron-grey beast.

He was on piece-work and came home with cuts on his hands, front and back and metal filings in his hair. She wanted him to have a bath. He wanted her to put on the two-bar electric fire and warm herself up.

'You haven't sat all day in the cold?'

'No, I went to see about a job but there was only bar work at the Prince of Wales.'

'Bar work's out.'

'I know. I was just saying.'

He would boil a kettle for himself, strip down and wash from head to toe in four inches of hot water, humming, smiling. He would throw the water down the sink, rinse the bowl and start again, a new bowlful for his beautiful hair. He would flick the fire on for her, both crimson bars sizzling bright. Singeing socks, burning dust, shampoo and damp clothes. It was a smell Maria would remember for the rest of her life.

She would watch as he dried his curls.

'You sit here,' she would say and try to move from the fire. But he was having none of it. Often she would simply end up on his lap, her arms hung around his neck like a drowning child. They were often silent, basking in their togetherness, listening to the quiet hiss and murmur of the glowing bars, Maria cradled against his chest, his hand on her hair, a still life photograph in a loose-leaf album. She knew, even then, that these were the moments to be savoured. The ones she would turn to again and again in some future time and remember that there had been a golden time between them when things were all good. She knew it would end. She knew he did not.

She knew he saw this as love's endless continuum, he believed he would graduate from lover, to guardian, to father, to grave. He wasn't taking pictures and folding them into his heart. He wasn't watching the two of them huddled together against the draught from the broken window, a slender, single shape under the blanket. She knew that when it ended he would have nothing.

Then one morning a man came to the door. 'Is your husband in, missus?'

She closed the door quietly and returned to the kitchen, to the making of a meal. She hadn't answered the man. Husband, he said.

She took the chicken and rinsed it under the tap then stuck her hand wrist-deep inside the little bird on the draining board, right up to the neck, and grabbed and felt the suction, the last gasp. She eased her hand out of the small rib cage with something between her fingers. It was the heart, the tiny heart. She slopped it all, the blood and innards, the slippery guts, onto the newspaper and knew then that she would leave him. She had to.

She walked away from the chicken. It would stink, just faintly, when he came home shortly after six. Half of their poor savings were hers. She wouldn't take more.

At the train station, there was a short moment when she cried but she stopped when she had to ask for her fare. By the time she was sitting down with her case stuffed between the seats, no one would have been able to tell that Maria's heart had broken for the second time. She saw then, in her reflection, her untidy ponytail, the obvious mend in her old check coat and the small, white chicken feather caught on her eyebrow and she knew why the caller had asked for the man of the house. She looked like a fool. She took the feather off and slipped it into her purse. She would keep it in an envelope for twelve years before it would disintegrate into fine, gossamer fluff.

Callum sauntered home just after six and found the fetid, pimply bird in the warm kitchen. He looked at the pale and naked carcass for a long time because he didn't know what else to do, it being obvious she'd gone.

He didn't call her name. Instead, he walked upstairs to their tiny bedroom and opened the shoebox. Exactly half the money was left. No one had broken in and taken her. It was much worse than that.

He went back to the kitchen and clutched the handle of the dull aluminium kettle as though to put it on the gas stove, to put a fire to it and make himself a strong, sweet, comforting tea. But he just held on to it, like a friend.

After a short moment, he banged it once on the side. 'There's an end to it,' he said.

That evening found him at their local, the first pub they'd gone to as a couple. But the snug was empty of her. And it found him later, hands in pocket, stalking around the bus station and it found him later still, peering through the glass of the locked-up train station. He walked then finally, with long arms, home.

Callum caught the chicken by the neck and shattered the wishbone up against the kitchen wall. He put his back to the wall, slid down and brought his knees up to his chest.

John F. Deane

EOIN FACHTNA, SCRIBE
Monastery of St Colmán, Achill Island, 983

Today there was silence and sibilance in the scriptorium;
Brother Conall's tongue was out, moving right to left,
brushing against his teeth; we choose a spiritual alphabet

imprinted on the soul with a reed-nib of water. Outside,
Brother Fergus hummed, loudly, in the barnspace, labouring
at the brewing of a strong ale; there is smell of mutton

from Brother Eogan's kitchen. Some days I am aware
that this is island, and I am island, the Devil herself – as
    always –
scours the darker spaces, stables, cellars – for this, at times,

is hell and this is harrowing. Down by the shore
a craftsman is shaping stone, chipping, till the Crucified
is outlined; I think of the years ahead, the precise chiselling,

the crafting to perfection. Faith is something like the sea,
gnawing and withdrawing, something like the moon when
    clouds
shift, parting, then thickening again. This afternoon I saw

blue smoke rise like soft-winged birds from Brother
    Fiachra's
fire: monastery detritus – hair from old tonsured heads,
spoiled pages, kitchen orts, torn vows ... I hoped to see

the Sacred Ghost hovering, but it was merely the kestrel
wrecking the carcass of a hare. Psalming is a rasping thing
like waves against fissured rocks, where fountains of sea-
    spray

flourish for instants on the surfaces, then worry down
in gurgles, swallows, sighs; sounding like prayers. Sheer
   will
keeps my hold on the island, keeps my shivering goose-
   quill

scraping at the page. Last night, psalter and sackcloth and
   cowl
felt like fire about me and I cast them off in anger; my soul,
sinking through dark water, down to unloving depths.

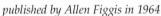

published by Allen Figgis in 1964

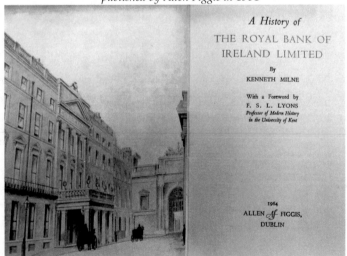

Bank of Ireland.

G.P.O. BOX No. 9.

Dublin, C.1.

23rd January, 1952.

Messrs. Hodges, Figgis & Co. Ltd.
    6, Dawson Street,
        Dublin.

Dear Sirs,

        We have to acknowledge receipt of cheque for £9. 9/- in respect of sale of five copies of the History of the Bank of Ireland, :-

5 copies sold ...	£15. 15. -	
Commission	£6. 6. -	
	£9. 9. -	

for which we thank you.

        We note you have on hand 16 copies.

        Yours faithfully,

                Secretary

Patrick Deeley

NORTH MAYO NIGHT

The 'rowboat' moon rears up on its prow
as though it has caught the swell
of the sea-blue sky. Dún Briste gives itself
away by the frothy whiteness I see

lapping at its base, while a jet slips, sparkle
after ruby sparkle, towards America,
and a star too bright to be a star ogles me.
The streetlights of Ballycastle shine,

the smell of a day that's done and dusted
hangs in the heather and on the air,
an unseasonably hot day in April
spent strolling the hills of Sralagagh. Lucky

to have lived, to be alive – is this
too blithe a thing to say? Not when I feel
lifted to rapture I can account for
only by the heady furze, the drowse of crows

silent at last in their rookery
become my pleasure here, the wear of sad
seasons and storm-scattered shapes
twigged to life, stirred to nurture once more.

It's a passing spell, our resonance
and room; the world finds ways to fail us all.
Still I call, recall 'rowboat', 'galleon' –
old words penned by an old poet long cast

adrift on the mainsail of his vessel,
in my fashion follow the push of the moon
through the bulked and blackened
addendum of the roosts, to break the gloom.

Kate Dempsey

SCIENCE HAIKU

Thumb on a touchscreen
tiny electrical charge
completes the circuit

Atmospheric dust
attracts water molecules
to form raindrops

From the inside out
coiled marginal meristems
divide into ferns

Sunlight scatters
atmospheric molecules –
blue dome of our sky

Magellanic clouds
Two galaxies ripped apart –
a slim bridge of stars

Is there an error
in our equations of space?
Call it dark matter

Smash them together
muon and anti-muon
a two photon burst

Your magnetic field
interacts with mine today
Science of the heart

Anne Devlin

from THE FORGOTTEN

Scene 9: Ext Park: In the Tree

BEE: If I stopped speaking it would be better.

TF: Not true, you use words only to defend yourself …

BEE: What's wrong with that?

TF: You aren't allowing yourself to begin to know what you feel.

BEE: Is that so? Then what do you think I was doing a few minutes ago shouting into the trees?

TF: You were being angry with yourself … you keep trying to ward off the anger and it keeps breaking through …

BEE: They're reading to each other …

TF: Don't change the subject … what feelings are you defending yourself against?

BEE: Feelings.

TF: Yes. What feelings are so frightening …

BEE: Paris. The bridge in Paris … Me saying goodbye to him … I don't know. I never knew what happened to me. I thought I was absent minded. It wasn't that I forgot love or couldn't get energised. It was something fundamentally wrong from the beginning. It was all these little parts, performances, but nothing took root in my heart or in my soul. And I'm trying now to bring myself together to remember, or to meet and hold the other bits rather like an orchestra or a little opera. But nobody ever tells you the greatest loss or how you can reclaim it … Is it possible?

THE FORGOTTEN: It is possible … It requires that you gather up your grief.

BEE: I haven't thought about him for so many years …

TF: Who?

BEE: He's the man nature intended me for.

TF: Ah nature.

BEE: I knew by the way he wrote his name he was the one … I could see it in the curve of the line he made … I pined … I shed 70 kilos … I lost so much weight I had to go to hospital … and I was shaking all the time … If I gather up my grief I would never stop crying … The things I remember are the things I didn't understand even at the time they occurred.

TF: For instance?

BEE: I remember that I had to say something … to someone … I want you.

TF: This was the man nature intended.

BEE: Yes. I remember he tied a bandanna around his head … it was red … the chair he was sitting in was pushed back against the wall and he was smiling at me … I began to tell a story, a stupid nervousness wouldn't let me shut up … and be still … the end line of the story was three words: I don't want you … I didn't know when I started speaking I was going to say that … I remember his chair crashing down against the desk … and I ran out of the room … I dropped my cigarette by the lift gates and walked down the stairs … So I know that I sabotage my own desire …

TF: There has been no real liberty for your body …

BEE: I need to get down, my limbs are stiffening.

TF: And another thing … hang on and I'll help you …

BEE: What's the other thing?

TF: … you can't count. I don't want you is four words.

BEE: I wonder if those two things are linked? *(Beat).* I don't believe it. They have my notebook.

TF: Bee … calmly … you are right about the numbers …

BEE: What about the numbers?

TF: The money …

BEE: I'm angry about the money aren't I? ... There was a pop song: *if her daddy's rich take her out for a meal; if her daddy's poor you can do what you feel*; I resented it ... it's like being a fat teenager, you never understand how some people can be thin ... food and the body are a bad combination ... it's not science, it's magic ... you either eat or starve ...

TF: So because you never understood the real equation ... you miss something vital.

BEE: Then ... I became a professional, jumped a class ... and just got used to money ... I've been rich for so long I've forgotten what a library is for ... until I got sick and the money dried up ... and then the problem was I forgot how to live without it.

TF: You know something, Bee? Nobody ever created anything by remaining in credit.

BEE: The worst thing I ever heard ... two people in the theatre, one says to the other: we'll not pay her the full rate ... she's a young actress. It's not what she'd used to. And I didn't say a word ... they didn't mean she was a young actress ... they meant she's not from our social group. Like those school teachers who used to say to me ... it's what you're used to ... to justify inequality ... so nothing changes.

TF: It might have changed if you'd spoken up for the actress.

BEE: It would have ... it most certainly would have.

TF: Why did you remain silent?

BEE: I remained silent about everything. I don't know, I just don't know.

TF: Defeat makes for timidity ... how were you defeated? Do you remember?

BEE: No ... not today ... I've got to go ... damage limitation.

Scene 10: Ext Park

THEA (*reads*): 'The brother was roaring through her life like a lion.'

GRANNY MAY: That's not a dream … is that fact or fiction?

THEA: I can't tell.

GRANNY MAY: What else does she say, anything about me?

THEA: She's coming … let's walk down to the shore … (*FX: sound of waves*). Have you not got your stick?

GRANNY MAY: I'll hold on to you and we can walk to Megan's rock.

THEA: Keep walking granny …

GRANNY MAY: Oh aye Megan … she was married to a sea captain and one day he went away and never returned, so she took herself down to the beach and she waited … until after many years when she was old and white haired a young and beautiful youth walked towards her … it was him back again … and she was found at that big white rock out there in the morning … dead, of course.

THEA: Of course, the sea captain had returned and was living around the coast with another woman, and it was her son who found mad Megan.

BEE (*approaching*): That's an awful story.

GRANNY MAY: That's why she haunts this shore … she walks up and down with a stick which is why for fear of being mistaken I never carry my stick onto the beach …

BEE: What are you two doing with my notebook?

GRANNY MAY: You left it in the garden, we though we'd bring it to you.

THEA: We're on our way to Megan's rock …

BEE: I didn't leave my notebook in the garden, I would never do that.

GM: What are you saying? That we took your notebook? … Out with it!

BEE: No … But it's such an invasion of privacy when I have lost everything else. It feels so disrespectful …

THEA: It was in the garden.

BEE: I don't know how it got there. I'm going to walk on. I'll see you back at the house …

FX: *Sound of waves and gulls …*

THEA: I feel awful.

GM: Oh stop. How else are we supposed to help her?

BEE (V/O): The sea is like a wall of water, I don't know why it won't lie down … I'm sure it should be flat and not vertical …

Martina Devlin

from THE NIGHT VISITOR

I would have preferred not to go to work for the Gilkinsons. Their farm was a lonely spot, a dozen or so miles from my home, and it was the talk of three townlands how they weren't able to keep a servant for any length of time. Sounds were heard there in the night. Mournful noises.

I was a sensible girl, not given to imaginings. I didn't seek out occasions to scare myself silly. Not like some, loitering by Gaol Square after dark, daring each other to go looking for the ghost said to walk there. It was a prisoner, sentenced to hard labour in Queen Victoria's time, who dropped down dead with exhaustion on the treadmill for pumping water. Why he should be the only one to haunt the place is beyond me. If ill treatment was enough to make ghosts of people, Omagh would be awash with the phantoms of unfortunate folk.

How and ever, what I liked or didn't like made no difference, and I went to the Gilkinsons. How could I refuse, when Mother begged me? My father, who was a ploughman, had been injured in a fall and wasn't earning. She cleaned the chapel for a few shillings a week, but it wasn't enough to keep the family. It fell to me to shoulder the responsibilities of adulthood, as the eldest of six. Fourteen years of age, I was.

'It's a bit cut off from the world, out there in the country. But that's all the better for you,' said Mother, trying to put a shine on it. 'Yourself and Miss Gilkinson will be thrown together for company. If she takes to you, she might help you get on. I hear tell she's a scholar, with a roomful of books out there. Didn't she teach school, once upon a time? Maybes she'd give you a leg up.'

Neither of us touched on the stories. About the child's wails heard after dark. Desolate sobbing that made sleep impossible, it was said. Mother knew mentioning books would please me. I had a bent for learning, and would gladly have stayed on at school, if my earnings weren't needed for the family. But needs must.

Mr Gilkinson himself came to fetch me in a horse and trap. There wasn't much public transport in our part of the world, back in the 1930s. Mostly, you had to rely on a neighbour's cart going your way for a lift. Otherwise it was Shanks' mare.

It was a bitter January morning, and we fairly raced along the roads, because he was anxious to reach home before the snow that was forecast. It held off till we were the length of Loughmacrory, where the first flakes fell, and he took the trouble to hap a rug round me. Soon after, we turned off the road and rattled up a track. 'My fields,' he said, pointing at the land. Another minute or so passed, and he spoke again. 'Thon's the house ahead.' I didn't get a right look at the farmhouse, on account of the snow flurry. There was just an impression of a square building, with a string of outhouses, all trying to hold their own within a blurred landscape.

Miss Gilkinson had a hot meal waiting for her brother and me. She let me thaw out by the kitchen range, and made sure I had plenty to eat, before showing me my duties. I was to help run the house, and prepare meals for the Gilkinsons and their hired man, Joe Sweeney.

The snowstorm continued into the evening, but we were cosy enough, listening to the wireless in the kitchen. When the clock on the dresser struck ten, Miss Gilkinson said it was bedtime. Mr Gilkinson bid me good night. 'It's fortunate I collected you the-day,' he said. 'I wud'n risk the horse on the roads the-morrow.' It was far from lucky I felt – homesick, rather. Still, I recognised I had a job where the master and mistress wanted to be kind to me. I was given my own wee room, off the kitchen. Miss Gilkinson said it would be warm as toast. She left a candle lighting there, inside a globe for fear of sparks, and said I could burn it all night if I liked – it was bound to be strange, the first night. But I was cosy in thon nook, and worn out from being transplanted to a new place. I wasn't uneasied blowing out the flame.

Some hours later, I woke up. The slap of air on my skin as the blankets were lifted must have disturbed me. There was a creak of bed springs, and a small, chilled body slid in beside me. I felt its skinny length press up against my back – the wee, bare feet hooking round my ankles. First one, then the other. Frozen, they were. Acting on instinct, I rolled over and threw out my arm to draw the night visitor close, thinking one of my brothers or sisters needed a cuddle, or to be warmed up.

But my arm landed on the sheet. There was nobody in the bed with me. At that, my eyes sprang open, and I realised I wasn't at home, after all. In another moment, I could see I was in the Gilkinsons' farmhouse. It was unusually bright, on account of the snow, and I could pick out the pattern on the curtains at the window. Whose weight made the bed springs grumble? Whose icy body slipped beneath the covers, trying to share my body heat?

All at once, I was gripped by an overpowering sensation of dread. My heart began to hammer, the blood roaring in my eardrums, but I had the presence of mind to fumble for the matches left by Miss Gilkinson. The candlelight showed I was alone, but my senses said otherwise. I squeezed my eyes shut, hunched my back against the bedhead, and gabbled my prayers.

Outside the window a twig cracked, and a slither and flop told of snow dropping off the slate roof. Tick-tock went the kitchen clock. I pictured it amid the Gilkinsons' blue and white china. All appeared to be normal. But my body was rigid with fright.

Time passed, my alarm faded away, and I began to relax. Eventually, I suppose I must have drifted asleep. The next I knew there was a clatter from the kitchen, and the candle had burned through. Quickly, I dressed and flew in, to see Joe Sweeney, with the range door open, poking at the embers. The master was sitting in an armchair beside it. 'Well, Sleepyhead. The animals have been seen to, and we're well ready for a bite of food.'

'What do you take for breakfast, Mr Gilkinson? Will I boil you a lock of eggs?' I asked.

'We have porridge during the week. My sister leaves it steeping overnight – thon's the porridge pot.' He pointed to a black pan with a lid on top of the range. 'Give it a stir. Remember to do it clockwise.' My surprise must have shown, because he added, 'Anti-clockwise invites the devil intae a house.'

Just then, Miss Gilkinson appeared, pushing clips into her hair. 'Robert, you're in already – I'm running late this morning.'

'Sure you're plain worn out from managing this house on your own,' said her brother. 'Joe and me'll take our ease be the range, and maybes there'll be a mug o' tae by and by.'

'How is it you weren't up?' she scolded me. 'We can't be keeping the men waiting for their food.'

But she was hurrying to the larder for bread, and didn't seem to expect an answer, so I said nothing. It was only later, as I was taking away his empty bowl, that Joe Sweeney stopped me in my tracks with a question. It wasn't to make conversation. There was intent behind it.

'What kind of a night did you pass, lassie?'

'Joe,' warned Mr Gilkinson.

'Don't you want to know?' asked Joe.

Mr Gilkinson gave a shrug that was neither yes or no, and Joe nodded encouragement at me.

I swallowed. 'Somebody climbed into bed beside me. A child, it was. Like a block of ice from the cold.'

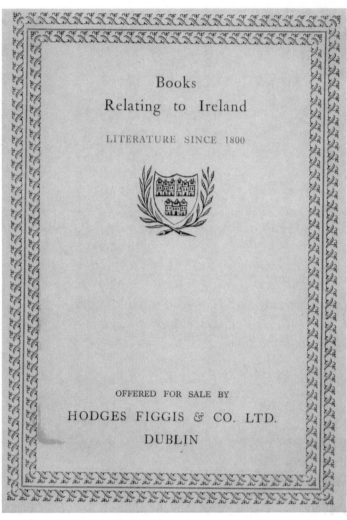

Books
Relating to Ireland

LITERATURE SINCE 1800

OFFERED FOR SALE BY

HODGES FIGGIS & CO. LTD.

DUBLIN

Hodges Figgis catalogue, undated

Moyra Donaldson

RETURN
Why are the horses so long without coming,
and let me suffer so much
– Kasper Hauser, the Child of Europe

Like the *viola d'amore*, our heart strings lie
below the heart strings of the horse
so that we harmonise through resonance,

and there is truth that lives outside of time
in vivid dream; the thin little sorrel beast,
the boy who kissed her dying eyes and lips,

memory perhaps, of when we were not the centre
of the universe, the locus of its consciousness,
not master, owner: we could yet set down the axe.

Vaslav Nijinsky dances the war in Saint Moritz
in front of the aristocrats; he dances *frightening things.*
Finished, he declares – *the little horse is tired.*

Nietzsche, weeping in the Piazzo in Turin, weeps
for the beaten horse, the beaten self – *sing me a new song.*
If I could remember where the bones were buried,

I would dig them up, the wings of scapulas, the skulls of air,
the golden saddle cloths; reconstruct the horses,
the black horse and the white horse and the horse of fire.

J.P. Donleavy

from A LETTER MARKED PERSONAL

He was one of the nicest guys you'd ever want to meet and had reached an age when he could take solace from the fact that he no longer had the whole wilderness of his life ahead to worry about. Especially in a business where sometimes you had to hurt people and you blamed yourself for wondering if you'd hurt them enough so that they couldn't hurt you back. But one of the facts of life he well and truly had learned was that adversity does get rid of loneliness. And then makes you really lonely.

He was living more than comfortably in New York City during a period when pornography was getting respectable, exercise had come into vogue and guys and girls were jogging all over Central Park. If you saw a little group of people you thought had collected to sympathize with a mugging victim, it was often the mugger himself who'd been apprehended by a half dozen fit and decent New Yorkers and more than a female or two among them. He once witnessed such a gathering and instead of an ambulance for the victim, a paddy wagon came along to relocate the culprit to jail.

'Hey, what the hell happened.'

'He tried to steal the lady's handbag. She held on to him.'

In short, this king of cities was becoming a better place to live and merited its reputation as the world's capital of money and entertainment. Not to mention beautiful women. In fact as he peered out of the window one day, breaking the law with powerful binoculars, he focused on a spidery window cleaner high on a skyscraper, then zoomed towards a street corner near one of the first bargain erotic lingerie stores he had established, spotting in the distance a stunning female creature whose mere existence by the store inspired him to feel he was engaged in one of the best businesses in the world.

He savoured the comfort that this was a metropolis where, if you didn't stand too close to the edge of the subway platform and if you gently minded your own activities and mumbled 'Have a good day' in as many directions as it might be called for and made a heap more than a few dollars and kept to routine and didn't let computerized bills drive you out of your mind, life could, at least for quite decent stretches of time, be sweet. As his had become with a still pretty wife and three children grown up and gone off into their own lives with the youngest just graduated from college, while Muriel, their mother, was free to attend a plethora of social activities between her beauty appointments and fitness classes. And they both knew, as seasoned New Yorkers, that you needn't say please to tell someone to get the fuck out of your way.

From the thirty-seventh floor of his newly built apartment block, he could watch the air traffic of helicopters and planes vectoring across the sky. Walking from room to room was a constant pleasure as was looking out over the City with a map and then, consulting a detailed guidebook of buildings, finding out what he was looking at. North to where the trees of Central Park ceded to Harlem and where, in this increasingly democratic New York atmosphere, white people might venture. But south to Wall Street, anybody of any colour or creed could try to make money, placing their bets on stocks and bonds and sitting on their asses waiting and hoping for a kill, but most ending up losing their shirts in a bust and, if they were stylishly dressed, having to cash in their cufflinks as well.

The thing he liked best about being comfortably rich was lounging in bed while Muriel was at a yoga class. He waited for Ida, the maid, to bring breakfast and then watched from his propped up pillow as the sun arose over Long Island and gradually hit the towers of Manhattan. It was his best time of day for inventing lingerie language to knock the market for a loop, and he never failed to find it awe-inspiring to come up with a name, like Japanese hug-and-tug silk knickers, for his latest creation. But then looking east to Brooklyn, where there were plenty of chimney stacks, he felt less inspired. The stacks were a reminder that whoever was sending up those smokey fumes maybe wasn't glamourous but was probably making money. Maybe even lots of it.

Then in the early evening, when he came home after his workout at The Game Club, it was Martini time. Into a shaker full of ice cubes, he poured his careful quantities of gin and vermouth and added a couple squeezes of lemon. Filled a Baccarat glass and played Mozart and Mahler on the piano. On a third drink, he toasted old friends and lovers gone till the tears came, then cast his eyes west over Central Park to dream past the River Hudson to Weehawken and speculate upon the future locations that still lurked out there for a lingerie boutique or two. And from that side of the river, one thing was for sure, it was limitless expansion. All the way west on the route of the old Lincoln Highway across the cornfields of Indiana and Illinois to Nebraska, the Rockies and California where, far out on the Pacific Ocean, the sun finally set on America.

He would occasionally contemplate having a big mansion and estate one day. Away from the fumes and grime, the firetrucks and police sirens reminding him of injury, murder and death. Plus, what the hell, it would really show them that he'd made it in New York, which you could easily think of as the lingerie capital of the world. With all his bank loans paid off, his credit rating purring, he'd even tested establishing outlets in the smaller boondock towns far out West where, price reduced, you could sell a heap of silk chemises, lace-trimmed camisoles and housewives' see-through boudoir wraps. Maybe a really big erotic lingerie store in Omaha. And the boondocks could be an experiment he could easily write off.

Meanwhile, the daily feasting upon the panorama of this soaring megalopolis was a treasuring preoccupation. It made him feel that a city he had arrived in as a bit of a hick was now his personal preserve to enjoy. A place in which he always felt that there was nothing he wanted and could pay for that he couldn't get. And what he didn't want or didn't like, he could easily avoid. Or at least have the offenders whacked. Like the multiplicity of sneaky knockoff artists nosing rat-like in his new season lingerie designs. Which, why not admit it, he purloined himself out of the erotic stratosphere of Paris and Milan to race back home with and put them on his own cutting tables. But that part of the business also provided the deep satisfaction he got from beating the competition with his own obviously superior quality and style and leaving them standing scratching their privates next to a mountain of inventory. But what a persistent endless bunch of conniving buggers they were.

He liked to choreograph his day. Following breakfast in bed and reading all the news that was fit to print, then taking a bath in the British manner, a Radox muscle soak, his ablutions done and further indulging in leisurely grooming, he carefully chose a shirt and tie to sport with his Savile Row suit and finally descended as an Anglophile to the lobby of Midas Towers. Even on a sunny day always carrying a tightly rolled umbrella. Avoiding eye contact, tapping his way through the building's damn nice lobby. Which, as the managing agents said, did not want for special features. Particularly the fountain and the piastraccia-veined marble floors from Italy upon which his leather heels clicked loudly. Four sumptuous leather sofas flanked by palm trees in large ceramic pots. A selection of papers and books to read. The latter being tomes that no one in their right mind would want to open never mind steal. And no visitor could avoid seeing the sign engraved in brass on the concierge's desk.

ALL VISITORS STRICTLY MUST BE ANNOUNCED

The management maintained that using the word strictly added an air of exclusivity. Which not even the police could ignore for less than three minutes before they drew their guns. One thing he'd learned early in the practice of business was to make damn sure you always knew who was coming to see you, plus have more than a hint of their agenda. And to put a stop to all wishful thinking that the folk coming were rich, charming and good-looking investors ready to back you to the hilt. Of course all they really wanted to do was board your gravy train and be certain that the gravy was already swelling up to the brim in overflow and, appraised of this in triplicate, they were going to make damn sure such train was not pulling out of the station without them.

Another big realization was that in trying to be the latest in New York was a waste of time. Because you were already old hat as soon as you were the latest. However, he was among the first to sign up for this ultramodern condominium Midas Towers, publicized as 'Better Than Tomorrow's Best'. And there was no doubt that the apartments were palatial without any sign of stinting. Marble foyers, galleries, herringbone wood floors and high ceilings. Even an attempt at a little Georgian splendour on an interior cornice or two. He also had the satisfaction, at least for the first few days after moving in, to be treated with such exaggerated consideration that he was tempted, with a smile of course, to say,

'I'm just an ordinary conservative guy with elegantly exotic tastes, who listens to Mozart and Schubert, but thank you for treating me in such a deferential way.'

Sometimes it amazed him that where he lived could matter so much. He still kept and spent time semi-secretly in his first down-market windowless office near the Flatiron Building, where he hung out alone for endless hours daydreaming and listening to music. And what the hell, it was always a bolthole for times if they ever got really bad. And if times stayed good, then it was a reminder of his long struggle up the ladder of success. But aside from his socialistic sensitive feelings, he was proud of where he currently lived. In the lobby of Midas Towers, he could gaze at the fresh flowers in vases on the marble-topped tables and sniff their scent while being lulled by the fountain of water spouting from the mouth of a stone cherub. He especially liked the idea that a waiting visitor, or more likely his wife, anxious to get to the theatre on time, could, instead of being irritated, read an out-of-date copy of *Who's Who in America*. He supposed too that the little verbal amusements provided by the Irish doormen, who were not that keen on his British affectations, were thrown in at no extra charge.

'Good morning Mr Johnson. So nice to see you looking just as well as you did yesterday when it didn't rain.'

'Ah, but it does from the fountain there. If you stand too close without an umbrella, the spray would ruin your shoe shine.'

Of course this play-acting was just to reassure himself, even in these safer times, and with now somewhere like an eagle's eyrie to peacefully lay his head, that he could continue enjoying all that he had fought so long and hard for without some son of a bitch street marauder relieving him of his life if he refused to be relieved of his valuables. Although for protection an umbrella wasn't as effective a weapon as a death-dealing swordstick, nevertheless he could skewer an unarmed someone deep enough in the belly or up the ass to make them wish they'd made a run for it.

HODGES ʄIGGIS

BOOKSELLERS SINCE 1768

IRISH CATALOGUE 1995/96

Hodges Figgis Irish Catalogue 1995/96

Neil Donnelly

from THE MASTER BUILDER
after Henrik Ibsen

Architect's office. It has been constructed from an extension to the main house. There is the main room and an inner room, up at back, off it, and doors to the house and street. Beyond the glass wall we can catch a glimpse of the main street stretching into the distance towards the outline of the mountains on the far horizon. KATHERINE, 22, is working in the main room. KENNETH, 72, and RAYMOND, 34, are up in the inner room busy working in silence on drafts and calculations, until KENNETH suddenly stands, distressed.

KENNETH: I can't, I can't, I can't. No! I can't go on with this any longer. No! No longer. No! *(KATHERINE goes to him).*

KATHERINE: What's wrong?

KENNETH: As if you need to ask. As if you need to ask a question you already know the answer to.

KATHERINE: Is it bad this time?

KENNETH: This time it's very bad. Very bad. Worst ever.

RAYMOND comes to them.

RAYMOND: Better get off home and straight to bed.

KENNETH: *Better get off home and straight to bed,* what's the matter with you talking to me as if I were a sick invalid.

RAYMOND: Alright, ok, look, maybe just go out for a bit of fresh air.

KENNETH: Fresh air in this town, you must be joking.

RAYMOND: A change of scene then.

KENNETH: A change of ... Jesus!

KATHERINE: I'll go with him.

RAYMOND: If he prefers.

KENNETH: I prefer nothing. I'm not going anywhere. I'm not going anywhere until *he* comes back. I'm not letting that bastard off the hook. I'm nailing him to that wall. Nailing him. I am.

KATHERINE: Can it not wait?

KENNETH: *Wait* – why should it have to wait?

RAYMOND: Sometimes it's better to wait, take a deep breath, count to ten, bite the tongue.

KENNETH: *Bite the tongue* – what's come over you?

RAYMOND: I'm just urging caution.

KENNETH: That's what's got us into the predicament we're all in – caution! Our over reasonableness, our patient understanding, our acceptance of our helplessness. Our wishing and our waiting, our waiting and our wishing. It can't go on any longer. It can't. I've let things slide too far as it is. Too bloody far I tell you. But never too late, never too late to stop the rot, never too late to call halt!

KATHERINE: Listen!

RAYMOND: Yes, I heard it too.

KENNETH: You're not going to talk me out of it. My mind is made up, I tell you. Made up.

KATHERINE: Listen, it is him!

RAYMOND: Yes yes, it is.

KENNETH: I don't care.

RAYMOND: Well I care and she cares.

KENNETH: It's nice and fine and dandy that ye all care so much.

RAYMOND: Just say nothing – keep quiet.

KENNETH: Why?

RAYMOND: Just button it.

KENNETH: Button it, he says. To hell with you!

RAYMOND: Please, Dad, please.

KATHERINE: Please, for all our sakes, please.

Pause. KENNETH finally gives in and they return to work. TOM HAYDEN enters. Well dressed, confident, but mainly bluster.

TOM: (*Whispers*). Katherine.

KATHERINE: (*Whispers*). Yes.

TOM: (*Pointing to inner room, whispers*). Are they gone?

KATHERINE: (*Whispers*). No. (*She resumes writing*).

TOM: Anything new? (*He is looking over her shoulder, stroking her neck*). Anyone looking for me while I was out?

KATHERINE: That young couple called in again.

TOM: What young couple?

KATHERINE: They want that house out by the lake.

TOM: Oh, them.

KATHERINE: They're very anxious to have the plans as soon as possible.

TOM: Are they now.

KATHERINE: They are.

TOM: Like everyone else, they'll just have to wait, join the tail end of the queue. (*She leans her head back; they are just about to kiss*).

KATHERINE: (*Loudly, as she breaks away*). They're coming back!

TOM: Who's coming back?

KATHERINE: The young couple is coming back. (*She crosses to his desk with a folder. RAYMOND enters*). Raymond, didn't the young couple say they'd be back this afternoon?

RAYMOND: Yes, said they'd drop in again.

TOM: Alright, we'll do our best for them but if they don't like it they can shove off and go somewhere else.

RAYMOND: You'd pass up a commission?

TOM: I don't know if they could afford the type of house we'd really like to build for them. They're not the type of people who would appreciate it.

KATHERINE: But they're lovely people.

RAYMOND: They're good people.

TOM: The world is full of good and lovely people.

KATHERINE: They are a steady couple with a sound future.

TOM: *Steady couple, Sound future.* In the heel of the hunt, what difference does it make. Gimme a break.

KATHERINE: You're in a very bad mood.

TOM: Sorry and all that but I'm in the mood I'm in and I wish I wasn't, but there we are. (*KENNETH appears*).

KENNETH: Could you put aside a little time for a quiet word?

TOM: Ah, the oft longed for, *quiet word.*

KENNETH: Katherine, could you excuse us?

KATHERINE: Of course.

TOM: You too, Ray.

RAYMOND: Take it easy.

KENNETH: I'll take it.

RAYMOND: Sure?

KENNETH: I'm fine – Go!

KATHERINE and RAYMOND exit up to inner room.

TOM: What's this – some sort of mutiny?

KENNETH: (*Quietly*). I don't want them to know how really sick I am. (*Pause*). Every day I have less and less strength.

TOM: (*Offers chair*). Take the weight off your feet. (*KENNETH sits*).

KENNETH: I'm worried about Raymond.

TOM: *Worried about Raymond,* what are you worried about him for?

KENNETH: What's going to happen to him when I'm gone?

TOM: He can stay on here for as long as he wants.

KENNETH: See, here's where there's a problem ... he wants to leave.

TOM: He wants a raise?

KENNETH: No, no, he's not after a raise, he wants to *leave,* to go and do his own thing.

TOM: Do you think he has it in him to succeed on his own?

KENNETH: That's what I'm not sure of.

TOM: He's a very competent draughtsman, I'll say that much for him.

KENNETH: That's what you were when you worked for me.

Katie Donovan

Deluge

I pass, scarcely noticing the raft:
a leaf, floating in the full bucket
beneath the water butt.
Clinging on, a sailor in the storm:
a soaked bee.
I bring it in, show my daughter,
this striped survivor
of the June showers.
Set on our kitchen table
the bee is offered bumble succulents:
mock orange, buttercup,
the florets of green alkanet.
First, it dries its fur,
by combing with hind legs.
When the wet is routed
its proboscis delves for nectar.
At last the wings
are energised to whirr,
so we venture out:
a mild night,
getting ready for another downpour.
Undaunted, the bee takes flight.
We smile, my daughter and I,
and, turning, find a frilled green moth,
flirting on a tassel like an acrobat,
taking shelter in our light.
At our feet, a snail glides,
smooth and unguent on slick ground,
a woodlouse clinging to its shell:
a miniature rodeo chancer,
catching a free ride
as the flood gathers.

Mary Dorcey

COMMON QUESTIONS AND ONE ANSWER

They asked her if she had children. They asked her
– why not. They asked her if she had ever wanted

children. They asked why not. You would have made,
they soothed, a marvellous mother. But what was

that, she challenged – she had never met a woman
who would award herself this title, or even one who

could claim to know what qualification it might entail.
But isn't it selfish, they replied. What? she puzzled.

Not to have any, they said. Why? she asked. Because,
they said, we all have to do our bit. To make a

contribution. To make more people, do you mean?
she ventured. Yes, they said, of course. To make

people to look after other people, she asked, until they
in turn make more people, is that it – on and on, ad

infinitum? Yes, they answered, is it not fundamental?
An unending chain? she asked. Exactly, to be unselfish,

they chimed. Well (for a moment, she considered) if
I had ever noticed an under-supply of people, I might

have thought the same. I might have felt, she said,
that I ought to do my bit. To make other people. But

even in this past century of rapine and of carnage, I
saw not the least shortage of mammalian production.

There was however to my eyes clear, a prolonged
drought of poets. Especially, she said, of women poets.

So I thought I should do my bit. To make some personal
contribution. To be unselfish. To add one more woman

to their number. And even now, thirty years after –
there are still more babies it appears to me, than poets.

And more women making them, than are making poets.
Especially, she said – women poets.

published by Hodges Figgis in 1903

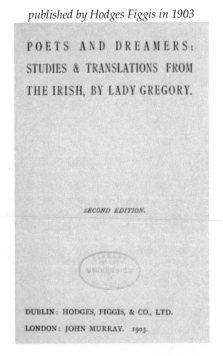

POETS AND DREAMERS:
STUDIES & TRANSLATIONS FROM
THE IRISH, BY LADY GREGORY.

SECOND EDITION.

DUBLIN: HODGES, FIGGIS, & CO., LTD.
LONDON: JOHN MURRAY. 1903.

Theo Dorgan

ORPHEUS
#9

Down in the villages I know they hear me,
how could they not? These builders of terrace walls,
tenders of vine, crop and flock, charcoal makers –
diligent, busy

people. I admire them, keep myself apart
all the same, can feel kinship without
needing to be among kind. Mine is not a
solitary art,

that's what I mean to say, and if they can hear me
when I play, they hear it all. The hesitant
runs, blank starts, whole liquid runs, they hear it all –
I can let it be

and so can they. Learning again how to play
as a child would, fingering without forethought,
not careless and not unconscious, just keeping
out of my own way.

Cork Examiner, 10 December 1979

Books and Christmas go together like HODGES AND FIGGIS

Cork Examiner, 10 December 1979

Garbhan Downey

A Letter to America

The US Special Envoy for Derry, Dave Schumann, writes home to his father:

Dear Pop

You're right of course. In this age of semi-illiterate messaging and fully-illiterate texting, hand-written letters have a real personal charm.

And besides, the era of safe email is over. Bad enough that every security agency on the planet (led by our own) has been violating our digital privacy for years, but now it's gotten so easy that any 12-year-old with a phone can punch in a few codes and rifle through our e-Bins. There's some comfort in knowing that steaming open a stamped envelope without a federal warrant still remains a felony. Who'd a thunk?

Not that I've anything to tell you anyway, that you couldn't read on the front page of the *Boston Herald*. Derry is up in arms that the reinstallation of a new Irish border could cut it right off from its suburbs and hinterland. They've had enough of being roped off. The Brits have screwed themselves even more royally with Brexit than we did with, well, pick a White House number ... And Derry is determined it ain't gonna be the scapegoat this time.

The big issue for me is making sure is that it doesn't become our problem – and that we don't get caught for a share of the border bill.

America is pretty much regarded by all in Derry as the kindly uncle. It dates back to World War II when the city was the largest Allied naval base in the North Atlantic, and we had a huge base here. The GIs were great mixers and were never afraid to spend money; many of them even married locals. Their generosity, and the fact that we'd already beaten Britain in a war, made us lots of friends.

We love them right back too, of course. Their hospitality to us is legion – even if 30 years of alcohol awareness messages have sailed right over their heads. But they tend to look to us a little too much for backup when their masters in Belfast or London don't give them the right answers.

For all sorts of reasons, I genuinely hope Brexit doesn't happen. The world needs more bridges, not walls. And besides, a new border would only encourage the folks here to revert to their previous occupation ... as world leaders in smuggling. No lie, they coulda taught Grampa and Joey K how to run liquor. Throughout the Forties, the entire US base (and all of Derry) was awash with fresh food, clothing, Guinness, tea, tobacco and hardware, all smuggled in from the neutral South. Meantime, the rest of the Empire was living off dried milk, canned potatoes and horsehair nylons. Building a hide in the boot of your car was as acceptable as watching pirate TV on the internet is today. The local priests refused to list smuggling as a sin in Confession – and would tell penitents that the biggest crime in Ireland was the border.

Not surprisingly, the Derry mayor, Monty Boyce, now wants us to intercede with the Dublin government on his city's behalf. Monty's understandably nervous that both the Brits and Europe are so eager to punish one another in the divorce that they'll force the other to build this unnecessary border and spend the rest of eternity, and billions of dollars, policing it.

The Taoiseach is actually quite sympathetic to Monty's cause. But his private office is marshaled by that old fascist, Joxer O'Duffy, who's never forgiven Northerners for setting fire to the British Embassy after Bloody Sunday. So, he's been refusing to allow any lobbying from the North to land on the Boss's desk. At all. Even from me. And given that the Boss's only other sources of information are a hostile Southern press – who would happily lay every single Northerner end-to-end across the Atlantic, just to see if they could drown – he's in serious danger of missing the full picture.

Anyhow, as part of my rotation, I get four two-minute meetings per year with the Taoiseach. So Monty gave me a letter on behalf of both Derry and the 56 percent of the North who voted against Brexit, asking the Boss to commit himself, publicly and irrevocably, to no new border. It was a very clear pitch, a one-pager, short and to the point, with just the one very simple demand. So as you can imagine, there was no way Joxer was going to let it in the door. He quite literally frisks you down. So I resigned myself to the Boss's statutory 'Please convey our most lukewarm wishes to your president' photo-call.

As always, before the meeting at Leinster House, I stopped in at the Hodges Figgis bookshop on Dawson Street to see if I could pick out a small gift for the Boss. And by sheer chance, I discovered a wonderful old book from the Royal Irish Academy full of maps and old pictures of Derry from Colmcille in the 6th century to the present day. So, if nothing else, I thought, I might at least get to remind the Taoiseach that we're all part of the one island.

When I strode up to the Boss's outer office a few minutes later, sure enough there was O'Duffy. He stuck out his and waited.

'Hand it over, Mr Schumann,' he said. 'We're in very sensitive negotiations to maintain our trade links to Britain, and we can't have the Taoiseach worrying over lost causes.'

I handed him the letter from Monty, which he opened, read quickly and then fed into his shredder. 'I realise you have to do these things,' he said, by way of apology. 'But so do I.'

I was then ushered into the inner office where sure enough the photographer was waiting for the grin and grip. So I handed over the map-book to the Taoiseach by way of a prop for the pic.

The Boss opened the cover and looked at the first page carefully. 'Excellent,' he said. *'Go raibh míle maith agat,* Mr Schumann. Such a thoughtful gift.'

He then pried out the page he had been studying and handed it over to O'Duffy.

It was the second copy of the letter Monty had given me.

'Please place that on the agenda for tomorrow's Cabinet meeting, Joxer,' he said. 'Top item, if you will ...'

Like I said, Pop, they coulda taught Joey K how to smuggle liquor.

So long and *slán*

Your loving son

David

Freeman's Journal, 3 November 1815

BOOKS

TO BE SOLD BY AUCTION,

On MONDAY, November 6th, and following days.
By Order of the 'Assignees of
Messrs. GILBERT & HODGES,
At No. 27, Dame-street.

THE remainder of their very extensive Stock of Books, in all the various Branches of Literature.
Duty to be paid by the Purchasers.
Sale to commence at 12 o'clock each day.
C. LEWIS, Auctioneer.

The House and Concerns No. 5, Anglesea-street, to be Sold.

Rob Doyle

from SONGS OF HATE

I'm staying on the top floor of the Museum of Contemporary Art on the edge of Zagreb. I've never been to Eastern Europe before, if you don't count the Czech Republic. I got here on Friday. It's now Sunday afternoon. I have beside me an opened 500ml bottle of Tomislav dark beer 7.5%. I've eaten today a banana and a handful of blueberries, and drunk a cup of instant coffee. I watched the end of a film, *Banshee Chapter*, which I had started streaming on Friday night when I got here but was too scared or distracted to watch until the end in a dark room. I also watched several porn clips, mostly of women pissing, which I was never particularly interested in before.

The plot of *Banshee Chapter*, in so far as I could or did follow it, is this: a guy takes the drug DMT, or rather a fictional variant of it called DMT-19, and vanishes. His friend, a pretty woman, goes in search of him, leading to revelations about the horrors unleashed by the CIA's MK-ULTRA program, in which unwitting mental patients were subjected to experiments involving LSD, DMT and other drugs. Demonic entities have been entering our world through the minds of those who took the experimental drug DMT-19. The film seems to have been inspired by H.P. Lovecraft's short story 'From Beyond'.

Last night Ana, the representative of the publishing house that arranged this residency, took me out for drinks and to see a gig with her friends. This turned into a binge that went on until 4am. Ana told me that she used to write feminist journalism in college but lost interest when it dawned on her that most feminists are sour dogmatists who hate men. I drank a bottle of Westmalle Tripel 9.5% beer, then a shot of rakia, then a bottle of Tomislav, then, in the club where the gig took place, several bottles of a beer called Budweiser Dark, and any number of shots of honey-flavoured rakia. I took the tram back to my flat in the museum at 4:50am. I went to bed at 6am, after watching videos of women pissing.

The book I am currently reading (on my Kindle) is *Mystery School in Hyperspace: A Cultural History of DMT*, by Graham St. John. It is some 600 pages in length, which is longer than many books I would be willing to read. I am also reading (in hardback) a collection of essays by Annie Dillard. I transcribed two short passages from the first essay into a notebook on which I have written the word 'Quotes'. I have another notebook on which I wrote the words 'Dalkey Anthology' and another on which I wrote 'Anything'. All three of these notebooks have navy covers. I have two or three other active notebooks of different colours (green, white) which have nothing written on them. The other day, on a whim, I gave away an attractive hardcover notebook with the word 'Hennessy' embossed on it and now I regret it.

On Friday morning, at Dublin airport and then on the plane to Munich, my nerves were frayed from too much coffee and my thoughts were horribly obsessive. To relieve this nervous tension I filled some pages in the notebook marked 'Anything'. I wrote about how quite a few people would have to die if I am ever to be happy. I ruminated on how I have spent much of my life fantasising about exacting brutal vengeance on people who have offended or slighted me, or about acts of sudden violence towards random people on the street. I wrote about how civilisation forbids me from acting on these urges (I smile, shake hands), so my instincts wither inside me, making me unhealthy. The rage is relieved only through sublimation in art. I changed over at Munich and when I got to Zagreb I was informed that my luggage had never left Dublin. A listless woman in a drab lost-and-found office took my number and gave me an overnight emergency pack which contained the following items: folding pocket comb and mirror; small tub of Colgate toothpaste; toothbrush; t-shirt in XXL size; razor; tub of shaving cream; tube of shampoo; small packet of detergent.

You told me that you are burnt out and hate books, hate writers, hate the reasons why books are written and the reasons they seem to be read, hate even your own work. Incidentally I used to live for hate but now I am often scared of it. Some say it is self-indulgent to write about oneself but there is nothing more self-indulgent than writing. I consider myself cowardly in some ways and brave in others. Outside my apartment there is a steel balcony on one side, and clusters of what I like to imagine are communist-era high-rises in the middle distance. The blue tram shuttles in and out of the city centre. The Croatian women are shockingly beautiful – as beautiful as the French but vivacious, game. Some of them have deep, masculine voices. Many of them are strikingly tall, as are the men. In a world without consequence I would like to have sex with a different woman every day of my life. I am angry almost all of the time, arguably without justification. Some of my friends have started having children, many of them have not. On Tuesday I turned 34. A friend emailed and said, 'What age are you, 34?' Seeing the figure on the screen was disturbing. But this also happened at 19, 28, 30. It's all relative. I turned 30 in San Francisco when my life was a mess, failure everywhere. Here in Zagreb there is a Museum of Broken Relationships which I intend to visit and write about. For years I have worried that I drink too much. For years I have been drinking too much. After I send this I will go out into the city. The birds that landed on the steel balcony have flown away.

Roddy Doyle

from LOVE

He knew it was her, he told me. He told me this a year after he saw her. Exactly a year, he said.

– Exactly a year?

– That's what I said. A year ago – yesterday.

– You remember the date.

– I do.

– You're throwing your life away, I told him.

He looked at me. He stared at me. He smiled. But said nothing.

He saw her at the end of a corridor, he told me. He knew it was her. Immediately. Before he *knew*. He saw her and knew it was her. She was exactly the same. Even from that far away. Even though, really, she was only a shape, a dark, almost black, slim shape – a silhouette – in the centre of the late afternoon light that filled the open door behind her. She looked exactly the same.

– She was never slim, I told him.

He shrugged.

– I don't even know what slim means, really, he said.

He smiled.

– Same here, I said.

– She was a tall shape, he said. – Not a round shape.

– So, she's aged well, I said. – Is that what you're telling me?

He didn't answer.

– Where was the corridor? I asked.

– The school, he said.

– What school?

– The school, he said again.

– We didn't know her in school, I said.

I knew he didn't mean the school we'd both gone to. We'd known each other that long; we'd met in school, in Fifth Year. It wasn't a school that girls went to and she hadn't been one of the girls we'd hung around with, after school. I'd said it – that we hadn't known her in school – to try to get him to be himself. To give me back an answer that would get us laughing. He was the funny one.

– My kids' school, he said.

– Hang on, I said. – A parent-teacher meeting?

– Yeah.

– The woman of your fuckin' dreams stepped out of the sun at a parent-teacher meeting?

– Yes.

– Thirty years after the last time you'd seen her, I said. – More, actually. Thirty-six or seven.

He looked at me.

– Yeah, he said. – Sorry.

I don't live in Ireland. I come to Dublin three or four times a year, to see my father. I used to bring my family but these days I travel alone. My wife doesn't like flying and she says she doesn't like my father. I don't think she's mad about me, either. But that's not fair. How can a fifty-year-old woman be mad about a fifty-eight-year-old man?

And how can a fifty-eight-year-old man be mad about a woman the same age, a woman he hasn't seen in more than thirty years? A woman he never really knew. A woman he didn't even see properly until she was halfway down the corridor.

– She kissed me, he said.

– In the school?

The man I knew – I thought I knew – would have answered, 'No, in the arse,' or something like that.

– Yes, he said. – On the cheek. She remembered me.

I don't know him well.

I used to.

We left school for good on the same day. He got work; I went to college. He had money, wages; I had none until after I'd graduated. But we kept in touch while I was in UCD. We both still lived at home, a ten-minute walk from each other. We listened to records together in my house about once a week, in the front room. He bought most of the records; mine was the house where we could blast them out. My mother was dead and my father didn't seem to mind, when he was there. He told me years later that he just wanted to see me happy. He endured the noise – the Pistols, Ian Dury, the Clash, Costello – because he thought it made me happy. I'd have been happy if he'd hammered at the wall with a shoe or his fist and told me to turn it fuckin' down. I'd have been happy if I'd thought I had to fight him.

– She remembered you?

– Yeah, he said. – She did. Immediately.

I looked at him again. I could see why she'd have recognised him. The boy – the young man – was still there. His head was the same shape. He'd worn glasses back then and he still did, the same kind of black-framed glasses. He still had his hair. It was grey now – or salt and pepper – but it had never been very dark. He'd put on weight but not much, and none of it around his face or neck.

– Where were you? I asked him.

– In the school, he said. – I told you.

– Where, though?

– Outside the maths room, he said. – Waiting.

– For your turn with the teacher.

– Yeah, he said. – There were people ahead of me. But I'd no one else to see. I'd seen all the others. We divided the list.

– Hang on, I said. – Trish was there as well?

Trish is his wife.

– Yeah, he said. – Somewhere else.

– You kissed the love of your life while Trish was in the building?

– Big building, he said. – It's a fuckin' school – in fairness.

That was more like the man I thought I knew. The man I'd always wanted to be.

– You kissed her, I said.

– She kissed me.

– Where was Trish?

– The home economics room? he said. – Woodwork? Somewhere else. We took four teachers each, to get it over with. Even at that, it took all afternoon. It's the only chance the teachers get to talk to adults. So, they fuckin' grab it. I was lucky.

– How come?

– I got to meet the maths teacher, he said. – A gobshite, by the way.

– And she walked in while you were waiting.

– Right place, right time. Yes.

– One of your kids does home economics and woodwork?

– What?

– You said home economics or woodwork. Trish was in one of those rooms.

– I just meant – like, for example. She was somewhere else, in one of the other rooms, you know. Way off somewhere in the building.

– Which kid was it?

I'd never met his children and I didn't know their names. We told each other about the kids, brought each other up to date whenever we met, and then forgot all about them. I hadn't seen Trish in twenty years. But I knew, and I wanted him to admit it: he remembered the date and the place but he couldn't remember the child.

– Holly, he said.

– You sure?

– Yeah.

'Lady assistants', Irish Times, 7 August 1973

PART-TIME
BOOK SELLERS

HODGES FIGGIS
RISH BOOKSHOP LTD.

require

Lady assistants to work 20-30 hours per week — times by arrangement. A knowledge of book selling is not essential, but applicants with business experience and/or languages will be preferred.

Please apply in writing to:

Mr. Figgis,

6 Dawson Street,

Dublin 2.

Catherine Dunne

from THE WAY THE LIGHT FALLS

1986: There are many things Melina remembers, so many.

The garden, of course. She can still see the way they used to walk straight out of the living room onto that green and fragrant space. Lavender, its scent humming from the moment they stepped onto the grass. Globes of allium everywhere: a whole orchestra of shades from barely pink to deep purple. Plum trees by the back wall, with their riotous spring blossoms bright against the tawny brick. And then there were those big, cumbersome French doors that led out and away from the house. Doors that remained flung open all summer long, despite the unreliable Irish weather.

Everything was bigger then. Wilder. Fuller of possibilities.

'Lovely fresh air, Mitros,' Mama would say, tucking the blanket around his soft, yielding body. Limbs that were overly fluid, a head and neck that seemed too heavy, as though they might become unmoored from the delicate stem of his spine. 'And you are *so* right – this cool, clean air is very good for you. Just what you need.'

Mama murmured to Mitros like this all the time, as though answering his questions, her shards of conversation ends in themselves. The words his sisters heard were part of the constant dialogue that he and their mother had been having ever since before he was born.

Mitros's part in these exchanges was, of course, invisible, inaudible to Melina and Alexia, even to Papa – but not to their mother. Her crooned words, Mitros's nodding silences and his occasional strange, deep grunts used to distress their papa, Melina realized that. But she also understood, at the level that lurks beneath the words we learn to speak, that Mama could hear all of her son's questions, his answers, his silent griefs.

Mitros was two when Melina was born. As she grew older, she was often astounded at her parents' courage. To have risked another child – her – when this plaintive boy had already captivated all of their time, their care, their love?

Alexia was there too, of course she was, she was six years old by then. Even the way Melina thought about her older sister was almost like forgetting; at best, it was acknowledgement by way of afterthought. Mitros was the beating heart at the centre of their family life: they all knew that.

By the time Melina came along, Alexia was already on the cusp of mutiny. She had always understood something she did not speak about until much later: until she became an adult. Her needs, her childhood, her life had acquired shape, definition, significance only in relation to their brother. Mitros's were the greater needs, the more challenged childhood, the most complicated life. This boy, who had followed her into the family. Alexia's presence was the shadowy negative, his the positive substance against which all of their lives ultimately came to be measured.

Alexia loved Mitros; she and Melina both did. But her love was guiltier than her younger sister's. She had a memory, or a sense, some kind of unspoken recognition of an earlier life, one that had been better off without him. A life that was not filled with being her mother's little helper, Mitros's guardian, her father's solace. Alexia always felt that something had been stolen from her. Her whole life, she said, fell away into a black hole somewhere in the wake of that theft. It had no way of re-making itself, no other way of reimagining itself, after that.

Melina had no such earlier memories, no such previous life. The moment she opened her eyes, it seemed, her entire family landscape had already been configured, all its contours shaped, its smooth ways made crooked. Each of them was in his or her preordained place. What she saw was her brother's jerking body, those sloe-black eyes, that lopsided smile-that-was-not-a-smile, according to those who said they knew. When she was old enough to wonder, Melina asked her mother why God had put Mitros's face together all wrong, why his hands looked like claws, why his feet sometimes pointed like hooves. Mama's eyes filled and she turned away from her small daughter. Melina never asked again.

In time, in the way that children do, Melina accepted that her brother was different. She loved him, hated his suffering. Then she accepted his suffering, too, and sometimes envied him the pure, generous, undemanding love that he seemed to wrest from everybody who knew him.

Unlike his two sisters, Mitros could do no wrong. All the wrongness had already been visited upon him, a whole lifetime's worth of wrongness.

He was the unsullied, the innocent, the perfect one.

Mitros loved to watch the movement of the trees in the garden. For hours, his eyes would follow the comings and goings of robins and sparrows, or the stealthy approach of next door's tortoiseshell cat. Melina didn't like that cat – she has never liked cats – and she doused it with basins of cold water on several occasions when it waited, all fur and expectation, under the nest-filled apple trees. It sat, tongue darting, under the knotty branches that made summer shadows dance on the wall between Melina's house and the one next door.

Once, Mitros laughed out loud at the cartoon-like leap the cat made, when Melina at last managed to take it by surprise. She sneaked up behind it, shoes discarded, her white, frilly ankle-socks already smudged with green. Her father always said that Mitros didn't laugh, that he couldn't laugh, but Melina did not believe that. She caught a flash of something rare that day, something that was not pain in her brother's dark eyes: they filled instead with a look that was radiant and bright and joyful.

At the same time, her triumphant whoop stirred all the light-filled spaces under the apple trees' flaring branches.

published by Allen Figgis, 1960, drawings by Leslie MacWeeney

Christine Dwyer Hickey

from BACK TO BONES

One morning she opened the bedroom curtains and found the tree waiting, long dainty fingers held up for inspection – oohhhh look at me, I've got *buds* – and about to turn her back on it, when the day caught her eye: the awakening back garden; the view down the slope and over the wall to Stranraer Parade, beyond that again to the Loch where the pearly-white haze of winter had finally lifted. So, spring had come then, despite everything.

She watched for a while the midday ferry shear its way over the loch, passengers on deck with their faces turned sunwards. She could see all the way over to Ireland. Or a mauve rim of Northern Ireland anyhow, from where she had come on a similar day a long time ago. Shiny new husband, a shield to the breeze, one arm haltered about her neck, the other pointing out the this and that of his Scottish childhood.

He had been worried that she would regret the decision, that she would be homesick – for what exactly? A neurotic Belfast, air charged with suspicion and fear – of people and bags and sudden noise in the street? Her own home then – with its brown stuffy rooms filled with that awful soupy light no matter the weather or time of day, with her mother and father quietly simmering away inside it.

She tried to recall the winter just gone. November was missing, December was vague. There had been Christmas of course – Christmas with Ruth. A weepy Ruthie in her sturdy Edinburgh house, cautiously decorated.

'You don't think Daddy would mind?' she'd asked more than enough times. 'You don't think he'd find it disrespectful?'

'It's only a few old Christmas baubles, Ruthie.'

'Poor Daddy. Poor, poor Daddy. To think he was here last Christmas, sipping his brandy, watching TV sitting on that very chair.'

A full week there'd been of that: comforting, consoling, fluffing tissues out of a box, fluffing out the same few sentences while she'd been at it.

'I know my darling, I know, but your father had a good life. He went the way he would have wanted to go – quick and clean, and on the golf course.'

Ruth, like a child – a forty-five-year-old child with no child of her own, no reason to pretend to be strong. And so she had been left to play mother. And why not – she was, after all, Ruth's mother. But the truth was she'd had enough of all that mothering business. Years and years of it. Max and Ruth barely left home when her husband had stepped into their place with his blood pressure pills and his cholesterol ratings and that hiatal hernia for God's sake, like a spoilt family pet requiring constant attention and discussion. All those years of fussing and ...

'I did not want to nag,' she said aloud. 'I never wanted that.'

Her voice in the silent house, an embarrassement.

A long day ahead of her. She considered getting back into bed, turning the television on and pretending that night had already come. The nights were so much easier to manage; it was the empty daytime house that got to her. The unused rooms, the lack of routine or some sort of formality – a set table in the evenings, scrambled eggs and newspapers in the sun-room on Sunday morning. Who cared about all that fuss now? Lately, she'd taken to going to bed after the six o'clock news: crossword, library book, flask of hot tea. The television had become her companion, turning it on and losing herself in someone else's drama, drifting in and out of sleep, while it took over and sucked up the hours.

She forced herself out of the room, wandered through the house for a bit, looking in doorways, before slipping out to the back garden. She walked the pebbled edges of the lawn before crossing it at a diagonal. She did that again. When she turned at the bottom of the garden, she stopped to study the rear view of the house. How odd it looked. Three upstairs windows – two small, one large. A clumsy black pipe tilted up the middle. The largest window was opened and she could see the pale green lining on the back of a curtain and, where the breeze had given it a twist, the darker green pattern of the curtain itself. But curtains were all wrong. She felt she'd never seen them before. The windows too, the pipe-work. Everything was unrecognisable. For a moment she thought she had wandered into a neighbour's garden and that she was looking up at the wrong house. But everything else in the garden was familiar: the bench and the cast-iron bird table filled with old leaves. It was the rear of the house that she didn't recognise – that window, those curtains and whatever it was that lay behind them. A bedroom – her bedroom, surely, it would have to be?

She could feel herself slipping. Her body was too light, her heart too large. She had lost the bedroom. She had lost the house it was in, and now she was losing herself.

She crossed to the tree and sat on the damp garden bench. Breathe, she told herself, come on now, *breathe*. Breathe long and deep. Head to chest, breathe now. Breathe. That's it. Gone. After a moment, she lifted her head to a pigeon twitching on the garden wall, an empty flower pot rolling on its side, and the cold, clammy ground under her slippered feet.

Back in the bedroom she placed her hands on the green curtains. The curtains were new. Of course. The material bought in the January sales in Ayr after the Christmas visit to Ruthie. A woman called Mrs Munty had made them up; there had been a wait of six weeks. A tiny button-bed house on the far side of Cairnryan. They had cost a fortune, and she could remember thinking as she'd signed the cheque, surely a woman who charged so much could afford to live in a better house?

That was the curtains, this was her bedroom. Everything back in place. Grief. That's all it had been. Impish fingers reaching inside her, pulling and twisting the switches. Grief, the insidious bastard.

More than once she had asked Ruth, 'He won't be home then in time for Christmas dinner. Your husband, I mean?'

'I told you Mummy, he's not due till Boxing Day.' Impatience in her voice. *I told you Mummy.*

'Oh yes, so you did.'

Photographs of him all along Ruth's mantlepiece. Two of them taken in a desert somewhere. She hadn't recognised him at first, surrounded by sand and soldiers, his big sunburnt forehead bulbing out from a receding hairline. He was a doctor, of course, a military doctor serving overseas. On Christmas Eve Ruth had given her a tour of the photographs, then she had taken down a group-shot of her wedding, pointing out all the little faces. How many years ago had that been? Fifteen? More? And five guests already dead. How many more she had wondered before she too could call it a day?

She remembered the wedding with fondness, though; all the men in their kilts. And the way they had danced! The boyish vigour. Light of foot and the sway of cloth at their backsides; speed liquifying the colours. One young man had nearly torn her arms out of their sockets as he whirled her through the Dashing White Sergeant.

And Ruthie's new husband with such a sprout of gingery hair. Where had all that gone to?

She had called him Max by mistake.

catalogue published by Hodges Figgis in 1930

No. 7—New Series 1930

CATALOGUE
OF BOOKS
ON IRELAND

*Including many items of great rarity.
Also sets of Periodical Literature
in exceptionally fine condition.*

HODGES FIGGIS & CO
20 NASSAU STREET DUBLIN

Martin Dyar

Val Jester in the Basement
of Saint Catherine's Bakery

From Catherine's heart I borrowed sanity.
This morning, the dawn a hemorrhage of trust,
I ate a husk of bread and instantly
teams of devils were exiting my brain.
I heard a bitter ruckus on the stairs,
and then a sorry tumult in the lane.
And later, my mind eccentrically calm,
I heard them racing north and south at once.
Even now, with my madness restored,
I know they met death when they met the sea.
Tonight, Catherine, through the cloud of your mouth,
draw from the earth the ableness of pain.
Then once more make of one who adores you
a song-creature secure in caves of wheat.

Alan Early

The Lost Letter

The world's greatest paranormal investigators just so happened to be the world's youngest paranormal investigators and tonight they just so happened to be sneaking into a haunted library.

Ex Lavender had just turned fourteen but was touching six foot tall and was as broad-shouldered as a rugby player. His sister Ellie was two years his junior, yet was often mistaken for much younger thanks to her petite frame.

It had taken Ellie nine seconds to pick the lock of the heavy wooden door into the library, and it had taken Ex another nine seconds to disable the alarm.

Nobody had asked them to investigate. In fact, nobody ever asked them to investigate, and they were losing count of the number of times they'd saved the world in secret.

'Tell me again what we're dealing with here,' Ex said as they crept up the stairs to the main library, with flashlights leading the way.

Ellie loved these moments, when she got to go over the details of a case. She felt just like her hero, a certain Mr Holmes.

'Marsh's Library was founded in the 1700s,' she said, 'by Archbishop Narcissus Marsh.'

'Good name,' said Ex.

'Creepy name. He still haunts the library today. When he was alive, he and his niece fell out. But she sent him a letter, trying to make amends. He never read it and stuck it in one of his books. After he died, he changed his mind. He spends every night searching the library for that letter. But then about a week ago, he got violent.'

'Any idea why?'

They stopped as they reached the doorway at the top of the steps.

'I have a theory. Over time, books have been lost from the library. I think the letter was in one of those and I think Marsh has just realised it.'

She put her hand on one side of the double doors and Ex put his hand on the other and then, together, they pushed.

The library was all dark wood panelling. Bookcases as high as the ceiling were half-empty because their contents had been scattered around the floor.

They stepped in and, as they did, the doors slammed shut behind them. Neither of them jumped because they'd been expecting it. Ghosts loved slamming doors.

'Hello?' said Ellie. 'Archbishop Marsh?'

Suddenly, the entire library glowed with a green luminescence. It wasn't coming through the tall windows or from the light fixtures above. It was emanating from every surface; from the floor, the walls, even the books.

Speaking of the books, as soon as they started glowing, they also started floating. They lifted off the floor and hovered out of the shelves. Every single book in the library was soon hanging in mid-air.

'Uh oh.'

The words had just left Ellie's lips when one of the larger books shot at her face. Ex was quick, however. He pulled something out of his jacket and sprinkled a white powder at the book. The instant the grains touched the dusty cover, the book stopped glowing. It fell straight down and slid along the floor to their feet.

Ellie breathed a sigh of relief and Ex held his weapon up to her; an ordinary salt shaker, filled with ordinary salt. Ghosts were as allergic to salt as vampires were allergic to garlic.

Before she could thank him, all the books flew at them.

Most people would have ran for the exit right about now. But the Lavenders weren't most people. So, they ran *at* the books.

Books are powerful things. Even the one you're holding in your hands. They are normally unassuming and quiet. But they're full of knowledge, and portals to other worlds.

The Lavenders were aware of just how powerful books were as they fought their way through them. They punched, kicked and ducked the length of the library. Ex lost his salt shaker at the midway point and had to wrestle one insistent medical journal off of him, while several copies of the Bible nibbled at the tail of Ellie's coat.

Eventually, they threw themselves into an alcove. Ex held the wired cage door shut. Dozens of books bobbed in the air outside, like sharks circling prey. One of them curled a page along its edge, as if it was licking lips.

'Hey Marsh!' Ellie rattled the doorway. 'We have something for you!' She took something the size of a large orange out of her pocket – a crystal ball – and held it up.

There were heavy footsteps then, coming down the length of the library. The books turned in the air to face the sound, and moved out of the way.

The ghost of Archbishop Narcissus Marsh stepped up to the door. He wore a black robe, and a dour expression. He gazed down his crooked nose through the cage at Ex and Ellie.

'Have a closer look.' Ellie pushed the crystal ball higher.

Marsh stooped somewhat, sniffed, and tilted his head as he peered into the ball.

When nothing happened, he looked back at Ellie and sneered. Then he reached his knobbly fingers for the door handle. Ex held firmer.

'Wait!' said Ellie. 'Look again. Stare right in.'

The ghost sighed but did what she said. And, as he looked this time, his eyes widened.

'Do you see her?' Ellie said in a low voice. 'Do you see your niece? Do you see how much she loved you? Look closer, Archbishop. Do you see the letter? Read it.'

His eyes went over and back as he scanned the words in the crystal ball, the words that only he could see.

When he was done, he looked up at the Lavenders with tears in his eyes.

He smiled.

And then he was gone.

The books fell to the floor and, a moment later, Ex and Ellie emerged from the cage.

'Case closed,' Ex said. 'What now?'

'Let's go home.' Ellie looked around at the untidy floor. 'I feel like snuggling up with a good book.'

Martina Evans

So

The best so was a *Now so!*
a triumphant there-you-are
that I tried out energetically
after wrapping a pan loaf
with the new peach-coloured tissue
that came in during the seventies
when people realised that
newsprint mightn't be a good idea
plastered on your bread.
So sugaring what, you so-and-so!
said Carol Carey before
she complained me to Mammy
for rolling six oranges over our black
wooden counter with my left hand
while reading from Maupassant
on my right. *I'll be on to your mother so!*
There was so as an alternative –
I'm sorry, but we're out of Barry's Tea.
Well, I'll have Lyons's so.
or *I'll have Lyons's so then!*
Pale Anne Helihan came in
shyly, her arms folded,
no preliminary
only a heavy silence
before she said –
I'll have a sliced pan so!
when there had been no alternative
in the first place.
Like an answer without a question
it was a back-footed scene
so shrouded in ellipsis that
I couldn't speak –
especially when Anne was so shy.

I didn't even get to wrap it.
The Keating's green and white
and red and yellow
wax-papered sliced pan
was good to go –
so all that was left for me was
to say *Goodbye so!*
to Anne's pink woollen
retreating back
as I pitched coppers
and silver from a distance
of approximately six inches
into each wooden compartment
of the cash drawer
hoping they would land and
they rarely did –
just so.

Irish Times, 22 September 1981

Hodges Figgis to shut city shop as trade slumps

By John Stanley

HODGES FIGGIS, one of Ireland's largest booksellers, plans to close down one of its two Dublin city-centre shops at the end of this year. The company's managing director, Mr John Davey, says the decision to sell its rented interest in Stephen Court, St Stephen's Green, has been taken because of the downturn in trade.

The firm plans to consolidate its city-centre business in its shop in Dawson Street and thereby reduce its overhead costs, said Mr Davey. "We expanded quite substantially three years ago — as it turns out just at the wrong time.

"We were going well until this year", he explained, but despite achieving 30% to 31% gross profits on average, "net margins have been non-existent for the past year".

operated an agreement whereby all books were sold at the publishers' recommended retail price. Now, following the break the sellers are operating a new prices code, which has been agreed with the National Prices Commission.

250% INCREASE

The price for an imported book is set with reference to a table which includes both the VAT and

Bernard Farrell

from THE UNDERTAKING

An undertaker's office. Disorderly, sparsely furnished – a filing cabinet, a desk, some chairs. On the desk a phone, a press-button walkie-talkie, a small tape cassette player. Entrance door at stage right.

At the desk sits DENNIS. In his 60s, he is usually morose, but now enjoying a mug of tea while listening to a tape in his cassette player playing Joe Dolan's 'Make Me an Island'. Then the walkie-talkie crackles into life. DENNIS turns down the music, as:

MARTIN: *(Voice).* Hearse to Funeral Home; Hearse to Funeral Home. *(Silence. DENNIS patiently waits).* Hello?

DENNIS: Martin, how many times do I have to tell you – you say 'Over' at the end and that's how I know you have finished. Over.

MARTIN: *(Voice).* Sorry, Dennis, I forgot. Are you receiving me? Over.

DENNIS: *(Patiently).* Yes, Martin, of course I am. Over.

MARTIN: *(Voice).* Oh good. Just to say we are now leaving the church for the graveyard. Over.

DENNIS: Grand. And did any mourners turn up? Over.

MARTIN: *(Voice).* No – no mourners – so I didn't have to give anyone a lift. Over.

DENNIS: Great – then you can get the chips on your way back – and we'll make a fresh pot of tea. Over.

MARTIN: *(Voice).* That'd be grand. And did you remember to take your tablets? Over.

DENNIS: I did – soon as you left. I feel grand again now. Over.

MARTIN: *(Voice).* That's good. I think you felt that way because you missed your breakfast. I'll call you again after the graveyard. Over.

DENNIS: Fair enough, Martin. Over and Out.

DENNIS turns up 'Make Me an Island' again. He sits back contentedly, closing his eyes. The bell tinkling of the door from the street alerts him. He turns to see ANGELA – mid-fifties, soberly and smartly dressed – looking tentatively in. It is raining outside and she is now closing a very wet umbrella. The music still plays.

ANGELA: Excuse me?

DENNIS: (*Casually*). Hello? Can I help you?

ANGELA: (*Unsure*). This is a Funeral Home, isn't it?

DENNIS: (*Suddenly alert*). Oh you want the Funeral Home? Yes, this is it. Come in, come in, please. (*Turning off the music, tidying the desk, fixing his tie*). My apologies – I thought you were just stepping in out of the rain or looking for directions. We don't usually get many personal callers – we operate mainly by contract, we specialise, so to speak. Sit down there now ...

ANGELA: (*Aware*). My umbrella is wet and I don't want it dripping ...

DENNIS: (*Seating her*). Never mind that – everywhere's wet today – it's grand there. Now, let me do this ... (*Takes out the Joe Dolan tape. Inserts another tape. We hear solemn, funereal music*). There, that's better, and apologies again. (*He sits*). The confusion is that there are two bigger Funeral Homes in the town and people tend to ...

ANGELA: No, I like this one.

DENNIS: Well, that is very good to hear: we are small but you can be absolutely assured of our complete, sympathetic and professional attention ... (*Probing*) ... at this sad time for you?

ANGELA: (*Sadly*). Thank you.

DENNIS: Now. (*Opens a large ledger*). If it's not too painful, I need to register some particulars, Mrs ... Miss ...?

ANGELA: Mrs. Now widowed.

DENNIS: Of course. My deepest condolences.

ANGELA: Thank you.

DENNIS: A terrible loss I am sure. And your good husband's name was …?

ANGELA: Reginald Johnston. I used to call him Reg but his close friends always called him Reggie.

DENNIS: Always a sign of great popularity – the shortened name. However, the authorities insist that we record the name in full. May I ask if you spell it with a 't' or without a 't'?

ANGELA: Reginald?

DENNIS: No, Johnson – or Johnston?

ANGELA: Oh – Johnston.

DENNIS: Excellent. I always preferred that version myself. (*Writes*).

ANGELA: And may I say, I would like the very best, irrespective of cost. The coffin, I mean.

DENNIS: Oh, of course, of course.

ANGELA: You don't have a selection here, do you?

DENNIS: Of coffins? Well, no. The thing is, our main day-to-day business is under contract to the Government – to tend to the final obsequies of those unfortunate, forgotten people who leave this life without relatives, without money and often without their minds and who require just a simple cross to mark the grave.

ANGELA: (*Concerned*). Oh I wouldn't be having that.

DENNIS: Well, of course not, Mrs Johnston, of course not. (*Takes a brochure from his drawer. Opens a page*). No, no, no, in your case, I would be recommending something from the top of the range: perhaps this particular casket? – exceptionally good finish in oaken veneer, genuine imitation brass handles, white satin lining – this would be my personal recommendation … and it comes at this (*Indicates*) very reasonable price, including VAT, if that is acceptable?

ANGELA: (*Looks at it*). Yes. Yes, I think that would be acceptable.

DENNIS: Excellent. So let me record that, with its reference number. (*Writes in the ledger*). Now, some questions about the arrangements. Your husband died at home, did he?

ANGELA: Pardon?

DENNIS: Your late husband – his remains are in your house, are they?

ANGELA: Reginald's remains?

DENNIS: Yes, his remains.

ANGELA: But what would they be doing there?

DENNIS: Ahh – he's still in the hospital, is he?

ANGELA: Reginald? No, he's in Aylesbury in Buckinghamshire, in England. That's where he was born, where I met him, where I married him, and where I saw him die, in my arms.

DENNIS: Ah I see. And now you want him brought back?

ANGELA: Brought back where?

DENNIS: Brought back here. To be buried in Ireland.

ANGELA: But he's already buried in England.

DENNIS: Is he? In a coffin?

ANGELA: Of course in a coffin. Ten years ago I gave him the best coffin that money could buy.

DENNIS: He's dead ten years?

ANGELA: And two months.

DENNIS: Ahhhh. So now you want him exhumed and re-interred here, in *our* coffin?

ANGELA: Oh no – Reginald would hate that.

DENNIS: (*Irritated*). So who, exactly, Mrs Johnston, are we making these funeral arrangements for?

ANGELA: For me.

DENNIS: For you?

ANGELA: Yes. There are so few people you can trust these days – that's why I am here and that coffin seems excellent.

Tanya Farrelly

from OUT OF TIME

Nick Drake pulled up outside the house named 'The Arches' and cut the engine. He was twenty minutes early and there was another car, a dark grey saloon, parked in front of his. He looked at the long white bungalow illuminated by the light cast from the half-dozen lamps that lined the winding drive, and wondered if it were, after all, a good idea to have come.

Shivering, Nick reached into the pocket of his leather jacket and his fingers closed round the pack of cigarettes that he kept there for emergencies. He noted that there were only two left. With trembling fingers he placed one between his lips and held the lighter to the tip until it burned crimson. He lowered the window, and inhaled deeply until the smoke filled his craving lungs and he felt the drizzle blow in on the damp night air.

On the passenger seat his mobile phone began to ring. He looked at the screen and saw Michelle's name flash up again. Rain drummed on the windscreen and the phone rang out, and then blipped to inform him that Michelle had left yet another voice message. It was her fifth call in three days. He knew that he should've called her back, but he didn't feel like talking to anyone. Talking meant making things real. And he wasn't ready for that.

A few minutes passed before the bungalow door opened and a security light clicked on. A figure stepped into the rain, pausing to pull up the hood of an anorak before hurriedly descending the driveway. With head down, the woman made a dash for the grey saloon car. The heels of her boots clicked on the tarmac, and the indicator lights flashed amber as she hurriedly unlocked the car and slipped inside.

Illuminated briefly by the interior light, Nick saw the woman pull the hood of her anorak down and run a hand through unruly dark hair. The engine started and the saloon turned and reversed into the driveway, the headlights momentarily blinding Nick as the car turned and disappeared down the lane by which he'd come. For a few minutes he sat and stared out the windscreen. He drew on his cigarette until there was nothing more between his fingers and the tip, and then he stubbed it in the ashtray, closed the window and stepped out into the rain.

The girl who opened the door was no more than seven years old. She looked at him with big brown eyes. Then a man's voice came from a room within. 'Kirsty, I told you not to answer the door.' The owner of the voice appeared from what Nick imagined was the kitchen. 'Go on in like a good girl.' The man put an arm round the little girl's shoulder to draw her inside. 'Sorry about that,' he said.

Nick shrugged. 'The name's Nick Drake. I've an appointment for 9 o'clock.'

published by Hodges and Smith, 1838

THE

HISTORY

OF THE

COUNTY OF DUBLIN.

BY

JOHN D'ALTON, Esq., M.R.I.A.,

BARRISTER AT LAW.

DUBLIN:

HODGES AND SMITH, COLLEGE-GREEN.

M.DCCC.XXXVIII.

published by Hodges, Smith and Co in 1866

LIMERICK;

ITS

HISTORY AND ANTIQUITIES,

ECCLESIASTICAL, CIVIL, AND MILITARY,

FROM THE EARLIEST AGES,

WITH COPIOUS HISTORICAL, ARCHÆOLOGICAL, TOPOGRAPHICAL, AND GENEA-
LOGICAL NOTES AND ILLUSTRATIONS; MAPS, PLATES, AND APPENDICES,
AND AN ALPHABETICAL INDEX, ETC.

Compiled from the Ancient Annals, the most Authentic MS.
and Printed Records, Recent Researches, etc., etc.

Ὄψις τε ἐμὴ καὶ γνώμη καὶ ἱστορίη
ταῦτα λέγουσά ἐστι.—HERODOTUS, *Euterpe*, ch. 99.
"I have related what I have seen, what I have thought, and what I have learned by
inquiry".—CAREY'S TRANSLATION.

BY

MAURICE LENIHAN, ESQ.

DUBLIN:

HODGES, SMITH, AND CO., 104 GRAFTON STREET,
BOOKSELLERS AND PUBLISHERS TO THE UNIVERSITY,

1866.

Elaine Feeney

WE HAVE ONLY TIME

We notice the bull's let out for spring calving & how our
    kitchen windows
are as vast as our attempts to listen. We have only time left
    to watch.

In Nida, Cormorants & Herons shit on trees, killing them,
    the skeletal branches
unwelcoming as all things underfed. They've tried coaxing
them. Brute force. Smoking them out. But still they stay &
still they shit & still the trees die.

Once a kid drew a graph on my whiteboard & plotted
himself between man | woman | & lust. Later at dusk I
marked my X | Y | lust | love on the palm of my
hand until sweat made the green dye flow.
I have only time left to melt.

The X on Mount Sinai is imaginable if you close your eyes
& feel a woman's breath on your neck. Everyone can cross
at this X – move back – go forward –
but everyone must meet. Woman describes herself as a
    protest singer

& tells me that once her father hadn't money to buy a slice
    of fruitcake.
The best raisins are sunk in rum, plump and sweet from
the bottom of caravel barrels that went places.

progress | regress | move on | stay

There is only time left to listen.

I see clinker-built as over lapped not flapped.
I see in colour.
I am waiting for the day I wake up colourblind.

I hear the crack when a horse breaks his leg,
and then they shoot him in the middle of his blaze,
dropping like a war parachuter over France.

I can't describe pain though I have felt it.

In the Via Dolorosa, I like to eat pitta bread & coriander
    hummus,
thinking in the present tense.
I don't say a word;
it's ill mannered to speak with mouths full.

We have only time left for silence.

Leave the swastikas on the river bridge in our town, boy
    said.
Fuck the swastikas to the river bed, boys said back, we are
    all of the earth.
I heard a crow tapping at the classroom window, curling a
    fist beneath my desk.

But I listen.
And tomorrow I listen & I unlearn like sands shifting.
When rivers rise on mountains & rush to the sea they
sometimes cannot
tell if they're river or sea; their questions only echo back
    from the caves.

John Fitzgerald

FIRST LESSON

Songbirds, flying at first light
can finish themselves
against the solid air of these tall panes.
And when they do,
the whole house shudders.
At least this slim wintered thrush,
still warm and opal-eyed,
speckled breast rusting up into
the loosed neck,
sprung claws now uselessly fierce,
can have its hushed removal
in the soft hands of two small children.
They whisper rapt exchanges,
grief eased by discovery,
held perfection, privilege of touch;
they don't need to question yet
the sudden brutal instant
when everything and nothing stops
and who and what you were
is of no consequence to the brightening day.

Gabriel Fitzmaurice

CREDO

I believe without the slightest hint of proof
And blunder on in faith and hope and love,
Unworthy to receive beneath my roof
A God, if there is one, beyond, above;
And still I come tonight to celebrate
In a damaged Church the God I've come to know
(An answer to a need that is innate)
Though distant from this soul down here below.
All of us have troubles, some believe
That God will help no matter how we're cursed,
I don't know if God will help us, but perceive
The good that comes from those who simply trust,
Accept, without the slightest hint of proof,
A God of love, alas, to me, aloof.

Patricia Forde

Wish Dream Curse

The Manual: Paragraph 447 Sub-section 12
Wishing on a star is an ancient custom on Earth. This in no way implies that such wishes should be automatically granted.

It's not that I hate humans. I really don't hate them but I do find them annoying, SO annoying. They seem to spend their time whinging and moaning, never happy with their lot and always wishing, of course. Throwing wishes around like snuff at a wake.

I wish I had blue eyes. I wish I lived in the city. I wish I were dead.

Oh don't worry. They don't usually *mean* it when they say that. You see, they don't think anyone is listening. To the wishes, I mean. But of course there's a whole department listening: listening and judging, granting and refusing – and filing. I do most of the filing.

Claude Carver is my boss. He runs the department. Picture a long double height room with high windows. High, so you can't see through them and be distracted. Then picture row after row of wooden benches. Ok. Now picture me. My name is Mia and I am thirteen years old. I have green eyes, slanted green eyes like a cat, with nice long brown lashes just like my mother. I have a nose. Just a regular nose and I have a large mouth. (In my opinion way too large). My hair is brown, nut-brown dad says, and long. And picture this: I am really bored. So bored you have no idea.

Here's what I am supposed to do:

1 Take a wish card from the main distribution area.

2 Read the wish.

3 Note the judgement already made by the main server.

4 File the wish in the appropriate place.

5 In very RARE circumstances question the judgement given.

Actually, that last bit isn't really true. Claude Carver doesn't want anyone to question anything. And usually, I don't. I read it and I file it. All of that was true until a wish came in from Cynthia Meehan. The computer had rejected it. It was a strange wish. I read it twice to be sure I had understood.

I wish this curse could be lifted.

That's what it said and it made me pause and think. You see, we don't often see anything about curses, because there is a whole other department taking care of that area. I should know. My brother Ross works there. He has a really exciting life flitting from one mysterious place to another chasing cursers and their curses. You see cursing is inclined to happen in exotic places nowadays. That's why this wish was even more surprising. It came from a human on the west coast of Ireland. Ireland is lots of things but it's not exotic. We get loads of wishes from Ireland. To be honest, they are one of our largest clients. Irish people seem to do little else *but* make wishes. They used to be big on cursing people too, but that was a hundred years ago or more. Modern Ireland does not go in for cursing. That's why the wish was so intriguing. It sounded like something from the dark ages.

I was so absorbed in the wish that I didn't notice the dark cloud that was my boss Claude Carver descending on me.

In Claude's world operatives are either good or bad. There is nothing in between. My parents had been good operatives. My brother Ross, who works in curses, is a good operative. To be fair, Ross is good at everything. He's clever and handsome and funny in a really quirky way. Everyone loves him, even Carver. My sister Baba, who works in Dreams Section A, is a good operative, she is diligent and creative and slightly nutty, which is all you need for Dreams. I am not a good operative, according to Claude, and he tells me that every chance he gets.

The first I knew of his presence that day was when I saw his meaty hand land on my desk. I looked up. His small eyes squinted down at me.

'Problem Operative 4457?'

'No sir,' I said in my best cheerful voice. 'No problem.'

I hated the way he referred to me as a number. What was wrong with my name?

'So why are you staring into space like a thing possessed Operative 4457?'

'I was just thinking sir,' I said. 'About this wish. It's very interesting, because it is about …'

'Has it been approved by the server?'

Claude spat the words at me, his thick lips trembling.

'No sir,' I said. 'It hasn't but …'

'No Operative 4437! There is no "but". If it has not been approved, then all that remains is for you to do your duty and file it. Is that clear?'

He was so close now I could count the hairs in his nose.

'Yes sir!' I said.

Reluctantly, he moved away. My friend Bronwen looked across at me and raised an eyebrow. Everything ok? I shrugged.

I looked at the wish again. It still troubled me. I was so immersed in thoughts about the wish, that it took me a few moments to notice the disturbance down below on the floor. When I did look, I got a shock. Someone was talking, words toppling over other words, volume way too loud for the workplace. It was my dad. My dad in his staying-at-home sweater with the patches on the elbows. My dad looking small under the great windows. My dad in my workplace in the middle of the day. He was talking to Carver, and even as I watched, he looked up and caught my eye. I knew then that he hadn't come with good news. My feet found their way to the stairs and I climbed down.

Carver started to say something but I ignored him. I looked at dad.

'What is it?' I said.

'It's Ross,' he said. 'He's missing.'

Órfhlaith Foyle

from THE AFTER-LIFE OF OSCAR HEAVEY

According to Dr Thomas Gilroy, Mrs Dolores Edge had summoned him to her place of business after Polly Salmon had gone into a surprising and nightmarish miscarriage on the early evening of the fifth of December 1927. He wasn't sure of the exact hour but he had finished his tea so it was definitely after half-past five. He was a nervous man and he had a slow heart. He was retired, but now and again was called to various homes.

'Did you do an examination?' Heavey asked.

'Naturally, Detective.'

'And what was there?'

'Blood, of course, and something akin to the afterbirth.'

'And the baby?'

'I didn't see the baby.'

'But you knew that there had been one?'

'Yes.'

'Did you ask about the baby?'

'Yes.'

'And what did Mrs Edge reply?'

'She said they had cleaned it away.'

'They?'

'She and that bit of an Abo girl that was with her.'

'How many months pregnant was Polly Salmon?'

'I don't know.'

'Mrs Edge didn't enlighten you?'

'No.'

'Did you assist her in the abortion?'

'Not an abortion …' The doctor's right hand wobbled to his chest. 'This is upsetting,' he said. He ran his hands over his hat brim. 'My wife is ill.'

'How long have you been retired?'

'Ten years.'

'Were you a good doctor?'

'I had many patients.'

'And you never disposed of babies?' Heavey asked.

Dr Gilroy shook his head.

'Describe how you found Polly Salmon.'

'Excuse me?'

'The state she was in after her … miscarriage.'

'I told you. Blood.'

'And what else?'

'Membrane trails …'

'So there was something of the baby there?'

'No. No there was nothing.'

'Dr Gilroy … I found the baby.'

Dr Gilroy licked his upper lip. 'I did not see the remains of the miscarriage. You must understand that I arrived at the end … the end …'

'The end of what?'

Dr Gilroy raised his hands and shifted in his chair. He stared at the door behind Detective Heavey's head. The damp from the walls made him shiver. He was innocent. He had merely arrived to a call for help. The girl on the table was pouring so much blood, and he had stood in the doorway, afraid for his shoes. He licked his lips. 'May I have some water?'

Heavey persisted. 'You came to the door and Polly Salmon was on the table, covered in blood, isn't that right?'

Dr Gilroy thought of his wife at home and he thought of gaol at seventy years of age. He had a good house and a near comfortable life despite his shakes and his seizing bones, and a wife who was constantly remembering her childhood. He licked his lips. He asked for water again.

'Not yet, old man,' Heavey said.

Fix her, old man. Dolores Edge had ordered.

Dr Gilroy had tried not to get blood on his shoes but even as he tiptoed in, the girl's birth blood seeped under. He slipped and clutched out at the table's edge. Her toe was at his face. Her blood had reached there. She was whimpering like a dog and he closed his eyes trying not to see between her legs. *Jesus, Gilroy, do your bloody job.* Looking into Polly Salmon's open and seeping vagina, Dr Gilroy saw the recent evidence of a traumatic and violent act.

He stared at the Detective in front of him who now picked up an instrument shaped like a forceps and held it to his nose.

'Carbolic,' the detective announced.

Dr Gilroy thought of the girl on the table. Wet blonde hair and a lace frill on the open neckline of her dress. A wedding ring also and her fingers were fat with fluid, her throat wide with fear. Her smell caught his nose; urine, faeces and blood and small shreds of afterbirth hanging at her vagina's lips.

'These instruments aren't your property,' Detective Heavey said.

'No,' Dr Gilroy agreed.

'So if they are not yours, they must be hers.'

'Yes.'

Heavey smiled at the old doctor. 'Perfect.'

Constable Adcock peeked his head through. 'Winston has Polly Samuel's photographs, sir.'

Heavey nodded and chose a blank piece of paper. 'Time, Constable?'

Adcock held the door open with one foot while he checked his watch. 'Just after midday, sir.'

Heavey wrote the time down. 'Date?' he said.

'Sixth of December, sir.'

'All that blood,' the doctor said.

He remembered the Abo girl scrubbing blood off her hands at the kitchen sink.

It just came out, she said. The girl looked at him with that absent face that other half-Abos of his experience had and kept looking until Dolores Edge said, *She's bleeding, Gilroy.*

Polly Salmon bubbled breath and spit. *I didn't want it. I didn't want it.*

She's going to die, Dr Gilroy told Dolores and the Abo girl.

Heavey placed a blank piece of paper and pen in front of the good doctor.

'Write down what happened. Sign it. Then Constable Adcock will get you some water.'

The old man took the pen and wrote for a long while. In the end he handed Heavey a simple half page statement. The Detective read it and smiled. 'I'll have that bitch swinging.'

Freeman's Journal, 30 November 1815

HODGES AND M'ARTHUR,

WHO for several years conducted Business for the Firm of GILBERT AND HODGES, respectfully take leave to inform their Friends and the Public, that they have commenced the

BOOKSELLING & STATIONARY BUSINESS,

At their House, No. 21, College-green.

One of the Partners has just returned from London, where he has made a Collection of Books in the different departments of Literature and Science, which they hope will merit approbation.

They avail themselves of this opportunity of stating, that they shall be most punctual in executing any orders with which they may be honored, relative to the supply of periodical Publications.

They beg leave to apprize those Gentlemen who had engaged the late Firm of GILBERT & HODGES, to furnish them with Reviews Magazines, &c. that they have adopted measures to supply the arrear which they may have incurred, and to continue to supply them soon after their publication in London.

Mia Gallagher

from CHIEF

The pub is in a shopping mall on the west side, the only outlet still open. It's all spindly plastic seating, chrome-and-plastic tables that jiggle when you set down your drink, stark overhead lighting and loud music blaring from the jukebox, the same music they'd heard on their approach. The jukebox seems to be there only for show, though, because any time Maeve suggests selecting a different track, the rest of the group shrug. The music is ugly Euro-rock, with schmaltzy faux-American vocals. Roxanne, Scorpions, Foreigner. Dalilah catches Maeve's eye and grimaces, but Uwe is tapping his feet, drumming his fingers on the chrome table-top.

Two tables away sit a middle-aged couple. The woman has hair like straw, a cheap bottle-job, and is wearing a leopardskin halterneck. Her tits are big in a German way and the halterneck does them no favours, dragging them down to her belly. The sort of figure Maeve dreads having when she's that age. The man is in a tight, pea-green poloneck and wears his thinning brown hair combed across his scalp. His skin, pale and gleaming, shows through the strands. He's got sunglasses on. He looks like a pimp, Maeve thinks, though she's never seen one. In front of them they each have a plate of wurst and sauerkraut, and a stein of beer. The woman eats quickly, drinks slowly; the man gulps his beer, picks at his wurst. He looks at Dalilah every time she gets up to go to the bar, his eyes sliding down her like snail-slime, clinging to every jut of her arse, swing of her hips.

Uwe makes another joke, banging his fist on the table. Foam splashes over his hand. The group laughs.

The woman in the halterneck pushes away her empty plate and, taking the hand of the man in the poloneck, lifts it to her mouth. Then she begins sucking him; little finger, ring finger, fucking finger, all the way across to the thumb.

Maeve thinks of the letter she read that morning, the spidery, inky-brown script. *Papa ran his index finger around her gums, very carefully, moving from her back to her front teeth. Elsa felt all of herself except her mouth begin to tremble.*

The man lifts his drink with his free hand, gulps, belches, glances across the pub at Dalilah's black arse on its spindly chair. He catches Maeve looking and stares. His stare is Robocop blank through the sunglasses.

'So,' said Papa. He said it soft; a light sound, wind whispering through trees. 'We may need some adjustment here. Otherwise, my dear, you run the risk of ruining your perfection.'

'Have you heard anything about your cousin's son?' one of the friends asks Dalilah, later, when they're all a bit more drunk. At least, that's what Maeve thinks she says. It's hard to hear with the music and everyone talking much faster.

'They're not *my* cousins,' says Dalilah. This bit is clear. 'We're not all related, just because we're Turkish.'

The friend sighs. 'Piss off, sow. I mean –'

'I know,' says Dalilah. 'Sorry.' She lights a fag. 'No.'

Maeve must look curious because Dalilah leans over. Her cleavage smells of peaches. 'The sister of my second cousin's husband.' She speaks slowly, as if to a child. 'Their son went missing two months ago.' She snaps her fingers. 'One second here, playing ball with his friends down by the river. The next, gone.'

Is she hearing correctly? Dalilah keeps talking, but now she's sped up again. Maeve doesn't want to interrupt, so she just nods, shakes her head. Then, at last, something she can understand:

'It's probably family. An uncle, wanting him back.'

Maeve nods. Dalilah's expression seems to beg a different response.

'Schade,' says Maeve, making her face look sorry. *Shame.*

Dalilah raises her eyebrows. Maeve flushes.

'Why not the *something*?' shouts someone.

Orangen Leute, it sounds like to Maeve. Orange People?

Dalilah starts to laugh. 'Oh yeah.' To Maeve, slowly again: 'The Orange People. It's a sex cult. You've seen them, yeah? So German. The Germans are always crazy for sex.'

'Freaks,' yells someone in English.

The table laughs, Maeve joins in. In the back of her mind, she sees him again, the rangy young man from the tram, with his acne scars and his orange clothes. The passport thief, her stalker.

'How is he with you?' says Uwe, much later, leaning in. His breath stinks of cigarettes.

Maeve has no idea what he's talking about.

'Has he *something something*?'

'Um. I don't know –'

'He won't *something* with Dalilah. That's because of me.' Uwe knocks his fist against his chest. 'He knows I'm *something*, yeah? He's afraid of *something* Turks *something* –'

Is he talking about Paul Bauer, her boss, the good dentist?

'Uwe, shut your mouth, you arsehole.' Dalilah is behind them, cradling five beers to her chest.

Uwe shrugs. 'I'm not saying anything.'

'He's a good man.' Dalilah glances at Maeve. 'All that last year, nothing to do with him. A mistake, ok?'

Uwe snorts, takes a beer, swallows.

'I mean it,' says Dalilah. 'Don't talk shit, Uwe. I'm not having it. He's a good chef.'

'That's not what you said last year –'

'I mean it, Uwe. Things like that happen. You can't *something* –'

Blame? thinks Maeve, grasping.

'– he did nothing. No badness done, ok. Speech like that, lying, it does no good. So shut it.'

The conversation turns. They're talking way too fast now, too slangy. The music is pumping. The bar is a blur, full of vague figures and foreign smells. Maeve wishes she was at home, in Ireland, with her own friends, her own family, in her own bars, in her own mind.

Susanna? she wanted to ask Uwe. Are you talking about Susanna, the girl who used to babysit the Bauer children? Something she did, something that got done to her? But there were too many other words in the way; inky brown spiders, stopping her mouth.

published by Hodges and Smith in 1845

THE

INDUSTRIAL RESOURCES

OF

IRELAND.

BY

ROBERT KANE, M.D.,

HONORARY MEMBER OF THE ROYAL DUBLIN SOCIETY, AND OF THE FLAX
IMPROVEMENT SOCIETY OF IRELAND;
SECRETARY TO THE COUNCIL OF THE ROYAL IRISH ACADEMY;
PROFESSOR OF NATURAL PHILOSOPHY TO THE ROYAL DUBLIN SOCIETY, AND
OF CHEMISTRY TO THE APOTHECARIES' HALL OF IRELAND.

Second Edition.

DUBLIN:
HODGES AND SMITH, GRAFTON-STREET.
LONGMAN AND CO., AND SIMPKIN AND CO., LONDON.
MACLACHLAN AND STEWART, EDINBURGH.
MDCCCXLV.

Carlo Gébler

from AESOP'S FABLES
a new version, illustrated by Gavin Weston

1: *The Good Things and the Bad Things*

The things on earth that did mankind good were vexed. Wherever they went, whatever they did, the things that did mankind bad followed close behind and spoiled whatever good they'd done. To see their efforts ruined was bad enough but on top of that there was the stigma that now attached to them: human beings (admittedly not the brightest), not understanding the way the things that did bad just followed in their wake, had come to believe that the things that did mankind good were *in actual fact* the authors of all their woes and to blame for everything bad. So the things that did mankind good flew to Olympus to ask Zeus if anything could be done to ensure they and the bad were never confused again.

'Oh yes,' said the god when they'd finished their presentation. 'From today, you'll live here with me on Olympus and the bad will live on earth. That's the answer.'

Since when the things that do mankind bad, as they live on earth, torment them continuously, whilst the things that do mankind good, who must travel from the sky (which is a long way away, of course) are only occasional visitors. This also explains why life seems to men and women like one long round of misery.

Small people (and Gods) often live in big houses.

2: *The Man Selling a Holy Statue*

A man carved a statue of Hermes and took it to the market to sell. He waited several hours but no buyer came near.

'I'll need to do something here,' he said to himself, 'if I'm going to shift this.'

He thought for a moment and then – inspiration.

'God for sale,' he shouted, 'who will give you whatever goods you want *and* profits – guaranteed. You demand, he delivers!'

'Well, if he's so good,' asked a passer-by, 'what are you selling him for? Shouldn't you keep him for yourself?'

'I know I should,' said the vendor, 'but he's so slow and I need the money – now!'

There are no faults in the thing we want badly.

3: *The Eagle and the Fox*

It seems unlikely but it happened; an eagle and a fox became friends and, believing that the more they saw of each other the more they would like each other, they decided to live as neighbours. So the eagle nested at the top of a pine tree and hatched her chicks there, while the vixen made a den for herself in a thicket at the foot of the pine and delivered a litter of cubs.

One winter's day, when the vixen was away foraging, the eagle, who also wanted food for her young, spotted her friend's cubs playing at the foot of the tree. She flew down, caught them all and carried them up to her nest where she fed them to her fledglings.

The vixen returned at dusk. From the fur scraps scattered around she deduced the whole story.

'It should be grief I feel but it's hate,' the vixen said, staring up at the eagle sitting looking cool, calm and indifferent in her nest. 'And all I want is to hurt you but I can't,' she continued. 'You have wings and I don't. You're a creature of the air, and I'm a creature of the land. I can't get at you.'

Her sense of impotence made her rage even sharper. She let out a long anguished cry: this was the kind of cry that the powerless typically make when they are traduced by the powerful and are unable to strike back. The eagle heard this cry but she paid no attention to it.

The next day, in a nearby hunter's camp, a goat was roasting on a spit above a fire while its discarded entrails were sizzling on the embers below. The eagle swooped in, snatched these up, and carried them away. 'They'll be a tasty titbit for my chicks,' she thought.

However, unknown to the eagle there was a spark lodged in the viscera and when she dropped the entrails down to her brood the spark fell out. It set the dry nest alight and the nest set the nearby pine needles on fire and within seconds the whole of the tree top was burning like a brand.

The vixen, in her den below, heard the crackle of flames and the piping cries of the eaglets. She ran out and looked up. The mother eagle was circling around the tree while her babies were leaning over the edge of their nest, shrieking.

'Save us,' the eaglets called.

'Jump,' their mother shouted.

One after another the eaglets jumped and one after another, as they could not fly, they plummeted and smashed into the ground right in front of the vixen, splintering their frail bones and dying instantly.

The vixen now got to work. She plucked then split the first eaglet carcass neck to tail then pulled the pink flesh free from the spindly chest bones with her sharp teeth. As she swallowed the first bloody mouthful of breast she heard the mother eagle overhead as she circled through the smoke making a strange noise. It was the noise the powerful make when the powerless pay them back. The vixen paid no attention.

Punishment is lame but it comes.

Patricia Gibney

from DEATH OF AN ARTIST

Crouching at the edge of the turret, she takes a final look at the scene in front of her. Vast fields of various shades of green, to which she can assign an artist's colour for each hue. Veridian. Hookers. Sap. Olive. Emerald. Not quite the fifty shades of green her father was apt to mention when he viewed Ireland through his rose-tinted glasses. And over there, iridescent oilseed rape radiates Cadmium Yellow on the upslope of a hill. She can even decipher the shimmering silver of the lake in the distance, but she knows that up close and under the sun it is Cerulean Blue.

She turns her head to her left. The twin spires of Ragmullin's Catholic cathedral and the single spire of the Protestant church nip through the azure haze that appears to be wrapping itself around her town, swallowing it up. To her artist's eye the haze is like a sinister fog resting on the shoulders of some macabre spectre. Between the spires, rooftops appear to shiver. Her town. Once. But no more.

To her right, the castle walls loom up around her, casting shadows long and deep. She grasps the crumbling stone tighter and wonders why the colour now appears to have drained from the landscape. Down below her, the gargantuan grey gargoyles are opening their mouths to scream at her. Warning or coaxing? Just in front of them, the man-made waterfall spurts water into a curved pond, in which helpless tiny fish swim round and round, day after day with no chance of escape. Just like her.

Clutching her hand to her chest she stems the palpitations of her heart with a sharp thump. Letting go of the ancient stone, she stands upright, her bare feet with Alizarin Crimson varnished nails, her only anchor to earth.

Standing.

Out on the edge.

On the edge of her existence?

No.

On the edge of her extinction.

A blackbird, plumage plumped, pauses on a chink in the turret and calls out. 'Chack, chack, chack.'

Turning towards him, she glares. With his yellow beak and black eyes he returns her stare. Mars Black. He nods, a slow deliberate bow, and with a flutter of his wings, he flies off towards the richness of the trees.

A slight wind chafes her skin. If she remains here any longer, freckles will bump up on her paleness. Orange hair floats about her shoulders, and her body trembles even though the sun is dominating the sky.

Will they miss her? Probably. But she knows there is one who will be glad she is no longer around. And she will be liberated from his torment. Yes, that is reason enough. She stretches her arms outwards, hewn stone beneath her feet, between her and eternity. Ready.

A whisper of a breeze glides to her ear. With her toes crooked around the crumbling ledge, she dare not look behind. Peels her eyes to the field of oilseed rape in the furthest distance. Nerve ends tingle beneath the hair follicles on her arms. A breath caresses her neck. Evil lingers on its tendrils.

And she is totally aware. In that instant. She is not alone.

Now that she has reached this height, in this space suspended between life and death, she changes her mind. This is not the way. She must face her demon tormentor. Is it too late?

Slowly, she attempts to turn, her resolve for escape diminished, replaced by a vow to fight. On this fortress castle, built by her ancestors and abandoned by her family, her fingers claw as she tries to find surface on the turret.

With the slightest touch, a cold finger nudges her shoulder blade. Bone on bone. Teetering, over and back, she stretches out her arms to grab something, anything. But there is only air.

He steps out and faces her. His laugh is sharp and manic. And he pushes again.

Her scream dies in the rawness of her throat. As she topples earthwards, the gargoyles appear to roar and the blackbird calls out loudly and the fish swim round and round in never-ending circles. She is wrong. He is not the one whom she had feared and in those seconds of her life's denouement, she knows that perhaps no one will suspect him.

But she has one last hope – the final painting she created.

As the colour fades, then washes out on her canvas of life, at last she is free.

And he is doomed.

published by Allen Figgis in 1969

Written by a widely experienced gynaecologist, this book outlines frankly the basic facts of marriage—the sex act, conception, pregnancy and labour—and will prove of great value to parents and teachers. There is a special section on the change of life.

riverrun

life
Michael Solomons

cycle

Karen Gillece

LOVE TOKENS
after Jules Breton's painting of the same name

The other gleaners have moved on to Monsieur Lefevre's field, but we three have fallen behind. We will catch up with them later under the shade of the trees where they will pass around jugs of water and we can moisten our tongues, shriveled by the dust and grain that fill the air where recently wheat grew tall and golden.

We are crafting love tokens. My knees hurt and the front of my feet are numb as I kneel under the searing heat of the afternoon sun. It warms my neck as my eyes fix on the wheat in my hands. I knot the tiny sheaf together and begin the delicate task of bending each strand back on itself. I look up at Eve and watch the neat latticework rising up through the rough stalks as she carefully twists and tugs. My effort is lumpy and brutish in comparison.

'Maman says that if you place a love token under your pillow as you sleep, you will dream of your intended,' she says quietly.

This elicits a snort from Annick. She does not weave and fashion the wheat, but stands watching us, hands on her hips.

'You will not dream of anything. With that thing under your pillow you will not get any sleep.'

'Maman says –'

'What would she know?'

Annick's cheeks burn under the sun. She brushes back a strand of hair that is stuck to her forehead.

'And who is it you hope to dream of?'

Eve doesn't answer.

'Some silly boy, no doubt. Probably not even old enough for the harvest,' Annick says.

She leans against Eve, a meaty hand on her shoulder, and turns her face to me. Large teary eyes peer over porcine cheeks, and my hands quicken, rapidly weaving and tightening.

'And you, Jeanne?'

I shift a little, my knees feeling the harsh prickling of cut wheat beneath them.

'Who has been lucky enough to capture your heart?'

'No one.'

'Ha!'

I look up at her face.

'No one.'

She stares back.

'No one indeed.'

Her voice is flinty and I realise that she knows.

My chemise pinches under my arms and sticks to my back. I look up at her, yellow hair uncovered and glinting in the sunlight, a thin mouth in her flat face.

'What about you? Aren't you making one?'

I feel the vinegary taste of the words as they leave my mouth.

Her eyes fill with hurt and instantly I regret it. A storm of ghosts has blown up around us, the memory of a young man intoxicated by the cry of revolution, pikes and stabbings and other unspeakable things.

Her hand drops from Eve's shoulder.

'They will be wondering where we are.'

She turns away quietly and moves through the field.

Round and round we dance, sparks crackling up from the flames, skirts lifting as our bare feet race, tempo increasing with every beat. Smoke from the fire rises, spiraling in laces that weave their way into the dusk. Our voices soar with it, touching the half-moon that hangs in the night sky.

The harvest is over, all the wheat has been cut and bound, each stray grain picked from the earth, rescued by our gleaning hands. And now we celebrate. The fires have been lit over the barren ground, flames leaping, sending up spluttering sparks that threaten our skirts as our feet pound the earth. Girls dance and men watch, quenching a thirst that has built up all summer. There are lewd remarks and bawdy laughter, and we dance with hair swinging, losing ourselves in the delirium.

My lungs heave, filling with heat, and I release my grip on the hot hands that bind me, breaking away from the ring, my place filled by another. I stagger past the men, ignoring their low voices and carnal glances, and remember the shadowy chin, his black eyes, a whispered urgency in his voice.

'You will come to me later, won't you?'

His hand pressuring the small of my back.

Escaping into the shadows, I find the path, a silvery ribbon stretching over the field. The boisterous singing and raucous laughter thins behind me as I hurry away, my pace quickening. The path twists and burrows into the sunless earth, leading me down to the river. I glance back to see have I been followed. Smoke rises from behind the trees, obliterating the stars in dense grey blankets. But there is no one there, only the low hissings of night-creatures in the undergrowth.

My heart pounds with anticipation. Stepping over weeds and hollows, I seek out shapes and figures in the gloom. I recall the touch of his hand on mine, the whispered instructions, my hurried promise. Something moves up ahead and I lean towards it, listening for a voice in the darkness, calling me to him.

A breeze moves through the trees, and the moon casts its light coldly and briefly on pale legs clasped tightly around a dark figure. Bare feet, soiled soles, toes curled in exertion. They move together rhythmically, breathing staccato. Untamed yellow hair, eyes closed over porcine cheeks, thin mouth straining and twisting in pain. And suddenly the eyes fly open, large teary eyes. They fix and stare – blue, melancholy, stinging.

The breeze dies away and the trees become still, merciful darkness returning. Their breathing follows me as I slip away. Finding the silver path, I start to run through the savaged wheat field, away, away. Something rattles in my pocket, brushing against my thigh as I beat through the field. I reach down and take it from my skirts, lumpy and primitive. I can hear the drums now, and the singing, and see the lick of orange flames through the clearing. Leaving the wheat field, I fling it into the darkness, returning my love token to the ground from where it came.

Shauna Gilligan

from When the October Wind Comes

The corpse lies frozen, the first in a line. A litter of bodies along the mountain road.

Over this body, once youthful, stands one of Franco's men, machete in hand. He works quickly, for he feels the cold of this awful place. He works quickly, for he wants to return to from where he came. He works quickly, for gold is money. This man is no longer a man; the red of a shirt no longer red but a dull iron or perhaps copper colour, a mix of blood and shit and filth. He works quickly for this man whose flesh is disappearing as the wolves have their nightly feast; this man is no longer in need.

He looks behind him, anxious to get what he can. Anxious to be the first to claim what he can. Some of the troops have already moved onwards towards the towns. Towns, he thinks, towns in these godforsaken mountains! Franco's man, who shivers now and can hardly feel his feet, surveys the long line of work before him. A freezing fog has fallen and he cannot see the end of the bodies and his hands are smattered with frostbite but still his fingers work nimbly. His pockets are becoming fat with teeth in which nuggets of gold sit, winking like light in fog.

It is difficult, this work, but he and his fellow soldiers have had their wits tested in the heat of the desert and the plains of Africa. The Asturian cold is nothing, and the mountains not more difficult to cross than The Altas; but the fighters, he has to admit, are something to behold in how they hide and dodge the fight: in the trees, in the mountain caves, like the savages that they are.

Their courage is something that he will never speak of. They die rather than surrender. They must think, he laughs, that they will be rewarded. The villages have been told, promised by the government that the Legion and the

Arabs will do no harm to civilians. Harm? Is that not just another word for war? Harm? But how is he to distinguish between civilians and fighters when they are all working together, these people, in this place where it seems, at times, that even death can be defeated.

He has been instructed to act *mercilessly*. And he, like his superiors, is nothing if not obedient. The tools he has been given will soon be worn from use: machete, pistol, rifle, and knives, long and short. He takes a breath and starts on the next man.

Celtic Studies catalogue published by Hodges Figgis in 1971

Celtic Studies

*A list of recent
Acquisitions
Antiquarian
Out-of-Print
New*

HODGES FIGGIS & CO. LTD.
Established 1768
5 & 6 Dawson Street,
Dublin 2,
Ireland.
Telephone: Dublin 776375

**AUTUMN
1971**

Anthony Glavin

from WAY OUT WEST

Nearly a year after he landed in Cleveland, Fintan finally got farther west. Farther southwest to be precise, 560 miles down I-71 and onto I-70 as far as St Louis. Picture him there nine months later: a June afternoon in 1977, within a stone's throw of the Mississippi. He stands at the lower end of the Arch, left cheek pressed against its chill, tracking its parabola of shimmering steel with his upcast right eye. It was the Arch that had caught his eye last September – like an arc of silvery water shooting up from a hose behind a tall office block, and pouring down onto the gold dome of the state capitol. The shirt salesman who had lifted him outside Indianapolis was heading for Tulsa, Oklahoma, but Fintan, unable to take his eyes off the massive sculpture, hopped out two red lights later, thinking to spend a day or two looking round.

That which he saw quickly slowed his gallop west. Not alone the Arch or the steamboats moored along the storied river he had first encountered in a tattered paperback of *The Portable Mark Twain* his mother Mary had turned up back in Donegal, but the city itself – entire neighbourhoods of grand houses and cobblestone streets, jazz clubs, a baseball stadium and towering brick brewery – its vibe utterly unlike Cleveland: not exactly Southern, but far funkier than what he had seen so far of the corn-fed Mid-West.

'Check this out, Jake?' he waves at a skinny black guy with a wispy goatee, who wanders over to lean his head against the Arch and eyeball it too. Jake is one of his clients, an ex-mental patient Fintan is helping to get housed as part of his new gig with the city's Social Welfare Department. It's a new job and one he largely likes, driving around to Goodwill or Salvation Army shops, helping a client pick out a bed or kitchen table, which together they trundle into the green van with its SWD-crest, then unload at whatever rented accommodation the client has secured, usually a Single Room Occupancy or SRO as Will, his boss, calls them. The clients are largely ok too; a good few, like Jake, Vietnam vets. A lot of them drink, which Fintan is supposed to take note of, but it's really none of his business, he figures, though he draws the line at swigging from the bottle which those who do drink invariably proffer. St Louis differs from Cleveland that way too – in that he himself is drinking less.

'Uh uh,' Jake says, jerking his head back from the steel base of the Arch. 'I don't dig heights,' so they head back to the van in the car park. Fintan doesn't mind how the Arch hasn't worked for Jake like it does for most of the clients he brings down here. 'Holy shit!' they shout, or something like that, after he gets them to sight up along the shaft, thinking it might startle them out of their heads – if only for a moment.

'I don't sleep in a bed,' Jake says in the Salvation Army shop on Union Road. 'Sleep on the floor, man.'

'What if you meet a woman?' Fintan counters.

'She can take me home!' Jakes grunts. But when Fintan explains how they can't use the bed allowance on a tiny black and white TV, Jake finally agrees to a bed. On their way over to his new abode, he tells Fintan of a marine buddy who went AWOL from a German military hospital only to end up in Ireland, where a guy with six kids whom he met in a Dublin pub took him home. Kept him for three months in a small shed at the bottom of his garden, the same shed, Jake says, where an aunt with TB had lived when the Irish guy was growing up.

That, too, was something different about America, Fintan had noted, the way you weren't squirrelled away somewhere if you weren't entirely sound in body or mind.

Not confined to a kitchen loft, say, like the mad brother in a house up the Glen who, according to Uncle Condy, used to call out from on high, 'More bread or I'll appear,' whenever his two spinster sisters entertained a caller. Nor packed off to a 'hospital' like his pal Rory's retarded younger sister, or to similar grim, grimy institutions around the country, if you suffered from cerebral palsy or epilepsy.

Take, for example, his boss Will, whom Fintan had first met at his interview two months before. The advertised position of 'Care Worker/Van Driver' was the first people-oriented job he had ever gone for, apart from bartending, and he had waited nervously on a folding chair outside the interview room. Nor had it settled his nerves either, when walking in he saw this bloke with an outsized head and shoulder-length, 'Wild Bill' Hickok-like, hair, seated in a high-backed wheelchair at the head of the table, a respirator tube tucked, hookah-smoking-caterpillar style, into a corner of his mouth.

'Take a seat,' Will had instructed him out of the other corner of his mouth, 'and draw a breath.' Said it like the shoe were on the other foot, the way a guy looking for work is the one with a handicap, and he wanted to set Fintan at ease.

The woman on the three-member interview board asked about his present job, so Fintan described The People's Food Co-op off Market St, which had been happy to hire as Produce Manager somebody who had actual experience of planting cabbage, spuds, carrots and onions, albeit on the other side of the Atlantic. Though produce manager was a bit trumped up for a general dogsbody position, one of a half-dozen full-time staff at the Co-op, who among themselves oversaw the five hundred or so members who exchanged three hours of labour each month in order to buy at cost the same dry goods and fresh produce that the supermarkets sold.

Sinéad Gleeson

CABLES

I pine for bridges
     those in-between places
         of metal and concrete
the promise of newness
      a road to elsewhere
     a future glimpsed through cables.

    In their old campervan
we dive down *Bulitt*'s hills,
     past tourists on Castro trolleys.
        Russian Hill, Bay Bridge,
    the dock crane AT-ATs of *Star Wars*
Fernet and ginger ale in Vesuvio
    a passing parade in Chinatown
as air show jets squeal overhead.

Can you feel content and homesick
    at the same time?

Above the bay's creased waves
    our host who left
    Ireland, and blossomed in the sun
offers us wine in unstemmed glasses.
    We clink to our good luck,
      salute the lonely rock of Alcatraz.

    Eight hours and 5,000 miles away
our children are sleeping
     in the bay of their beds
    and we think *we could live here*
    growing lemons, or olives
     nursing vines
that will grow tall as each child.

Hodges Figgis shopfront, 104 Grafton Street, c 1900

Julian Gough

MAGMA
for Rob Doyle

He was tense, it was hot, the white cotton of his shirt sticking to his skin like he'd been shot.

He turned abruptly into the silence of the shady alley; away from the fast cars roaring, frenetic, along the main street behind him; breaking the sound barrier, breaking the taste barrier, banging bad rap out of half-open tinted windows.

'Losing your game by the lake, the mistake
You can't take back what you've done, you fake.'

He'd soon forgotten them, the cars, his friends.

The alley seemed infinite and, after a while, as it wound through the stone-fronted buildings, with nobody moving, not a dog, he felt he was walking a trail between cliffs; and when he saw the pulsing red light coming from around the next bend of the alley, he thought for a moment of volcanoes, magma, glowing clouds of hot ash, and he jolted to a halt, suddenly sure a tide of lava was about to sweep towards him.

The old town had indeed been half-buried in lava, a century before; but the volcano had been dormant for decades, and when he'd calmed his heart in the terrible silence and walked around the turn, it was to see an abandoned ice cream van, silent, its lights turning and flashing.

He stopped, laid his hands on the smooth metal flank of the van, and remembered his first time at a club – a cube of smoke jolted by blasts of light – dancing to songs older than him. He began to mumble a hit by the Human League. *'I was working as a waitress in a cocktail bar ... When I met you ...'* Lost songs.

A woman of about his age walked into view, from around the back of the ice cream truck. In the moment before she saw him, he glimpsed in her calm face an entire other life, a life with more kindness than he had ever known, a life with spectral views through early morning mist of the dormant volcano, a life in a world with no evil; he could see their flat, they were at a table, eating fish, yes, anchovies, and olives, they were laughing about something, there was a sword on the wall, but it was ironic, it would never be used, this was a world with no evil; and then, as the woman noticed him standing in the shadows of the alley by the ice cream truck, its lights sweeping across his face, his clothes, he remembered what he had done, and, as she stared at the blood on his elegant shirt, he began to cry.

A kilometre beneath their feet, the liquid rock began to move.

Eamon Grennan

STRUCK NOTE

Here if you look up this instant is the silver
sliver of a moon pendant in blue-becoming-indigo

as if the whole sky had been conjured one
note at a time by Satie whose rain-drop music

moves its tapered feet inch by fluid inch and
won't for anything be hurried yet strikes out

on its own its own note of lucid gymnopedic
passion its passionate exact lucidity striking

like a swallow skimming water then silent.

published by Hodges Figgis in 1895

LOCH CE AND ITS ANNALS

NORTH ROSCOMMON AND THE DIOCESE OF
ELPHIN IN TIMES OF OLD

BY

VERY REV. FRANCIS BURKE, M.A.
DEAN OF ELPHIN, AND DIOCESAN REGISTRAR

DUBLIN
HODGES, FIGGIS, & CO. (LTD.), GRAFTON-STREET
PUBLISHERS TO THE UNIVERSITY
1895

Sarah Maria Griffin

FOR CAIT

i am embers from the barbeque sitting in the grate
tender pieces of this summer evening
i am swinging in a hammock i am elderflower wine
i am eating blue flowers with her mother

i am a last bus neglected in favour of sleeping in the shed
just like that night the november before last
i am the folk opera on the radio
telling of orpheus before talk starts then of the underworld
in the suburbs:

i am ghost stories described rather than told
we are too old to be scared in the garden when it's dark
white transit vans are still sinister somehow because
because we know they had bad things inside

i just love the couches in your sitting room
my father bought them from a priest in a bunker
don't they look like they come from a knockin' shop
then i am those couches, that bunker, that priest

i am a belly full of savoury things
i am the madeira cake eaten late,
i am a lemon swiss roll unopened
i am the twelve firelighters that luke tosses
to the belly of the beast
i am the giddy new flames

i am the next log that you bring to the fire
in the shadows it could be a beast in your arms
or giant eddie and small oscar the cats
i am eddie, i am oscar: i recline, boyish and regal,
on a deckchair and sleep

i am wood lying then in the grate,
splitting open on the furnace
with the hotness creeping through skin into my belly
my new cracks blue flames in my gut
tiny bursts of lightning

come morning when the ashes are swept into the grass
i will then be sleepy, unshowered on a 145 bus to the city
remains of the night grey and earthen beneath the grate
i am still glowing though they disappear

Hodges Figgis hosted a Yeats exhibition in 1965

WILLIAM BUTLER YEATS
1865—1939

And pluck till time and times are done
The silver apples of the moon,
The golden apples of the sun.

The Song of Wandering Aengus

A HUNDRED YEARS HAVE PASSED SINCE THE BIRTH OF
William Butler Yeats. In this century, both in Ireland
and throughout the rest of the world, his writings
have come to be regarded as among the finest literature of all time. It is, therefore, with very great
pleasure that we are in a position to celebrate his
centenary by presenting this Exhibition. Such would
not have been possible without the kind assistance of
the Librarian of Trinity College, of Mr. Colin Smythe
and of Mr. Micheál Ó hAodha to whom we are most
grateful.

HODGES FIGGIS AND CO. LTD.

Kerry Hardie

REAL ESTATE

For thirty years
we have walked around
inside each other's lives.

We pay bills, hang out the wash,
comfort children who wake.
Sometimes we bury our dead.

This is the room we inhabit,
fragile as glass
with the light passing through.

Yeats exhibition catalogue, 1965

Lisa Harding

from OVERSPILL

They say you shouldn't look directly at the sun – the explosion of colours and shapes straight after is like looking down the lens of a kaleidoscope. If I shake my head a bit to the side I can imagine I'm turning the lens to the right, changing the picture each time, click, click, clickety-click, a smorgasbord of stars, shapes shifting: rectangle to square to circle to oblong to triangle to itty-bitty grains twirling and swirling like multi-coloured snowflakes. Yaya and I used to love to stare down that lens and she'd make up stuff about fantastical creatures, deep sea creatures mainly and that night I'd dream I was riding on the back of a wave, exhilarated, we were always riding waves, until He came along. They say that my memory is unstable, that I couldn't possibly remember what happened before the age of four but that time is more vivid than any time since, it's when I had her all to myself and the world was shifting, lilting and I can still hear her song in my ear, 'My beautiful blue eyed boy … my Irish bonny …' and she'd jiggle me in her Kangaroo pouch when I was her only roo. What they did to her in that place I don't know, but the sunshine and the laughter was gone. 'Mania,' they call it in here, the swimming and the tickling, the squealing, the staying up all night, the sometimes not eating for long hours, but when we did, it was all my favourites: fish fingers and ketchup and orange juice. The dancing in the rain? That was part of the 'condition' too Tommy. I don't mention the stealing.

It's all her fault, you see, this tendency of mine, this 'condition', it's inherited, not my fault, over and over again they tell me this, it's not my fault, handed to me in the stars, packaged in a most unique way. I'm unique, they say. Good, I say. But maybe you could put that special part of you to better use? I can't think of any better way of using my talents, which are distinctive and bright and beautiful. My eyesight is dimming. I need brightness.

People could get hurt, a person did get hurt. Yes, I say, that was my intention. The smell of sulphur lets me climb back into Yaya's arms where I am held high and jiggled, where the world tilts and spins, where the sun glares bright and pin-pricks my eyes, warming them and the space around me, my cheeks are hot and flushed, Yaya's cheeks are burning, burning, burning and I blow on them. He had no right to do what he did, say what he said. No, they say here. No, he didn't or no, he did? No, he shouldn't have said what he said, but sometime people's intentions are good, yet misguided. They were not good, I say. Perhaps they came from a good place, they say, he was the one responsible for getting you back from the foster family. That I don't remember, nada, blanket-blank, I'm not even sure I believe them when they tell me this. You were four, they say. There was only her and me and Herbie, and then her, me and Him and no Herbie. She might have died, they tell me, your mother, without his input. 'Input'. Sounds like what it is: computer language, heartless.

Have you any remorse Tommy? Do you feel any remorse?

That word doesn't land in any part of me. Yaya's free now, free to dance barefoot in the puddles under the light of the moon; staring at the moon doesn't hurt your eyes in the same way that staring at the sun does. I can still feel the spinning after though, I am Moon Boy, I am Stardust, I am a whirling particle of dust, I am the liberator. How Tommy? How is it that you see yourself this way? You destroyed people's lives. Only one, I tell them, the one who deserved it. And your mother? We spoke about it, the three of us, getting away, starting again, but three became two, and nothing happened, and each day she disappeared more and more. Maybe that was just as well, Tommy, you know the way people say things and don't mean them? Oh yes, yes I do, how well I know they do.

Where was she? Downstairs, in front of the TV, where she spent most nights. How did you know it wouldn't get to her too? I was there, remember? I started the thing, I was in charge. But you weren't Tommy, were you? Not really. No one is in charge once a thing like that starts. But I felt like I was conducting the orchestra of heat, blaze and thrill, licking and whooshing. The curtains surprised me, they went up so fast, they were particularly spectacular. It woke her up, you know? The light was reflected in her eyes, a different kind of light from the flickering of the screen, a blazing, alive-light full of purpose. Would you have left her there, Tommy? No, no, of course not, no. But no one went for him. That's not what your mother says, that's not how she tells it. Her eyelashes were singed, her fingertips seeping. Isn't it amazing that no other part of her was touched? I say. But it could have been worse Tommy, so much worse. No, it happened exactly as it was supposed to. I see, they say, you really meant this to happen? Think carefully Tommy, very carefully before you give your answer, you meant for this incident to play out exactly as it did; it wasn't a prank that got the better of you, ran away from you, got out of control as these things are prone to?

No, I say. No, it did get the better of you, or no it didn't? No as in no. It didn't get the better of me, I was fully in charge, the way Yaya was that day in the park when they came to get her. You do remember? You remember being taken away from her? I remember I was tripping over my feet, my two left feet, and I remember the swans that seemed huge and everywhere that day. Why would she have given you away Tommy, if she was fully in charge? Up until that point, she was there, then she was gone. They took her away from you? Yes. That must have been hard. If

I could remember it. Then he came into your life and you blame him? Your mother might not be here now if it wasn't for him. I wonder are they talking about the same man I am. I won't say his name and when they do I wipe it from their mouths. Yes, Tommy that's right. Bleep. And I was responsible, I am responsible, although they keep trying to make me say that I'm not, it's not my fault, beyond my control, in the stars, I'm too young to be held fully accountable, I heard one of them say. I liked the sound: woosh, whoosh, whooshing, the crackle and the fizzle, the heat, the rage, the speed, the stealth, the beauty of the thing, the smell, the smell which doesn't remind me of anything else – it's all its own thing, its own unique thing.

catalogue published by Hodges Figgis, mid 1960s

CELTIC STUDIES

HODGES FIGGIS & CO LTD
DUBLIN

James Harpur

IONA
from 'Kells'

Evening was slanting the boat
from Mull towards Iona
a journey the echo of a shout,
and I was staring at the water
as deeply as a gold panner.
Behind, Dalriada rose
in heather-lit mountains, the border
of a kingdom of shadows.
I came for traces of Columba
and found nothing but stone
in the wind-sleeted abbey,
grave slabs sliding into ruin,
the slatey boarding house
of widow hush, netless glare.
No clues on the coastal paths
or the rhythmic machair's
hummocky grass and furze;
or at the 'cove of the coracle'
where Columba saw, at last,
that Ireland was invisible;
or on Síthean Mor's rise
where a circle of angels appeared
as he prayed alone on his knees
and they caressed the air
with beating wings, an oratorio
of swans, alighting in a halo.

Jack Harte

from KILLING GRANDAD

The scene is set for the Battle of Moytura, the epic battle of Irish mythology. The outcome will depend on hand-to-hand combat between the two great warriors from either side, Balor of the Evil Eye, and Lugh Lamhfhada. Balor presents as an old man with just a staff, but with a knitted cap down to his eyebrows that might (or might not!) conceal his weapon of mass destruction. Lugh presents as a glorious young warrior in golden raiment. They might (or might not!) be grandfather and grandson. They meet on the field of battle, with the two armies staying well back.

BALOR: (*With irony*). Who is this come to brighten our lives on the lonesome Bricklieve?

LUGH: I am Lugh. Lugh of the Long Arm. Leading the army of the great Tuatha Dé Danann, against the might of the Fomorians. The battle will be fought here, so you should get out now, old man, before the action begins.

BALOR: Lugh. Mmm.

LUGH: Yes, Lugh. And I have come to challenge Balor of the Evil Eye to single combat.

BALOR: Challenge whom?

LUGH: Balor. He before whom the whole country crouches in terror. He who can destroy a whole army with one glance of his infamous Evil Eye. So clear off. You might get hurt.

BALOR: Mmm. Over-dressed for the occasion.

LUGH: What did you say, old man?

BALOR: All this colour … this display. Don't you think it a little inappropriate for these surroundings?

LUGH: What's wrong with these surroundings?

BALOR: You.

LUGH: What's wrong with me?

BALOR: You're confusing the plant life.

LUGH: Oh?

BALOR: They don't know which way to turn, to you or to the sun.

LUGH: (*Laughing. Relaxing. Flattered. Setting down his spear*). Funny you should mention that. When I approached Tara of the Kings, the warriors assembled there said, 'Is the sun rising in the west today?' I must have made an impression.

BALOR: You did.

LUGH: Oh. (*Looking more closely at* BALOR). So my fame has even reached this god-forsaken place, has it?

BALOR: (*Ironically*). Your fame has preceded you. All that blather has made for a good story. And good stories travel.

LUGH: (*Taking up his spear and adopting a more bellicose pose*). What blather?

BALOR: (*Imitating and mocking him*). Tell the king I am a poet.

LUGH: Oh, so you heard! I *am* a poet.

BALOR: So is everyone who rhymes 'bushes' with 'thrushes'.

LUGH: (*Aggressively*). I served my time.

BALOR: No doubt. Turning the boring details of someone's boring genealogy into boring quatrains.

LUGH: I was not bored.

BALOR: Ah. Then you are a true poet. They invented such chores hoping the poets would die of tedium, or go away. But the dull-witted poets didn't even notice the tedium.

LUGH: They were not bored.

BALOR: Probably too drunk.

LUGH: I had many other skills.

BALOR: Yes, a regular jack-of-all-trades.

LUGH: A master of all arts and crafts.

BALOR: (*Again imitating him*). Tell the King I am a harper. Give me a harp, and I will play you a lullaby.

LUGH: I put them all to sleep.

BALOR: Well done, well done. Would it not have been a greater feat to have kept them awake?

LUGH: Be careful of your mockery, old man. Don't you realise I am also a warrior.

BALOR: Typical. When all else fails, threaten. (*Again mimicking LUGH*). Tell the King I am a warrior.

LUGH: That caught his interest.

BALOR: Why wouldn't it? With a war imminent. He needs fodder for the battles.

LUGH: I am not fodder. I am the one who can end the war, who can put an end to all wars.

BALOR: Oh, spare me. Whenever I hear such a claim, I brace myself for a long and bloody campaign.

LUGH: There will be no long campaign.

BALOR: You are optimistic.

LUGH: We are ready for a decisive battle. The Fomorians have landed all over north Connacht and are advancing on Moytura here as we speak. But our forces are massed here to the south and are ready to meet them. Goibniu has his smithy ready, and will replace with three strokes any weapon of the Tuatha Dé Danann that is broken in battle. Dian Cécht and his physicians are deployed by the well below, and will restore to health every warrior of ours who is injured. Ogma and our other champions are ready to crunch with their clubs the bones of their opponents until the fragments are flying on the wind like hailstones. Morrigan, our goddess of war, will rain down fire and blood on the Fomorian warriors so that their vision will be blurred and our warriors can slaughter them all the more easily. Their severed heads will be rolling down the slopes of this mountain. All this you will witness presently. Unless you scamper. Now.

BALOR: All worked out, eh? But what of their champion? What of Balor of the Evil Eye? As you have said, he can put paid to your whole army, with one hostile glance.

LUGH: I will put paid to Balor first. I will challenge him to single combat. And when I have dispatched him, the Fomorians will have little stomach for the battle.

BALOR: But what if you don't dispatch him?

LUGH: (*Looking at him incredulously, as if such an idea had never occurred to him*). Of course I will dispatch him.

BALOR: Why so sure?

LUGH: It is predicted that I will kill him. (*Emphatically*). It is my destiny.

BALOR: Destiny! Mmm.

LUGH: You are trying my patience, old man. With your snide innuendo. Now clear off, until I issue my challenge to the great Balor. You won't want to be around when we start fighting.

BALOR: Why bother fighting? If it is your destiny to kill Balor, then it will happen anyway. If you do not kill him in combat, it will happen by perhaps a trivial accident. Am I right?

LUGH: Are you trying to confuse me?

BALOR: Destiny is destiny. It can't be circumvented. Right?

LUGH: What will be will be.

BALOR: Then why get worked up? Why all the sweat and anxiety, when the outcome is already determined?

Anne Haverty

from FIDELITY

The little blue-painted station was gone, along with its odourous fug. The new Gare de Glassonville erected in its place, a steely and hygienic structure, was a fine example of Fernande's detested *modernite*. And things were different from those former days in another way as well. Today nobody was here to meet me.

Afterwards, after Jean Luc could no longer be glimpsed waiting at the end of the platform the moment you got off the train, a time followed when Fernande would be waiting. And later again, after the new station was built and the concourse at the top of the escalator became the rendezvous for arrivals and their collectors, she would be standing there anxiously scanning the faces as they rose from below. Locating yours among them, her anxious expression would be swiftly replaced by the bright Ledon smile of welcome. A smile which by then you'd have to see as a sign of special valour.

Nowadays Fernande was keeping away from train stations. She was keeping away from all public places, shunning even familiar and smaller urbanisations like Glassonville, even in as far as she could, the little town of Nagour itself. The car in the garage was coated in dust. There's no way to evade modernity when you're out and about in a car and Fernande had come to hate what she called *la modernite*.

'*La modernite. Je deteste*' she was sure to proclaim at some point when we talked on the phone. Maybe modernity's push to turn people into islets of solitary consumption exacerbated the bleakness of her newly-imposed solitude at home. Solitude had always unnerved her. The minute she noticed one of us wandering off alone towards the garden or heading upstairs with a book in search of a nook somewhere to have a quiet read she would start to fret.

Fernande regarded the wish to be on your own as akin to wantonly opening the door and inviting in *le cafard* – the black insect of black moods that was always lying in wait to sink its pincers into you if you weren't vigilant. Or you could foolishly let in the thing that brought about the condition of being *ennerve*. This, while not as fearful as *le cafard*, was also to be avoided. What made her happiest was to see us all settled close together in front of the television or companionably setting out together for a Sunday promenade.

The little forays she was obliged to make on foot to the shops or to consult the doctor about her heart tablets offended her. The faces she passed in the street, new faces she didn't recognise and young faces in which she couldn't discern the lineaments of people she should have known, were reminders that to them too she was also unknown. The mass of new apartments for recent arrivals that crouched on all sides beyond the little ancient streets of the town she saw as constructed deliberately, maliciously, to encourage anonymity. The bips and chirps from the gizmos in which people had taken to ungraciously burying their heads in public she took as a personal assault. This was why I was going to have to get the bus to Nagour.

'I don't mind getting the bus,' I assured her. 'I like buses.'

But this wasn't as easy as it sounded. The bus station was deserted, as empty of buses as it was of travellers and I couldn't find Nagour on any of the timetables posted on the stands. I decided to go back to the train station and ask at the information desk. On the way as I was passing the new *cafe de la gare* I decided to turn in there. They should know about the buses.

The cafe's lugubrious *patron* could tell me nothing. *Bouf,* was all he said, shrugging his magnificent shoulders. Then he went back to the brisk pulling of beers. The bus station seemed to be unexplored land to him.

I got a Stella and took it to a corner table and gazed at the sugar wraps and the fag ends and the random oblongs of drowsy sunlight littering the floor. On the tv there was the usual football game that nobody was really watching. From the zinc where the rest of the clientele were lounging over beers and espressos fragments of conversation drifted across, mostly idly repeated *boufs* and *c'est ca's*. A cheerful rounded woman in a black dress, a little helpless on heels that looked too spindly to carry her, was keeping the talk going. One of those women to be found often in a French cafe, whose connection with it is unclear but amiable.

I would drink the Stella. And then I would go and look for a taxi to take me to Nagour. Or possibly not … The temptation that I'd been keeping at bay all morning now came brazenly into the open. Why couldn't I call it a day? Wasn't the absence of buses a sign, an offer of reprieve? Because I had done my best, I had tried. With a good conscience I could call Fernande, tell her how everything was conspiring against me. She would sob and I'd have to cope with that. But then I could get the next train back to Paris and stroll down the big avenue to that little street, it wasn't far from Châtelet, and meet Gus in the bar where we often met. He'd be so pleased to see me back. But I'd have to hurry.

There would be another day, I would tell Fernande. I'd have to keep it vague though, we didn't have that many days left in Paris to spare. Gaining resolve, I took a draught of Stella.

The cafe was suddenly filled with an urgent clamour. The woman in the black dress came towards me, flapping her fingers and urging *vite, vite*. Everybody seemed to be looking at me, calling *vite vite*. Waving his arms like a mountainy sheep-herder the patron whooshed me towards the exit. He wouldn't let me pause to give him the money for the beer. Go, go, he insisted. Quickly, the bus is leaving. A fellow who'd been waiting at the door went loping ahead of me up the street, turning around often to make sure I was following. At the bus station a lone bus stood ready to depart, its engine eagerly chugging.

We moved off, the driver and his passengers turning alternately to beam at me and wave to my guide. He went on waving until we turned onto the boulevard and he was lost to view, replaced by the camouflage-patterned trunks of Glassonville's lines of plane trees. They had grown stouter since I'd seen them last.

So very kind, I thought, those people in the cafe. The kindness of strangers. Possibly the sweetest of relations between people, because the most ephemeral. Allowing us to mutually ignore our faults and limitations. With a stranger you don't have to know what they may be really like, nor they you. And for a brief moment you're persuaded you're worthy of them as they're persuaded they are worthy of you. A shared moment of harmony. Of simple happiness that self-congratulation does nothing to taint.

I lapsed back into my seat. I was going to the house of a friend. A place where I was known, known all too well. Few of us can do with being known so well.

Claire Hennessy

You Learn to Dress for It

The work experience girl has cuts up and down the underside of her left arm, which is your first port of call if you're right handed. I see them in the kitchenette the first day, when she stretches up to the cupboard in the kitchenette for a clean mug, and that night I spend too long dragging my fingernails along my own arm. The thin white lines disappear too quickly, nothing like the dark pink left by the days when blood pushes its way out of you with that gorgeous sting.

Her name's Lisa and I'm supposed to be keeping an eye on her because Christine's off sick this week. It'd be a good time to have an extra set of hands around if they were any use, but sixteen-year-olds are almost always more trouble than they're worth. I keep having to find things for her to do that need doing but that she can't fuck up too badly; I try not to yell at her when I see the email she's sent back to a prospective client, all smiley faces.

'The thing is,' I say, doing my best to sound chirpy and encouraging and Christineish, 'even though we're in design and kind of artsy and creative, we still need to seem professional.'

Lisa nods, though I swear she's getting a little teary. 'Sorry.'

If she cuts herself because of this … 'It's cool,' I make myself say. 'Just learn from it.'

We've scissors around the place, even though we work almost exclusively with digital images now. I keep thinking about them, the cold metal, the point. I always went for knives. Anything that can cut meat. Now, though, I'm thinking about the scissors, and it's her fault. You see the red slashes and you want them, like those no-smoking signs that make you wish you had a cigarette.

I watch her reaching for things, waiting for them to appear again, but her sleeves cling to her arms Tuesday, Wednesday, Thursday. You learn to dress for it.

Finally on the Friday I get her, the sleeve slipping up just enough for me to grab her arm. 'What's this?' I ask, like I don't spend my days deciphering patterns.

Her eyes widen and she shakes me off. 'Nothing,' she says, in what has got to be the least convincing voice ever.

And then watch it spill; how things are all too much, how it's easier to feel this than that, and God, her eyes, her eyes are like she's having a fucking revelation. The talking, the telling.

'I'm not going to do it again,' she says like she really means it, unprompted.

'Good,' I say, and then I turn back to my desk, and the scissors have made their way into my top drawer, sharp and ready to usher blood into the air. At the end of the day she comes to me with her school's work experience evaluation form, and I tick boxes and wonder when it happens. When we grow up, past the age of rescuing.

Aideen Henry

THE QUEEN OF POLYESTER

Let me set the scene. You are sitting in his house beside a roaring fire, logs spitting sparks, feet roasting, Loved One by your side, your hand in his. Your last time to touch. Usual crap on the box. Doorbell rings. In walks a rotund figure in pink polyester, blonde hair flying. Thick face and body. This Vision brandishes a bottle and demands glasses from newly-cowering Loved One. He scuttles and goes fetch while she shakes your hand by the fingertips.

She bears news and wedges corpulence into chair with great flamboyance. Vision takes charge. You rack your brain, was there some talk from Loved One of an alcoholic neighbour who might ramble in? You can't remember. Anyway, she speaks of life generally in a weary but excited vein and repeats your name to you many times. Whoever Vision is, she has been practicing your name.

You sit and smile, one should be kind to the eccentric, possibly insane.

Loved One returns and clarifies that Vision has 'high-powered important job'. Loved One can read your mind, well, what do you know.

'A boss of some variety,' you say, while you smile at her and at the unlikelihood of this being true. You never can tell but. What with the greatest buffoons fast-tracking it to the top.

She squints at you trying to read you, irony not in her armoury. Loved One pours and clinks glasses. With her.

'Cheers,' they smile. The cock crows.

But we are on a farm, so that's ok.

Vision presses on with her news turning all her attention on you.

'Six years, wasn't it?' She looks at you but she is speaking to Loved One. A talented multi-tasker. You are jealous.

'Six years that we were together!' she continues.

All of her sentences earn exclamation marks.

'Six years,' LO affirms and sips. Not the alcoholic neighbour then.

His lips look thinner on the rim of the wine glass.

Now for her second question to LO, the one she doesn't know the answer to.

'So how long are you two seeing each other?'

'A month or two,' LO slices in fast.

You glance at LO.

The cock crows a second time.

She presses her advantage.

'You mightn't know,' she continues, warming to her topic, 'that he's still married, I bet he didn't tell you that!'

She is pleased, her news was clearly weighing upon her.

'And,' she says, she's just getting into her stride now.

What else could she possibly reveal?

LO couldn't be demented, could he? Syphilitic? Bulimic? Surely not, you peer at his teeth.

'And,' she says, 'he didn't tell you he spent the weekend with me just two weeks ago, I'm sure he didn't tell you that! We went to see a play together in the Abbey, *Anna Karenina*, didn't we?'

'We did,' he says, companionably.

You are impressed. That she would pay to watch catharsis on stage when it must be the bread and butter of her daily life.

So that was the family funeral LO had to go to then. Alone. Now you see.

You look at them both.

And then you look at the door.

Any minute now a transgender Mongolian uncle will burst through that door to balance this fantastical scenario. The uncle will be your secret lover, brother, cousin or twin or maybe hers. Take your pick.

Where was I?

Mongolian transgender uncle never arrives. You suspect you hear him wheezing behind the door but no, that's her ladyship. Flesh has to be moved with each breath and she is now reaching the high notes of her aria. Did I mention she is loud? Loud isn't in it. A high brassy alto of a voice, with screechy undertones. LO is a cattle dealer, used to stampedes and the like. And you are in his farcical sitting room, beginning to wonder why.

Before she comes to the clincher, she wants to know your views.

'My what?'

'Yes, I want to know what you have to say about this! Well, let's have it!'

'I don't … with strangers. And you … to me, anyways.'

And intimacy by proxy doesn't count. No, don't say that. Best keep it simple.

'She keeps her cards very close to her chest,' LO elucidates to her, helpfully.

'Do I,' you ask LO, 'with you, really?'

'Yes,' LO smiles at her.

The cock crows a third time.

Not deterred she presses valiantly on.

'He told me, didn't you,' she asks LO, 'that he loved me, not two weeks ago!'

The cock is sucking lozenges and considering emigration.

You nod sagely.

He confesses, good Catholic that he is. And it's a brave confession. Not just an affirmation, no. Not a twitch of a nod or an eye-closing auction type assent, and he has plenty of practice of those, selling his bulging Belgian Blues. He gives her back the full sentence. Certainly dutiful, though a little hit-and-miss about to whom. But maybe you mistake obedience for duty. Maybe you need less empathy, more threat in your intimate relations. Less mush and more edges. Steel ones perhaps. There are lessons to be learned here. You must listen carefully.

And the finale?

'Jeremiah!' she cries.

I know. It was destined to end in this comedic way with a name like that. I mean, really. Jeremiah?

'Jeremiah!' she beseeches, starting to look almost magnificent. Maybe she's the one.

'You have to make your mind up!' From some deep place, a note of desperation. She's definitely the one. 'You're going to have to choose between us!'

Ah, there is a god. Your lines have finally arrived on the teleprompter. Better late than never. You've found your entrance, well ... you stand.

'There is no choice,' you mumble, after all there's only space for one diva in this room, 'you can count me out.'

You exit, relieved to have finally figured out and successfully fulfilled your role in this postprandial drama.

Sadly, no Transgender Mongolian Uncle awaits you outside the door.

HODGES FIGGIS & CO. LTD.

Booksellers and Publishers

5 and 6 DAWSON STREET

DUBLIN 2

FOUNDED 1768

TELEPHONE : 76375/9

DIRECTORS :   Allen Figgis   Frances Figgis   Neville Figgis   Thomas Figgis   George Hodgins   Joseph Murray

NANF/AW

William O'Brien, Esq.,
84, Northumberland Road,
Dublin 4.

11th November, 1966.

Dear Mr. O'Brien,

    I must ask you to forgive my delay in writing — Due partly to a trip I had to make to London, and partly to the fact that I didn't want to bother you with money matters, at the time of your settling into a new house.

    You will remember of course, that in my letter of the 30th August, we offered £650 for all the books, pamphlets and magazines in the book-room at 89 Pembroke Road, (excepting the Anglo-Irish literature case). On a more leisurely and detailed examination however, I have come to the decision that this sum is a little niggardly, (partly inview of the fact that several of the Journals turned out to be in complete runs, and are therefore more valuable to us than isolated copies). For this reason, we are increasing our figure by a hundred pounds, as we consider that it is only fair that you and Miss O'Brien should have a share of this extra value. Incidentally, we are still pining a little over the mislaying of the Skeffington/Joyce pamphlet — If at any time this turns up, we would be very grateful for it. *given to Mr Figgis.*

    I very much hope that both you and Miss O'Brien are now comfortably settled in your new home, and will enjoy many peaceful years there, un-upset by further moves.

    With best wishes.

         Yours sincerely,

         ......DIRECTOR
         W.A. Neville Figgis.

UNIVERSITY BOOKSELLERS   :   NEW AND ANTIQUARIAN BOOKS   :   AGENTS FOR ORDNANCE SURVEY

Typescript letter from W.A. Neville Figgis to William O'Brien offering him a further £100 to add to the £650 offer for all the books, pamphlets and magazines in the bookroom at 89 Pembroke Road, 11 November 1966 (NLI)

Phyl Herbert

WHITEOUT

When I answered the door he was carrying a sack of firewood. Freshly fallen snow was thick on the ground.

'You'll need a fire in this weather.'

I knew exactly how he liked his coffee, two sugars, just a drop of milk. After living with someone for twenty years you get to know things like that. Another thing I knew about him was that he didn't like chatting. If he thought I was talking too much, he'd look at his watch and say, 'Is this going to take long?' You learn to say nothing. Can't even remember when we had parted company.

'Remember that form you got for me to have my pension paid into the bank?'

It was his first month of retirement. A new beginning.

He coughed and then said, 'There's nothing keeping me in this country.'

I looked at him and knew there was something else he wanted to cough up.

'Do you think if I emigrated from here they'd pay my pension in another country?'

'Where are you thinking of going?'

'Back to Thailand.'

The penny dropped, I'm a bit slow like that.

'Have you got a woman there?' I held my breath.

'Yes', he said. I felt a lump jump into my throat. I swallowed it.

'I'm happy for you.'

'I met her on my last visit. She worked in the bar where I drank.'

I looked at those elegant hands as he stirred his coffee. Hands I had held. I wanted to scream at him to stop stirring. He looked at me then as if I was his mother.

'She's been ringing me since I got back.'

Then he floored me.

'Will you come over for our wedding in September? I want you to give me away.'

Michael D. Higgins

THE PROPHETS ARE WEEPING

To those on the road it is reported that
The Prophets are weeping,
At the abuse
Of their words,
Scattered to sow an evil seed.

Rumour has it that,
The Prophets are weeping,
At their texts distorted,
The death and destruction,
Imposed in their name.

The sun burns down,
On the children who are crying,
On the long journeys repeated,
Their questions not answered.
Mothers and Fathers hide their faces,
Unable to explain,
Why they must endlessly,
No end in sight,
Move for shelter,
for food, for safety, for hope.

The Prophets are weeping,
For the words that have been stolen,
From texts that once offered,
To reveal in ancient times,
A shared space,
Of love and care,
Above all for the stranger.

Rita Ann Higgins

It Suits a Narrative

It suits a narrative of the 'big, bad State'
and the 'big, bad religious congregations'
– Mary Higgins, CEO of Caranua,
The Irish Times, 20 March 2017

Some applicants will never be happy
and grievances suit a narrative,
of the big bad church
and the big bad state
and the big bad building
with the big bad gate.

We ration our compassion,
while all ye say suits a narrative
of the big bad state.

We ration our compassion
but we'll give you a couch.
We ration our compassion
but we'll give you new windows.

We are the keepers
of the church's money.
As keepers we divvy and we pay
but not to you directly, we won't give you money
but we'll give you new teeth
a new radiator, a brand new funeral.
What more could you ask for?

It's not that we want your pain
to be everlasting,
but by the same token
it suits a narrative for ye

to come on national radio and complain
and say we have no compassion.

We have oodles of it,
but we ration our compassion.
If we give you stuff without humiliating you
it will be no fun at all.

So fill out that form and then fill another
and another and another
and one for your sister
and one for your brother
and while you're at it
fill one out for your mother.

Don't listen to the guy who said,
criminal records are given out
like holy communion to people in institutions.
We all know he stole an apple
otherwise why would he have been there?

Some applicants will never be happy
and it suits a narrative,
of the big bad church
and the big bad state
and the big bad building
with the big bad gate.

Sophia Hillan

from UNDER THE LIGHT

I don't know if I've mentioned before the effect of the street-lamp outside our house. It is hard to explain, but it casts a curious light on all it touches: it lends to people and things a nostalgic air, softening outlines, making a kind of gentleness. I have often remarked its effect on my children as they come in from school on winter evenings. In an instant they become ethereal, ghost-children, spirits of Christmas yet-to-come. Even my husband, when he is with them on their walks, or weighed down with books at the end of the day, seems a boy again, their brother rather than their father.

It was under the lamp that I saw, for the first time in many years, the woman who had been my girlhood friend. By its light, she became eighteen, nineteen perhaps – about the age she was when my husband left her for me. I'm not proud of that, but it happened; and since I'm telling you this story you might as well know. Did I feel any unease, seeing her after so long a time? No: well, perhaps a faint twinge, nothing more.

Neither the illusion of youth nor that slight access of sentiment lasted more than a moment. Indeed, it was something of a relief to note, as she came down the path, that she looked her age every bit as much as I do – more perhaps, because she has let her hair show the grey. *Dunkel blond*, she used to be, in German class. *Cheveux blonds foncés*, in French. And I admit that it was nearly a source of satisfaction to me to notice a slight, arthritic limp as she walked. It meant that I could safely welcome her to my home: I might even find it in myself to pity her.

And yet, I forgot to pity her as she entered the hall, and I saw her clearly. Avril. I was suddenly overcome with emotion at her presence, and was for a second, no more, almost overcome with the old passion to tell her everything – of my mother's dementia, my father's protracted death, that time I – well, perhaps not that, but unaccountably, something about my life with David, who once thought he loved her. Yes: I had missed her. Before I knew where I was, I had thrown my arms about her neck and held her as my children used to do me, not wanting to let go. I couldn't see her face, the cool, familiar eyes, but I did not sense reluctance. I was, at last, nearly glad in my heart that David had asked her to come.

For, yes, I am ashamed to say that I had not really wanted this visit – except for residual curiosity to see what she had become, and to meet this husband of hers, the television man, American. He turned out to look quite remarkably like the young Jack Nicholson. You know, *Chinatown*. His name was Hubert – or it could even have been Humbert – but it hardly matters, because I immediately thought of him as Jack, and am nearly certain I called him so at least once. He was attractive, no doubt about that. She did all right. All the same, left to myself, and despite hearing about her stellar career from my one or two remaining school friends – I lost many over the whole business – I would not have asked Avril to visit.

It was David, of course, David, dazzled by her appearance at some charity function, David coming home full of it, of her, so pleased, so like himself again that I had not the heart to deny him what he wanted. In fact, it was I who found her, after he had virtually destroyed the telephone book by riffling so hopelessly through it. I said: 'David, there's the internet,' but he wasn't listening so in the end, inevitably, it fell to me. He phoned, though. I wasn't doing that; and of course they couldn't come on the first two dates he suggested – busy people, busy, busy – so I put a spoke in the next two they suggested. Those dates would have been perfectly all right; but, well. Anyway, they got something in the end, and I agreed, but – and I don't know why – once it was definite, the prospect sent me into a state, a panic like that time when I was so ill; or no, not at all like that, not really. I don't get excited about things any more. Still, I cleaned and polished and did absurd, unlikely things, like sending the curtains – the curtains, for God's sake – to be dry-cleaned. They shrank, of course. I cooked and I froze and I dived in and out of this cookery book and that cookery book, and changed the menu a dozen times, and rejected each change at three o'clock several mornings. Yes, well, the freezer is certainly well-stocked. We could survive a siege right now.

And then, the evening itself arrived. There she was, real, tangible, almost ordinary, in my house. I began to wonder why on earth I had been nervous. I had everything planned. We would have a drink, perhaps two, to ease any tension, and some light preliminary conversation, and then the meal, which could take up a leisurely hour and a half if I got the intervals right. I would keep the talk to general topics and if anything, anything came up about that old business, I would bring down our baby, our late bonus, as a – as whatever. I had made sure the bigger ones were taken care of, staying with their grandparents or their friends, but I made sure the baby stayed with us. I was torn, yes, between wanting Avril to see what David and I had, and not wanting to underline the fact that she and what's his name, Jack, have no children. I'm not cruel. Yet I knew, if I had to, I would bring the baby down.

Desmond Hogan

SKIN

I first met Skin at a showing of *Three Little Words* in the convent hall in which Gloria DeHaven played her mother, vaudeville artiste Flora Parker DeHaven.

Sister Perpetua was the projectionist and all the orphans in their nursery-blue, knew that when Saint Perpetua was led into the arena in Carthage for martyrdom she refused the chiton of Ceres, goddess of food growth, stripped naked, was transformed into a man, and, like Vincente Saldivar, trounced her opponent.

Skin's name was Anterus Benskin. Ant he was sometimes called. Anterus after a pope who was a freed slave.

Lilies of the valley had been dug up from the convent garden in Loughrea and given to the nuns here. They grew in the dark, in the shade when Skin got a job as a hot towel shave assistant to Trixie Leech – Trixie Leech's father was known as Ha'Penny Shave – ten pounds a week, and moved into a room over a window where the Venetian blinds were permanently down and where there were two horse chestnuts permanently in the window.

The nuns gave him a gift of a one-button jacket with drape collar when he left the convent.

Eyes blue as an epidemic of sloes, turtle-brown hair, high swept crescendo roach, cornetto roach, he already had a downtown look.

Trixie Leech got perfumes from Fred Dolle of West Madison Avenue, Chicago and there was the smell of witch hazel and the Australian eucalyptus tree in that shop.

On the wall was an advertisement for American shoes Fred Dolle had sent Trixie Leech – Buster Brown in a scarlet brimmed hat, with page boy hairstyle, with his dog Tige – beside a photograph of Jim Montgomery of Sunderland baring his teeth.

I used to go to the Society Fruit Stores every Friday evening when *Photoplay* had come in and I first found Skin doing the same thing when Shirley MacLaine in *My Geisha* was on the cover.

The Society Fruit Stores was run by Mrs Killigrew, President of the Opera Society, who strode Society Street in Dubarry country shoes with a look like Irene Handl in *The Pure Hell of St Trinians*.

Miss Shelsbury who conducted the opera had studied music in Heidelberg and was called the Heidelberg Jaw after a fossil jawbone, 400,000 years old, found in the Neckar River vicinity 1917.

Heidelberg Castle survived rampaging by the French in 1689, 1693, being struck by lightening in 1764. Accessible by cable railway.

Miss Shelsbury was like that. You had to take a cable railway to communicate with her.

She'd slapped Lady Winckley on the face for not singing 'Oh, dry the glist'ning tear' from *The Pirates of Penzance* right when Lady Winckley was wearing the picture hat, white earrings, white suit with black collar, black belt, large black squares with *moiré* blue and red around the squares, which she'd driven from the country in, in her Vinvet Continental.

Shirley Anne Field – she's shown those Hollywood starlets how! Elvis Presley breaks loose in the swinging, swaying, luauing South Seas – Hawaiian style! Has James Bond met his match?

Jill St John – Hollywood's reluctant siren in moss green jump suit on purple cushion. Liz Taylor, buccaneer earring right ear, cinnamon brows, light giving fuchsine edges to hair, raspberry lipstick. Anita Ekberg, blue pin-stripe bikini, slits bottom part. Silver-blonde Belinda Lee in strapless blue dress on a Second Empire sofa. Eva Gabor in gold *lamé* sheathe dress. Anne Heywood in chain mail dress.

One Friday evening a *Photoplay* which featured Rock Hudson, Sammy Davis Jnr, Hayley Mills, Leslie Caron, Elvis Presley, had a Win a Holiday in New York offer.

I had to buy this copy of *Photoplay* because I wanted to go to New York.

I went to the house of my godmother – no children of her own – who had a Frans Hals – who always owed money to the barber or shoemaker of Harlaam – reproduction in her sitting room, his Cavalier rollicking at a joke.

There was a lampshade in the sitting room with a motif of Japanese court ladies and she sometimes turned on the lamp when I was present though it was afternoon light.

On the Feast of the Epiphany – little Christmas – she always baked a Battenberg cake – Victoria sponge, apricot glaze, marzipan.

One day when I arrived in the house she was kneeling on the ground, beside her hoover, weeping.

I asked her for 1/6 to buy *Photoplay* so I could win a holiday in New York which she gave me and I purchased *Photoplay* but word got back to my mother and *Photoplay* was confiscated as had been a letter from Elisheba, a New York pen pal, seized from the letter box on the way in from morning mass, shortly before – 'It will interfere with your studies!' – and I was walloped up the stairs and locked in my room.

From my room, caught in floods, the bushes looked as if they were gifts wrapped in water. Ditches just above water.

The golden plover had already come here – gold spangled back – and my godmother who was from Mayo, a Paul Henry reproduction also in her sitting room where the clouds were like things saved up, never spent, had told me that in Mayo the golden plover was called the yellow whistler and its flight whistle sounded like someone weeping because it was carrying the soul of an unbaptised child condemned to the skies forever.

Declan Hughes

ISLE OF THE DEAD

Mary sometimes wonders how often the others remember they once might have killed a man. But then she doesn't remember very often herself. It feels like something that happened at a party long ago (and it had happened at a party, if it had happened at all). Someone she kissed when she shouldn't have, slept with even, and now she can barely recall it occurring except for a stray detail, a ridge of scar tissue at the base of his spine, perhaps, or the cry in his throat when he came. It certainly doesn't tug at the memory, let alone the conscience, the way she had thought it might. *The conscience.* What a long time it's been since she's used, or even heard that word. And she teaches English and Religious Education at a Catholic school.

There was no way of knowing which of them had actually struck the fatal blow – if there had even been such a thing. They had gone out of their way to ensure that. Now, in the clear light of day, it simply seems like something that had happened to someone else.

And it is the clear light of day, a bright and fresh Halloween morning on the road to Galway. Motorway, to be precise, the M4, and then the M6, a couple of hours from Dublin to Galway if you put your foot down, and there isn't much point to a motorway if you don't. It's one of the positive legacies of the boom, this road. And like most of those legacies, it has its downside. What if you don't want to get where you're going quite so fast? It used to take forever, this trip, slowing in Kinnegad and Tyrrelspass, in Kilbeggan and Moate, absolutely crawling through Athlone and Ballinasloe and Loughrea, especially if you hit a cattle market, and you usually did. It felt tedious then, sure, but tedious to a purpose. Mary misses the delays now that all the towns are bypassed and you can be beyond Galway and on the road to Clifden in two hours. She misses the gradual falling away of the day-to-day, the anxiety slowly dissipating until somewhere on that long stretch from Ballinasloe past Athenry, the fields stretching out on either side, the sea floating in and out of view, something dreamy and expansive on the stereo, you began to feel yourself escaping, breaking your bonds, slipping your skin. Going out west. What happened in Dublin stays in Dublin.

Now the trip is too short, and Dublin is still snapping at her synapses with its to-do lists and its time-poor demands, its balance-the-books and its profit-and-loss, and she is grateful for a horse fair outside Oughterard that holds her up for twenty-five minutes.

Not that her anxiety levels are likely to drop the way they used to; more that it will delay arriving at her destination: George Fitzgerald's house in Ballyconneely, where the eight of them will be together again for the first time in twenty-five years.

There had been the days of drama, the when-will-you-leave-her years. After the second child is older, after the third child is born, after Carole gets the all-clear. And then one day it was too late. And funnily enough, like the boyfriend you fear will dump you but feel nothing but relief when he does, it was all right, at first, anyway. She discovered she had no real wish for him to leave his family. It was too late by then for her to start her own, and she had gotten used to living by herself. And the distance worked wonders. She could feel the need off him every time they met. She could fluster him so easily, with a quick glance at her watch.

'Are you in a hurry?' he would say. 'I thought we would … I thought you wanted to …'

And the big face would fall. Sweat on his heavy upper lip, thick fingers drumming on the bar top, eyes dimmed in a fog of lust.

'The only thing I want is you, Tom,' she never quite says. She never speaks her feelings. Which has the double effect of making her feel, in the serene solipsism of the day-to-day, as if she doesn't have any, only to be overwhelmed, in the unlived-in apartments and ghost houses and disused hotel bedrooms, by the strength of her emotion when he leaves. Because he has somewhere to go.

For Mary, everything is the same as it has ever been. She teaches at the school she attended as a pupil and she lives in the house she grew up in. 'As a child,' she might have said, but Mary doubts whether she was ever really a child. A watchful, anxious little girl, just she and Mammy after Daddy's sudden death, sitting quietly on never-ending Sunday afternoons while the aunts twittered on about who had made it into the bank or the civil service, who had the shop or the pub to fall back on, how clever Mary must surely go for the teaching. Mammy always encouraged her to behave like a grown-up, to believe that's what she was. Once, when her presents had been exclusively books and clothes the previous Christmas and she had asked for a particular doll for her birthday because all the girls in her class had one, Mammy looked at her reprovingly.

'I don't know now. Is it a second childhood you're having?'

She was ten years old.

Sometimes these days, from the window of her childhood bedroom, now her walk-in wardrobe, she is taken by the amber glow of the sumac tree in its autumn glory, or in the winter classroom by the slate glint of the sea, sights she has known for as long as she can remember, and she feels as if she has never really gone anywhere or done anything in her life, as if she is five and fifteen and forty-five all at once, infinite and invisible, unbound and confined. At moments like these, Mary senses a tiny, fleeting joy, and then she feels very small indeed, small and sad and alone. And not a little angry.

Rosemary Jenkinson

MAY THE ROAD RISE UP

I grab my bag. Go straight to the Housing Exec and present myself as homeless.

Homeless. It shocks me.

Sorry, Mia, says the client adviser, but realistically you have no chance of being housed, being single with no children. Unless you were intimidated from your home – were you?

He's almost willing me to lie but being chucked out my friend's gaff for partying could hardly class as intimidation.

The Homelessness Test – yet another points system! I feel like a lab rat, analysed, tested, stuck in a cage. Wouldn't even mind a cage – it would be somewhere to sleep.

I sit and wait while he phones round the hostels. Head on me's nipping like a scrapyard dog. This time last year me and Ryan were sitting with a travel agent, booking a week's holiday in Rhodes. Spacious room, ensuite, sea view. No wonder I got into debt.

Great, we've got you a room.

Ensuite, sea view? I'm thinking.

The only thing is, you can't bring any of your own furniture.

Oh, what a shame. I'll have to leave the Louis XI armchairs in storage. (That one came out loud – stop the sarcasm, just stop it). Look, thanks for helping me, I mean it.

Whip round to the hostel. The support worker gets me my bedding, takes me up to my room, unlocks it – that many keys she's like a jailer! The room's small, strip lighting, the only colour in it is the mould. But I'm grateful. Have to sign a licence, agreeing to the house rules.

VOICE OVER: *No pets, no alcohol, no non-prescription drugs, no visitors unless they're signed in, no chip-pans, no noise, no theft, no threats and no sectarian remarks.*

Whacked out, head slaps the pillow but I don't sleep, swish of the mop on the stairs, whump of the heavy fire doors.

Have to be out by nine the next morning. Eight whole hours before I'm let back in. Go to the dole, apply for a few shelf-stacking jobs, then out on the dander, the meander. All autumny now – leaves brown and crispy like they've been deep-fried in the sun. In the evenings I go to the hostel 'library', full of shite like the *Da Vinci Code*. Get to know the residents like Anna who keeps sneaking her Jack Russell in under her coat and is on her second written warning. I don't know why Anna can't have her wee dog with her, keeps her warm at night – and, believe me, Economy 7 is more about the economy than the fucking heating. I sneak her dog in for her a few times, but one night I'm coming in, meet the support worker on the stairs and there's this face exploding out my jumper like something out of *Alien!* Support worker near cops a heart attack! First written warning.

Here, says this girl, Hayley, who's been living there a year. Don't you be bringing that mangy mongrel in here again or I'll stab you.

I don't meet Hayley's eye. She's beaten the bag out of five girls this year, says Anna, she's a schizo. I start avoiding the 'library' as I realise it's the site of Hayley's fight club. Now I know why we're turfed out every day, the hostel heart-scared of fights, cliques and factions.

VOICE OVER: *(muffled). Fuck you, you cunt!*

(Sound of violent thuds). Hayley. Welcoming a new girl.

Support worker turns a blind eye, locks herself downstairs with her panic button. Not her fault, it's the government's for closing down secure units for schizophrenics.

Next morning, I'm still scared. Pack my bag. There's nothing worth taking. You know those distressed jeans? Christ, all my clothes are distressed. There's an old sleeping bag where they keep the bedding, take it instead.

And out I leap and the sun's shining, the city's chocker-blocker, shoppers, workers, walkers. 57p in my pockets. I try to phone Paddy but they've cut my connection. Chuck my mobile in the bin.

Bimbling about, end up in Bedford Street. At the old boarded-up building opposite the Ulster Hall. Sit on the steps, feel the warmth of the sun on the old faded sandstone. Arse covered in pigeon shit but never mind. And I see this bottle of cheap wine planked behind a pillar. For the first time, I really see this other world. An oul fella wanders over, clocks my sleeping bag. Ginger John, he's called, raddled by the booze, more wrinkles than a Schnauzer. But kind. A younger fella, hoodied up, with no teeth. Bouncing the gums at me, but I can't hear a word he says. Frosty you call him, cos he always feels the cold.

We'll show you the craic, Mia. Give me a sandwich, a drink. It's getting dark, so they ask for boxes out of Centra just as it's closing. Then we nip down a side street. Ginger John sleeps in a doorway at the back of Centra. There's another store down a bit and he tells me to park myself there for the night. Not a soul about. Bit of bubble-wrap under the bap, sorted. *Bed*ford Street – aye, well it found me a bed alright. Still a bit cold but.

Here, says Frosty, passing me a Kapake. A Co-codamol. Knocks you out.

Has a whole ton of them in his jacket – more packed than a drugs mule! Wash it down with some wine.

And that's me. Gone without trace, no address, no phone, what a relief to be out of the system! So low I feel elevated.

published by Hodges Figgis in 1886

THE

LAKE DWELLINGS

OF

IRELAND:

OR ANCIENT

LACUSTRINE HABITATIONS OF ERIN,

COMMONLY CALLED CRANNOGS.

BY

W. G. WOOD-MARTIN, M.R.I.A., F.R.H.A.A.I.,

LIEUT.-COLONEL 8TH BRIGADE NORTH IRISH DIVISION, R.A.;

Author of "Sligo and the Enniskilleners";

"History of Sligo, from the Earliest Ages to the close of the Reign of Queen Elizabeth."

"There, driving many an oaken stake
Into the shallow, skilful hands
A steadfast island-dwelling make,
Seen from the hill-tops like a fleet
Of wattled houses. . . . . ."

"The footprints of an elder race are here,
And memories of an heroic time,
And shadows of the old mysterious faith."

DUBLIN:

HODGES, FIGGIS & CO., GRAFTON STREET.
PUBLISHERS TO THE UNIVERSITY.

LONDON:
LONGMANS, GREEN & CO., PATERNOSTER ROW.
1886.

reprinted by Beaver Row Press, Dublin in 1983

Jennifer Johnston

THERE ARE EASIER WAYS OF MAKING A CRUST, BUT THIS IS THE ONE I'M STUCK WITH

I have recently finished my tenth novel.

I find this quite astonishing, as back in 1969, or whenever it was that I finished my first one, I felt I had possibly about three novels in me; three pieces of work that were queuing up in my head to be given their freedom and that, I presumed, at that far-away time, would be that. Thoughts and ideas, though, beget other thoughts and ideas; the queue in my head lengthened, queue jumpers shoved and pushed, the feeble were left to wait at the back of the queue, while plays, monologues, characters, notions, dreams and fantasies that I never thought existed in my mind scrambled to the front. Sometimes the feeble would gain strength in the waiting, sometimes they would just shrug and go away.

If the above gives the feeling that I have very little control over what I write, that would indeed be true; to carry on the analogy of the queue, I am the bus into which these ideas climb and when we all reach our destination they get off and go their ways out into the world. The bus is then empty and ready for its next passengers.

I came to writing in a disorderly fashion at the age of thirty five. I was married, I had children, I was living a pretty good life in London, doing the things I liked doing, seeing the people I liked seeing, but for several years a voice in my head had been insistently saying: 'This won't do, you know. You have to do something with your one and only life. Hanging in there is not good enough.' Except, of course, that expression had not then been invented; I use it now because it amuses me to do so.

I have never yet worked out whether it was the voice of a good angel reminding me, somewhat magisterially, that I owed the world some effort, or a bad angel screeching: 'Get noticed, don't allow yourself to slip through life without being noticed.' I don't suppose it matters very much which it was. The persistence with which it spoke made me eventually move. Even then when I started first of all to write I never enjoyed it. It was dogged no surrenderism that made me sit there day after day writing, re-writing and then, over-critical and over-anxious, tearing up page after page in despair. It seemed quite a ludicrous way to suddenly start spending my days.

It was the day that I realised that I must finish a piece of work before bringing the critical side of my brain into play, that I first began to be a writer. I was then starting to learn from my own mistakes.

Lesson number one: nothing is real until it is finished.

It is impossible to judge the weights and measures of a piece of work until the pattern has been established and the last full stop is in place. Then you have something to work with, to mould, cut and carve.

Let me give you an example of the sort of odd thing that happens when I start the writing process first on a new book: when I began tentatively to get *The Invisible Worm* (book number 9) down on paper I had quite clearly two women in my head. One, a Dublin woman, who walked briskly each day on Dún Laoghaire pier, hail rain or snow and talked to herself, made jokes to herself, was in fact healthy in her head; the other, Laura, who lived in the country and waited and wished for darkness to envelope her. At that time I was not quite sure why she had this strong desire and whether it was for death or the peace of madness. I had the notion that these two women would meet and that out of that interaction the book would grow.

Instead, after a few weeks of writing Laura took up more and more space. Her story, she insisted, was the one that had to be told. She demanded that I search out her secret. No meeting, no interacting, was necessary. So the Dublin woman got shoved to one side; I gave her no more thought.

She was, I thought, erased from my life. Luckily though, she was only biding her time in the shadows of my mind, because as soon as *The Invisible Worm* was out in the world, she moved inexorably to the front of the queue and refused to go away until her story also was told.

I was grateful for her reappearance as the nightmare of emptiness is always close to the mind of all writers. It is a terrifying notion to feel that you have typed the last sentence, put the last full stop on the last page, typed 'The End' for the last time.

The woman, by this time called Stella (a ghastly name, and it wasn't until I was well into the book that I realised why she carried it) trailed with her a whole lot of thoughts about love, lies, betrayal, secrets, power, marriage, mothers and daughters; also magic and the strange quirks of fate that make writers discover themselves. I was also having daytime dreams of this man/angel hovering above me, his huge wings shimmering in some kind of light. For a long time I couldn't work out why he was bothering me so in the hope of some sort of exorcision I wrote out a description of the vision that was in my head and having pinned him to the page I found that he became the centrepiece of Stella's story.

It took me a long and wearisome time to write *The Illusionist*. In fact having written about thirty five pages, I lost all energy and interest in it. I shoved all my papers away and instead concentrated on other things: I adapted one of my books for the stage, I wrote a film script and a couple of short plays, until one day my daughter said to me: 'Why are you trying so hard not to write your novel?' Cheeky lady, I thought, but after a day or two I became filled with intolerable guilt, rather as if I were killing someone by inattention, so I got my papers out and began to reacquaint myself with my characters and their lives. I tried to find out why I had wanted to write the book in the first place, tried to hear once more Stella's voice.

It took a long time. I had to edge myself back into the book, line by line; some days I wrote no more than a sentence; some days I sat in rage staring at a blank screen. I resisted the temptation to work on anything else and gradually I began to understand what I had been writing about; I began to feel the return of energy and confidence. It was almost like recovering from an illness.

The book is written both in the past-recollective tense and in the present-reflective tense. Each section is written in Stella's voice. This basically means that the timespan for the book is twenty four hours and also, at the same time, part of a lifetime. This seemed to me to be the easiest way in which to tell seamlessly the parts of Stella's story that I felt I wanted to tell.

I never write in chapters; this means that I have to find some other method of punctuation. It is therefore in *The Illusionist* the movement backward and forward in time that acts as punctuation. Maybe to the reader this will seem a little arbitrary, but I hope not. I hope each move has its sense both in time and also in the general rhythm and thrust of the book.

If there is a fault in this particular book, it is maybe that it floats in a somewhat abstract way along the side of society, of the reality of life. I hope this doesn't diminish the work in any way as I set out, as I say in the early stages of the book, to examine a sliver of a life and to make some sense of the trailing thoughts that came along with Stella.

I prefer always to leave things unsaid, making the whole process of writing and reading a dialogue, rather than a lecture. I think a lot of readers are bothered by this, preferring to be told how to react to situations rather than to join in the joyful exercise of creative reading.

I loathe the notion of the writer as some authoritarian figure. The reader must be given freedom to range at will within the laid perimeters of each writer's work.

When I started first to write *The Illusionist* I saw the opening section as the first scene of a play: indeed I wrote it as such. I wrote stage instructions and all, setting the scene and then a couple of pages of quite good, wry and energetic dialogue. I then moved on to explain why I had started a novel in such an untraditional way. People who are not involved in theatre believe that they will find plays difficult to read; a challenge they don't want to accept. So, after the dialogue came to an end, I wrote as follows:

'I would like to flesh out this room in which I sit; you see when you write a play you have to leave space for the director, the designer, the actors. They too have their place in that act of corporate creation, each of them in their own way enlivens, transforms the words on the page into an illusion of reality. For the reader you must be more specific, no point in saying … a room full of light and shade. Two long windows. That won't do at all. The reader needs to move, breathe in that room, smell the smoky scent of the newly-lit fire which spits sparks from time to time onto a hearth rug already freckled with tiny burns.'

I realised after I had returned to work on the book that this, though in its own way quite good, intelligent reading, and the dialogue and stage directions that had gone before it, had to go. It was giving out the wrong signals; it was creating a mode that I might find myself having to use later in the book, and as I moved back in with my characters I realised that this would be inappropriate, so I plunged straight in, beginning as I meant to go on, speaking with the voice of my heroine … if that is what she might be called.

'I sit in a room full of light and shade.

I dream.

I dream of her entrance.

She will come into the room as if she were coming onto a stage, or anyway that's the way I see it from where I sit, from where I think about it.

A fire burns in the grate. From time to time it spits sparks onto the hearth rug and I make a mental note to chastise the man with the horse and cart from whom I bought the neatly-chopped logs of wood, when next I see him.

There are trees outside the window, just coming into leaf and the light in the room is filtered through the acid green of newly-born leaves. A bright cold light. I imagine she will be dressed in black.'

This is neater, more appropriate to the tenor of the book.

You can get yourself mightily snarled up by trying to be too clever! Having said that I also have to say that writing is all about tricks and trickery, sleight-of-hand, illusion. Never be afraid of using tricks, just don't make them so obvious that the reader feels overwhelmed. The art of trickery is in the subtlety ... now you see it, now you don't.

Here a few notions of advice spring to mind, though I don't suppose I have much to offer by way of advice that you don't already know.

Read.

That is the great imperative for any writer and shouldn't really have to be said, as I presume all writers are readers. I don't otherwise know how you would come to that gate that has 'I have to be a writer' written on it, let alone push it open and go through. Reading gives you courage, because the more you read the more you realise the risks that writers take and you understand that if you are idiot enough to want to be a writer, you are also idiot enough to take the risks involved.

Jump without the safety net ... it's not easy, but it's been done before.

Think carefully of the importance of the first ten pages of your work. This is when you have to trap your reader. This moment is when you have to catch the reader's interest. This moment is when you have to intrigue, amuse, seduce, whatever it may be you wish to do, this is when it must happen. I would hate to admit to the number of books I have thrown aside, never to pick up again, because I have not tasted the magic in the first ten … or perhaps I should say twenty pages.

Here, just for your delectation, are three openings that captured me instantly:

'*On the day they were going to kill him, Santiago Nasar got up at five thirty in the morning to wait for the boat the Bishop was coming on.*' – Gabriel García Marquez

'*Stately, plump Buck Milligan came from the stairhead, bearing a bowl of lather on which a mirror and a razor lay crossed. A yellow dressing gown, ungirdled, was sustained gently behind him, by the mild morning air.*' – James Joyce

'*I have been in love with Evelyn Conlon for twenty four years and four months less eight days. We have made love twice. The first time was twenty three years ago. The second time was yesterday. Does that make this a sad story; make me a comic figure?*' – Frank Ronan

No fireworks, just good confident writing and the promise of pleasure to come and probably mysteries. I love mysteries. Perhaps that's really why I write.

Remember that every character, no matter how small has to have the possibility of real life. When you first start to write you tend to use the minor characters rather like bits of furniture, or props in a play, but they too have to have the reality of the major characters. The reader doesn't have to know their life histories, but has to believe in their humanness. If you don't believe in the humanness of your subsidiary characters neither will your reader.

Writing is trickery. Never forgive this. The better the writer, the less visible the tricks, but they are nonetheless there. Even the shaping of a piece of work is trickery.

To be an artist is to be an illusionist, a weaver of spells.

Read what you write out aloud to yourself.

Phrases, sentences, paragraphs have to sound right as well as make sense. Even abrupt and unsettling prose has its rhythms, and those rhythms help to give substance and an atmospheric sense to what you write.

I really can only tell you about how I feel, about my attitudes to the way I work and as you may have gathered from what I have written above, I am a writer who does not enjoy writing. I like the notion of being a writer, but not the practise of writing. This is not to say that there are not moments when I look at a piece of my work and say to myself: 'Yes, that is precisely right.' But by and large I find the whole process quite painful, but compulsive.

I see no other way of living my life.

What else is there to say?

published by Hodges Figgis in 1959

DENIS JOHNSTON

in search of

Swift

DUBLIN
HODGES FIGGIS & CO. LTD.
1959

Neil Jordan

from BALLAD

He would come to love him, though love was the farthest
thing from his mind as he was pulling the boots off in the
dead field with the burning farmhouse beyond. The
shooting was over and the light was coming down and the
carts were departing with the ones still alive, the groaning
ones, as he remembered them and he was scouring for
whatever he could find in that shadowy thing that was all
that was left of the daylight. It was called the gloaming,
that hour, he would learn much later in the fields around
Kildare where they both, with families now attached,
made their last home. And in that gloaming the red jackets
gleamed a little brighter than the blue ones. This one must
have been deserving of someone's love to have caught his
attention, a mother's love, perhaps. There would be an
annoying kind of goneness to him in those first few days,
of something barely human, that was hardly there. He
would have been a goner alright if the one he later called
his Tony hadn't turned the body over to get a better
handle on the boots. They were fine calfskin, covered in
mud and scuffed bare round the bit where the sword
rubbed off them. It was the right hand boot he tried first,
with the smooth bit that the sword scuffed, because, of
course, the right would have been his sword arm.
Something cracked and a low moan came out of the corpse
with what must have been the only breath it had left. And
he didn't know it then but realised later that he had
cracked his shin back into place with the effort of turning.
It had been broken somewhere inside of the boot and the
body that he now realised had some breath in it moaned
with the pain. And the scavenger, because that's what he
was then, knew the corpse was alive and with that odd
knowledge came some odd responsibility. And he would
think, in subsequent days, about how it all could have

been different. He could have put his bare foot to that elegant throat and squeezed out the last breath. He could then have fingered it to see if there was a wallet, a watch and chain maybe, a cigar-cutter and whatever other fancy ornament an officer carries. He knew he was an officer by then, with the turning, because it had exposed the muddied braids on the front of his red coat. There were dark bits that weren't caused by the mud of the swamp which he knew must be blood. So he could either have used his foot or just left him to die with the light that was going down. But he didn't, and maybe that's what began it all. The officer became his charge, and later he became the officer's and they were tied together forever after for reasons he would never fully understand. Out of such accidents are we made, he would later think. Out of such accidents was his mother dragged from old Ethiopia, chained to a plank in a hold in a ship over the white waves of an ocean she never knew was there before. Of course a kind of luck came with the accident; he was given another life after he had nursed the broken one back to health. And the life he had had wandering those swamps in the Carolinas had little to recommend it. He could have made it to Charleston maybe and believed all of the King's promises or he could have joined the Continentals and tried to curry favour there, or he could have run away among the Creek Indians looking for his father. But he did none of those things.

He twisted off the muddy boots, the right one all bloody, and fitted them on his own bare feet. The officer's eyes opened a little and he could see they were greeny grey, not the colour of the moss on his muddy cheeks, but close. There was nothing but mud and muddy moss in that gloamy evening, mud that the dead bodies sank into, mud that the horses had churned into grey soup. There was one horse lying in a lake of it, trying to turn over and get a foot once more in the wet sludge, and he thought of grabbing the reins and pulling the beast upright and thereby doubling his luck, but he saw that the two back legs were broken and the horse would be of no use for anything but feed. Then he heard the one he had left, whose boots he had already fitted on his feet, give another moan and utter a few breathy words. The words were, Don't leave me here.

published by Hodges Figgis, 1922

University of Dublin,

TRINITY COLLEGE.

WAR LIST,

FEBRUARY, 1922.

DUBLIN:

HODGES, FIGGIS, & CO.,

BOOKSELLERS TO THE UNIVERSITY,

20 NASSAU STREET.

Ann Joyce

BLUE DRESS

He walks the shore,
his past divided into lots like flotsam.
Winter wears itself into his face,
bleaches the bones of his memory.

Today, only his body is present.
Some freighter or tug has claimed him
like love lying on the ocean floor
waiting to hook a name.

Edging the island, that space between
water and clay, belonging fully in neither,
he fills with the memory of ocean
and the memory of her at the pier,

the morning he sauntered out to the boat
carrying her silhouette across horizons.
He falters, like an aspen bending
to the tune of a breeze, his hands cupped

with water knowing the sea can unlock
whatever picture he summons.
And yes, her dress was blue,
so clear now he reaches to touch her face.

Joe Joyce

from 1691: A NOVEL

The fleet anchored off a spit of land that stretched out into the centre of the bay, surrounded by wet sand as the tide receded. Major General Hugh Mackay stepped ashore from a tender, relieved to be back on solid ground, and took his first look at Ireland. To his left and right were hills and ahead of him the sun was going down like a great light shining from the interior, dazzling and inviting at the same time. It obliterated any sight of Dublin beyond the scatter of stone houses in front of him. A cross between the hills and valleys of his native Scotland and the flat land of his adopted Holland, he thought.

Soldiers were coming ashore from the ships and forming up into groups and being led at a quick pace across the sands. Shallow barges were being hauled into place to take their cargoes into the city's quays.

Across the sands, out of the sun, came what appeared at first to be a chariot, a horse driven at speed by a man standing wide-legged on some kind of crossbar. It came closer and he could see there was a bench of some kind behind the driver and another figure sitting there. It came off the sand and pulled up on the grass in front of him with a stopping swerve.

The passenger jumped off and Mackay recognised a Dutch officer on General Ginckel's staff who hurried over to him. *'Mijn excuses voor het te laat,'* the officer said with a slight bow. *'Welkom bij Ierland.'*

Mackay acknowledged the apology and welcome with a slight incline of his head and the Dutch officer snapped an order in English at two of the red-coated soldiers standing nearby. They picked up his trunk and brought it to the carriage.

'What is that?' Mackay asked the officer, pointing at the car. The driver was still standing upright with the reins held tight as if he was holding back the small horse.

'They call it a Ringsend car,' the officer said. 'After this place. They're the only cars that travel across the sand here. You're unlucky the tide is out and the ships can't come in further.'

This whole journey had been unlucky for Mackay. It had taken a long time from Holland, through England, and, worst of all, worse even than the North Sea, the long stomach-churning crossing of the Irish Sea. The harsh northerly winds which slowed the convoy down had died away at last as they came into Dublin Bay in a sunny calm which came too late to help his mood.

He should have been here weeks ago, should have had plenty of time to acquaint himself fully with the situation, but there had been one delay after another. Actually, he thought with a touch of residual bitterness, I shouldn't be here at all, having to take orders from a man like Ginckel whom everyone knew had been but a stopgap commander for King William's forces in Ireland.

'General Ginckel wishes you to come immediately to a council of war,' the officer said as if to remind him of who was in charge.

'Right now?' Mackay replied in English, his Scottish accent underlining his irritation.

'It's about to begin,' the officer switched to English, a note of apology in his voice. 'I fear we will miss the start. The general expected you earlier.'

Mackay got up beside him on the heavily patched seat and the driver let the horse go, taking off with a jolt that almost threw them off. They were shaken from side to side as the horse galloped across the ribbed sand, passed the marching men and splashed through a shallow river without breaking a stride. Mackay felt his nausea rise up again.

The officer paid off the Ringsend car man with three pence at Lazy Hill where his carriage was waiting and they got on board. The city gradually took shape and they passed by Trinity College and went along a rutted road of big houses to the Dam gate and into the narrow streets of the city itself. It was still busy with many people about, the streets narrowed even more by hucksters' stalls selling rabbits and chickens and sheepskins and tin utensils.

The carriage made its way slowly up the hill to the castle. The wheels resounded on the wooden drawbridge at the entrance and they halted for a moment at the iron gates until the sentry waved them through into the courtyard.

The interior still bore the marks of the fire which had devastated it some years earlier, and of the controlled explosions required to stop it spreading to the magazine in the tower. Some of the buildings were still ruined, the long gallery on their left only partly repaired, the reconstruction interrupted by the momentous political and military events shaking the three kingdoms in recent years which had led to the rapid changes in control of the city from Protestants to Catholics and back to Protestants again.

The carriage turned to the right and came to a halt between what had been the old parliament building and a line of old wooden houses untouched by the fire. The Dutch officer led him at a brisk pace up a stairway and announced him into a room of uniformed men standing around a large table.

Mackay hid his disdain for his new commander in a bow to Godard van Reede, Baron de Ginckel. A cavalry officer in his native Holland since he was 12, Ginckel, like Mackay, had been among the force accompanying William of Orange to England to claim his wife's throne three years earlier. Those who played preferment games and indulged in intrigues had little time for him, seeing him as a good general officer, solid and dependable, but lacking in imagination.

But King William preferred to put his trust in his Dutch and Danish commanders, even in the French Hugenots, above most of his English and Scottish officers who had forsworn their allegiance to the former king, James, his father-in-law and uncle.

detail from Hodges Figgis catalogue published in 1968

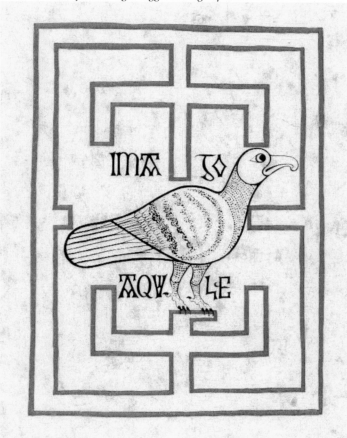

Hodges Figgis catalogue published in 1968

CELTIC STUDIES

NEW SERIES

CATALOGUE 23

HODGES FIGGIS & CO. LTD.

Established 1768

6 Dawson Street, Dublin, Ireland.

introduction, Hodges Figgis catalogue published in 1968

Spring 1968

Dear Customer,

We hope you will welcome this catalogue and that it may prove to be not only a vehicle for the promotion of our trade, but also a helpful bibliography for your future reference. Seldom, if ever before, has it been our privilege to offer such a collection of books in this field, and we are particularly pleased to do so now for two reasons.

Firstly, this is our first catalogue to have been prepared by Pádraig Ó Táilliúir, who though a recent addition to the staff of H.F. will need no introduction to many Celtic scholars. An acknowledged authority on Celtic books, he has joined us with a view to maintaining and increasing the reputation our firm has long held as specialists in this branch of scholarship, and we hope you will agree that this, his first offering, is worthy of very careful consideration.

Secondly, 1968 is upon us and this is our firm's bicentenary year. For two hundred years we have stocked books on Celtic subjects, and this catalogue seems a fitting way to celebrate the tradition. We hope that you will agree, and look forward to the continuation of our friendly relationship in the years that lie ahead.

HODGES FIGGIS & CO. LTD.

To facilitate Libraries and others who will require copies of this Catalogue for reference purposes, a limited number will be made available in cloth covers at 8/6

Colm Keegan

Sunday – it's hard to get up
Put my feet to the floor and rise
Walking into who knows what
To arrive again between two states
The feeling of everything falling away
wanting something to come along.

Sit and open up the old laptop
fuck around with some metaphors.
Stitch meaning to where there is none
bind things together that shouldn't go –
Death to rainbows, loss to hope.

My children watch from the sofa
Looking up at me like I'm a god.
My heart is a bucket
Lowered into a well.
How far down before there is water?

John Kelly

from WORK IN PROGRESS

Sometime around midnight, the city humid and slow, Michael Brennan is walking home along Seventh Avenue when he sees his father, the late Art Brennan, standing on the sidewalk outside Village Cigars. Art Brennan has been dead for a very long time, buried beside Michael's mother on an Irish hillside, but even so – there he is, as large as life, popping a cigarette from the pack and slotting it between his lips like a movie star. It seems those American brands can seduce him still – Vantage, Winston, Newport, Pall Mall.

Michael steps sideways into the bright lights of Dieter's Flowers and hunkers down in the deep cover of irises and lilies. He watches closely as his father – dressed in a cream-coloured raincoat, white shirt, black tie, black trousers and brogues – lights up, takes two long drags, then hails a cab like he owns the place, his hand raised as if to bless the sudden flow of yellow swerving hard towards the kerb. When the anointed cab obediently stops, he flicks his cigarette to the ground and gets in.

Michael takes note of everything – the way his father settles in the seat, checks his watch and then, with a simple nod of his head, directs the driver southwards. He's like a new man these days, thinks Michael, a slight smile of pride playing on his lips, and he looks the part too – like a born New Yorker in fact. It's almost as if Death, if that's what you'd call it, has given Art Brennan something of a second wind.

This is not the first time that Michael has seen his father in the neighbourhood. During the Blizzard of '96 he almost bumped into him coming out of the Cherry Lane Theater on Commerce Street. Then one night in the Vanguard he saw him seated at a table (presumably reserved for somebody else) with a glass of whiskey before him on the marble top. He spotted him twice on Bleecker and then discovered him standing stock still at Sixth Avenue and Waverly on that terrible day when the Towers came down.

The wide wash of traffic moves and manoeuvres and Michael gazes south. Red lights and white lights – horns in gentle jabs as a thousand cabs accelerate and shunt. They change lanes and break hard – a rolling cavalcade of yellow southbound hearses and he knows that his father is in there somewhere. The late Art Brennan deep in the night-time flow. The thought of it. His silent father on the town.

A sudden voice from the back of the store.

I can seeeee you!

Then a poke to the nape of his neck and Michael, startled, turns to find Dieter, New York's most muscular florist, gazing down at him over the tiny red rims of his glasses.

Jesus, Dieter, you scared the life out of me.

Dieter folds his arms and his biceps bulge.

May I ask, Michael? Are you in some kind of trouble?

Michael takes a last look along Seventh Avenue and gets to his feet. He feels suddenly dizzy. Light in the head. The wild energy of colour. The thick funereal smell.

I'm fine, he says. Just thought I saw someone.

Oh, we've *all* been there, honey!

I wouldn't bet on it, says Michael, steadying himself. You haven't been *here*.

Dieter tilts his head and feigns alarm.

Oh my! He says. That's most *misterioso!*

Misterioso indeed, says Michael. That's the word right enough.

Dieter makes his wisest face and presses a finger to the side of his nose.

I tell you what, he says. These tulips. Why don't you take them home to the lovely Sally B – gratis and free. She is, as I *hope* you know, a princess.

That she is, says Michael. Thanks Dieter. You're a kind man.

Michael exits Dieter's Florists and, clutching his bunch of tulips, crosses Seventh Avenue and ducks into the Kettle of Fish for his nightly vodka martini – an essential ritual of some twenty five years standing instigated by his oldest New York pal, Tony Strode. A proper drink, Tony said. The clearer the liquid the better it is for you. And so, reasoned Michael all those years ago, if a vodka martini was good enough for a real New Yorker like Tony Strode, then it would always be good enough for him. Straight up. With a twist.

The Kettle, which is just across from Michael's apartment on Grove Street, is quiet tonight – no Packers fans or tourists – a monumental mercy. All peach and golden with its year-long ropes of Christmas lights, it's not at all what it used to be (in fact it isn't even what it says it is now) but certain solid elements remain – the bartender for one thing. He knows his trade and because Michael has arrived with the obvious air of a man who needs to get his thoughts straight, the drink is served in total and respectful silence.

Michael takes the first sip – a substantial sip – and savours the hit. A proper drink indeed. Good for the constitution and sacramental in its burn. He stares long and hard at the glass, gently fingering the stem as he tries to analyse things yet again – what it means for the only son to see the only father, here and there, time and time again. And, just now, on Seventh Avenue. Outside Village Cigars.

Dad, he whispers to himself. *Sláinte.*

They'll tell you, of course, that there's no such thing as ghosts. No such phenomena as phantoms, wraiths or dark, perturbèd spirits; and no such slips in the system as to ever leave the shades, content or otherwise, to linger on the spot. But Gotham is full of them and Michael's patch seems especially populated. The West Village. Sheridan Square – right at the intersection of Washington Place, West 4th Street and Barrow Street – an old Sapokanican trading post – and Christopher Park, where Grove Street meets West 4th. No wonder the spirits gather constantly. No reason why Art Brennan, a departed Irish schoolteacher, shouldn't join them for a cab ride or a smoke. No reason at all.

order form, 1930s

To Messrs. HODGES, FIGGIS & CO.,
    20 Nassau Street, DUBLIN.

    Please send me the following items from your Irish Catalogue, No. 7, New Series :—

....

....

....

....

....

....

....

....

....

....

....

    Name...

    Address...

    ....

Date ....

Brian Kennedy

THERE WAS ONLY SO MUCH ONE HOUSE COULD TAKE

It was as if the house had waited for every last voice to leave before it would allow itself to grieve properly. Drip by drop the cold, stagnant liquid suddenly leaked from the dark tank in the attic, escaping along the copper veins where years of tears had been collected through the thin skin of the ceilings, slowly and reluctantly at first, until it could hold back no more and it gushed forward for all it was worth.

You see, the house had been there at the very start when the bright young couple first turned the key in the lock of the precious newly-painted front door some 60 years earlier.

Oh, the laughter in the air then, the parties, the love, the songs, the disagreements, the frustration and, of course, the new nervous sex in the still of the night.

Hopeful coats of paint were gifted to every available surface and slowly but surely the bedrooms were filled with four healthy children, all girls. Over the years it was understandable, for a while, that the carpet began to get ignored or that the windows mightn't always be as clean as they could be, but the house knew they were investing in the future.

Sure enough, the husband got promoted and new radiators were clamped to the waiting walls of every room and the heat was sometimes enough to make you want to open a sash window just a touch, even in winter. Christmases were survived, birthdays remembered, homework suffered, colds were nursed, boyfriends were kissed and toast was burnt with a fork against the grill of the gas fire.

'Jesus, I tell you, a man shouldn't have to live with so many bloody women under one roof!' the father would proclaim safely behind his newspaper as the bickering between his wife and the girls propelled with each passing year and gnawed away at his fraying nerves until he took to the pub for his nightly escape. Once settled at his usual snug he was a man of few words but many pints. Of course it never stopped him expecting and wearing the immaculately-ironed shirts that appeared as if by magic on a wire hanger behind the main bedroom door every morning or indeed the plates of perfectly-timed and cooked steaming food that tasted so good that it had him reaching for extra bread to mop the dish clean.

Inevitably, one by one the daughters suddenly outgrew the house and left. Room by room the parents reclaimed the peace they'd secretly wished for as the entire house fell evermore silent.

Himself was the first to get sick shortly and cruelly after he'd only officially retired a few months, still wearing his tie every morning at breakfast. His wife nursed him like she had a newborn child again needing constant attention. It was only at the very end when she woke up for the last time next to her cold companion that the house had a reason to temporarily get full again. All at once it was like the daughters had never been away at all and their bitter voices scalded the air with accusations and blame while their mother wore out the rosary.

After the wake and the rain-soaked funeral, she decided to stay on in the house against their wishes, even though not one of her four girls had offered an alternative as they fled back to their own lives before the dish cloths were even dry. Gradually the deafening silence got the better of her and she rented some of the bedrooms out in an attempt to curb the increasing loneliness saturating every cup and corner. There was a kindly, smiley male nurse from Kildare, a substitute teacher from Dublin with a lisp, and a divorcee from Sligo who gradually took up residence, but they eventually all moved on too, one by one and then people just stopped answering the ads altogether.

Inevitably nature got the better of her attempts to brave the stairs as she only got weaker and cursed the occasional guilty postcards that were hastily written and spat through the tight mouth of her front door that was only ever knocked on now by strangers asking her for money as they looked beyond her into the cluttered hall.

Last thing at night the house would creak at her not to be silly, her children would come back, she'd see. Things would get better.

It was early one Monday morning after a sudden bout of flu the week before that the house tried everything to revive her. The high-pitched hissing of the immersion heater, the tiles on the roof shifting in the wind, the door slamming because a window had been left open, but nothing could or would wake her now, because it was her turn to be dead.

The house was in denial. Sure, didn't it only feel like yesterday that himself and herself had moved in and filled its four walls with so much life?

Sure enough as the house had predicted, the children did come back after the milkman raised the alarm. 'See,' whispered the house triumphantly to itself and got all hopeful.

Oh how the girls wailed and cried over their mother's exhausted coffined old body in front of the unlit hearth any time a nosey local came to pay their respects and wolf down the tea and sandwiches, only to wave them off with gritted teeth before retiring upstairs to their separate childhood bedrooms with their strange spouses, plotting about how much the old dump was worth. The old dump indeed! It was enough to break the house's heart. One by one they began to ransack the former family home and that's when the fighting really started in earnest. Screaming vicious rows erupted over who was entitled to what.

'Daddy would have wanted ME to have it, not you!'

'Oh is that right? Sure you fucked off to England the second you were able.'

'Listen to her – the stupid, oul put-on accent on you. You sound like you were born with a silver spoon rammed up your arse!'

'Mammy insisted that I was to have her watch because I'm the only one that inherited her fine bone structure and tiny wrists. Youse three are more like daddy's people, peasant stock!'

'How dare you, she told me you never even remembered her birthday.'

On and on the bickering went with not a single thought for the poor house's feelings. Oh no.

They left vowing never to come back until, of course, their cars would return unannounced under the cover of night and cart off pieces of furniture and rugs and the good china while the poor exhausted dark house slept unaware until the next morning.

The final straw came when the oldest remaining daughter drank anything alcoholic she could find in the cabinets and vomitted all the way up the empty stairs, roaring that she'd torch the fucking kip before she'd see the other bitches get a penny. That was it as far as the house was concerned, they'd really gone too far now.

When the last bulb was snapped off, the last door bolted shut and the last footfalls troubled the gravel driveway carrying away the last hope of happiness, it was only then that the tears had permission to leave the attic.

Tears for every time the old woman had prayed for her failing husband to get better, for her daughters not to be so jealous of each other, to ring home more often, for the world not to be so broken, for the lord god in heaven not to be so quiet, for her own body not to be so sore.

There was only so much one house could take before it was time to let go.

Victoria Kennefick

Á LA CARTE

In Cassidy's Restaurant
I watch you slice a hunk of meat
on porcelain.

Your winking knife presses
to relieve muscle from fat,
soft as toothless gums.

The steak wants you to eat it,
is begging even, like a palm.
I have not eaten meat

all my adult life – its juice
an embarrassment, but now
I cannot look away. The fillet

pulsates on your plate.
Would you like a bite? you say,
extending a sinew on a fork

towards my lips. In front
of me, leaves, nuts, seeds.
To be honest, I say, *I'm starving.*

Brendan Kennelly

To Miss McKenna
my teacher at St Ita's College, Tarbert, Co. Kerry

What you have given us we shall not forget
Or easily improve on.
To be a teacher is to give, and not
To measure profit in the giving;
To make the shapeless days
Part of the art of living.

In the years' design of love,
To be a teacher is to be a learner;
To have the most profound and holy sense
Of sharing every minute experience
Till it is seen as part of the complete design
And, at the same time,
To feel the impact of a permanent farewell
To those who once seemed near.

It is a shaping and a scattering,
A moulding and a breaking,
A deliberate seed pitched on the wind,
Flowering or withering
In the individual heart and mind.
It is a sense of decent possibility,
A chance to open to the world,
To see into onself
And to perceive the link that lives
Between the two.

This is a little of what you give
And have always given.

For this, we thank you,
Teacher, friend and most unusual woman.

Kerry, 2017

galley proofs of Dream of a Black Fox *(1968)*

3221.—ALLEN FIGGI?.—DREAM OF A BLACK FOX.
Galley 1.—11 on 12 BEMBO 21 ems. Titles in 14 Bembo

DREAM OF A BLACK FOX

BRENDAN KENNELLY

FOR PEG

The Tippler
Out of the clean bones
He tipples a hard music;
Cocking his head,
He knows himself sole master of his trade.
Hence his pride.

A goat ran wild
Through field and hillside,
Was tracked, caught, tethered, tamed,
Butchered and no man cried.
And the Tippler got his bones.

courtesy of Phyl Herbert

published by Allen Fiiggis in 1967/1968

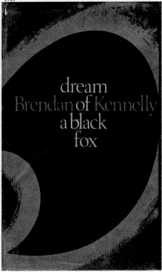

published by Allen Fiiggis in 1969

Adrian Kenny

from A CHINESE DIARY

December 1996: Evening in Sichuan. The terraced fields are like lace spread over the hills. Water fields reflect the sky. Men with mattocks on their shoulders walk home along the tops of earthen banks. Women drive home white geese. It was like a scene painted on an old china bowl. Old men sat under wide-brimmed grass hats, fishing in ponds from which white mist rose. Smoke rose from the cottages: some roofed with black clay tiles; others thatched, with beautiful plaiting along the ridge. The eaves sweep down over walls of ochre mud. A low watt bulb filled each doorway with a lamp-yellow glow.

Next morning we were down in warm countryside among orange and banana trees. The land was dry, there were more water fields, the hat brims were as wide as bicycle wheels. Farmers waded thigh-deep behind wooden ploughs drawn by buffalo grey as the mud. The old men wore scarves wrapped about their heads. Further south into Yunnan, the scarves closed over on top and became full turbans.

A boy sat opposite, busy with a notebook and pen. As we approached Kunming he told me he had written a poem: 'On Returning Home'. When I said that I was soon going home, he translated it. The last line was so beautiful – 'I feel safe at home with my father's earth-coloured face' – that tears came to my eyes. That and a 24 hour journey together, but he left without a goodbye.

A clear sun in a blue sky. Swallows were chirruping swooping above the station square. A prostitute, about eighteen, with a big smile in a wretched face, plucked my elbow, said *'Erse yuan'* – twenty yuan, two pounds. Not a twinge of assertion temptation. Tribe people, talking loudly, strolled about in vivid clothes. Two women chatted and laughed as they leaned against a noticeboard showing photos of condemned prisoners. Countrymen sat on their heels selling fox, wolf, wildcat skins. Some girls wore t-shirts, open blouses; others wore beautiful stiff white masks. Outside a shabby mosque a boy struck an empty gas canister with an iron bar and sang the call to prayer. In the park a man was singing, a crowd stood listening, a woman sang in reply. I drifted through the freedom and freshness, remembered only as warm dusk came down that it was Christmas Day. I was away, alone for the family festival – and able for it.

Next morning, to celebrate my achievement, I took a bus going up the mountains, eastern foothills of the Himalaya range. It was night when we reached a freezing frontier town; wind was baying down the main street. The huge expensive tourist hotel was empty except for a girl attendant standing at the head of each corridor, holding a tiny hot water bottle to her breast. One of them showed me to a room.

Alone there, my calm collapsed. Sudden anxiety panic, then the sweats began. Two Noctamid, but the racing thoughts went on. Why? Why have I never grown up? The question of my life, and I still don't know the answer. I dozed at dawn, woke to a blue cold morning. As the sun rose above snow-tipped mountains, my fear melted and pride returned. I was alive. I had done it.

A few miles down the road was Dali, an ancient walled city which had escaped the Cultural Revolution. Fierce stone lions sat by the entrance gate, young cherry trees were in flower. An old woman tripped across cobblestones on bound tiny feet. An Italian girl stopped to greet me – 'Buon Natale' – and passed on the news that Marcello Mastroianni had died. We agreed he was ham, but a great old ham, then we went our ways.

The happy chance meetings when you travel alone. Sitting in the sun, I was approached by a teacher who asked me to his school, to talk English to his class. Afterwards, in thanks, he showed me around. An ancient pagoda was there to dominate the earth's evil spirits – but also marked the manhood of a sleeping giant. A similar ambivalence in the temple, where Buddha sat in peaceful contemplation next to the village god – black-bearded, like a dragon devil, eyes bulging with rage, waving a crooked sword like a thunderbolt.

Together we looked in on a folk music session. It could have been my childhood Mayo. Countrymen in old suits and hats played drums and cymbals; a woman in a cardigan played bells: the remains of Tang court music, the teacher said. More old men sat in a sunny garden, one trouser leg rolled up, peacefully rubbing their bare knee, smoking big bamboo water pipes as they played Mahjong.

The teacher led the way to a poor crowded restaurant. 'If you want a good meal, go to a crowded place. If you want a good bus, go to an empty one.' The Chinese are great for these wise sayings. Hearing I was a writer, he pronounced 'You can't be a writer if you sit in your room. You must experience life, go down to the bottom of experience.' He asked if I was famous. When I said No, he intoned 'You are thirsty, and the water is far off.'

Finally he took me to the Catholic Church, at the end of an avenue of trees pollarded in French style. I asked if any Catholics were still there?

'Some old and crazy people, I think.'

Two very old, very small women were locking the door for the night, but they let us in. Red paper lanterns hung from Norman arches, a tea bush in a pot of clay stood before a statue of a pink cheeked Virgin. One woman plugged in winking fairy lights about a crib. The other explained that the church had been built by French priests when she was 2 years old. Now she was 92. Some people still came there from the outlying countryside; fifty had come in for Christmas. They showed me a photo of their priest, who had died the previous year. Together they knelt at my feet and asked for a blessing. The best I could do was to kneel beside them. I felt their peace breathe on me. All my desires felt part of my desire to be good.

On the bus back to Kunming I met the Italian girl again. She too had been ambushed by the teacher, and taken to his school. A full moon was on the wane, floating alongside the windows as we talked. Lower down the mountain road we met the rising sun. We parted at the station square.

Women guards in navy uniform stood on the platform, exactly a carriage length apart; heels together, white gloved hands raised in salute as the train pulled out. It made me cry again in happiness. I had endured, seen the beauty of China, and its goodness. Now I could go home to work in peace ... I thought.

Des Kenny

THE READING EXPERIENCE: A BOOKSELLER'S TALE

My first visual memory is of books. Walking home from school with my brother, we were within yards of the house when I dodged away from him and ran out onto the road after some marbles. An Eason van came over the brow of the hill. The driver hadn't a chance and I ended up in a coma. Some days later I woke up lying in a cot. Walking down the ward towards me was my father, carrying oranges and books. This is my first memory. I was five years of age.

We all had the usual growing up children's ailments, but staying home from school wasn't all negative as we were supplied with a continuous flow of books … The Famous Five, The Secret Seven, the myths and tales of Ireland, stories of minotaurs in caves, of Viking warriors rising from the sea, the Richmal Crompton books on the hapless William – I always wanted to be just like William … *Treasure Island*, stories of pirates and knights all thrown in together, *Gulliver's Travels*, a mixum gatherum of books that fired our imagination.

As we grew older, books were our lifeblood. We stacked, packed, dusted, shelved, catalogued, mailed them, but I can't say that I ever opened a book without a warm sense of anticipation. No matter how forbidding or dense the book looked, there was always the possibility of something new and exciting or even a cracking read.

Towards the end of my secondary school days in Coláiste Iognáid, I had an exceptional reading experience. We had a rather volatile (though never abusive, either physically or mentally) French teacher. His was the last class on a Friday. We were all thinking of football, girls, records, anything but French. About five minutes into the class, the teacher, a Jesuit priest, suddenly banged on one of the desks.

'Cuigigí bhur leabhair ar leataobh,' he said.

We waited with bated breath. He reached into the pocket of his cassack and took out a book.

'I believe you are all of an age when you should expreience this book.'

He opened it and from then every Friday at last class, he read J.D. Salinger's *The Catcher in the Rye* to us until it was finished. This was momentous for a number of reasons. Although censorship was not as stringent as it had been, the book was almost certainly still banned in Ireland. In reading it to us, the teacher paid us a valuable compliment, although I don't think we all appreciated it then. The more I thought about it in later years the more I realised that it was an inspiring example of the full reading experience.

Three or four years later, after three happy years in UCG and a mediocre Arts degree, I found myself living in Paris with a *bourse* from the French Government studying for a masters degree in comparative literature at the Sorbonne. Arriving in a very wet and dark Gare du Nord on 26 October 1970 at 5.30pm full of hope, elation and with little money in my pocket and no place to stay, I discovered quickly that Paris wasn't going to exactly welcome me with open arms.

Out of sheer loneliness and because of a permanent lack of money (despite the fairly generous grant) I found myself night after night sitting in those warm cafés that allowed poor students spend a couple of hours over one tiny café express, reading avidly the short stories of Guy de Maupassant, the twenty volume family series of *Les Rougon-Macquart* by Émile Zola and other French writers such as Gustave Flaubert, Albert Camus and, for lighter reading, Georges Simenon.

Towards the end of my Parisian séjour, I became involved in a haphazard soccer team. There were eight different nationalities on the team. We never won a game and never really got to know each other. But we still created some sort of a vague bond. After our last game, we were sitting on the terrasse of a café in some Parisian suburb and began to discuss our futures. The African was the son of a tribal chief and he was going to learn from his father the skills of leadership. The two Arabs were also going home to follow in their fathers' footsteps; the Swiss was going to work in a bank; the Canadian was going logging, while my French friend was somewhat vague as to his future.

Listening to all this I suddenly said: 'ye know ye are all richer than I am, but I am wealthier than the lot of ye put together. My life will revolve around the great riches of the imagination. It will be peopled by powerful word weavers of spells and dreams. I will share their magic, beauty and inspirations with the world. I am going to be a bookseller.'

Three weeks later I ended up behind the counter with my mother and said 'here I am.'

published by Hodges Figgis in 1942/1947
Lord and Lady Longford (of the Gate Theatre and Longford Productions)
published many books with HF in the 1930s and 1940s

Kate Kerrigan

from THAT GIRL

Cork, Ireland, 1965: Noreen felt quite certain she had just had an orgasm. It was not what she had been expecting from only her third time making love with John. The first time had been somewhat uncomfortable and awkward. The second had been pleasant enough but really they were just getting into the swing of it. Then today – their third time? Well, it had been something else altogether. An *orgasm*. What else could that mighty, shuddering, glorious cacophony of ecstasy have been?

Noreen flopped across her fiancé, John's, chest, smiled broadly and laughed a little. After a minute she leaned on one elbow and gazed up at him. John was looking very pleased with himself indeed. As well he might.

'Ouch,' he said, 'that elbow is sharp.' Her elbow was the only thing about Noreen that was angular. Fully dressed, she had a broad, traditional build that, while it didn't suit all of the fashions of the day, made her perfectly delicious when she was naked. At least John thought so. Noreen was boundlessly sexual, mound after glorious mound of flesh, as white and soft as powdered sugar. Irresistible. John considered himself something of a saint to have held strong as long as he had. It was nearly a whole year since they had gotten engaged and, in the end, they were only here on her insistence. With broad features in an honest, open face Noreen wasn't considered the most beautiful girl in Carney but John didn't care too much about that and neither did she. She was clever and funny and kind. She was all he had ever wanted. Noreen was John's girl. And now she always would be. She gave him a playful dig with the offending elbow and reached across him for the cigarettes.

'Just tell me. Did I have an orgasm, John?'

'Jesus, Noreen. Isn't it enough for you to be doing the thing without talking about it as well? Who cares?'

Sex had been Noreen's idea. Of course, John had *wanted* to do it. He was a man, after all. However, sex before marriage was a risky business. She might get pregnant, too early to pass it off as post-marital.

She gasped with exaggerated horror. 'I can't believe you just said that. Everyone cares. Every woman is entitled to an orgasm *every* time she has sex.'

'Who says? I never heard that.'

'That's because you never read.'

'Ah, that's grand. It wasn't Father Carney then? Phew.'

'Well, did you feel anything?'

He laughed.

'I surely did.'

'I mean from *me*, not *you*.'

'I dunno, sure didn't I pull out before … Ah Jesus, Noreen, you have me at it now as well.'

'It's just that if we are going to have sex …'

'Make love. Noreen, please. Can you at least put a nice name to it?'

'… and do this terrible thing that'll have us in purgatory for all eternity …'

'That is correct.'

'Well, then, at least I want to be sure I am getting the most out of it. It says here,' she pulled a copy of *The Feminine Mystique* off her bedside table 'that every repressed housewife in America feels they should be "having orgasms while waxing the family-room floor". They are having orgasms all the time.'

'It's a wonder they get anything else done.'

'They don't. American women aren't allowed to work. Only do housework and have sex. And orgasms are mandatory.'

She took a pull out of her cigarette and blew smoke up at the ceiling. 'I wish I wasn't allowed to work. Da has me killed out in that pub. I'm on again tonight.'

'Ah no, I thought we'd go into Fermoy and see a movie.'

Noreen tried to look disappointed. Truth be told she preferred real-life to the movies and would rather be in the pub. Catching up on local gossip and dealing with rowdy drunks was better than chewing on a bag of Emerald Toffees and cooing over some romantic Hollywood nonsense with every other couple in town. John was so predictable. Life was so predictable. At least on a Saturday in the pub, you might get a bit of trouble.

'Old Kathleen Molloy passed on this morning, so Da has to get her ready for the wake.'

'At least he hasn't got you fiddling with dead bodies.'

'Yet …'

Noreen knew that her father wanted her to take over the funeral home as well as the pub. Once she and John were married, Frank Lyons would get the son he craved.

'Besides, I prefer live bodies,' Noreen said, running her hands down the front of John's bare chest. 'Will we go again? Just so I can be sure?'

'Ah Noreen. Now, we have to put a stop to this carry on now. Honestly. We'll be married soon and then we can be at this whenever we like.'

His voice was saying one thing, but his body was saying quite another.

'Noreen, stop now. Really, we can't be at this messing.'

But it was too late. She had already clambered on top of him and he was drowning under a mound of sugar.

Irish Independent, 4 December 1979

Marian Keyes

from ICELANDIC DIARY 2017

June 8th

Today's the day for going to Iceland. But when I wake from my anxious slumber I have The Fear. I want to stay at home in my Irish bed and eat my Irish meals and watch my Irish telly.

This happens to me *a lot*, whenever I'm due to go away. Six months beforehand, I'm always dying to go. Three weeks beforehand I'm always dying to go.

Ten days beforehand, I'm always dying to go.

But seven hours beforehand, I am *not* dying to go.

Instead I'm dying to stay at home. This sort of homesickness-in-advance is happening to me more and more and I strongly disapprove. I suspect it's something to do with getting older and seeing as I only discovered five days ago that I have a favourite spoon (also a favourite bowl, a favourite glass and a favourite cushion) – another characteristic of old age – it's quite a worry.

A few weeks ago, in preparation for this visit, I read 'the book.' And 'the book' told me that Icelanders work very hard, are very materialist and crave all the newest consumer toys. Apparently, most Icelandic homes are jammers with abandoned Nutribullets, Nespresso machines, automated pancake makers, racing bikes and Fitbits. I also read that the Icelanders aren't particularly friendly. Neither of these facts overlap with my idealised, wish-fulfillment picture of the place – I've decided they're well-read, liberal, Bjork-style nature-lovers who take every one on their own merits. This is odd considering the only thing I know about Iceland is from watching subtitled crime telly yokes, in which people are – by dint of the subject matter – murderers or the people trying to catch them. But I'm fiercely bonded to my notion of Icelanders as intelligent, easygoing gods and goddesses so I've faced up to the facts in the guidebook, the way I face up to all unpleasant truths, by going into deep denial.

Despite everything my spirits rise and rise even further when there are a reassuring number of hairy, beardy mens at the departure gate. This – I am certain! – is a mere preview of what I will see left, right and centre when I land. On we get and all around us on the plane they are spaking Icelandic, everyone sounding like they've either just committed a crime or are about to solve it.

The flight passes in jig time – Iceland is very, very near, only 2 hours – and when we land the pilot makes an announcement. Great news! The weather in Reykjavik is 7 degrees and there's a northerly wind! I've just spent 2 SWELTERING weeks in London, my feet are in utter RIBBONS from sandal-triggered blisters and my eyes are permanently squinched from trying to filter out the glaring sunlight. Summer is misery for me and I'm craving some 'mild' weather.

Even at the airport, I can smell the sea. Outside, the sky is blue and the wind is brisk and blustery and something about it reminds me of trips to the seaside on Easter Sunday when I was a child – innocent, hopeful, happy, and pure.

51 kilometres from the airport to the centre of Reykjavik and yes, on the drive the entire place looks like an outpost on another planet. Strange flat lava fields stretch wide and away, then miles off in the distance, charcoal-coloured mountains rise suddenly. Now and again clusters of car showrooms and other big warehouse-y buildings bloom at the side of the road, everything looking as if it was thrown up five minutes ago.

But the centre of Reykjavik is charming and cute, reminding me a bit of them there lovely towns like Tromso and Trondheim that I visited on a Norwegian cruise a hundred years ago.

We go to a restaurant that we saw on *Rick Stein's Long Weekends* when he went to Reykjavik. One of the other tables got a giant plateful of something ferried to them, it was the same size as a joint of beef but the chef had been blowtorching it and I deduced it was a cod's head. Himself expressed doubt. I, however, was certain. So certain that I summoned the waiter chap over and quizzed him. He confirmed that it was indeed a cod's head and I had the good grace to not gloat.

June 9th
We 'rise' early. We've had a bad night's sleep because:
a) The sun never set and the room stayed bright all night.
b) There was a ferocious racket from the music venue next door.
c) The British general election was yesterday and the exit polls were exciting and every time I turned in the bed, startled by the daylight at 4 in the morning, I'd find Himself glued to his tablet and looking sheepish.

But we arise and go to the breakfast buffet where amongst the other delights is a large bottle of cod liver oil in an ice bucket. (We decline). Other than that the breakfast is tame. Except! Skyr! Do you know of skyr? It's like yoghurt only far, far, far nicer! And thicker! And yes, all round better! I first had it in Denmark and I've been excited about having it again.

Right! Off we go whalewatching. The day is bright, blue, blustery and very sunny. Cold, still, but it doesn't matter. Reykjavik is beautiful. It's a small little place. Hard to know what to compare it to, but it's small.

Out on the boat it's perishing, but we get padded suits if we want them. (I do, Himself doesn't). We see loads of minke whales. Then! We change boats and go puffin-watching and this is a DELIGHT! There are thousands and thousands of 'nesting pairs' on an island that looks like one of the ones in Clew Bay on a bizarrely sunny Sunday in July. The sky is blue and the water is navy and the island is luminous green and the puffins are cute. They're a bit too heavy for their wings so they have to flap like billy-o. (Naturally I identify). They are monogamous – which I approve of – and they mate for life.

At 4.30 myself and Himself 'repair' to a bookshop in the centre of town (about 20 seconds walk away) for the Icelandic launch of *Watermelon*. It's a hoot! And mind-blowing in a good way. It's 22 years since *Watermelon* was first published and it's great to have it translated into Icelandic! Lovely people come, including 4 generations from one family. There are babies and women and mens and all sorts and every Icelander I meet has about 16 different jobs. They're playwrights and magazine editors and chefs and field and track coaches. (And that's just the one person).

Then at 7.30 we go with the publisher and translator and translator's friend to a café and for my dinner I have pink skyr.

published by Allen Figgis in 1972, paperback edition

In *mutual self-protection two children move through adolescence enjoying a beautiful intimacy, united in their struggle against the hatred and hypocrisy which surrounds them, and unsuspecting that their narrow social circle must one day condemn such love as shocking and sinful.*

The Ailish O'Breen
half brother

published by Allen Figgis in 1972, hardback edition

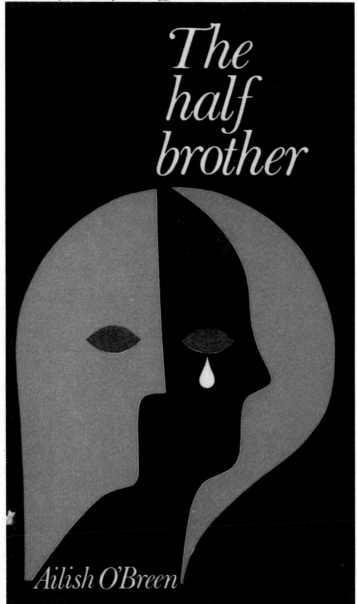

Jess Kidd

PYRO

Colette crawls through the gap in the witch's hedge. She knows the others are watching her arse and she's relieved to be wearing tights, although the day is too hot for them and they snag as she goes.

The others aren't watching. They have thrown her bike into a field and have pedalled off sniggering.

Colette has little going for her. She has a round tummy, small eyes and a sweaty fringe. She wears the plaid skirts and knitted ponchos that belonged to her older sisters. There are years and years of wear in them, maybe decades. Colette is the slowest on a bike, in a race, on the uptake. She loses every bet and every dare and gives up at the first sign of danger. She suffers the shame of failure, but has no backbone. Like all soft, shell-less things she feels hurt deeply. Otherwise, she's never spiteful and often kind, even to wasps. In this way Colette is older and wiser than her years. Which are ten.

Colette knows she screamed as she fell and the others heard. They will be biting their hands and laughing on the other side of the hedge. She waits for them to call out to her, to ask if she's all right, but they don't.

Colette pulls up her skirt. There are scratches and a bad graze that gives her a hot, swoony feeling.

Tears come. Because she hadn't wanted to go through the hedge, because her leg hurts, because to get out of the pit she'll have to pull herself up through nettles. She sits down with her sore leg held straight and sobs until she can't see.

The woman is wearing a nightie. Colette looks away as the woman comes down the ladder in case she isn't wearing knickers. Colette knows that women who wear nighties in the afternoon are either lunatics or trollops.

The woman wears butterfly clips in her hair, except they aren't clips because they crawl. And they aren't butterflies, because their bodies are hairy stalks and their colours are dark. This makes them moths. Colette resists the urge to scream by pretending the moths aren't real.

'I've antiseptic out the back,' says the woman, whose name is Gertie Moran.

Gertie says she's a hundred years old, which Colette knows can't be true. Gertie has a hunchback and long white hair, which is pretty despite the moths. She has eyes the colour of hot treacle and a fierce point to her nose. Her hands have atrophied into rheumatoid claws, all knuckles and gnarl.

Colette smells the burnt-out house before she sees it. It has glittering carbon walls, twisted doorframes and heat-buckled windows. The sky can be seen through the blackened ribs of floor joists.

'There was a fire.' Gertie says.

'Oh,' says Colette.

'Before the fire ...' Gertie looks around her, baffled as to how to explain.

Before the fire the house was whitewashed. It had tucked-in blankets on iron beds, gables and curtains, a range and a dresser, swept chimneys and brushed floors, polished mirrors and china plates. A hundred years ago, when Gertie's parents were alive and Gertie was little older than Colette. They walk through the burnt-out house together,

Colette, hushed at the sight of it, Gertie, recollecting a straight spine and unfurled fingers.

Out back there is a lean-to, a chair, a table with a plant on it. Gertie dabs Colette's leg with a sponge and makes sympathetic noises. Colette stares sympathetically at Gertie's hump.

Then, because it's rude to stare, Colette counts the bird droppings on the table, the singed leaves on the plant and the feathers on the ground. The feathers glow bright crimson even in the shade, like little wispy flames.

Gertie brings the scones. They're burnt too; black rocks. There's jam, only the lid has melted onto the jar. Gertie bites into a scone making a little dry rasping noise as she looks out over the garden.

Gertie helps Colette find her bike. Colette promises to return next Thursday. Gertie will make a trifle.

Colette knows what to be frightened of.

Bad men who'll take you for a drive, put their hand up your skirt, dig a hole and bury you in it.

Supernaturally: zombies, ghosts and banshees.

Somewhere between worldly and otherworldly evil lies Barry Walsh.

Barry Walsh stops her and asks where she's been. Colette says nowhere. He tightens his grip on her handlebar and she tells him. Like all soft, shell-less things she feels hurt deeply.

Colette sits on her palms and looks out over the car park at the back of the pub. Barry does the talking.

Barry makes a convincing case, although they would agree with him anyway.

Your woman caught Colette in a mantrap and force-fed her poisoned scones.

Either way she has it coming.

They'd give her a fire.

Colette says nothing. She watches a crisp packet skitter in the breeze up off the sea and thinks about Gertie's hump and the trifle she'll never have.

Night unwinds over the bay and in and out of the sleeping town. A vixen cries and a badger answers. In the burnt-out parlour of her burnt-out house, Gertie unbuttons her nightie and slips it over her head. She turns and turns about in the moonlight on the one-time hearthrug, which is now no more than a scorch mark. Throwing shadows, drawing crescents, far beyond the reach of human arms. As she turns there's a whirring beat, then the whisper, like wind under wing, then silence.

The guards find a melted petrol can on the porch but it hardly explains the conflagration that lit up the sky above the uninhabited Moran cottage. Barry Walsh said they also found the burnt-out body of a hunchbacked witch. When they touched her she fell to dust.

Colette is not the only person to notice the moths. For the next few weeks they are everywhere. Circling light bulbs like dark warnings, combusting in candles, igniting on hobs. Colette falls asleep watching them dance. One night she dreams of a bird with blackened feathers, preening itself in Gertie's midnight parlour. It shakes soot from its wings, revealing burning crimson feathers and flies up through the floor joists. In an arc of fire it turns out over the ocean, flares once and is gone.

Claire Kilroy

from DARLING

I encountered a mound of briars. It was as high as my
chest and tore at my clothes as I attempted to plough
through it. I heard my pocket ripping off and was gratified
by the violence of the sound. Look at me! I suppose was
my logic. Behold my suffering! I was without my anchor,
our names carved in stone. You don't need to hear this.
Which is why I wait until you're asleep.

I got caught before I even made it halfway across – of
course I did – and when I tried to double back, a hundred
hooks snagged my legs and over I went on my back,
toppling like a statue off a plinth. I let myself fall. I was
ready to come to a stop. The jittery energy drained from
my body as if a plug had been pulled, and that was it, I
was done. I started to cry, in shame as much as anything,
on my bed of tiny nails. A grown woman stuck in a bush.
The girl I used to be would never have, blah blah. I tried to
wipe my nose with my sleeve but it was caught in the
thorns, so I lay there snivelling and looking at the sky,
limbs pegged down like a tent.

I grew calm as I abided there with the other wild
animals and after a time the forest absorbed me into it.
Birdsong, squabbles on branches, the drone of insects – the
volume crept back up. Woodpigeons reembarked on their
conversations. They were probably talking about me. I was
alone, I realised. *Alone* alone. Alone as in how we face
death. Green is my favourite colour, I thought, gazing up
at the leaves. I hadn't had time to think in so long. My
world had become too chaotic. A balance, the great balance
I hadn't known had been looming over me all those years,
had abruptly tipped. I was sliding off. Plus I had forgotten
to drop the black bags to the clothing bank. And you,
abandoned and irresistable, just waiting for another

woman to gather your warmth into her arms. A bitter flare of jealousy. I closed my eyes but I didn't understand. I'm sorry that. I never meant. A creature was approaching in speculative bursts across the forest floor. I tracked its progress without opening my eyes. A bird? Too loud. It got closer still, then stopped to regard the felled giant in its midst. Badger? Fox? That's when something pronged my scalp. I launched up and out of there with a shriek, by which time the creature was gone.

On the other side of the briars was a lush and hushed clearing of green. No human had set foot there in years. It was a glorious little glade and I immediately thought of you: hey look! But you were gone, oh, oh. I was so tired, so beyond myself. Mother Mary, come to me. But who was ever there for her? Who mothered the mothers? Weren't mothers people too? Weren't they the ones on the hardest station of all? I took the tub of pills out of my pocket and tipped a few onto the palm of my hand. My wrists were all scratched up. Good. My husband had wanted to punish me? Well. Well, well, well.

I had forgotten to bring water. The pills tasted vile.

Stepping on the mossy carpet detonated a booby trap of screeching. Birds sprang into life at my intrusion, a pair of them flapping and shrieking. They appeared to be shrieking *at me*. I shooed them away but they wouldn't desist. They had lost their minds too.

'Jesus,' I said to them, 'what is the problem?'

It was a crazy little pocket I had happened upon. Then I saw it.

There on the forest floor, purplish pink among the vivid greens, and just about heavy enough to bend the grass, was a foetus. It was no larger than my big toe and at first I thought it *was* a big toe. 'Fuck,' I cried as I twisted to avoid stepping on it, at which the birds lost it altogether. Don't stop, I warned myself, but I had already stopped. Don't look, but I had already bent over to look.

Disproportionately large head, tiny body, all elbows, purple eyelids sealed shut and a yellow beak. It's skin was as thin as clingfilm. A hatchling.

The birds ramped up their protest. 'What do you want me to do?' I asked them. 'It's dead. Your baby is dead.' I don't know why I was so callous about it. My mind was reeling. The tablets had lodged in my throat.

And then it moved. The hatchling opened its beak. Gasping for air or food or life. It understood on some level that it was dying. Even a tiny brain is large enough to register panic. And pain. Should I put it out of its misery? Step on it? 'Oh Christ,' I said to the birds, 'where's your nest?'

I glanced around the forest canopy. But how could I climb a tree? Even without the stitches, I could not have climbed a tree. So I burst into tears again. It was you there, darling, dying in the grass with no one to help you because everything vulnerable was you, everything tender was you those days, and these days, and very possibly all my days. The overhead screeching was as disorientating as a burglar alarm. I couldn't hear myself think. It seemed shriller than before though we appeared to be down to one bird now. The dowdy one, the female. The male and his petrol sheen had fucked off and the mother was beside herself. I reflexively looked around for someone to help, to advise, but I was deep in the forest, darling. I was lost.

I knelt down to pick up the hatchling to ... what? Give it back to the mother? Here is your dying chick? Just before I made contact with it, she dive-bombed me. The mother actually dive-bombed me, her beak or claws briefly connecting with my scalp. I sat back on my hunkers in surprise and admiration. Her slightness, her drabness, her courage. She put me to shame. I stood up and backed off and she alighted in front of her young, setting herself and her fierce heart between us. She was nothing, she was no weight at all. I could have blown her away with one puff.

Babies die, I thought as I regarded her. That is the world we live in.

I did not make this world, I thought.

If I could, I thought, I would make a different world. I would make a different world for you and me, darling. And for this brave bird.

But I can't.

I can't.

published by Allen Figgis in 1960

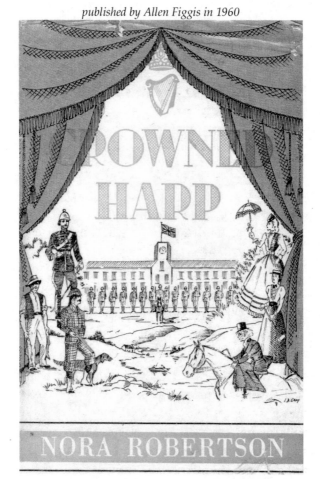

Crowned Harp: Memories of the Last Years of the Crown in Ireland

Thomas Kilroy

from THE TRIALS OF WILLIAM SHAKESPEARE

QUEEN ELIZABETH enthroned, a glittering image. SHAKESPEARE kneels before her with head bowed.

QUEEN: Rise, Shakespeare! (*Shakespeare stands, head still bowed*). It is unlike you to seek an audience like this. Not your style. You were always the quiet fellow. Although, we welcome you. Certainly more so than some of those idiots who pester us daily with their claims to this, that and the other. Do people pester you, Shakespeare?

SHAKESPEARE: Constantly, Your Majesty.

QUEEN: There! You see! Idiots!

SHAKESPEARE: This is not on my own behalf, Your Majesty. It is on behalf of someone else.

QUEEN: Someone else! Someone else? And, pray, who is this someone else?

SHAKESPEARE: The Earl of Southampton, Your Majesty.

QUEEN: (*Very angry*). What? What is this? Do you dare to question the judgement of the court? Do you dispute the evidence? The verdict of nine earls of the realm and sixteen barons to boot?

SHAKESPEARE: No-no, Your Majesty, never!

QUEEN: We should hope not, for your own sake. Careful, Shakespeare! Be very, very, very careful of what you say next –

SHAKESPEARE: Yes, Your Majesty.

QUEEN: Actually, we are intrigued. What is it that makes you step into such dangerous water? Hm? We are told by our informants that you do not allow your right hand to know what your left hand is doing. Yet here you are now, ready to put your head on the block. For what, may I ask? Inform me!

SHAKESPEARE: The fate of Lord Southampton means a great deal to me, Your Majesty. A great deal.

QUEEN: Is it sex? Of course we have heard the gossip. The tumbles of you and Southampton were the talk of London for years. You are a cock-lover, Shakespeare? Isn't that so?

SHAKESPEARE: The death of the earl would mean the death of part of me.

QUEEN: Are you two still servicing one another?

SHAKESPEARE: Our – (*finding the word*) – relationship is in the past, Your Majesty.

QUEEN: He is notoriously promiscuous, you know.

SHAKESPEARE: I know, Your Majesty.

QUEEN: Was he unfaithful to you?

SHAKESPEARE nods.

QUEEN: With a boy?

SHAKESPEARE: With a woman.

QUEEN: What a shit he is! Cannot stand him, you know, Harry Wriothesley. Cannot stand the sight of him. He will ride anything that moves, apparently. We can recommend other males of our acquaintance who can give like service, Shakespeare. If you still have the inclination, that is.

SHAKESPEARE: This relationship, Your Majesty, cannot be replaced.

QUEEN: I see. You are indeed a prudent man, Shakespeare. And now, this!

SHAKESPEARE: I am sorry that I have troubled Your Majesty with this request.

QUEEN: Enough fol-de-ro! Persuade us, Shakespeare. Go on! You are a man of words and we love words. Let us have your delivery, then. Make your case. What could possibly persuade us to free Southampton?

SHAKESPEARE: With respect, Your Majesty. The offence of Lord Southampton is not as grievous as that of the Earl of Essex.

QUEEN: (*Explosion of rage*). Essex! How dare you mention the name Essex in my presence! Don't you ever speak that name in my hearing! Ever! Do you hear?

SHAKESPEARE: Forgive me, Your Majesty, I did not intend –

QUEEN: Intend? You are an upstart, Shakespeare! (*Fierce effort at control*). One must not give way to turbulence. It weakens the heart. In spite of all, we are still intrigued. We are still curious as to what you would say in support of your outrageous plea.

SHAKESPEARE: Such clemency would cast a glow of light upon Your Majesty.

QUEEN: (*Suddenly curious*). How so?

SHAKESPEARE: It would mark Your Majesty as having severe authority and benign pity in equal measure. In such a balance there is perfection. Such a largeness of temper is a model for all princes everywhere, to be equally an unflinching judge while possessing limitless mercy as God's representative on this earth.

QUEEN: Bravo! I do believe we should employ you, Shakespeare, as a royal speechwriter.

SHAKESPEARE: I am overwhelmed by Your Majesty's generosity.

QUEEN: Indeed. What was it, Shakespeare, that drew you to this man? You may be frank with me, you know. Nothing shocks me.

SHAKESPEARE: (*Pause. Choosing his route carefully*). It was ten years ago –

QUEEN: Yes-yes. Go on! Go on!

SHAKESPEARE: The plague was rampant in the city. The theatres were closed. A year of indoors, with curtains drawn. Holes in the houses blocked up against the cursed infection. A year of night. A year of darkness everywhere, every day.

QUEEN: And what did you do?

SHAKESPEARE: I wrote poems.

QUEEN: Good Heavens! (*Pause*). Was it the flesh, Shakespeare? Was it that which overpowered you? You may confide in me.

SHAKESPEARE: I wish to confide in you, Your Majesty. You are the only one to understand.

QUEEN: It was the white limbs of this spoiled brat, was that it? Laid out. Waiting for you. You were crazed with anticipation? Was that it? Tell me the details, Shakespeare. You may be as free in your language as you wish.

SHAKESPEARE: Every sinew, every muscle, every nerve. It was as if my body was set alight. As never before. Never since.

QUEEN: (*Pause*). And is that all?

SHAKESPEARE: It was as if I had passed beyond nature itself.

QUEEN: Were you both completely naked during this – male excitement? Details, Shakespeare, details! Where are the damned details?

SHAKESPEARE: I cannot – cannot remember.

QUEEN: Good God, surely you must remember something like that?

SHAKESPEARE: I believe I may have lost consciousness.

QUEEN: That's a lot of bollocks, Shakespeare, and well you know it. You are not the type to lose consciousness. Ever alert, ever awake –

SHAKESPEARE: I am trying to respond as accurately as I can, Majesty.

QUEEN: I am thoroughly bored with all this.

THE ROYALTY THEATRE.

THE PROGRAMME OF THE IRISH NATIONAL THEATRE SOCIETY.

President, W. B. Yeats. Vice-Presidents, Douglas Hyde and George Russell. Treasurer, Fred Ryan. Secretary, George Roberts. Stage Manager, W. G. Fay.

Performance under the auspices of the Irish Literary Society, Hanover Square, London.

SATURDAY, MARCH TWENTY SIXTH, NINETEEN HUNDRED AND FOUR, AT TWO IN THE AFTERNOON.

PRICE TWOPENCE.

Advertisement for Hodges, Figgis and Co in theatre programme for National Theatre Society plays staged at The Royalty Theatre including: The King's Threshold, a play in one act & in verse *by W.B. Yeats;* Riders to the Sea, a play in one act *by J.M. Synge; and* In the Shadow of the Glen, a play in one act *by J.M. Synge, 26 March 1904 (NLI)*

Sealy, Bryers and Walker, Printers, Dublin. 951. 3. '04.

Deirdre Kinahan

from THE LOST ONES
for Meath County Council Arts Office 2017

1926. Michael is a young man wearing a dress and fur coat. His make-up is smudged. He is holding a wig in his hand and has a hair net clipped tight to his head. He has been running.

They'll have to hang me if they find me.
So I'm asking you not to scream. Not to tell.
I need you not to tell.
Because I'm a mess of a man.
And not in the way you see it.
You see I always came at the world arse-ways.
From the very first.
I was actually born that way.
Breach.
Wrong way round.
Nearly killed my poor Mother or so they say.
I know she never forgave me for bringing her more than the usual pain. But then as the years wore on I think she might have forgot which one of us it was, because she had that many children screaming and running wild around the Spire of Lloyd.

That's where we lived. In a small cottage, on a small hump at the foot of the Spire, outside Kells. The Spire is a lighthouse in the middle of the fields and more than thirty miles from the sea. It's a folly built by the local toff ... stupidity and pomp locked in stone. Sure what else could you be but queer living in the shadow of a thing like that?

But then I've lived in 'interesting times' ... isn't that the phrase?
'May you live in interesting times'.
English words for a Chinese curse.
And a curse for sure.

One I've found myself in the mess of ... more than once.

Sure amn't I running now?
Running from the Peelers.
Do you hear their whistles?
Their excitement?
Their crushing boots!
It'd remind you of one of the hunts at home.
Perhaps I shouldn't have worn my fur?!
And I was only dancing.
Dancing in Soho.
But for a man like me, with a man like mine.
Dancing can be awful dangerous.

I wasn't always 'Me'.
I was once a boy, a man called Michael.
Michael Doyle.
But you can call me Josephine, or Rosaline.
Which do you prefer?
I chose Josephine at the end of the war in honour of my
Mother but not so sure that she would enjoy the
compliment I switched it later to Rosie ... or Rosaline.
That was the name I chose for Roger.
Roger Casement.
He is my ghost and my lover.

The first time I saw Roger I was just out of short pants but
he looked at me like I was a man. He was stood on a cart in
the centre of Kells, an Irish man with an English Voice
talking of *Freedom* and *Gaelic* and *Poems*. My Father told me
he was an English Knight that saved Africa from slavery
and murder but all I seen were slender hands and hips that
swayed as he boomed.

I stood right at the front of the crowd and heard nothing.
He left, as suddenly as he had arrived in a frenzy of cheer
... but not before he caught my eye.
Grey. Slate grey. Like marble and sky, his eyes.
And they could see ... what was it?

What was it they could see in me?
What was it caused him to stall?
To stop.
To shake my hand.
And whisper low his name.
Casement. Roger Casement.
He took my breath away.

There's a plot by the Spire of Lloyd. A Famine plot. And my father used to tell us stories of the people who lay there; their privations, their hunger. How they shuffled down from the hills on famine days like spectres, their arms as thin as parchment, stretched, outstretched, barely able to mouth a whisper, lips green from sucking grass and eyes wild with want. He could tell a story my Father.

And that was where we met.
At the Spire. Me and Roger.
At the dead of night.
In a nest of the dead.
Maybe that was how it started?
I started?
Though I was always different.
Always the dreamer. That's what they called me at home.
No use for cutting out on the bog. No use for milking. Too slow! Because my head was always stuck in the clouds and that made me a solitary youth. I never seemed to understand the passions of the living; the politics, the girls, the town, the push and shove of ordinary life. So I surprised myself as much as anyone when I went and joined the army, the British Army.

I don't know what I thought I was fighting for. Ireland? Home Rule? The chance to dance? Because in truth it was just a way out of Kells, to a different place where I might find other men who could make me feel like he did.

So I signed up for the killing in 1914. The killing and mayhem and slaughter. And I was only days in Belgium when I saw battle. Men, boys, shadows of boys ordered forward into the screaming gun. And all I could think of was the step, my step, in my boots. Feet so swollen that I couldn't take them off but feet that still found strength to carry me on. Slipping, gripping in the grime and blood and flesh and pleading that was my new world. I feared. I feared that I had followed my peculiar passion into hell itself!

You have to understand that when I ran out from my trench, I ran out over the bodies of the boys that I had shared tea with that morning. I ran out over their screaming and their bloody dismemberment as the enemy shell cut right through them, and me. Arms, legs, corpses, flew about my head like birds. Thick muck blasted up and fresh graves made but still my feet ran on like I was the last bead on a string of rosary, broke, and scattering madly across the land.

Finally I reached the other side.
A German trench.
And one German that had been left behind.
I remember his eyes.
Always the eyes.
Shining.
Holding me in them for just one moment, before thrusting with his bayonet.
The glint of his eyes.
The glint of the steel.
But my hand.
My arms.
They seemed to have a life of their own.
And they reacted faster. And I saw blood, thick and fresh and red, oozing out of that German mouth. That full pink German mouth.
And I saw the shock on his face and the shock in his eyes as I pierced him again and again right in the chest.
It took my breath away.

Susan Knight

BAD PENNY AND PIG

George Parkes was watering his window boxes. The blue lobelias, sweet alyssum and geraniums were coming on well, but the petunias looked shrivelled. Too much direct sunshine, perhaps. There were some gaps, too, in the colourful mix. A few days before, George had uprooted every last one of his pansies, unable to bear any longer the hopeful expression on their little faces.

He could deal with the gaps. But what to do about the petunias?

The front door slammed hard below his second floor bedsit, so hard indeed that his windows rattled. George Parkes knew who it was. Hadn't he heard her heavy feet clumping down the stairs past his door a moment or two earlier. Now, accidentally on purpose, he upended his watering can so that its contents sloshed down just as she emerged from the house. The cascade missed her but she looked up in surprise and spotted him before he had time to draw back his head.

'Watch it, Fatso!' Her voice as grinding as a road mender's drill.

Fatso! That was a joke. What right did she have to call anyone fat, her with her big tits and big arse and thick legs carelessly exposed in a mini-skirt? Stuffing her ugly face all the time with burgers and chips and chocolate bars probably. His, on the other hand, was a glandular problem. Nothing he could do about his size and it was cruel to mock.

She was staring up at him now, mouth twisted in a sneer. Penelope, Bad Penny, as he thought of her. Always turning up.

'How are you this fine morning, Georgie Porgie? In the pink? Pink as a pig?' She laughed, an unattractively-harsh sound. Penny smoked, he knew that for a fact, the way she and her friends chucked their fag ends everywhere. If there was a God in heaven, He'd make sure she got terminal lung cancer. The sooner the better.

'George Porgie, pudding and pie,' she chanted. 'Kissed the girls and made them cry.'

Oh, it was so funny. Wasn't it so very funny! Penny must have thought so, whole lumpy body quivering with mirth, almost choking on her laughter.

Enough.

That's enough.

You can only push a man so far, after all.

George shoves the window box off the ledge so that it hurtles down to where the girl is standing, directly beneath him, laughing like a drain. It happens so fast she doesn't have time to move. The box hits her square on the head and she is knocked to the ground, spread-eagled, her mini-skirt riding up obscenely, exposing the tops of thick thighs, pale as porridge, while dark blood snakes down over the stone steps.

'It was an accident,' George tells the copper, 'a tragic accident. You see she always slams ... I mean to say, of course, officer, she always slammed *the door so very hard. I've noticed the boxes wobble before but of course never imagined anything like this happening ...'*

They are scooping her up now and shoving her in a rubbish bag.

The copper is making notes, a regular Dixon of Dock Green, *him.*

'That a box would fall right on her head. Right on her conk ...' George starts to laugh. 'What are the chances of that ...'

'Bulls-eye,' the copper says and laughs too ...

George stared dreamily out the window, a smile on his moon face. By now Penny had lost interest in him and was sashaying down the street, big arse wobbling, greasy hair swishing down her back. He watched her go, then picked a rogue weed from among the geraniums and pinched it to death between his fingers before letting it drop to the scrubby patch below.

published by Allen Figgis in 1969

Epic in proportions, written with a poet's fluency, this big novel of life in pre-Revolutionary Ireland is now published for the first time in English outside the U.S.A. It will confirm Padraic Colum as one of the major figures of the Irish renaissance.

riverrun

The Flying Swans
Padraic Colum

Conor Kostick

from ETERNAL VOYAGER: THE WHITE DRAGON

Later, with their tents up and with a lively fire drying his clothes, Eternal Voyager felt more cheerful and even found he was paying attention to what Silver was saying: something about her plans for when this expedition was over.

'I know what you're thinking. Why bother with the weeks of grinding necessary for a *Dragonslayer*, when I've got four weapons with better damage to time ratios?'

'*Dragonslayer*, the pike right?'

'Well, a glaive-guisarm, but yeah. So, the point is the resistances on the *Dragonslayer* will get me – on average – three extra minutes against elder blue, red and white dragons. For black and green dragons, obviously my *Longsword of the Ages* is better.'

'Obviously.'

'With a *Dragonslayer* I only need to group two seventh level dtt-classes, with decent gear of course, and we could take an elder dragon. Actually, if I was grouped with you, the two of us would win most of the time. I was running simulations. The crucial difference is that I survive nine minutes, not six. And if we had a reasonably competent group healer class with us – though, admittedly, they are as rare as a honest innkeeper – it's almost without risk.'

'Erm Silver?'

'Yeah?'

'Can we talk about something else, other than *Epic* gear?'

The barbarian frowned. 'Like what?'

'Well, philosophy, say.'

'Philosophy?'

'Yeah. Do you have a philosophy of life?'

'Sure, I have a philosophy.'

'Great.' EV looked at her, taking in the solemn blue eyes that looked back at him through long braids of blonde hair. For the first time since they had begun their long trek, he found himself interested the next utterance that would come from her mouth.

'If it moves … hit it. And if it doesn't move …'

Eternal sighed. 'Hit it until it moves. I know. All tanks think that's a clever line. But seriously. What makes you happy? Really now.'

Silver didn't answer at once, but drank some of the beer from her magic horn. 'That's a good question. Let me think about it.'

So EV let her think. Presumably, she was not used to using the parts of her brain that were not devoted to playing *Epic*. Above, slender clouds caught the silver moonlight, stars visible between them.

'I'd have to say, in all honesty, nothing beats being in a team of top *Epic* players and crushing the enemy.'

'Like at Wizard's Ford?'

'Meh. No. I was stuck behind a wall most of that day, up on the south hill, dodging the missiles of the ogre catapults. I mean, say, a group of six taking down Djarinja or something.'

'I see. And are you happy then, because you've achieved something difficult? Or because you anticipate respect and admiration from your peers?'

'A bit of both. That and the pure survival on the cusp of death thing. It's like, only in those moments does all the grinding and questing become worthwhile. It's pay-off time. Know what I mean?'

'Yeah,' said EV, 'I do. But that still begs the question a bit.'

'Huh?'

'You're happy that the questing has paid off. But why invest so much of your time doing questing in the first place?'

'Oh I see. Well, you're right. I guess there's a level at which I do this because that's who I am. That's what I do best. You don't become the best tank in *Epic* just as a means to an end. You gotta love the getting there.'

This, it seemed to EV, was a reasonable answer and matched his own understanding of Silver's nature. It crossed his mind to probe her to see what her character was like outside the context of being a barbarian warrior in *Epic*. Did she go to parties? Have lovers? Enjoy avant garde music? His suspicion was that all the time Silver was outside of *Epic*, she was planning for her next adventure in the game. But rather than test that theory and push her to identify a deeper meaning to her existence, he preferred to sleep. His legs were warm at last, though they ached with the day's effort.

'Your turn for first shift, right?'

'Aye.' Silver gave him a nod and EV crawled into his tent.

Nick Laird

Manners

I am interested in the possibility of reasonable conduct.
Reasonable conduct is part of the ordinary course of things.
Also violence, though one must resist this. Life is only life

at one remove hanging from a hook wrapped round with
waves of sound and waves of light and gravitational waves
of feeling hot and cold and sad of every kind, peckish,
    bored.

Also quickened with touches of transporting fear and love.
I hold mine out in front as a black single-breasted suit I am
inspecting to see if it is suitable for attending the funeral.

I am slapping dust from its shoulders. If we're suspicious
of meaning, Dragos, that's because meaning has, historically,
had very hard edges. The point remains and it's to be
    someone

else, not repeat again how I am not you and never can be.
What I do know is that already, that already our silence
has as many selves as citizens. Regard the corner of one

citified moment, descending a staircase or writing an email
to her mother about the ironic chanting at the
    demonstration.
I still get up in the morning and breakfast. I am still burning

toast. I am still interested in the possibilities of radical formal
shifts and tonal ambiguities. I still require ceremony to
    practice
ending properly. I still feel bad about the death of that
    clothes moth.

Caitriona Lally

from WUNDERLAND

I wait for him to come out of the building. He's a bit more comfortable with me now, not so much a jumpy stray as a slightly anxious pet. He walks over to me, his tongue working in his mouth like he's worrying a mouth ulcer or easing a bitten tongue.

Hey, how was work?

Fine.

All set for the graveyard?

Cemetery, he says, it's not connected to a church.

Cemetery, I say, adding cold to my voice but it makes no odds, he doesn't notice small vocal sulks. If ever there was a time to obliterate a brother it is now; I know how Cain must have felt, maybe Abel was a nit-picking pedant of a brother. He draws me back inside, Reilly does, sends me back to my insides. What's the point in speaking words when they're sent back to you with red pen all over them? I feel patronised and misunderstood, as if subtitles were put on my accent in a television documentary.

I tell myself he can't help it, I tell myself it's the one thing that makes him feel good so let him have it, but I can't do it with good grace. It's not so much his reactions that bother me: I'm angry at myself for not anticipating his responses and taking steps to avoid them. It's like physical pain: the problem is not simply the pain itself, the problem is when you forget the pain and go about as normal until you're suddenly felled by it.

We walk in silence to the train station. Strange how it feels local now, it feels like my station even though after tomorrow I may never see it again. We walk up the steps and stand waiting for the train. I want to ask how many stops we're going and whether we have to change lines, but when I compose these questions in my head, they are never anything but dull and would lay me open to being ignored or insulted.

When the train comes, I follow Reilly on board. It squeaks and rattles and I'm glad. I like a thing to act and sound like itself – too smooth and you forget you're on a moving object, neglect to notice the stations; on a bockety one, you have no choice but to get involved.

I stare out the window. Sometimes it seems as if cities show their worst sides to train windows – the dirtiest most graffiti-strewn buildings, the unpainted backs of houses, the roofs coated in bird-shit. I wait for Reilly to speak and when he does, it's to say 'We get off here.' I follow him out of the train. It's soothing, after years of leading a child-pack, to follow and be shown and be led. I like package holidays and journeys that require nothing from me. I like long-haul flights: the air stewards decide when your bedtime is and when your wake-up time is through lighting and mealtimes. Your head might be thinking dinner but there's breakfast on your tray.

We change train and pass through suburbs and allotments. I close my eyes because keeping them open and waiting on conversation is a pain in the eyeballs. When I feel Reilly moving, I open my eyes.

We're here, he says.

Right.

It doesn't cross his mind that I haven't uttered a word, not so much as a vowel, since we got on the train but I try to put gloomy thoughts from my head. You need to keep your spirits high when you're dealing with the dead.

It's the second-largest cemetery in the world and the largest park cemetery in the world, he says.

Oh?

I try to appear interested without frightening him off with too much interest, skittish beast that he is.

What's the largest?

What?

If this is the second-largest, what's the largest cemetery in the world?

Why would you want to know that, what does it *matter* what's the largest? Why, whenever there's a list of biggest brightest best, and you name the second or third, does everyone want to know what came ahead?

Human nature I suppose.

He snorts.

That's what they say when humans behave like fools.

He talks as if he's not a member of the human race. We walk on. I clamp down on any thoughts of conversation topics.

Iraq, he says, after a silence wide as a cruise ship.

What?

That's where the largest cemetery is. And there are one and a half million people buried here, compared to five million in that cemetery in Najaf, Iraq.

Have you been?

No.

Have you been here before?

No.

He reads things, he stows knowledge from books, he knows so much about things from internet research, but he never *goes* to those places, he never *sees* these things unless he's brought. Even then he manages to act superior; I envy him that.

There are 230 gardeners looking after the place, it covers almost 300 hectares and there are 17km of roads.

Ah numbers, Reilly, you fly in my face with your numbers but what do they mean? I can't take in 17km of roads with my bare eyes, I can't imagine what 300 hectares looks like, I don't think I know 230 people in the world.

Gert, I don't know, I really don't know.

He looks like he's been extinguished.

Are you happy, Reilly?

What the hell kind of a question is that?

Ok, I'll narrow it down. When are you happiest?

He thinks for a while.

When I've charged my phone and cut my toenails.

That's it?

And when I've topped up my travel card.

Jesus, it's like he's climbed into his coffin already.

Let's walk, I say, you need to get out of your head and into the trees.

We walk. I like the peace of the graves in the middle, that's where I'd like to be buried, rather than the outskirting ones that face the road. Visiting a graveyard near a busy road, it feels rude to be alive.

published by Allen Figgis in 1963

An Chomhairle Ealaíon series of Irish Authors
Number Five

The 1916 Poets

Edited with an Introduction by
Desmond Ryan

1963
ALLEN FIGGIS
Dublin

Simon Lewis

APGAR SCORE

It seems degrading the way you're taken,
how I imagine animals are grabbed
before their throats are slit at the butchers.
You are on a towel, pink and screaming.
The nurse is happy and gives you a two,
sticks her latexed finger into your mouth.
Wiping away the vernix, all you do
is numbered: heartbeats, sneezes, coughs.
It's less than five minutes into your little life
and you've already been given a value.
Today the nurse says you're an eight
or nine. I look at you being wrapped
in swaddles of towels and blankets
ready to spend your life trying to reach ten.

published by Allen Figgis in 1963

The 1916 Poets

Padraic H Pearse Joseph M Plunkett
Thomas Mac Donagh

Edited with an Introduction by Desmond Ryan

Brian Leyden

from HERE WE ARE

Her throat feels scratchy and she drinks bottled water to keep hydrated. After the processed air on a red-eye flight from Palermo her nasal passages are blocked and inflamed. She sneezes, dabs the end of her nose with a fresh tissue, and submits to her illuminated screen. She responds to an inbox full of unanswered emails.

The coach travels at speed along a stretch of motorway, opened since she left the country. With stops to drop off passengers, and the space of time needed to retrieve bags from the luggage compartment visible from where she sits looking out at the countryside through the juddering begrimed window, the journey from the airport takes three hours, followed by another forty-five minutes of laboured headway along coastal roads plastered with signage for the Wild Atlantic Way.

It is late afternoon when the rattling provincial bus with the fleet Irish red setter livery drops her in the centre of Mullaghmore village, a seaside resort popular with holidaymakers, where families stroll along the waterfront and the pier, and yachts anchor serenely in the harbour's picturesque square basin. She stands to look at the aged fishing boat fleet. Tied up along the cut-stone pier, the ramshackle steel and wooden-hulled boats sway unattended against a weave of dangling ropes and car tyres. Between the roadway and the Alexander Nimmo designed pier, the stripe of greensward is neatly mown. Past the harbour mouth, sail-boats bob at anchor. Bright sunlight, clear seawater, and solid stone masonry: the very essence of a safe harbour.

On the near side of the old-world pier a bulky white camper van sits beside a portable office with a sandwich-board advertising stand-up paddle board lessons, sea angling trips, snorkel safaris and scuba diving. There is no sign of the drive-on-drive-off ferry, and apart from casual strollers the harbour is quiet. Most people are on the water.

Up along the main street, though, the shop selling ice-cream cones is doing steady business. Eithne's Sea Food restaurant, where Tara orders a coffee and a meringue flavoured with chocolate and seaweed of all things, is packed with diners. She takes a seat outside at one of the plastic tables. A group from the riding stables clip-clop past in single file. The horses drop fresh manure, mashed by the wheels of the cars using the parking spaces along the seafront.

She has the wi-fi hotspot code and is tempted to take a quick look at what's happening overseas, but she binged on the Brexit Referendum coverage earlier on the bus. The seafood chowder the waitress brings to the people at the table beside her looks good, but she is still a little queasy from the bus. For the moment she is happy to sip hot coffee and have the meringue melt in her mouth into an intensely sweet lozenge with a delicate, medicinal aftertaste of iodine. A short hard cough causes a stab of pain under her ribcage.

She sits back to ease the discomfort and watches a man and a boy prepare to board a small craft on the far side of the harbour. First, he fetches a fishing-tackle box and rods from a blue minibus, and a woman beside him helps the boy into a life jacket. The mother passes the boy a little blanket or rug of some sort, and the man leads him by the hand down the cut-stone steps. When they are safely aboard the lightly-bobbing craft the boy sits tight while his father unties the mooring ropes and moves to the cockpit to stand at the wheel. He throttles up and takes the boat out. The woman waves them off. After the boat clears the harbour she delays on the pier.

The figure of that solitary girl on the pier triggers a spasm of distress and guilt. Her mind flashes back to the look on the face of nineteen-year-old Mai from the Gambia, her helpless terror transformed into hysterical relief at the prospect of rescue from the sinking rubber dingy fit for twenty passengers and carrying one hundred and thirty nine terrified souls in choppy seas, eighteen nautical miles off the coast of Libya. A survivor of robbery, imprisonment, beatings and rape after a two-month journey through Senegal, Burkino Faso, Mali, Niger, and the unspeakable Baai Walid in Libya, Mai was just one amongst the thirty desperately screaming women with children rescued during the first of two SOS Méditerranée-coordinated missions in one night. It felt like a betrayal to be indulging her sweet tooth and drinking coffee instead of being at her post on the MV Aquarius looking after those in peril at sea.

As soon as the ship docked to re-fuel and take on fresh supplies she was obliged, on doctor's orders, to take shore leave. Also, after seven years apart, the last thing she wants is to meet her husband here on his home turf, but she needs a divorce.

The cough kicks against her ribcage again. Pummelled by the waves at sea in the cold night on the 'rescue daughter' RHIB they'd used to pull Mai and the others off the trafficker's sinking boat she has ended up with a serious chest infection on the brink of pneumonia. Practically everyone they rescued had skin burnt from immersion in engine-fuel saturated seawater and the same harsh cough.

She closes her eyes and begins a 'mindfulness' exercise to focus on her breathing, calm her anxiety and neutralise the discomfort. She becomes aware then of the summer air warm on her skin, of the sea and saltwater, horse manure and freshly-mown grass, and some otherworldly, elusive quality in the air, a fragrance particular to this small corner of Ireland, a quality in the air found nowhere else in the world. It ignites a shiver of nostalgia and estrangement.

Paula Leyden

Surprised by Joy

She sensed the words before they came; she heard them through the silence that draped over him as he lay next to her. 'I've been thinking Alice ...' Mick said, breaking through the shroud. She didn't answer. She didn't want to hear him tell her that he had found another. More suited. More whole. Still they lay there, side by side, two bodies that had known love and wonder.

Mick O'Donnell had grown up too easy, his mother always said. That was his problem. As if everyone should have at least one problem that they could call their own. She said it without trying to hide the pride in her voice, because, after all, it was she who had raised him. Mick didn't remember it that way. Sure, no one had slapped him round the head or pressed burning cigarettes into his pale soft skin. He had not sat sewing sequinned t-shirts for young satisfied girls whose stomachs rolled over the top of their jeans. None of that. But still it had not always been easy being his mother's son.

Alice, whose surname was given only when necessary, had definitely not grown up too easy. No one ever pretended she had. Mick remembered so clearly the first time he'd met her, standing outside Ryan's with the smokers. 'This is Alice,' Donal had said, he paused, 'Ó Griofa.' The name hung in the air between them as if somehow it might burst. Griffin, Alice always thought, would have been easier to hide from.

Mick, after asking himself the unspoken question 'you mean *the* Ó Griofa?', looked at her more closely and felt a telling warmth creep up his cheeks as he stood there in front of her, watching her as she watched him. 'I'm Mick,' he said. She nodded her head, before her attention was taken by a thin lad whose hair flopped listlessly around his face. Mick hated him instantly. It was later he got her attention back and then they talked. About things and thoughts and coincidence; how strange that the two of them, so different, both liked books set in the deep South; how tales of slavery and loss made them read a book through to its end.

Emboldened by her laughter, he asked her about her mother. Lightly. Had Alice forgiven her? As if he was asking her about the weather; or enquiring after which subjects she liked in school. She said she would rather not talk about it right then, at that minute, if he didn't mind. Her voice was dull as she spoke and she turned her head away from him. Mick felt a prickle of shame and replied quickly that of course he didn't mind. He should not have asked. During all the time he then came to know her, she never answered him.

'Alice,' Mick said again, insistent 'Why so silent?' There was worry in his voice, she could hear it. She knew then that it had come to this. He was scared to tell her that he no longer wanted her. The rules in Alice's world were simple: expect nothing, keep your head down and show no emotion. She had broken those rules with Mick. She deserved what was coming to her.

He had come to love her quickly and surprisingly; it was in the way she looked at him, as if she already knew him. Alice was wary. She'd not known unconditional love. Her mother loved only herself and father was a faded lost memory. Micks easiness made her awkward. He had no knowledge of hurt and he looked at life with eyes open and pleased. He minded her carefully after that first blundering question and slowly she started to believe that perhaps, one day, she might love him back. Her body she gave easily, distractedly. This sometimes made Mick wonder how often it had been given before him, in this careless manner, as though somehow it didn't belong to her. He tried not to keep those thoughts in his head as they blurred his vision of her.

Still they lay, side by side, in the silence of the room that was now familiar to her. He turned on his side to face her, but she didn't move. Dread filled, she could not speak.

That first night they left the pub together. Mick had offered to share a taxi home with her, that way he would know where she lived. That way he would not lose her. She came home with him, in a matter of fact kind of way. When he asked for her address for the taxi driver, she shrugged, 'We can go to your house, if that's what you want.' He did. That first night was not easy. Alice was passive in the face of his urgency. She was used to being wanted and had known it only as an inquisitive desire in the boys she had known. She had no reason to think Mick was different. When she left him still sleeping the next morning she walked without looking back. Another day. Like the day before and the one after. But Mick found her, after two days of insistent looking and that was where it began.

With time she started to believe the things he said to her. He had satisfied his curiosity, and usually that was enough. But not for him. He still wanted her. Slowly she allowed him to love her in his own contented way. And slowly she began to love him back.

Until now. As she lay there on the narrow bed, hardly daring to breathe, she thought of that first night and the way he looked at her. She should have turned away then. When he asked her about her mother, that was an easy time to turn away. But she hadn't. If she had known, on that first day, that this night would come, that she would be here next to him with her bones aching with love for him, she might have kept a small part of herself in storage. But she had not known until now, and now it was too late. She closed her eyes and breathed in his memory, trying it out to see whether that would be enough. She filled her head with the sound of his voice, the lightness of his touch, the rumble of his laugh. It wasn't enough, it never would be. His breath was soft on her cheek. She opened her eyes and looked at him. He did not move, he watched her watching him, then closed his eyes. He could not face her, she knew that, he could not bear the words that had to come.

'What is it you want to say to me, Mick?' she said finally, her voice lost in the air stilled above them. He opened his eyes and smiled, 'Hah, you can speak. You have a voice. I can hear you, but maybe I have nothing to say any more.'

He closed his eyes again.

Alice was confused. His words were playful. His face was easy. Her words tumbled out. 'If you want to go, you may go. I will not think badly of you but I will think of you often. I will see you in everything, I will hear you even when you're not there. I don't want to but now I cannot help it. So go if you will,' she said.

Mick sat up abruptly and pulled on the light cord next to the bed, flooding the small room with brightness. He stared down at her, 'Alice, have you lost your mind? Go? Go where? Me? What are you thinking? I'll go nowhere at all other than here, not even you can chase me away.'

He lay back down and held her so tightly she felt she would never breathe again. 'Here I am, Mick O'Donnell, with you, Alice Ó Griofa, and nothing you can say will change that. You hear me?'

'But Mick, what did you want to talk to me about?' Alice said, her mind slowly clearing from the fog of false mourning it had created.

'Nothing important. I just wanted to hear your voice.'

Michael Longley

MATISSE

Wielding a colossal pair of scissors,
Cutting out from the costliest paper
The world's peculiar shapes, he instructed
From his wheelchair beautiful assistants
Where to position – floor to ceiling –
Each adhesive genesis, cloud formations
Reflected in estuarial waters.

He covered a stain on his studio wall
With a swallow's cut-out shape, then added
Other birds and fish and coral and leaves,
Memory replacing the outside world
And his imagination a lagoon
Where, immobile, he swam every day
Contemplating his submarine kingdom.

published by Hodges Figgis in 1903

A LAY OF OSSIAN AND PATRICK
WITH OTHER IRISH VERSES BY
STEPHEN GWYNN

DUBLIN HODGES FIGGIS
AND CO LTD. LONDON
MACMILLAN & CO LTD.

Paul Lynch

from BEYOND THE SEA

It is not a dream of storm weather that follows Bolivar into the town but words overheard last night, perhaps in Gabriela's bar, that give him the feeling now of a dream. He thinks it might have been the chatter of Alexis or José Luis, who knows, they are such troublemakers. And yet this feeling of dream persists. It is the feeling of a world once known, but forgotten, asking from over the sea.

His sandalled feet follow the road over the crumbling bridge. Past the empty beachside cabanas. Past where the nesting sea turtles scallop the beach. His eyes seeking out beyond the lagoon but his eye is drawn toward the shore. An oilcan lies washed-up and surrounding it a glittering of dead popocha fish. He walks onto the beach fixing his baseball cap, stands over the fish and counts them.

He thinks, it is just a dozen or so, but still. Even the beggars won't touch them. There is a sickness in the rivers and no one will ever explain.

He studies the indigo dawn for trouble. He studies the clouds and the wind. That the ocean has a hue is a lie among men. He cannot remember who said this. For the sea contains all colour and in that way everything is within it. This might be true, who knows what you hear.

The plastic white seats at Rosa's café lean like drunk sleepers to their tables. He slaps at a net full of beach balls hanging from the palm-wood. Damn it, he says. Angel is not waiting. He kicks a seat past the beach screen and the back of the seat cracks when he sits. His hands rest on the spill of his gut and he studies them. Such hands are too big, perhaps, and he has often thought this. A forearm for a wrist. A thigh for an arm. Shoulders for a neck. But what else do you expect for a fisherman?

He turns his head and shouts, Rosa!

From here he can see the panga boat he thinks of as his own alone and high upon the beach. The blood-coloured hull with *Camille* painted in white. Angel is not there either. He can see the ghosts of two men, his earlier self and Angel last night and how they sat in that panga – moon-drawn effigies of fishermen drinking beer amidst the bodiless shouting and the gaunt light thrown by the bars on the strip.

He calls again for Rosa, can hear that crazy Alexander at his singing, the old man's voice a glass-bright tremolo. He leans until he can see him on a cooling box of some undetermined long-ago colour. The flashing of nails as he repairs sea-worn nets. Each day Bolivar tries not to listen yet still he listens for such songs evoke in him feelings he cannot explain. Sometimes a feeling like guilt. Sometimes a feeling of being alive long ago, as though he had lived the life of another, and what are you supposed to make of such a thing?

Loose sand rolls across the matting. He puts a finger to his nose and gouts snot. Rosa!

It is the Guadalupe Virgin from her high shelf who watches Bolivar as though he were an apparition gliding through the hanging beads of Rosa's door. There is Rosa asleep on a hammock, she is always asleep. He reaches for the remote control and turns the TV on to a game from the night before.

Rosa! he shouts. Have you seen Angel?

The woman stirs with a vexed sound. With slow feet she swings out of the hammock and stands in the half-light tying up her hair. Just her eyes he can see as if they can draw all there is of the light toward them. He blinks at her twice and an old part of his mind thinks of her as some witch in the dark until she rolls up the screen and her body finds its expression. His eyes following the light as it falls upon her loose-shirted abdomen, upon her glossed hands and thighs. His eyes prizing her the way a man prizes a woman.

Has Angel not turned up yet, Rosa?

That box of limes, Bolivar. Did you bring them? I asked you last night.

He is either here or not here. I have just a few limes to take with me on the boat.

How Rosa seems to sigh in everything she does. Her body is sadness bending to the fridge. She pulls from it two beer bottles, the movement of hinging upwards is a weariness that does not belong to a woman as young as this. She uncaps both bottles without looking. Rests a stare upon some faraway thought out past the lagoon.

Bolivar holds her with a look as he takes a long drink. Then he wipes his mouth with his wrist. A goal sounds on the TV and he leans for a moment out the beaded door.

You will not believe it, he says. Remember that great fish kill last year that nobody would explain? I saw some popocha dead on the beach just now.

He watches the way her right eye pinches when she drinks. Watches this cool brick room where she lives. A hammock and two palmwood chairs and a box refrigerator. The trace odour of sweat. Her clothes hanging off nails. He studies a redoubt of dark in the room as if for sign of a man. But who would want to listen to her sighing all night? he thinks. There is good sighing and there is bad. It is bound to get to you one day.

What is the forecast, Rosa?

Did you look at the TV?

I thought I heard talk last night at Gabriela's but it looks good from here.

She stares at his sun-browned feet, the sandals taped together, the plump spread toes. The big toe on his left foot missing a toenail.

Bolivar turns his foot inward as she looks at him.

She sighs again. I have so much to do. Now I have to go get those limes.

He hears his own words pass unthought out his mouth.

Some day, Rosa, you should marry me. I am only a fisherman, it is true. But I will pay off your TV. Maybe even buy you a jeep. I will buy you some furniture for your clothes. I'll give you all the limes you want.

They listen to Alexander laughing to himself.

Bolivar turns toward the door and the old man begins again to sing.

That fool, he says. Whoever knows what nonsense he sings.

Rosa says, those songs are sung to the bones of the dead.

Bolivar pulls at a piece of wall plaster.

This place is falling apart, Rosa. One of these days the wind and the sea will carry you away.

Rosa shrugs. I do not think today will be the day.

Aifric Mac Aodha

RÓS EILE
Freagra ar an dán 'A Rose' le Peter Fallon, Irish Times, *Feabhra 2017*

Ach fuil
an ghrá
an fhuil
ab áil

le fáil
iontaofa
deireadh
scríbe.

Deanna
an chroí,
más bocht,
ní buí.

Bláth na
bladhma,
'fhir na
feidhme

ceart do
nádúir.
Masla
táille

sop na
gcairde,
is súil
in airde

coiscthe.
Ach 'chara,

os buí
an t-eadra,

ná séan,
antráth,
an fiach
go deargadh.

catalogue published by Hodges Figgis in 1931

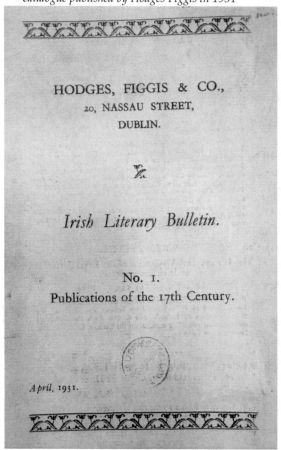

HODGES, FIGGIS & CO.,
20, NASSAU STREET,
DUBLIN.

Irish Literary Bulletin.

No. I.
Publications of the 17th Century.

April, 1931.

Gearóid Mac Lochlainn

HEATWAVE EILE

Bhí an boladh bréan ag análú
ó leithreas briste síos sa Choirceog Beach
róláidir inniu. Dofhulaingthe.
Bhí mo phoill sróine ag damhsa
le *sewage* an *heatwave* órga
a ghlac seilbh ar an chathair
seachtain ó shin.
Bhog mé go dtí an gairdín ar chúl a' tí
le bheith ag caitheamh.
Bhí an áit folamh go fóill.

Tháinig mé go luath roimh lucht na gcapall
le píosa de *Séamus Ennis – Dialann Taistil 1942–45*, a léamh,
leabhar a fuair mé ó Áine sa Cheathrú Póilí
ar *bargain* praghas ...

Bhí Ennis ag seanchas faoi *Ediphones,*
wax cylinders, tyres a phléasc sna *potholes* ar dhrochbhóithre
Charna ...
Thosaigh mé a mhachnamh faoi tharr Mac Adam
agus Dunlop ... agus *inner tubes* ...
nuair a tháinig Arutura isteach
agus é ag iarraidh orm líne nó dhó a chumadh
fá choinne amhrán nua *hip hop* Gaelach s'aige ...
Bhí sé ag gearán go raibh sé dúthuirseach ag iarraidh
bheith *liked*
ag daoine geala, agus tuirseach de Ghaeilgeoirí Dearga
nár thuig a chuid Gaelachais ar chor ar bith! ...

D'éist muid le píosa den amhrán ar *Mac* s'aige,
muid frámaithe ag seanfhocail Ghaeilge ar an bhalla in aice
linn –

NACH RAIBH FEAR BRAITE RIAMH I DO
CHUIBHREANN
GO RAIBH DO DHEOCH LÁN BRÍ IS BEATHA
DIA IDIR SINN AGUS AN URCHÓID agus araile …

Trasna uainn thar bhalla eile bhí seanséipéal na mban rialta,
brící rua ag crithlonrú, dreoilín agus lon ag ceol
sna driseacha a d'fhás thar an bhalla.
Bhí seanstaighre iarainn meirgeach
ar thaobh na láimhe deise
chuig doras an halla damhsa ar bharr a' tí
a bhí druidte le fada an lá.

Go tobann thuirling scamall ón Chnoc Dhubh.
Bhí beirt fháinleog mhístiúrtha agus faoileán ag
peannaireacht
is ag líníocht leo sa spéir liath …
Stop an ceol.
Thosaigh Arutura ag seanchas liom faoi mhuintir s'aige –
Ní raibh siad róthugtha don rud scríofa,
don pheann ná don phár,
rud a thug an cine geal leo
nuair a tháinig siad leis na bíoblaí.

– Tá *totems* níos tábhachtaí ná teanga, arsa sé,
Ba *hippopotamus* mo mháthair mhór.
Níl cead ag éinne lámh a leagan orthu
gan bheannacht s'aicise.

Rinne sé adharca beaga ar a éadan lena mhéara
– Agus cad é mar a déarfá i mBéarla … bíonn
siad amuigh ar an mhachaire?
– *Gazelle* …?
– Sea! Is *gazelle* mé féin. Clann *Antelope*!

Agus cén fáth nach gcreidfinn é?
Nach seanchapall mé féin? a shíl mé …

Níl ann ach seal ár gcuarta.

Bhí *staff* ón King Kebab ag cúldoras na cistine
ag snórtáil línte sneachta roimh am oibre.

Las Turo dúidín agus tháinig cumha air.

– An rud nach dtuigeann daoine geala
faoi Mugabwe, arsa sé, ná …

Go tobann,
bhris *hum drum* leictreachais
agus raiméis innealra ó na *generators* is *coolers*
a bhí ar a' dé deiridh le fada,
isteach ar an chomhrá.
Clagarnach, cniogaide cnagaide …
Thart orainn bhí crónán cáblaí,
cluncanna agus clancanna seaninnealra,
cuisneoirí ar crith, ag croitheadh a gcnámh,
ag cogaíocht le cluncanna is clancanna eile,
Nuts, bolts, blades, belts, shudders, shakes
miotal ag sú isteach aer te na maidine,
meaisíní, ingearáin sna ballaí.
Ní raibh dul as.
Maraíodh ár nglór ag an challán chrua.

Ansin, stop sé de gheit,
Sos cogaidh. Tost …
Puth gaoithe sa bhrothall.
Scuabadh an scamall ar shiúl.
Scaipeadh na liatha.
Phléasc an ghrian anuas orainn arís
ó bharr an tSléibhe Dhuibh,
gathanna gréine ag spréacharnach
ar smidiríní de ghloiní briste ón oíche rua roimhe,
soilsí órga ag rollagú inár súile
leis an toit liath gorm dubh airgead,

muid ar snámh le scáthanna *hippopotami* faoi uisce,
ag rith trí mhachairí le *antelope* adharcacha,
greadadh na gcrúb, cosa in airde,
fáinleoga místiúrtha ag peannaireacht arís
trí ghormacha na spéirlíne,
Ar feadh bomaitín bhí muid beirt
chomh Gaelach leis an ghrian ...

Chaith muid ceann eile is thit muid siar
isteach sa *heatwave*.
Bhí an saol ar a sháimhín só
i gcroílár na Ceathrún Gaeltachta
ciorraithe.

published by Allen Figgis in 1970

A seal-hunting expedition in a motor-boat off the coast of Donegal, described in the delicate, evocative prose that has made Monk Gibbon renowned as a stylist, takes on extraordinary qualities of natural serenity and high adventure—". . . interest nowhere flagging, because (the author's) intentness of eye and mind nowhere lapsed." (Æ.)

riverrun

the seals

Monk Gibbon

John McAuliffe and Igor Klikovac

NORTH
from the Bosnian

This morning I carried out from a dream
a wish to travel north. I did not see mountains
or snow, deep fjords and cathedrals of ice,
just the word, tapping its thigh like a dog-trainer.

In an old photo-album I searched for the proof;
maybe this time I needed to go farther, somewhere more
    northern.
I went through the books whose tenants flee north,
but even the Japanese masters (who alone
show nature as if poetry did not exist)

would not help. Somewhere, in an old text,
or perhaps in an orange juice ad, they say that
all music travels south, and all words are northbound.

Perhaps, I thought, the wish was not a wish. The dream
was that, when the time comes, things are not given up,
    but lost …

Niamh McBrannan

from THE DEVIL'S OWN JOB

It was news to me that I was to be built into a two-seater sofa. Up until this, human furniture really wasn't my thing. The deal was that I'd infiltrate the event to find out anything related to the missing bodies. At most, I expected to have to don an apron and attempt to carry around a drinks tray without dropping it. Instead, I found myself interred within a steel frame under six inches of black leather-covered polyurethane foam, invisible except for my unkempt upstyle protruding at one end and my ankles and feet extended at the other, the latter in seamed stockings and six-inch black patent T-bars.

At least I hadn't been upcycled into a standard lamp or a coffee table or worse, a footstool. Whatever about the additional exposure required, which would have been both painful and chilly, I just couldn't cope with being so suburban.

We were in a furniture warehouse in an industrial estate on the outskirts of town. Even prior to the additional human components, these fixtures weren't just any old office furniture. Here were the contents of the swiftly-vacated offices of the Central Bank of Ireland, which had recently fled Dublin 2 for the financial services district on the quays. Departed to a shiny new future in what might have seemed like a shiny new neighbourhood, if you didn't know the neighbours – notably, a nearby greasy café, sinister nightclub and run-down hotel, the self-appointed bastions of counter-gentrification. If I was the Central Bank, I'd have run a mile.

Meanwhile, its old boardroom tables, designer desks, generously-padded executive chairs, watercoolers – the whole shebang – had been sold off in a single lot and were now temporarily redeployed as props for a performance artwork, or so I'd been told.

Tonight was the preview of Morgan Le Frey's latest work, a 'shocking challenge to conventional perceptions of pain, shame and the human body' according to the publicity. I didn't mind what it challenged so long as it involved somebody else's body fluids and not mine.

My current position, flat on my back in the dark base of a sofa, with muffled hearing and zero vision, unable to move more than a few millimetres in any direction, did not provide optimal conditions for information gathering. Stifling a rising sense of claustrophobia, I squirmed, trying to face the direction where the mics were being tested. I managed to shift the overhead padding a fraction, enough to create a sliver of light and a breath of air. Squeezing a hand underneath me, I scraped off the debris embedded in my back, my fingers identifying a couple of coins, a scattering of crumbs and a crumpled scrap of lace, thong-like.

Just as I became marginally more comfortable, the world caved in and my upholstered roof distended, bellying downwards as far as my nose. A significant weight had deposited itself on the seat above.

'Hey,' I yelled, 'you up there, shift over to the far corner, will you? You're sitting on my face.'

'If only these items could talk,' came the oblivious rumble of a rich baritone. 'The stories they could tell.'

'Gordon,' I hissed, recognising the art dealer's voice. 'Gordon Wentworth. You're smothering me. No, this is not part of the performance. Move your arse.'

'Constance!' Wentworth said delightedly, shifting himself heavily and spilling his wine in the process. A trickle of Bordeaux ran down my cheek. 'You're an installation – aren't you marvellous! Are you working for Morgan? What a genius – she's a true visionary.'

'I'm only here due to a mix-up with catering,' I said. 'Is Morgan out there?'

The volume of voices had increased all around us. 'Tell me who's here – do you know any of these people?'

'I know *all* of them,' Wentworth said. 'And all about them, unfortunately. You learn so much from people's taste in art – which for this lot is non-existent. Nice shoes, by the way.'

'Seriously,' I asked, 'is this art?'

'Excuse me, but you're not supposed to talk to the masters,' came a female voice from nearby. 'And it's not bleeding *art* they're here for, it's the furniphobia, isn't it?'

'I think you mean *forniphilia*,' I said, informative as always. 'A form of bondage in which a person's body is incorporated into everyday household items. What you said, on the other hand, would be a *fear* of furniture.'

'If you could see yourself from where I'm standing,' said the voice in its stage whisper, 'you'd have a fear of furniture yourself.'

'You're very pass-remarkable, for an object. What are you, anyway? Gordon, help me out here.'

'Mid-seventies teak veneer, sub-G-Plan-esque, mirroring the unloved architecture of the building for which it was designed. Probably Blaney-Kortel, a wildly trendy design firm for five seconds in nineteen seventy-six.'

'I'm a bleeding corner display unit, amn't I?' the voice snapped. 'I said to them I'm not doing anything involving clothes-pegs anymore, I said, I'm still numb from the last time. Asked to be a filing cabinet, but I got this instead. I've a built-in downlighter which is fecking blinding me, splinters in my arse and these crystal decanter things are sticking into my chest.'

'And a fine chest it is too,' said Gordon. 'Aren't you supposed to enjoy all that pain and objectification?'

'Gimme a break,' she said, adding, 'Master.'

'Ssssh,' Wentworth said. 'It's Morgan. She's on the podium. She looks pale, poor thing.'

A high, clear voice spoke through the sound system and the hubbub died down instantly.

'Tonight's event is cancelled,' said Morgan Le Frey. 'Apologies to all of you. We had planned, as part of it, to honour the late Rex Ryeland's last wish. His instructions were to have his mortal remains ... utilised ... by his favourite photographic models in a live webcast, and then portrayed on the cover of the magazine, *Chicks and Stiffs*. Unfortunately, this cannot be achieved tonight ...' She paused for a moment and waves of whispers swept around the space.

'... as Rex Ryeland's corpse has disappeared.'

Without warning, the weight lifted from above me. Wentworth was gone and, judging by the rush of hurried footsteps and retreating voices, so were the rest of the crowd. And then silence, except for that damned bell ringing. It took me a moment to identify the persistent clamour. A stream of sweat ran into my eyes. I coughed as the smoke caught in my throat.

'Hello?' I said, wriggling, pushing unsuccessfully against the unyielding structure. Louder, 'HELLO? Anyone?'

There was no response, not even from my fellow furnishings.

Joan McBreen

TULIPS AT RODMELL 1941

February. Too cold for spring.
A river the colour of violets
beckons her, fast flowing.
With no memory of last year's
yellow flowers, she carries
her shadows inside her as if
in a black laquered box,
its lid tightly sealed.

Her last letter found by Leonard
on a mantelpiece,
was torn open, her words of love
too heavy to be carried
by the living for decades,
forever housed in a lighthouse
as near and far away,
as her body in the river.

Eugene McCabe

UNTITLED

The shouting was the first thing he remembered. When he began to cry with fright it got louder. It was very near his face. It made him stop crying. When he could crawl about the kitchen he could hear his father behaving in the same loud way with his mother. When he saw him hit her across the face with the back of his hand he was very shocked but found it difficult to hate him. When sober he was great fun. He pretended to be a horse raring up, making snorting, horsey noises while he clung to his back. There was a potent smell from his breath. His mother told him it was brandy. Very early on she began to teach him nursery rhymes and fairy tales. He especially liked the one about *The Boy who Cried Wolf* and *Little Red Riding Hood*. When he began to look frightened she told him it was over a hundred years since a wolf had attacked anyone in Normandy. That was a little girl of five snatched from her doorway in daylight by a lone, hungry wolf. For twenty kilometers around men came that day with dogs, wolfhounds and guns. The wolf was dead by midnight. It wasn't shot, it was ripped to pieces by hounds. As far as she knew they were rare enough in France now. They come up from Italy where they were still prevalent. When she was a girl you could sometimes hear them howling in the dark, especially in winter. Every night she prayed when he was in bed till he was able to say his night and morning prayers without prompting; 'May the most holy, most sacred, most adorable, most incomprehensible, ineffable name of God be forever praised, blest, loved and glorified in heaven, on earth, under the earth and under the sea, by all the creatures created by God'. He could also read children's books with big print when he was six. *Gulliver's Travels* was his favourite. He wondered how he managed when he had to pee or do big business because there was nowhere to hide in the land of the Lilliputians who were no bigger than his little finger 'If their tallest trees were below his knees where could he go?' 'The sea,' his mother told him. 'He swam out for a mile or so and relieved himself.' He laughed a lot at Gulliver urinating on the Queen's palace to stop a great fire in the royal apartments. The queen was outraged and gave an order that he be blinded and starved to death for this terrible indignity to the royal person. Gulliver walked away from this ridiculous sentence that saved the palace from burning down. There were other worlds to explore. When Thomas was about seven he was taught by their farm labourer Phillipe how to milk the quietest of the four cows. Phillipe was a simpleton with a squint and stutter who got no wages but was happy to have a bed on the loft. He was well fed in the kitchen. Once he was overheard calling Tommy, Tommy. The master gave him a severe lecture about that. Phillipe was in love with Felicite, the maid servant who was kindly and gave him money to buy tobacco. She could also be naughty and teased him when there was no one about by holding up her skirts. She was wearing no knickers which made Phillipe put his hand inside of his trousers and jiggle vigorously with his eyes closed. It was a few years before Tommy understood what he was doing. Some times the master came into the byre to see how his son was progressing under Phillipe's tuition. He would sit down with the bucket between his knees and the milk would come in such a strong flow that it made a froth on top. No matter how you looked you couldn't see his hands moving at the teats. There were big veins on the back of his large hands; 'That's how it's done lads, technique. When I was a young fella on my Grandfather's farm I could milk eight cows in less than an hour!'

Patrick McCabe

from THE BIG YAROO

And that was a right setback, I have to say, finding myself heaving up my entire guts like that, at a time when, realistically, I ought to have been over the moon, what with the magazine now more or less complete, and that old boy racer machine sitting down there waiting for me – raring to go, all polished up in the shed.

As I did my best to get back to the way that I'd been before – pulling them up on the screen one after the other – all the images I'd collated of Skerries and North County Dublin in the sixties, along with the map that I'd saved from Google Earth.

Doing the best I could to convince myself once more just how good it was going to be – once I got out through those gates and away off down the open highway, before zipping through the city, out then to the coast road to breathe the sea breeze, with it all plain sailing then to my destination.

– Lambay Island, here I come! I cried, look – no pedals!

But making sure not to forget to stop off in Portrane, to say goodbye to all my old compadres in their new home, regarding which I have had nothing but good reports, in all the emails and texts that they've been sending. Describing it, variously, as 'a dream!' and 'a perfectly sumptuous near-hotel!' With Dismal Tony adding a humourous note – suggesting that he's sorry he 'didn't go mad long ago.'

The most important of all as regards the departure was to have everything planned right down to the very last detail, leaving nothing to chance. Because the last thing I wanted was a repeat performance of my very first escape attempt, which turned out to be a complete calamity, sometime in the early nineties. However, I knew damned sure that that wasn't going to happen – because I wasn't going to let it.

No, every possible eventuality would be explored – right down to the exact times of the trucks which I knew to be travelling on a daily basis all along the M50, from Newry and many other places, to the city of Dublin.

But I happened to discover that the Newry times suited me the best and that their vehicles passed very close to the hospital. No, there was no need to worry – this time my escape was going to be heroic, I told myself. And final!

O man, I really do have to admit it – that that first shambolic attempt at a bust-out was a true disaster, an embarrassment really.

But I think, in all honesty, that it was just because in those days I had been too impulsive – and that, most definitely, is no longer the case. You want to see all these charts and booklets and timetables I've gathered up. Why, I'm nearly as bad as my dear old father.

Who you usen't to be able to see at all, sitting there beavering away at his desk, buried under this avalanche of coins and stamps and books of approvals – not to mention radio guides, as I mapped my way through the avenues and byways of the country of the imagination that I called my 'City of Sound.' If only I had been more like him back in the nineties, I thought, and paid a little bit more attention to what it was I was supposed to be doing, then all of my 'Great Escapes' wouldn't have been the balls-ups that they were. But, of course, when you think about it, it has also to be considered that, even then, back in the nineties, and even in the early noughties, you didn't have anything like the technology you have at your disposal today.

So maybe, to be fair, it wasn't all that surprising – notwithstanding the fact that, apart from Tom The Weaver's funeral, I hadn't been outside the walls of Electric Mansions ever since the year 1962.

Anyway, whatever conclusions you might reach regarding my navigational and other assorted ineptitudes on those occasions, their cumulative effect is to render me a lot more efficient and alert – providing me no end of assistance and mental support for my great big exit this coming Easter Sunday.

And my preparations, even if I say so myself, have been second to none – downright obsessive and fastidious to the last.

I mean, you don't want to find yourself being smashed to a pulp by one of those great big lumbering Newry mastodons, do you?

So that's the reason I will be leaving nothing to chance.

I won't be sorry to see the last of Dickon Courtney, though – because he was here again last night, along with Roddy. Who has clearly come under his influence and has begun to derive some form of squalid pleasure from mimicking both me and various people from my past.

It was horrible last night – but I won't, thank God, have to endure it for very much longer. It was like a black circus.

With their three faces melding as they appeared – gradually emerging in the steam of the bathroom mirror. At first you think – ha ha, it's a laugh. But then you realise, very slowly, that it isn't.

No, it isn't a laugh, said Philip – he was the boy whose mother I'd murdered.

I was sorry for doing it – but he said he didn't care.

He looked a lot like Roddy, Philip did – with the very same blazer and the exact same stripey tie.

– I don't want to hear any of your self-serving lies, he said, because we've had quite enough of those from you already.

What they were wearing was really the outfit of a 1950s schoolboy, but now they all – including Philip – especially Philip! – looked the very exact same as Roddy McCoy. With those same long lashes, blank and terrifying eyes, and a limb at the end of which was a stained meat cleaver. Also his voice – it didn't resemble that of a human being –

mocking my name as he repeated it over and over: Martin Mooney, what a silly name!

What on earth made you select that for your replacement, you great big silly piggy wiggy! What a fool you have turned out to be – but then we never expected much else!

My head was spinning and I could hear the thunder of the sluice jets as he nodded his head – the very same as the fibreglass model on its plinth marked: butcher boy, wearing a tall white hat and which always used to be outside the shop, long ago in the days when I was young.

He continued speaking in the same robotic voice.

You think you can escape us, don't you piggy?

Please, I implored.

You think by changing your name you can be free. But you can't, little piggy. No, you can't, you see – and never will. Not if you call yourself Septimus Corncrake McIvor. Never!

Then he said he wouldn't waste time.

Close your eyes, I heard him demand. As I hesitated.

Do it, he said.

Before I heard an appalling squelch – Yeuurgh! – as the sharp implement descended with one swift movement, parting the flesh of my lower shoulder and upper arm.

Tee hee, he said, that's a corker!

Then he instructed me: look in the mirror!

There was a polished piano with flowers in there – and an orange fire glowing softly in the grate. On the wall there was a picture of a waterfall that seemed to flow with the rhythm of a perfect dream. No wonder, I heard him whisper, that they sometimes say that we are the roving, restive voices of those who are no longer living! He struck me again, and another fountain of blood came gushing out.

Poor fellow, he said, look again in the mirror!

Having no choice, I did his bidding.

Colum McCann

STILL I RISE

The bougainvillea probably wasn't as red as I like to remember, but still it flowered. The ironwork gate did creak a little, but there was birdsong in the garden. The hybrid teas were plagued with summer greenfly, but for the most part they bloomed. The olive trees in the back were slightly stunted, but the olives themselves didn't seem to mind. The terracotta roof tiles cracked a little in the heat, but the house never let the rain in. The children routinely took a broom to the beehive in the vestibule outside the front door, but they never got stung. The brass-plated numbers on the front door were hung a little haphazardly because the handyman didn't wear eyeglasses, but Ahmed was an old family friend and we didn't want to embarrass him. The baby carriage was a little tattered and torn, but we used it for an antique flowerpot in the sunroom. The doormat was woven with cheap fibres that tore when the ledge of the front door swung open, but Salwa liked the shape and the style. The large vase on the credenza was glued together after one of my fits – when things began to crack – but the dried flowers we kept in it were still pleasing to look at. The crown moulding in the living room wasn't perfectly straight, but the height of the ceiling made up for it. The painting along the western wall was hung in a frame that always seemed crooked, but we loved the summer seascape at Latakia. The candelabra was always one lightbulb short, but it cast a gentle light over the painting. The bookshelves were a little lopsided, but they were happy to hold all of Salwa's endless tomes, philosophy, anatomy, physiology, math. The office wall was spider-cracked, but we covered it with our university citations. (I must admit my solitary one from the law school hung, a touch embarrassed, alongside her three). The drawers in the desk sometimes stuck on their rails, but we could always fish the crumpled envelopes out. The inkpot stained the mahogany, but we liked the patina. The door swelled whenever there was a rain, but with a good push you could still lock it shut. There were tiny nailheads that appeared in the floorboards over the years, but the worst that happened is that we ripped our stockings as we walked across. (I can still close my eyes and see Salwa's slow tall saunter, across the room, sometimes with Areen in her arms, sometimes with Mahmoud, often alone, late at night, with a book). The piano keys were slightly off-colour, but it didn't affect the timbre of the music, sometimes we played like we were still in Allepo. The faucet in the kitchen leaked, but we began to like the sound of the dripping. The grandfather clock didn't tick anymore, but the sound of the faucet replaced it. The refrigerator hummed loudly, but it was comforting enough late at night, we even began to miss it when the blackouts began. The silverware was slightly stained, but we kept it in a beautiful oak box where we hid the money we needed. Our photo albums were home to silverfish, but we used the little plastic pockets to keep our documents dry when we took the rickety boat. The stairs upstairs creaked but it was a way to know – once, back then, way back then – that the children were safe. The clawfoot tub had a little iron stain, but the bath was deep and it looked out to the garden where Salwa watched me tending the roses, not like here in Chapelizod where I paved the garden to make room to park the taxi. The bed where we lay was lumpy, but Salwa's beauty smoothed it, I assure you, it still does now, even when she comes home at dawn exhausted, her hands feint with disinfectant. (She never mentions her first dissertation, but she works within sight of the Sam Beckett bridge, maybe she remembers it, and Darwish too, as she vacuums around under all the fluorescents). The bedside lamp had a frayed electric lead but it still went on with a careful click. The mirrors on the landing were speckled with age, but we could see ourselves clearly. (We moved along the corridor. One suitcase each. The stairs creaked once more. My arms were too full to hold the children's hands and we had to hush Areen with a little touch of bourbon that I put on my finger, just to help her sleep). The trees outside the window were dark, but we still felt they were gathering not waving. (All along the streets of Dublin, the people wave me down, they get in and out, my meter flashes on and off, the ceiling light pulses). The hallway may not have thrown out a whole lot of light, but it was enough. The bannisters may have been a little wobbly, but they still took our weight. The pencil marks on the children's doors may have been scruffy, but they marked the height at which I will always remember them, no matter how tall they grow over here.

published by Allen Figgis in 1966

I SEND MY LOVE ALONG THE BOYNE

By Elizabeth Hickey with illustrations by Nano Reid

Thomas McCarthy

FALCONS HUNTING

Imperceptible disturbance there in the gloaming:

We raise our eyes to their ghostly presences,
A pair of falcons soaring above our windows –

See how steady they are in the air together,
Earth's most beautiful hunters taking the blue air

Of early June, as we are in the private hours
After Whitsun love-making. The crumbled

Sheets of feathery cloud, high as falcons,
Even higher, are love's unmistakable signature;

And these great high creatures, double nibs of life
Creating a single brushstroke, Chinese calligraphers

Of a long romance, just bank together
And sail into a fresh up-draft. The conjugal air

They recognise, I'm sure, the sudden, un-called for uplift
That gives an even higher viewpoint. Such love

Between falcon and falcon is impossibly human.

Mike McCormack

from THIS PLAGUE OF SOULS

Scanlon remembered one summer when Olwyn had gone through a sudden mania for refurbishing the house.

He had woken one morning to find her at work with a cordless drill, already having removed three of the doors from the other bedrooms. He had not questioned her because Olwyn in those days was operating to an energy and logic all her own. Her designs and structures went completely over his head. He had merely stood back and let her at it and she had not stopped till doors and carpets were piled up in a heap at the sod fence at the bottom of the garden and she was standing over them with a can of petrol which had been set aside for the lawn mower.

The house itself was now hollow sounding, all its separate spaces flowing into each other in a way which confounded the notion of a house; there was a sense of lawlessness about the place Scanlon could not abide nor put his finger upon. And the atmosphere of the place made it impossible to sit in any of its now disjointed rooms with their raw concrete floors and the faintly echoing sounds which seemed to reverberate back to him. Nor did Olwyn stop with doors and carpets. Now that she'd started everything seemed to offend her and in that comprehensive way of hers she moved chairs and tables out into the garage also and put in a call to some charity shop and then took off in the car to look for new replacements.

When she was gone Scanlon stood in the garage listening to the car turning out onto the road and looking at the furniture stacked up against the wall. Something about chairs on tables and tipped upside down on top of themselves filled him with unease. The fact that he had grown up with some of these pieces and that many of them had been in this house since his parents' marriage filled him with an uneasy sense of betrayal he would not have thought himself capable of.

Scanlon took that moment to have a look at himself standing there in the shaded light of a garage which smelt of oil and cut grass. He saw a sullen man with a sloped belly whose back now curved onto itself for balance and whose longish hair now reached down over the neck of his t-shirt. A man who had not yet given up his youth, who had a clear unwillingness to move into middle age.

On a sudden impulse he pulled the little coffee table from the pile of furniture and dragged it out into the light and onto the grass slope in the middle of the garden. Then he went back in to get the small armchair which he brought out and set beside the table to face out over the fields and the dark mountains in the distance. And for the whole of that summer Scanlon spent every available moment sitting there, gazing out over the small fields beneath blue skies and allowing the feel of open, rolling space to clear everything from his mind. By rights it should have been time spent developing or clarifying some new idea or scheme but all that summer, under the blue sky, Scanlon found himself to be unusually vacant, his mind a welcome empty space in which nothing of any importance took root. And Scanlon was happy with that; it was a curious pleasure to feel himself so reluctant to commit to anything whatsoever. Nothing at all suited him very well.

Even when the carpenter came to replace the doors and architrave and put down the laminate floors Olwyn wanted throughout the house, Scanlon had sat gazing out over the land at some distant thing on the horizon visible only to himself. And if Olwyn had thought that the presence of this burly tradesman who went about his work whistling through his front teeth would waken in him some feelings of territorial jealousy she was mistaken. For a full week, during which the house resounded to the sound of saws and hammers, Scanlon had taken the opportunity to vacate the house almost completely, going so far as to take his meals on his lap outside and drinking bottles of beer while staring out over the hills. Come evening, when the sun went around the front of the house and the shadow of the trees spread over his chair he had snoozed beneath a blanket with his head thrown back and his mouth open. He had maintained the same pose of silent indifference when the truck from the poverty agency came to take away the rest of the furniture. At one stage he had opened his eyes to find Olwyn standing over him with her lips pursed and her arms folded. He said nothing, just closed his eyes and dozed off once more. He imagined that she had turned on her heel and done a good job of stalking back into the house; he resigned himself to getting the silent treatment for a couple of days. Olwyn did not like being crossed in these small matters. So for the rest of that summer Scanlon had sat in that armchair, alternately awake or snoozing and gradually, by way of a benign thoughtlessness, found himself spreading out into the wider scale of the world.

And then Autumn came, the days shortening and the light lowering about the house. The temperature fell in mid September and Scanlon began to feel the cold. Something began to stir in him once more, just the slightest shift in his mind. He went inside and got a map and spread it out on the kitchen floor.

Barry McCrea

from THORN ISLAND

Two great things have happened to me in the course of my existence: a series of religious visions, or hallucinations, when I was six and a half years old, and an extraordinary, mysterious stroke of fortune the week I turned forty. What connection there might be between these two events must be, in a way, the story of my life. The group of neighbouring children, with whom I spent my earliest youth climbing trees and hiding in bushes, started life out thoroughly folded in upon one another, bunched tightly together like petals on an unopened flower; as we grew up, the flower blossomed and the petals grew apart. Until I was well into my 30s I had assumed in a tacit, unacknowledged way, that all the people one had been close to would gather back together, that the petals on the flower would stretch themselves out, as though for exercise, but then all eventually curl back into the tight bud they had come from. Only when Simon and Caroline Keaveney's father, Dónal died, did I discover what everyone else knew, that the petals on a flower keep opening out further away from each other until one by one they wither and fall away.

Nonetheless, I suspect that the origins of the great fortune which unexpectedly came my way, the very week I turned forty, and in the very month that Dónal Keaveney died, can be located back in that early cluster of friendship, and specifically in a series of pious manifestations that befell us as six- and seven-year-olds in Ireland in May 1982. For a long time I liked to think of myself as a young man making his fortune by going from the provinces to the city, but the source of this weird luck must surely be in the maritime, middle-class outskirts of Dublin and in the anachronistic, almost rustic childhood I had there.

Our world was centred on a patch of grass within a small cul-de-sac which looped off a street called Islandview Park, within a suburban development of semi-detached houses on the outskirts of Dalkey. On one edge of Islandview Park lay empty fields, and on the other it sloped laterally down to Dalkey village and to the granite rim of Dublin Bay, on whose littoral edge, frosted with seasalt and ancient barnacles, my first school, Loreto National School, was perched. The Islandview housing estate, cradled laterally between hill and sea, is where my life began, and where so many things about my life – including, I am convinced, my sudden, recent wealth – were forged.

The social composition of the whole of the Republic, Islandview Park included, was to be completely upended as the new millennium opened a demented economic boom (by which time I had already galloped west across the Atlantic in search of eternal youth), and Dalkey was to become a shorthand for prosperity and opulence. But when I was a child Dalkey was divided into three basic social and geographical sections, which could be distinguished by the favoured form, in speech of the parents' generation, of the second person plural: first, the part of the village that people nowadays think of as 'Dalkey', a synonym for wealth, rows of austere Victorian mansions along the sea towards Killiney, huge draughty houses which were inhabited back by either well-to-do Catholic doctors and lawyers or by old Protestant families, genteel and sometimes penniless, all of whom who addressed their children as 'you'; second, what my parents called 'Old' Dalkey, the labyrinth of labourers' cottages and council housing in the heart of the village, teeming with children who called their grannies 'nana', grizzled men who wore Claddagh rings and drank in the pubs, and mothers who smoked while pushing prams, all of whom called their children 'yous'; and finally, ourselves, the middle-of-the-road, Goldilocks zone of 'the Estate', inhabited by middle and lower-middle-class migrants from rural Ireland, Guards, teachers, nurses and civil servants, who considered themselves foreigners in Dublin and called their children (us) 'ye'.

The houses on the Islandview estate were built largely in one go, at the end of the 1960s, some years before I was born, during Ireland's first, quieter, economic boom. Before then it was, as they say, all fields: dairy farms and pasture and woods, as it had been when Dalkey was a thriving medieval port, its green waves plumbed for herring and its earth lightly tilled and grazed for buttermilk, to fill the bellies of the Vikings, Anglo-Normans and Gaels who lived out their short, guttural lives there. When I was a boy in the 1970s and 80s there were stretches of green and undergrowth left scattered throughout the estate, relics of the countryside strewn here and there, substantial patches of ground not yet covered by the quiet concrete blankets of four-bedroom semi-detached houses. Our house thus faced onto a small field, dotted with clumps of brambled bushes and trees, most notably a big sycamore from which a rope with a wooden seat had been hung long ago by children who were now no longer children. Everyone referred to this field as the Green, and it was the undisputed centre of life for the whole of the Estate.

The Green was special also because of the presence of the Keaveneys' house, the only detached house in the whole of the estate, the only one with a name – *Radharc an Oileáin* – instead of a number, bigger than all the other houses, the place where I first learned about so many things, love and money and smoking and playing cards, where I learned dozens of songs in both English and Irish, where I had a shy, out-of-the-ordinary friendship with the luckless Jem Staunton, and where, conversely first I intuited that I was due some special fortune in my own life.

Radharc an Oileáin with its exceptionality and grandeur seemed so identical with the Keaveneys, so thoroughly indistinguishable from all the many other things that made them special, that the story of its having been built by Jem's father Gerry, the builder responsible for the whole Estate, for himself, and especially the idea of the Stauntons themselves – with their denim skirts, public bickering, and constant air of petty economic struggles – inhabiting the elegant rooms and corridors of the house was hard to credit or picture. The counter-factual history, whereby the Stauntons would have been the castellans of the big house, and the Keaveneys squashed into number 100, not even on the Green, was rendered all the more unimaginable by the fact that Jem Staunton spent so much time as a teenager in *Radharc an Oileáin*, and cut such an alienated figure there. He stood formally in corners like a tradesman's boy who was there to deliver vegetables or coal, always looking around him as though fearful of breaking something or soiling the white walls. He stayed out of the house if Dónal was there, and could sometimes be found lurking in the garden waiting for the others to come out.

This is where and with whom it all began, where the pip was planted that would grow into the strange, lonely tree of my life. I started out there with great hopes and high expectations of what lay ahead; for many years I was disappointed and now, *tout d'un coup*, it has all changed. I am of the firm belief that the extraordinary good luck that unexpectedly, or at least belatedly, came my way has its origins in a sudden flurry of happenings in the May when I was six and a half, a set of events which bound me forever to the Keaveney family and their impulsive patriarch, Dónal, and so it is first to these occurrences, rather than to the odd, ageless existence I was living in America when the cheque arrived, that I now turn.

Rosaleen McDonagh

SNAP

Her Confirmation photographs were not what the journalists wanted. They used the one on the internet.

That morning. Trying to catch her eye. She looked so innocent in a school uniform that was too big on her. But her make up and hair told the world she was a sixteen-year-old beoir. There had been a lot of work put in to softening her father to the idea of secondary school. He wasn't too gone on her staying on. The mention of her cousin, Kathleen, doing her Junior Cert made him give in. The thought of another father giving his daughter free rein was eating Tom. In our time, marriages were done between families. Fathers did the asking. Mothers did the refusing. Tom struggles with the way young ones do things these days. He had hoped that Charlene would marry David, his brother's son. But our daughter made her own arrangement.

'How did this happen?' he shouted. 'Are you sure this is what she wants?' My nod was slow. In the lead-up to the families meeting, the tension in our home was like hard frost. Tom was anxious and ragging with Charlene. The anger he held was hidden. Sometimes he looked at me, silently judging, even though he had as much influence over the children as me.

We reluctantly agreed to the wedding. 'She's my only girl,' Tom said quietly as he shook Gerard O'Donovan's hand – the hand of his future son-in-law. The O'Donovans were people we didn't know. The school had been complaining that Charlene had lost interest and wasn't turning up for some classes. The teacher, her voice, her tone, the words she didn't use, suggested we were forcing an under-aged girl to get married.

'It's our name. They'll know who and what we are.' Her big fear was the hotel. 'Surely it's our money they want?' Charlene flung her arms around him. 'You outsmarted them all, Daddy,' she gushed when Tom told us he paid a settled fella off the street to make the hotel booking and hand over the deposit. Charlene wanted the biggest dress, the biggest cake, the biggest carriage and the biggest wedding.

That evening Tom was late home. He had been playing cards with some of his brothers who lived in the site across the road. He opened our door, put his head into the other trailer where the boys were and, on his way back towards our bedroom, stopped at Charlene's room. Waving twenty euro and kissing my neck. Pushing the money into my bra. 'Poker or snap?' was my question. We were giddy. Unbuttoning his shirt. Emptying his pockets, Tom put his phone near the lamp, beside the bed. It made a noise a few times. It was late, we were busy. The phone could wait until morning.

He helped the kids get dressed for school. Shouting at the young fellas to put his phone on charge. Edward ran into the kitchen, pale faced. Tom demanding, 'Give me the phone, what are you doing?' The boy must have been trying to delete it. Tom grabbed it off him. But there it was. The picture of Charlene. My baby girl posing naked.

Gerard's family got to us first. We tried to hold Tom in the trailer, but it was no use. The mother stepped out of the van. My sons struggling to pull their father towards the entrance of our trailer, his face red with rage. Gerard's father was dragging his son away from Tom. Gerard's mother was using a dirty tongue on Charlene. Gerard was shouting and pushing his mother back into the van.

Tom was screaming at me to take Charlene into the trailer. The two fathers got down to it. Ripping off shirts. Then the young men joined in. The crowd scattered at the sounds of the sirens. Arrests made. Bloody faces and bruised chests. Both families met at the Garda station. Comments about family feuds were made by the Guards. Nobody made a statement. Eventually, the guards just got bored and gave a warning to the men.

In the days that followed, Charlene moved into the spare trailer with her brothers. Patrick told me she was just lying in bed like a ghost, not eating or talking. Tom barely spoke during those days. He sat up at night. In bed my body shook with pain. His sobs broke my heart. Mumbling 'why did she do this to us?' Then, on the second night, walking past him to check on our sons, he grabbed me. Sitting on his knee, cradling his head. Still no words passed between us.

Neither of us could bring ourselves to look at or even walk in the direction of the small trailer where our daughter was hiding. After two days, Tom told me to go over and talk to her. It took me a couple of hours to find the courage. My hands were shaking carrying a tray of her favourite sandwiches. Putting the tray down on the ground. Knocking on the door. Knocking harder the second time. Screaming for Tom, who put his hand through the window of the trailer. Shards of glass, splashes of blood bounced from my face to my clothes, reaching for the inside lock on the door. It flung open. Hanging high, in her wedding dress, with her legs dangling. Charlene.

The light sleepers are keeping an eye out on the entrance, making sure journalists and media types are kept away from us. A television flickers in a trailer at the other end of the site. Dogs are barking. Yesterday, after the funeral, the O'Leary lads – all under the age of eleven – used a tray of eggs to get rid of a photographer. Tom's chest rises heavily beside me. He's neither awake nor asleep. Mothers shout their children's names all across the site as if they were singing. That's how I used to call for Charlene.

Bernie McGill

from SMALL STEPS

Granda is what Mumma calls 'set in his ways'. That's what she says when we're in the Spar and people ask after him, but sometimes, to Dan, when she thinks I'm not listening, she says he'd drive you round the bend. He wasn't like this before the stroke, she says. Now all the small things that Granny took pleasure in doing for him when she was alive have become the bars from which he can't escape. One small thing out of sync can spoil his day. I don't want Mumma going round the bend, wherever that is, I want her to stay here with me, and Shortlegs, so I do my best to help. Granda can only go from his armchair to the kitchen table, or to the bathroom, or to his bed. His daily radius is very small. I worked it out. If you take the TV as the central point, I reckon it's about twenty steps. That's not much, and Mumma says it's shrinking. My new school is nearly three miles away and the nearest cinema is twenty-five. If you include Glasgow, and France that time we went on holiday, then my radius is nine hundred and ten miles. I think if it was as small as Granda's, I would want everything in it to be perfect too, including the tiny yoghurt and the twelve apostles' spoons, so I think that that's ok.

Granny collected the full set of spoons, including Judas, though Mumma says she wasn't much fussed about him. Granda doesn't mind what order they come in, so long as we never give him the same spoon twice in one day. Just to be on the safe side, we lay them all out on the shelf and select them from left to right. This morning it's Saint James the Lesser. I always feel sorry for him. Just because there were two Jameses doesn't mean that one has to be lesser than the other, because he was younger, or shorter, maybe, than the other James. His symbol is a club because he was beaten to death. The Bible is a violent place. We never bothered much with the Bible before but Granda has a huge one, with a cream fake leather cover, and gilt edges and coloured prints inside. There's a picture of Abraham with his arm outstretched, the fingers spread over Isaac's face and an ugly, curved blade in his other hand, ready to cut his son's throat, and then the angel at his shoulder, saying it was a test, just in time to stop him. Imagine if the angel had been three seconds late? I don't like the pictures but I can't stop myself. I keep going back to look. Granny bought the Bible off a salesman, Mumma says, and paid it in every week. Mumma's name is in the front under Granny's and Granda's names and my two Great Grannies' names and my Great Grandas' but they didn't put my name in. It's because I wasn't christened, Mumma says. You have to have been christened to have your name written in the family Bible. Shortlegs is not in it either. Sometimes when I'm in the green cave and I imagine it really is a mouth and that it might take a notion of closing and swallowing me up I wonder what that means. If I'm not in the Bible does that mean I'm not really here? But that's nonsense. Mumma would notice if I disappeared, and Granda, and Dan too. I don't know about Lucy. Lucy's not the sentimental kind.

Granda likes the knife with the white plastic handle that has a chip out of it and the fork with the diamond pattern and water in the Famous Grouse glass, half from the pump, half from the freshly-boiled kettle, to take the chill off. He likes one pancake toasted till the edges go crispy and he likes the butter melted with one soft poached egg on top. 'Matthew, Mark, Luke and John, God bless the bed that I lie on, and if I die before I wake, I pray to God my soul to take.' Granda says this before he takes his tablets, as soon as he sees the apostle's spoon. Mumma says it's a bedtime prayer but Granda can't help himself. I ask Mumma what God will do with Granda's soul when he dies and Mumma says that Granda hopes he'll take it to heaven where Granny will be.

'Is she?' I ask Mumma.

'Is she what?' she says.

'Is Granny in Heaven?'

'I don't know,' Mumma says, 'but that's what Granda believes. And you'd think he would know. They were married for fifty-one years.' She nods towards Granda. 'If I ever get like that,' she says, 'you have permission to whack me over the head with a sledgehammer and have done with it.' She doesn't mean it, though. I don't think she means it.

Me and Granda and Shortlegs all have the same bedtime. Mumma helps Granda and I put Shortlegs in the back porch and I get everything ready for the morning. Granda likes his tablets in the blue egg cup with the tiny yoghurt exactly beside it to the right and the apostle's teaspoon beside that, bowl face down. I leave everything out except the tiny yoghurt which has to stay in the fridge until the morning. Granda needs it to swallow his tablets down, and then the water in the Famous Grouse glass to wash down the yoghurt and once that's done, he turns his eggcup upside down so he knows that that part's done and the next part is crispy pancake and soft poached egg. Granda can't remember things he's done three seconds ago, but on his better days, he can remember sinking the well for the pump and he can remember building the wall of the boiler house and Great Granda teaching him how to use the shotgun and he tells me all about these things. He remembers when his own granny lived in the other end of the house with a door that faced the front when their door faced the back so that there were two houses the exact same, joined together, but facing in opposite directions, like two pieces of Lego. But he doesn't always remember who I am. 'Catherine,' he says when he looks at me, and then 'Kate,' and then, 'Cassie' at last. He can never get to me without passing through Granny and Mumma first.

Afric McGlinchey

NOTE TO SELF
all this is provisional
– Michael Symmons Roberts

The cobbled streets are wet,
disconsolate; the usual solitaries.
I am shuffling under a cloud of shapes
and contradictions, old spectres moving
back and forth across my path. I want
to redact every mark of my profligate pen,
drown every journal, erase every stick.
The pressure increases. A man
in a doorway says *some moon, huh,*
and I sense that the moon, like me,
is under construction. I shake off regrets,
like city foxes shaking off the rain.
In the sky, there's always something
meteoric. Or, at least, lightning.

Iggy McGovern

THE CROSS OF CONG
i.m. James MacCullagh 1809–1847

A cross to bear a piece of The True Cross,
oak-cored, embellished with gold filigree;
some craftsman courted eye-strain to emboss
the founding names of Prelate and Ard Rí.

Long centuries of candle-lit procession
have dwindled to a solitary friar,
upon whose death the parish gains possession
and hawks it to the youthful city buyer.

One hundred guineas of his private wealth
establishing a national collection;
a brilliant mind, who suffered much ill health
of that same mind: How deep the disaffection

when he can bear no longer his own cross?
Admire the gift, commemorate the loss.

Royal Irish Academy,
28th August, 1844.

Sir,

The Royal Irish Academy, having succeeded in securing to the country the Dawson and Sirr Collections of Irish Antiquities, are again engaged in the endeavour to prevent the dispersion of an equally valuable and interesting collection—the last of the kind that can now be made in Ireland—of ancient Irish Manuscripts.

These Manuscripts have been brought together, at a great cost, by the long continued assiduity of Messrs. Hodges and Smith of College-green, who, with a patriotic desire to see them lodged in the library of some public institution in Ireland, have refrained from disposing of them elsewhere during the last year, in order to afford the Academy the opportunity of making an effort for their purchase.

The extraordinary exertions made within the last few years, in bringing together, at a cost of several thousand pounds, the large collection of Antiquities and MSS. already deposited at the Academy House, have left the Academy unable to do more in the way of direct contribution towards the purchase of Messrs. Hodges and Smith's MSS., than to subscribe from their corporate funds, a sum of £100 ; but the Council, zealously assisted by a noble and patriotic member of the Academy, Lord Adare, have succeeded in obtaining from Her Majesty's Government, the liberal promise of £600 in aid of the purchase, on condition of the residue of the purchase money being made up by subscription.

The total purchase money agreed for is £1312 10s., leaving £712 10s. to be so subscribed. Of this sum, £502 13s. have been already contributed, as will be seen by the subjoined List of Subscribers, and it only now remains to make up the balance of £209 17s. to secure to the Academy and the country, the possession of these inestimable materials for the promotion of one of the most important branches of British Literature.

In order to make up this balance, the Council of the Academy have deputed their Committee of Antiquities to make this appeal to the liberality and patriotism of such Noblemen and Gentlemen, as they might hope would be disposed to aid the Academy in such an endeavour, and I am directed by the Committee accordingly to solicit your assistance ; and at the same time, for your information on the nature and value of the collection, to submit the enclosed abstract of the Report on which the Council's proceedings for the purchase have been grounded.

I have the honour to be, Sir,
Your obedient, humble Servant,

GEORGE PETRIE, V. P.,
Secretary of the Committee.

Leaflet signed off by George Petrie and issued by the Royal Irish Academy, then based in 114 Grafton Street, calling for subscriptions to purchase Messrs. Hodges and Smith's collection of Irish manuscripts (NLI)

Claire McGowan

from THE KILLING HOUSE

Margaret, *1993*

They'd told her, back when she'd first started doing their dirty work, how it was likely to happen. There'd be a knock at the door, hard and demanding, and when you opened it there'd be a bag over your head. That was for two reasons – to stop you seeing them; and to stop them seeing you. So you'd be less human, somehow. Not an ordinary woman in her kitchen, a mother with a daughter due home from school any minute, but a tout, a traitor.

Then you'd feel rough hands on you, pushing you into a car. They wouldn't speak to you. They wouldn't have to: you'd know who they were. And you'd know there was no point in arguing or fighting, because they had no say in what happened to you next. They were just the delivery men.

Then the car would drive for a while, and if you could see the light under the rough sacking you'd be able to tell you were heading to the country, from the sound of cows and birds and the low green shade to the darkening air, and then the car would bump over a rough track and a cattle grid or two and it would stop. You'd be dragged out, in the same rough way, and you'd be marched and sat down on a hard chair and your hands would be tied with rope, and you'd know from the noises and smells you were in some kind of farmhouse, way out in the country, where no one could hear what they did to you next. And that was when they'd take off the bag and then you would really start to panic because you'd know that if they showed you their faces it was all over for you. You'd pray they had a balaclava on. A balaclava meant there was a chance.

So far, it had all gone exactly as they'd told her, except that they'd left the bag on for a long time after she'd been pushed into the chair, while she'd watched their feet in heavy boots move about and listened to their low voices rumble. Snatches of words here and there were all she'd caught. *What – Fecking woman – Paddy.* The floor of this place was bare earth, cold and dirty. It made everything echo. For a moment she allowed herself to imagine today had been different. That she hadn't found the word in the dirt on her car two days back – TOUT – and she hadn't stayed in the kitchen writing that note to her daughter, and they hadn't come for her, she'd made it away in time. Or that she'd never have started any of this in the first place. Because it had been going on for years now.

It had been so small at first. Glance at confidential papers she was copying in the law office where she worked, the one where they defended so many Republicans. Maybe make another copy and slide it into her handbag; sure no one would notice, and what harm would it do? Slip the copy to Edward, the names and addresses of suspects, people to keep an eye on. They were bad men, even if they were her own side. Murderers. She told herself these small acts – a name here, a nod there – might lead to a better future, where her daughter could grow up safe. Her husband not get killed on the job.

She began to tremble, from cold and shock. Thinking of her daughter, who would by now have come home and found the house empty and dark, the curtains open. Who'd have read the note left on the worktop. Called the police maybe, called her father. Maybe they were looking for her already. Maybe they were almost here to save her. Of course, even if they did, everything would change. Her arms contracted; she'd gone to touch her stomach automatically, but her hands were tied behind her. She was so vulnerable. She tried to remember had they ever killed women. A few times. Not many. And surely not one who was –

There were footsteps coming towards her, and a hand on her head, tugging on strands of her hair as the bag came off. She stifled a cry, blinking in the cold light. It was all so stupid. Tied to a chair, of all things. They'd been watching too many gangster films. Someone stood in front of her, blotting out the light from the bare bulb so she couldn't see their face. A man, of course. A big man, tattoos on his hands, a bomber jacket. Smell of tobacco and bubble gum. Paula always wanted to buy it with her pocket money but Margaret wouldn't let her, said it looked vulgar to be chewing like a cow. As if that mattered now.

'Margaret,' the man said. Surprisingly musical. The accent from over the border. 'I hope they didn't hurt you.'

She shook her head, wrong-footed. Maybe this was going to be ok? 'My daughter ...' She could feel the cold of it around her neck, Paula's cheap little necklace that she'd grabbed off the kitchen counter as they took her. It was all she'd had time for, and for once she was glad her untidy daughter always left everything lying in a trail behind her.

'No one's going to touch your daughter, come on now. We don't hurt weans in this organisation.'

She could have asked did they hurt women but she knew the answer: if they really deserved it, then yes. And she deserved it, no doubt about that.

He pulled up a stool and moved closer, and she could see his face now, her eyes had adjusted to the gloom. He was a good-looking man. A full head of black hair, fine soft lips like a woman, sharp blue eyes. Not what she'd expected; a thug maybe, with a broken nose and shaved head.

That was when Margaret realised *she could see his face*, and that meant he was not wearing a balaclava, and that meant she was in much, much more trouble than she'd even been afraid of. That meant she probably wasn't going to make it out of this alive.

back cover of travel book published by Allen Figgis, 1962

BERNARD SHARE went into advertising in 1952 armed with an inappropriate qualification from Trinity College, Dublin. Spent 3 years teaching English in Newcastle University College, New South Wales, fitting in a lot of travelling on the way there and back and in the long vacations. Again working in advertising in Dublin. Has made an accidental hobby of editing odd magazines—[*Icarus* (literary), *The Irish Jewellery and Fancy Goods Journal* and *Campaign* (advertising)]—reviews fiction for *The Irish Times* and has published travel and other articles in Ireland, Britain and Australia. This is his first book.

Medbh McGuckian

The Star Parasite

My thought became a kind of algebra
where the X sank to the bottom
as your arms submerged
into more like a pure V.
The brown rectangle and warmer browns
of your raised and squared-off arms,
drenched with an inner glowing,
reversed the typed B.

Geometic ghost, you clasped your hands
at a certain distance from my nipple
that nailed itself to your chest
as clearly as your wedded face.
The round bee-stung lips of the wine glass
opened their splendid dead-ends
to your black tongue's nocturnal squares
like a shapeless town, poorly explored.

The imaginary triangle of your Ionian
torso overlapped the real, angel-sealed
diamond of my smaller breast,
and the almonds of your thighs
arched me from the second foot
into a kneeling woman, standing woman,
crouching woman, using the same curves
to frame an arch of trees in the late forest.

Complete tree, furrowed with big veins,
I weighed you on the floor
like the drop-leaf of a table
before the shape is finally reached.
My breasts were repeated twice,
once as a sloping melon slice,

an immaterial gleam of light
whose pathway may be closed or narrowed.

And once as the brown-tipped steeper
cone, commonly found only
in young girls. They read to me
like shells on an antique piano
or a violin alongside an anchor,
stranger to me in their nudity,
forever decaying and undiscoverable
as the street incision and its surface.

The walls seemed to swing backwards,
threadlike through the increasing shallowness
of the pedestal fruitbowl, through everything
that makes a place the same place,
so what had no place
was at home everywhere.
Your fingers deadened, one after the other,
vivid and mingled, on your calf and kneecap.

You marked off their divisions, grouping
their muscles and bones like banished elements,
like teardrops repeated over and over
or a language with only one word.
And set them on your thorax,
abandoned, like one of your senses,
your gaze stepping down your share
of the house, its suggestion of hips and eyes.

Lisa McInerney

FIND MY WAY BACK

All I had to do was book the flight, pack up some bits, sell off the others, *annyeong* and out the gap. Except what happened then? I'd get back to Ireland into thunderous complication because I had fucked things up beyond forgiveness, beyond explanation even. There were boys in Cork I knew would be happy to kill me. I thought that the Shades would demand that I help them with their enquiries, given the way things were before I left, or the way I'd left things … I didn't know what enquiries they might have had. I didn't feel the reverberations from all that way away. I bounced around the world. There was no discipline or form to what I was running from. A sense of dread, I suppose, potential that spidered off into all of the ridiculous places I could imagine.

That was the clamouring stuff, the lurid stuff. There was the practical stuff too. Like whether there would be any opportunities at home. What would I get out of a studio job at home? Twenty quid more than I'd get on the dole? Whose couch would I be crashing on? Even if there were studio jobs in Cork, everyone in Cork knew me, everyone in Cork knew what I used to do when I was a young fella, and it doesn't matter how hard I regret that, I can't take back any of it. Even if I could I wouldn't know where to start: how do you measure what damage you did when you personally saw the last of it wrapped tight in a half-kilo block on a table top just before a courier took it away? All I can be sure of is the damage it did to me, but who'd care? I could show photographs of bruises, medical reports, prescriptions, receipts for days spent on the tear, trying to drink away all sorts, and who'd fucking care?

And the private stuff: who was I in Cork? Did I like who I was in Cork? Was it better for my son to see me how I really was or to see me as a distant but respectable fella? If I came back to Cork would I just turn into my own dad?

Would you ever want me back?

'Find My Way Back' started coming together just after we'd made the EP. I didn't think it was a song, at first. It was just me jotting out knots and bumps to see how I felt about them in a different format. Writing things down is a habit you got me into. Do you remember? You brought me a notebook after I had that meltdown on the Jazz Weekend and told me if I wasn't going to talk to you to write stuff down instead. D'you know what I used to do with it? I used to write letters to my mam. I used to write letters to a woman I could hardly remember. I dunno what I was at. I was a bit lost. I was doing a lot of drugs. Making one insane decision after another, decision being too confident a term in this context. I still dunno how I survived it. I think I only survived it because I went up a gear after I found out Diarmaid was on the way.

So I would write shit down, first to my mam and then to myself and then thoughts that weren't addressing anyone in particular, just lines that went well together. Do you know you made me a songwriter? I know you didn't mean to. Is that a kind of alchemy? Is that always going to be the way with you?

I was writing down all of these thoughts about going home and they started looking like desperate wayfinding and so I saw what the song might look like. They come out like that, sometimes, like a shape rising a welt in a mass of words.

Desperate wayfinding. Home terrified me but I needed to be home. As much as I wanted to stay away, reinventing myself, designing a new, sharper, tidier nature. I had to turn my face back to all I'd done. I had to rescue what was still healthy and I had to tend to all that was sick or brittle. I had to go home. I had to book the flight, pack up some bits, sell off the others, say *annyeong* and be brave for the first time in my life.

Danielle McLaughlin

from THE CHALK SCULPTURE

After Loretta had gone upstairs, I settled myself on the floor of the studio, my legs stretched out in front of me. The house had once been the parochial house, and it still carried a whiff of the sanctimonious in the plainness of the doors and stairs, the sedateness of the cornicing. It had direct access to the shore, and its own private beach, though in the three months that I'd been coming here, Loretta had never once invited me to see it. It wasn't for want of hinting on my part, and one afternoon, perhaps after I'd hinted that bit too strongly, she said, rather crossly, that it wasn't a beach as such, more of a rocky inlet with a strip of shingle.

It was a wet day, but humid, and I hadn't worn any tights. I observed my legs, pale and dappled with old bruises, noticed how well they complemented the floorboards. The timber had turned grey from all the clay ground in over the years, a flinty grey, with here and there shades of flax and bone. I'd measured every inch of this floor on my hands and knees, photographed it, sketched it on gridded paper over a series of afternoons. I'd marked in pencil the location of Locke's chair; his work bench still with its rasps and chisels; the cast-iron statue, half-stoat, half-man, that had stood so long in one place that when I moved it, I found two perfect imprints of feet on the floor. The floorboards would be taken up and carried away, transported to the city to be laid down again exactly as they'd been, even the used rags arranged carefully in a pile.

I was sitting next to the Chalk Sculpture, my head resting lightly against the top of her thigh, in the shadow of her jutting belly. The 'chalk' wasn't strictly speaking chalk at all, but a soft gypsum alabaster Locke had experimented with in his middle years. The sculpture had languished for a period in a disused milking parlour in Clonakilty, and when we'd begun to clean it there were parts that had a greenish tinge, other, lower, parts coated with a residue of cow dung that had taken a long time with a small brush to remove. I wondered, without caring much, if the chalkiness was getting in my hair. I would have to remember to brush it before going to the school.

Through the front window I could see my car parked on the patch of gravel beneath the trees and, out beyond that, the sea. An untended field sloped to the shore, with the ghost of an old pathway, a tiny modulation in the tilt and shading of the reeds, running like a fault line down the centre. I imagined Robert Locke taking that path after a morning spent chiselling and shaping. I wondered what sort of a husband he'd been. I often wondered about that, wondered about it even more than I wondered about matters that were part of my job. But thoughts of other people's husbands led inexorably to thoughts of my own, and things were not particularly good between Philip and myself, it was not exactly Walton's Mountain, and so I blinked away the image of Robert Locke, husband, striding through the reeds. I looked down instead into a crevice between floorboards. I thought about how there must be particles of stone down there that were last touched by the hands of Robert Locke, and how the next person to touch them would be me. I bent closer to the floor, banged the boards with my fist, to see if I could stir the tiny relics. At what point in all this Loretta returned, I can't say. All I know is that I heard a low cough, and when I looked around the curved headland of the belly, there she was, staring at me. The expression on her face was difficult to read: bewilderment, maybe, or sorrow, a trace of outrage. All these things, or perhaps none. I thought I detected discomfort, possibly embarrassment, whether for herself or for me, but I might have been wrong in that. I didn't know Loretta very well, I doubt many people did.

I scrambled up, shamefaced, like a child who'd been caught stealing biscuits. I dusted off my legs, smoothed down my skirt. I felt guilty, then annoyed with myself for feeling guilty, because was I not, after all, in the same room where she'd left me? It wasn't as if she'd caught me pocketing the silverware. But Loretta had that effect on people, or at least she had that effect on me.

'I think I'll bring you down to the room, if that's all right,' she said. 'My mother's almost ready.'

It was always *my mother*, never Eleanor. She picked up my bag, and handed it to me. Then she walked me down the hall, waited until I was seated at the little circular table.

'We won't be long,' she said, perhaps by way of warning.

frontispiece from Dublin Fragments, *1925*

Maria McManus

PRONE

my heart
                    wanted a place
                    howled out
                    from far in

the dark conjuring
a dreamed house

the roof
a shelter
an observatory
a gamelan of rain

safe corners
for what
            was fragile
broken
delicate
too young
& tender
to venture out
alone
prone to bruising

windows
winning sunlight
flowers
championing
a path
cheering the door
and these bees
among the lavender

a bed
linen
your arms
that night
we slept
entirely without
moving

& when I woke
you were still
holding me

published by Hodges Figgis in 1925

DUBLIN FRAGMENTS

SOCIAL and HISTORIC

BY

A. PETER

DUBLIN: HODGES, FIGGIS & CO.
LONDON: JOHN MURRAY
MCMXXV

Alan McMonagle

from LAURA CASSIDY'S WALK OF FAME

To the theatre, then, and step on it. Have marked the important July date in my diary, and need to find out more about the audition. Give Stephen Fallow a feel for the sort of roles I can do. Let him see that this part has my name written all over it, that he need look no further for his leading lady.

Harelip is on the front desk. Aka fire-breathing dragon. And a look on her that lets me know I am a brave person showing my face around here. During auditions for the lead in *Alice in Wonderland,* she – Harelip – was another one who had convinced herself that I was stalking the theatre director – correction, make that *former* theatre director. *Following him about the streets. Turning up at his house at that hour of the night. Staging a sit-down protest on the roof of the theatre building because the part had gone to someone else.* She had called the guards. And a fire engine turned up and a pair of burly firemen raised a ladder and a set of firm hands gripped and removed me from my sit-down perch. But as I kept saying at the time: A quick goo in the dictionary under the word enthusiasm would have provided a more accurate indication of my intentions. Not on me if Harelip's – along with a few others – interpretation of the word happened to be a little different than my own. Simple as that.

Look at the sour head on her. In her spare time she probably strangles kittens. I limber up some suitable words for her in case she makes any sudden moves. Too late. She has spotted me and is already jabbing buttons on her phone. I turn on my heels and step back outside. And on the steps I walk straight into none other than Stephen Fallow.

'Hello,' I say. 'It's me again.'

'Do I know you?' he asks.

'You probably remember me. I was here the other week. You know, when the press release went out about your new production. I'm Laura. The actress.'

'Laura?'

'That's right. I saw the notice in the paper about the auditions. This is going to be huge. I can tell it is.'

'You're very kind.'

'And you are so modest. It's a very attractive quality. This town has been crying out for a decent production for ages and it is obvious you are the right man for the job.'

'That's very nice of you to say so. Now, if you ...'

'No need to thank me. Thank that remarkable CV of yours. The West End. The Royal Court. Broadway. Sydney Opera House, for God's sake. I bet you've got some stories to tell. Have you? Some good stories to tell.'

'Well, I don't know about that.'

'And I think someone is being modest again. I saw the call for auditions in the *Advertiser*. And you're keeping the play's identity a secret. A reprisal of a famous movie from the 1940s. Hmmm. I bet I could take a good guess at what it is. What's your favourite? Movie, I mean.'

'Eh ...'

'I know. It's a hard one, isn't it? I have several favourites. *Woman Under the Influence*? *Letter from an Unknown Woman*. And *Women on the Verge of a Nervous Breakdown*? *Three Women* is really good too. That's a lot of women, but there you go. Have you seen *Three Women*?'

'No, I haven't actually.'

'It's really good. You should see it. I'm surprised you haven't. A director like you. I suppose you haven't time. You're so busy – directing. Hey! Do you want to see my Gloria Swanson or Barbara Stanwyck routines? And Gena Rowlands? I do a very good woman on the verge. And a tomboy. An out and out thug even. My femme fatale is pretty good too. I can do pretty much anything except a damsel in distress. I draw the line at those. Best of all, though, is my woman on the verge. I can do it now if you like.'

'Well, I'm a little busy at the moment.'

'Of course you are. I've been reading all about you. All the productions you've already been involved with. All the actors. The *Advertiser* said you are on the list of people to look out for. Well, I'm on the lookout. Be in no doubt about that. Are you sure I can't do my woman on the verge for you? It won't take a minute. You won't be sorry.'

'Maybe next time.'

'Something else, then? Go on, just say it. Anything you want me to do. Quiet. Loud. Listening. I can do a great listener. Someone who is just waiting for the other person to shut up so I can start. I can convey plenty with my eyes. If I'm in the mood I can have an entire world going on behind them. You know, like Garbo You'll see. I can do it now if you want.'

'Now is probably not the best time.'

'What about an accent? Not a problem. A farmer's daughter? A cockney? A sophisticate? A daughter of Dracula? A southern belle? You know, the way Vivien Leigh does it. I'm a fast learner too. And I can memorize. Do you know I can remember lines I heard as a little girl? Reams of stuff. Would you like me to do some for you? I can do it now.'

'I better go.'

'Before you do, are you sure you can't say what it is. The name of the play. A clue will do. What *kind* of a play is it? Romance? Family drama? Black comedy? Something psychological, perhaps? Like I say, I can do it all. Anything, so long as it's not a musical. It's not a musical, is it? Don't get me started on those things. The first time I saw one I actually thought I was going to throw up. Not for me, thank you very much.'

'Well. Goodbye now.'

'Oh, yes. You have a masterpiece to put together. See you at the audition. And don't forget – anything except a wetbrain and I'm all yours. Oh wait, can you give me any tips?'

But he is already walking away from me. I understand. He's a busy bee. He needs to rejoin his crew. I watch as he disappears inside the theatre, give him a friendly wave when he turns back towards me. But there is no time to stick around to see if he waves back. Harelip has turned up, warpath face and all, and it is time for me to scarper. Not to worry. I've gotten to say my few words. It won't be long now. Soon I will be part of their little gathering, swapping theatre ideas, offering my own suggestions to their eager ears.

It's going to be fun.

Isn't is, Laura?

Yes, it is, Laura. Indeed it is.

dustjacket of Dublin Fragments, *published in 1925*

Eoin McNamee

from THE VOGUE

She showed him a monochrome photograph taken just after her parents married. Her father burly, authoritative, wearing an evening suit and black tie, hair Brylcreamed back from his forehead. He was smoking a cigarette. He looked capable of violence, a back street enforcer with a lethal swagger. She didn't recognise the background. The west end of a city somewhere, cruel and vibrant, men with hard eyes in well-cut suits, the women's mouths looked like faces slashed with open razors. Her mother wore her hair up in a French bun, her eyes heavy with mascara, dark lipstick, her waist nipped in. This was the couple who should have had a child, not the lost parents she remembered. This street mother would have been different, reeking of gin, spiteful, directing cutting remarks. There would be fights, slammed doors. As a child she said she worried that these parents were in the house somewhere. That another hard-bitten life awaited her.

When the house was empty she would go into the bathroom and take down her father's cologne and smell it, a masculine odour under the sweet tones, a low-life rankness.

She talked into the night in the gas-jet hiss of the Superser, the caravan close and airless, the whorled intimacies examined, Kay a tender-hearted rationalist. She talked and did not ask him about himself. Reticence must be allowed its moment. There was space in her life for the close of heart. Her father spoke little and she knew how silence worked. Her mother showed her how to operate within the confines of a man's silence, whole days would go past without anything being said. He would have been better off in an order of contemplatives, his quiet became a rich, monkish thing which left Kay easy in the realm of the untold.

'It's like a film,' she said.

'What is?'

'You. A stranger comes to town. All of a sudden things start to happen.'

'Things happen anyway.'

'You fit the character though.' A man who sat at her fold-down table, laconic, burdened.

'I just want to fulfil my client's requirements and get out of here.'

'How do you do that?'

'Identify the body.'

'How, you got DNA, forensics?' She liked the tech words, the way things could be broken down, codes retrieved, recreated under lab conditions. Authorities would be involved, serious people in white coats. You could defer to them. We were all made of the same things, differently ordered. We were all dust blown across the universe in cosmic gales. You could gaze upon what was eternal in your bones, the star matter, the icy filigree of self.

'There's nobody to compare it against. No DNA samples. Anyway, it's not the kind of proof the client is looking for.'

'What then?'

'Her clothes. I know what she would have been wearing.'

'Where are they?'

'They'll be at the morgue.'

When he was in the shower Kay opened his briefcase, thumbing back the brass clasp. She felt hunched over, thievish, looking back over her shoulder, dry-mouthed.

The briefcase interior smelt of leather and copying fluid. There were photocopies of land registry documents. She opened them out, trying to keep them in the correct folds. Things had to be returned to the case in the right sequence. The banquette light cast her shadow against the wall, a crabbed, underhand figure. She put the legal documents aside. There was a dental record in the name of Reay Wilkinson. Police reports on absconded teenagers, press cuttings from local papers, the paper yellowed, brittle along the folds where they had been opened out, reeking of harm. They looked like scattered documents retrieved after a catastrophe. Copies of statements and court documents. Committal orders. Documents rendered illegible by damp stains. An envelope containing photographs.

They'd photographed themselves in a place Kay didn't recognise, a planked interior, utilitarian materials, an old single bedstead with a blanket thrown over it, a pot-bellied stove. Polaroids, the colours otherworldly, the emulsions fading, red-eye giving the older boy a feral look, Reay acting tough, glaring at the camera so that you wondered what outlaw world she imagined herself, what on the run interlude, death's agents on the trail, what flinty-eyed G-men of her imagination. Cole stood to on side, unposed, not looking at the camera, hands in his pockets.

In the side pocket of the briefcase there was a blue envelope with a single sheet of paper in it, the paper watermarked Basildon Bond which made her think of letters from another era, close-written intimacies. The envelope was addressed John Cole Solicitor, Water Street, Shotts. She opened the letter. A newspaper cutting. 'Body Found at Cranfield.' Question marks had been added in blue pen, certain phrases underlined, illegible words scribbled in the margins, the writing crabbed, seeming worked at under a dim light. The signature full of threat, other agendas, indiscernable malices.

There were more photographs taken outside. Kay thinks she can place them by the shape of the mountains behind them, somewhere on the western edges of the aerodrome. Harper and Reay are paddling. Reay's wearing a cheesecloth shirt and has her hippy skirt bunched, holding it up in one hand. He has his trousers rolled up and a hankerchief folded over his head. They're a parody couple, industrial workers on an annual jaunt to a seaside of donkey rides and kiss-me-quick hats. She's acting a knock-kneed matron and he's a banty little trade unionist. The sun glints on the waves behind them, what might pass for happiness in burnished glimpses. She imagined buckets and spades, candy-striped deckchairs, the heatstruck ephemera of a day at the seaside. The boy taking the photographs, happiest when he's just out of frame, a figure at the edge of the crowd.

In the bottom of the case there was a hardback copy of *Horseman of the King: The Story of John Wesley*. The dustjacket faded and torn, the red cloth binding showing through. She wondered if this was how Cole saw himself, a carrier of the flame, a man with a staff set out on the road, burdened, carrying light into the pilgrim dark.

Paul McVeigh

from In Plain Sight

His father had such an easy way with kids. Boys. The kind who never seemed to be at home. Always hanging around street corners. Whose names were always on other kids' lips.

Giving something back to the community, he was, his father. More power to his elbow. You couldn't fault the man for that. Well, unless you looked hard at the surface of him where there was a hint of something underneath.

There was something in his father's smile and the laughter that came too quick – and from the throat, not the belly. Most didn't notice. The odd one would, over the years. A child too old for his body. One who had already encountered kindness that was not to be trusted.

His father had bought a van. Blue. Used. It only had to go short distances. To the swimmers and back. The odd daytrip out of the estate to a park or a river.

His father would make his son come along even though it was clear his son didn't want to. Never wanted to.

His son hated the rough boys and he hated swimming. Not that he could swim. But he knew if he could, he would. Maybe that was unfair to say, then. It was the event of swimming, all that it entailed, not just the trying to move in water bit. Getting naked, he hated most. That's why he would let the other boys get changed first. And why he had a secret trick to be doubly safe. He'd put his togs on under his trousers, after school, before going to the swimmers.

Once, when he'd left it to the last minute, his father called for him and he didn't have time to change. Thought he was so super speedy he'd pushed changing back later and later, each time, almost as a dare. Almost as though in some hidden place inside him he wanted to lose this game with himself and end up naked in the changing room with the other boys. He envied their carelessness. They acted like it was fun. Laughing at each other and talking like they'd never given a moment to who saw their bare bodies when he came out in hives at the thought. It was what he dreaded most. Being exposed like that.

Maybe some part of him wanted to get caught, wanted to be punished for being the way he was. As though someone else lived inside him and this someone wanted the worst for him. Maybe it was God.

That's why, on that occasion, when he didn't have time to put his togs on before, he couldn't go swimming. He just couldn't. That's why he panicked. Why he fell down the stairs breaking his arm.

He'd stood at the top of the stairs, his father calling. His fingers felt for the walls either side and the tips glided along the bumpy surface of the wallpaper print. He saw the hall at the bottom of the stairs with the front door open, the grey path outside cut short by the doorframe. The family coats on the wall on the right, above about where he would land if he made it all the way down.

He didn't have much time. His father shouted for him, a final call. He took a sharp breath and his heart responded with a drop hitting lower in his ribs than he'd felt before. Panic fizzed cold through him. His heart stopped jabbing and started knock-out punches with each beat. He had to do something.

A shadow head bobbed on the path outside, a body followed, coming towards him. He let go. Closed his eyes and gave himself up to the world. His right arm went of its own accord. With his eyes closed he saw clearly the blue arms of the sky open up to embrace him and the pillow-white clouds arrange to break his fall.

His father didn't take him to the hospital. No point in spoiling the swimming for the other boys. And children in pain was what mothers were for.

In order for no one to know he wore his togs to the swimmers, he had to get into a corner of the changing rooms and make a bubble around himself where time slowed. He would stay silent and fold his clothes, ever so neatly, while everyone else went on fast forward. The other boys always pushed each other, always laughed, filling the air with their shouting, amplified and echoed by the tiled room. Boys made so much noise. Took up so much space. Spared no thought. They'd fight their way to the pool and in their wake, clothes lay in messy piles on the floor as though their bodies had evaporated. As though their mothers were about to come and clear up. As though, at this young age, they'd already learned the world was theirs to leave behind.

Seeing the changing room empty, he made his way towards the exit to the pool on the balls of his feet because he hated the cold of the tiles. Shouting came from the toilets to the left where stragglers lurked. He padded past through freezing-cold, ankle-deep water. 'To clean your feet' he'd heard his father explain before to one of the dirty boys.

Around the exit wall, bathers rinsed themselves, swimming hats and goggles, in cold showers. They seemed not to notice the cold. They were not the same kind of human as he.

The exit brought him out to the middle of the pool where he stayed watching the boys with his father at the shallow end, wondering when they might notice he wasn't there. He waited, toes curled around the lip at the waters edge.

His neck cracked backwards, his chest kicked forward, knees buckled, as hands on his back pushed him into the water to the laughter behind. His arms went out as the water swallowed him whole. He blew with all his lungs and the bubbles thundered against his nose. His fingers tried to grab but the water wouldn't be held.

Paul Maddern

IN THE BRILLIANT DOMAIN
i.m. Debi O'Hehir

I surrender to the cold body of the lake
and slide beneath to a time

when a dancer echoed the grace
of courting swans in slow *port a bras*

and a gardener skimmed leaves off a pond
and remembered a lesson on meniscus

and a pianist lingered over Middle C
but recalled the forest and moved two octaves down

and an artist put charcoal to paper to enter her study
of gold horses and the fulcrum of their movement

and when I surface in the cold body of the lake
it is to this artist in a field and to those same gold horses
   galloping.

Mary Madec

THE EGRET LANDS WITH NEWS FROM OTHER PARTS

I wish it were to a place
emptied of memories

not caught in the gauze of those thin trees
as the river heaves, bursting banks
until I'm up to my knees in its detritus.

The hill above, which I have walked
so many times, leaves me once again breathless
at the summit, as if it were the wrong road.

What I didn't know then
hops out like a harlequin from behind the hedges
mocks me on those lonely walks

with the smell of gorse or woodbine in my nose
where I thought a sweet scented world was consoling me,
not telling me I'd make better memories somewhere else

in another world, from where the egret came,
his cascade of white plumes flowing down
as he stoops and dallies in the inlet

long enough for me to notice him,
then raises to the span
of his brilliant majestic wings.

Why should it mean anything?

Emer Martin

The Hag Takes the Limbo Babies on a Day Out

I am the hag. I am this land you call Ireland. When I die, even as a hag, my legs will curl up like a dead spider. I am not restless like ye; forever shape-shifting from fish to rodent, to ape, to human. You can find me in amber 130 million years ago. Before I was a hag, I was a spider for so long. It was when you came to my shore that I took your shape. Later I regrew my eight arms: I can't shaky my spidery ways.

'Spiderlings, spiderlings,' I call on the abandoned mountainside on Bolus Head, in the Barony of Iveragh, Co Kerry. I poke my withered arms into the earth of the limbo graveyard, and retrieve those little ones who you wouldn't even take into the afterlife with you. 'It's time for a day out,' I coo to my limbo babies. 'A jaunt up to Dublin. I can only take 8 of you this time. So I'll have one spider hand for each.' We bus it up to Dublin. The limbo babies open their mouths and make popping noises with their lips. Grateful to be out of the ground. I spit on a tissue and wipe some of the dirt from their faces.

'This will be educational too, you know. Next stop the National Museum. Can't all be fun and games, storytelling at the Leprechaun Museum, crawling about the tunnel in the Wax Museum. Up and down the slippery steps in the Phoenix Park, hearing the roar of the lions at the zoo. We'll do all of that, but I have to see my bog bodies too. I haven't been able to talk to them since they pulled them out of me. I've heard they've created a fine exhibit in their honour.'

In the National Museum I ignore the stares of the guards. We are quite the sight, the old hag trailed by eight, mucky, crawling limbo babies. I check in my bag and march off to find the bog bodies. While they were under the earth I had some contact with them, gave them a bit of motherly affection over two and a half millenniums. I thought I had so much to say. But as soon as I enter their tombs I can say nothing, except remember. They lie under glass. The Iron Age seems like yesterday; my little rotten precious Limbo babies press their tiny noses to the glass as I hold one in each arm. They gasp at their kin, the perfect fingernails, the emptied out lives, the cut nipples. Sacrificed men. I remember the Iron Age nights you went down, boys. I remember the faces on those who killed you. I remember them cutting you under the nipples so you could never be king. I remember your last meal. How you looked to the sky at the new gods coming like flashing streaks of light. You were pushed into earth, into me, your old hag mother, old hag God, Ireland.

'I told you that I would come, lads,' I whisper. I'm worn out from our excursion today. There is a bench beside the bodies and I sit. 'Is it ok now?' I ask them. 'Is time the great healer that everyone keeps saying it is? For me, you see, time goes in spirals; everything keeps coming around again but at a different level. Whisht now. They are all gone, your murderers, but you are still here. Take some comfort.'

A bog body replies: 'Fame is poor revenge, indeed. Would I have not chosen another night? Just one more night under the ancient stars before my sacrifice?'

I touch him, tender is this hag. He shivers but lets me. A man like what's left of him can't be fussy.

'What took you so long?' He asked.

'Arra, don't whinge. I'll never let you down. I'm not human.'

My limbo babies are getting fidgety and scuffle around the place. I have to keep an eye on them or they'll be up to all sorts of mischief in the museum. Two have disappeared already. Some French tourists are staring at me with their mouths hanging open. They snap pictures on their iPhones. Here I am, Ireland herself.

'Every culture holds a sacrifice as its igniting force,' I whisper. I don't like that they are already uploading my image to social media sites. I get ready to leave, looking around for my little spiderlings.

'Yes, I was their bog Jesus,' he says to me through his black skin. His perfect fingers twitch and clench. 'Aren't all sacrifices really acts of convenience? Isn't there always someone to get rid of?'

More tourists gather and everyone has a phone out to record the moment the bog body moved.

'Shh,' I said, 'wipe your tears, hush now.'

'Was it worthwhile? What is Ireland now?'

'Hush now, maybe someday you'll be back inside me. Maybe I'll gather you up.'

'They sucked the fluid out of me like a spider.'

I let go of his hand; he did look rather like an empty school bag. 'Nothing to do with me. I gave you all the affection I could.'

'*Is fuar cumann caillach.*' He snaps. The affection of a hag is a cold thing. So it is, spiderlings. So it is.

Before I cause a riot in the museum, I run off to gather my bold wee spiderlings. We'll go in the shape-shifting boat past St Patrick's Cathedral. The man in the Viking Splash Tour gives us a funny look. An old hag and her eight dead and decaying babies. There are so many crows following us that he keeps glancing in consternation at the sky above. But we have cash so they give us our plastic Viking helmets and off we go. He tells us about the grave of Dean Swift. The inscription on his tombstone reads: 'Here lies Jonathan Swift, where savage indignation can no longer lacerate the heart.' I wish I could lie somewhere like that.

Into the water by the canal, the babies all clap in delight. One claps so hard her finger falls off. I pick it up and pocket it. Last stop before we go home, I buy all my putrid limbo children a Happy Meal. If they can never sit close to God they can at least have a happy meal. As they eat I watch them for signs of happiness and I think I see a glimmer. I sigh as they snuggle up to me. I hate to have to put them back inside the mountain on Bolus Head. But they wouldn't last long here. Not on this diet.

We make our way to Busaras and I don't know Dublin all that well so we get lost in Marlborough St. What I see here shocks even me, who has been witness to all since the Devonian, since the Cambrian, since all the world was one big country of Pangaea. Since I, Ireland, was two halves that collided. I, who had once been moored by Australia. I have witnessed years in the millions. I see it has come to this. Was it for this you crawled out of the water? Was it for this you came down from the trees? Was it for this you walked the land bridge from Africa? Was it for this you set out on small boats from the foggy coast of Iberia and made first landing on Bolus Head? The lost junkie tribe on Marlborough St gathered in shivering clusters. The light gone out of their eyes worse than even in all the famine times. What really shocks me is that everyone else is moving about, oblivious, while their own people stand soul destructed as they wait for the dealer. There had been more life in the bog bodies.

Suddenly, my handbag gets snatched. 'Lousy junkies.' I find myself howling. 'No one cares about ye. Where will you pawn a hag's handbag?' My limbo babies begin to cry and it almost takes the good out of the happy meal. Since we have no bus fare, I have to mount onto the roof of the Kerry bus. Their bodies are so flimsy; one loses an ear to the whipping wind. I gather them closer to me, spider hag, wrapping my hairy old arms around each of them. At the end of the journey some of them pretend to be asleep, just like real children do. Just so I have to carry them. Exhausted, I tuck them back into the dark deconsecrated mountain, my wee spiderlings. Rest now far from God, no grace granted to you, only me here to take care of you. *Is fuar cumann caillach.* The affection of a hag is a cold thing.

Máighréad Medbh

UNTITLED

Emotion is a continent full of tourist traps.
Won't you buy that faux gold cup with its fadeable legend?
Who wants only to be home and mementoes of the same
    old?

Do you, though, buy the fickle jungle that tricks
you into non-composure at the brim of the prurient river,
where it swallows the path by the edge of its long mouth?

Retreat from this to silverhanded *bonhomie*. He is
not done yet, the voluble guide, and pulls you to him,
the commentary coaxing you from your stubborn
    ignorance.

For now. You will go trekking alone year after year
and re-require the kindness of the random, in face
of another uncalculated chasmic challenge.

The volcanic landscape looks harmless in its *petite mort*,
baked only by the sun. But as with cakes too sweet or too
    hard,
what yields imprisons, what does not, disappoints.

Mary Melvin Geoghegan

AT THE US AMBASSADOR'S RESIDENCE
11 September 2017

There's the deer –
up in the Phoenix Park
watching in the green Ford van
chasing those rum and butters
as our father bursts open the bag.

Now, queuing outside the gates
the poet Kevin Power walks by.
In the knot of arrival
– his reading confirms –
and the view spills open a world
all manicured, green and alive.

Geraldine Mills

from RETURNING GOLD

From the hole up near the ceiling, the sky was letting in a trickle of grey light. A shaft of it struck the far wall; a beam of hope in the darkness. He, Hiram Brock, had survived, lived to see another day though he didn't know how long he had been there with the way they mixed up day and night on him. Bright lights shining in his eyes or covered in darkness and no way of telling which was which. His captor pushed lumps of bread, crawling with maggots, into his mouth. He had gagged on them.

Soon his hair would begin to fall out, his nails. Starvation a slow death. Maybe it would be a blessing, to be gone, let it all be over with. Just drown him, let his breath be taken from him.

But then a picture of his dead wife, Effie, appeared before his eyes. *Give me your word that you will see our boys, Starn and Esper, grow up to be good men, to make a difference.*

That was enough to pull him back from the brim. He shook his head and stood up. Whatever it took, he would do it. The Sagittars would not defeat him.

Up, up, up.

The flame sings its own rising song as it fills the balloon with hot air. Esper and I move above it all, leaving the people of Colmen Island behind, Veltor smiling his wolf's smile beside us. Nothing to do but let the wind take my brother and me home. Home, the sweetest word, sweeter than the honey waffles in the bag at our feet, sweeter than the birds that fly out for their day's work.

Collywobbles are starting up inside me at the notion of being back in the sky again. The last time we did this we nearly died; how close I was to losing my brother, thinking I would never see him again. But the world is a brighter place this time. No storms, no cloud suck. Just the bluest of skies, as we move along at our ease.

When we begin to lose altitude, I release the valve, give it another blast of air just like Lili showed me before we left the island. The flame whooshes through its wide-open mouth of fabric and we soar, right back up into the sky again. Lili's words continue to echo in my ears: how the wind has a mind of its own and the balloon listens only to that. No steering on my part will get us back home, so I read the wind and try to make it work for me, up and down to get to our destination. Up and up again.

The UltraCharge rests against the burner. The gauge says: fifty percent. At my feet, the little box with the queen bee and her brood is quiet, the buzzing has settled down. This balloon is a royal carriage for the special creatures we are carrying on board: royalty. Lili's words as strong as ever: 'That's your job now; handle them carefully if you want to save your territory.'

So, we mustn't let them come to any harm. You are better than all the gold in the world, I whisper to them. You will bring Orchard Territory back to life again.

'So, brother! What's the plan?' Esper leans over the side of the basket, Veltor on his hind legs, beside him, peering over with him. Down below the hexagon houses of the island grow smaller and smaller. Soon we won't be able to see them at all. Going further and further away from Colmen: the world that minded us for that short sweet time and brought my brother back to himself.

Another twist on the valve brings us above and beyond the trees. Soon we are drifting over the cliffs where the five Sagittars who tried to steal the gold met their end, dashed to pieces on those rocks, never to be seen again.

Then we are moving out to sea, the wind still in our favour, just the right strength to keep us going.

'You enjoying this, Veltor?' My brother says, his arm thrown around the neck of his wolf friend.

I unfold the map and straighten it out across the top of the basket. 'Lili suggested we head towards Mannioc if we need to refuel,' I say.

'What distance did she think that would be? A kilometre, two?'

'Less, about half the distance from Orchard to Galyon.'

'But look here ...' and my brother points to where two humps of land sit in the middle of the sea. 'It looks like Mannioc is quite close to Serpens.'

'You're right, we could land on either of them. It's just such a pity we cannot take a more direct route, like Vasuri Island, since that's the obvious one. They wouldn't be exactly happy to see us return. We ruined our chances with them, or at least, Malfas did, but we won't be able to explain that one away.'

'After the way we left them,' my brother says, 'not a diddly-squat. It's a real bummer. Bet I know why you want to go back that way, though. You just want to see Leone again.'

'Don't be a dizzard,' I say, as I punch him in the side and look more closely at the map so he won't see my face go red. His words bring me back to that evening when she showed me around her part of Vasuri. She's the first girl I was really able to talk to since my sister died. I push the feelings way down, not wanting to let my brother see. Remembering that dank hole that they threw us into. Malfas shouting and screaming that he would kill them, the chase of the dogs and then the mad dash for the raft. He ruined it for us when he tried to steal their pyrite like that.

I check the UltraCharge; it's down to thirty percent now. We sail on and on. Lili warned us not to let the charge run out, else we're two boys falling out of the sky and no one to see us fall.

Lia Mills

from TICKNOCK

The searchers are out again. A helicopter strafes the
hillside with cones of light. Its staccato *thrum* splinters
Emer's dream. Chips of light and sound rattle in her mind
like nuts in a blender, shattering sleep, casting her to the
surface. Outside, searchlights hover and loop across
midnight grass, misshapen shrubs, needles of rain – a bad
night for anyone to be out. There'll be some unfortunate
lost or hiding in the woods or on the mountain. *Good luck
to the lost and the hunted* is about as close as Emer ever
comes to prayer. The noise from the chopper swells. It fills
her head. When it stops the abrupt silence leaves an
internal echo – somewhere between a memory of sound
and sound itself – ringing like a bell.

The searchers move on but Emer and the house go right
on throbbing. She doesn't want to think about where
Clodagh might be on a filthy night like this but an
impression forms against her will. Clodagh on the run, out
of doors in the violent dark of this night's storm, gives way
to Clodagh underground: earth in her eyes, carnivorous
roots growing down through the bony frame of her
unbreathing ribs, splitting them apart. Others nearby,
beside and above and below her, this whole benighted
country a shallow, overcrowded grave.

Clodagh. When she comes to Emer's mind in such
jagged small hours she seems buried, underground. If
that's so, if she's dead, then at least whatever torments she
faced are over with. Let her rest in peace. No. Emer refuses
such treacherous thoughts. There's a crowd in her head
now, jostling for space, muttering, but that part of her that
will always be Clodagh's mother no matter what turns her
back on all of them, retreats from what it knows it's doing.
Not wanting to hear, it doesn't listen. It banishes dirt from

Clodagh's mouth, pulls worms from her empty eye-sockets and fills them again with light and life. A nod to what the rest know is just about possible. Possible, but unlikely. Clodagh might be alive somewhere, in hiding. Even if what has risen in Emer's mind is true and she's confined somewhere underground, she could be anywhere, doing anything. She could be an ordinary commuter on an underground train in any city in the world. She could be working in a rich woman's basement, washing and ironing. Down a mine. Caving. In an adventure centre, she'd have liked that.

Sometimes Emer catches sight of herself on the edge of these visions. She lets Clodagh see her standing there but she's careful not to ruin it. She doesn't rush up to her or call her, doesn't open her arms or reach. She waits. Let Clodagh decide, does she want Emer there or not? Does she want to be found? Many don't. A person walks out of her life and people assume she's come to grief, when her grief might have found her long before. It could be grief she's leaving behind. As Emer has reason to know.

She fights her way to sitting, breathes deep, tells herself that was no vision she had, only an uneasy ledge her mind rested on in its downward search for sleep. No chance of that now that Clodagh's in her mind. She may as well get up. She feels for her slippers with her feet, pads the length of the hall, the short stairs to the kitchen. She fills the room with light, drives away the sound of wind and rain with the radio and the swell of the kettle, rattle of cup, teapot, spoon. Everything slower and clumsy because of having to use the wrong hand. Her damaged wrist itches under plaster that's due to come off tomorrow. No – she looks at the clock – later today.

Waiting for the tea to draw she stares at the black square of the kitchen window, beaded with rain. In memory she finds her daughter, walking away from her that last time. Through this same window she saw the red of Clodagh's parka blurred by threads of water, movement – as though she was running – into a distance that grew and lasted. If she'd only known. In her mind's eye that deep strong shade of red is taken up by green, crumbles to brown, fades to black. Was that a car she heard, or thunder?

Then or now?

She pours the tea, laces it with whiskey. Time confusions are nothing new in this house, the one she was born and raised in, the house she came back to with her children when she left her husband. At the time she was careful to make it look as though he left her, so as not to injure his pride.

That man's pride was a shocking thing, alive, as vital to him as a lung or a heart. It drove him. She'd learned to soothe it every way she could. She gave false reasons for leaving, reasons that could have been true; reasons that were true enough, or became so. He knew where she could be found but she had protection there and not so much as a hint of another man to stir the whispers. She told everyone she was waiting for him to join her. When he didn't come they thought the loss was hers, that she was the one who'd been abandoned.

That's if they thought about her at all. Here's a thing she's learned: public attention, even during the biggest and most crushing of scandals, is a fickle thing. Like her husband, it doesn't stay in one place for long.

Geraldine Mitchell

Bone Dance

The graveyard's expectant
     as an empty stage, but
         there's no guarantee
     they'll dance to-night.

We let on we're not scared,
     tell each other stories
         – his family, mine –
     the TB, the suicides,

the longest living and
     the soonest dead. We try
         to calculate the density of
     corpses, cubic meters, multiples of

bones, the depths they must descend to.
     We wrap our minds
         round Earth's broad girth,
     make lists of wars, add to the bony heap

life's ordinary debris.
     We sit bone white under
         a mandible moon.
     Quiet as death.

And still no clickety-clack,
     no clatter,
         no clash.

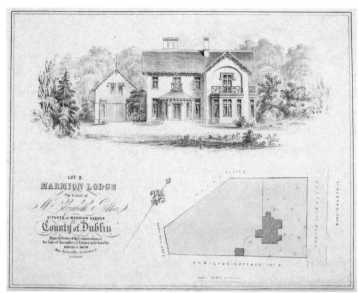

Marmion Lodge. The Estate of Mrs Elizabeth Pittar. Situated in Merrion Avenue, County of Dublin. Made by Order of the Commissioners for Sale of Incumbered Estates in Ireland by Hodges & Smith Map Agency-Office, 104 Grafton St, Dublin (NLI)

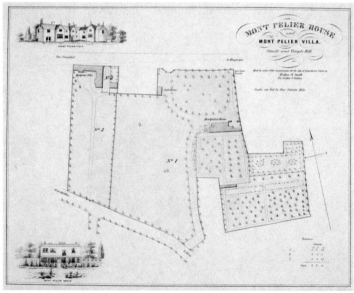

Mont Pelier House and Mont Pelier Villa, situated near Temple Hill. Made by order of the Commissioners for the Sale of Incumbered Estates by Hodges & Smith, 104 Grafton St. Dublin, circa 1850 (NLI)

Noel Monahan

DELIA, WOMAN FROM OSTUNI

Delia, Old Stone Age woman from Ostuni,
You still have charms and have me wondering
If men invented praise words about your beauty,
Your passion for dress and jewellery, red ochre in your hair,
Bonnet of sea shells, beads of ox and horse teeth.
You bear witness to past ages. Huntress of the hills and
      moon,
Ripple-dancer to rhythms of hammerstones and choppers,
Your great needs: to find and eat food, bear children.
Only twenty years old when you died,
They laid you to rest
In a grotto, one hand under your head, pillow of flint chips,
The other hand protecting your unborn baby
And I stare at your bones in the museum and wonder
Has anything changed? All life born unto death.
Mother Earth, tragic Delia, on life's journey.

Mary Montague

ITCH

I lie awake
under the duvet's warm and weighted air
in January's hard dark –
streetlight-orange seeping
around the edge of the curtain,
and, outside, a robin's faint tremolo.

I have been woken
by the dunt of thoughts,
their itch of words

that I must scratch

again. So

here

I am
bracing myself –
talking my body
out of its need
for warmth,
my brain
out of its craving
for sleep –

now – I reach out

switch /

on the light.

Sarah Moore Fitzgerald

from THE LIST OF REAL THINGS

'He has cracked the secret of living!' Bee announced the night before Granddad's birthday. He was going to be ninety.

Bee and I watched him from our bedroom. I could see him humming away to himself in the garden, carrying something bulky in his arms and disappearing into the shed.

I'd been trying to encourage Bee to go to bed but as usual she had zero interest.

'I think it's highly possible that he is part of a team of magic people. His immortality is a great comfort to me, Gracie. In this world so full of endings, it's wonderful to know that Grandfather will always be here.'

'For the thousandth time, stop saying things like that.'

'Why, when it makes me so happy to say them?' she sang.

'Oh, Bee, because they're not true, and besides, I worry that you're getting your hopes up about things that can't possibly be facts. Nobody's immortal. Not even Granddad, however much you might like to believe it.'

Talking about death was an awkward thing in our house on account of the subject being completely taboo, but it didn't deter Granddad Patrick.

'Most of my friends are dead,' he proclaimed quite merrily in the middle of his birthday speech the next day.

'Thank goodness for the wonderful little Bee here and Gracie. Thank goodness also for Jemimah and Celia!' He held up his glass in the direction of two people who'd just come through the door. It took me a while to recognise the Misses Allen who had huge feathers in their hair, velvet hairbands, enormous netty dresses that rustled when they moved and make-up on their faces, which was something we had never seen on them before.

'I never knew they were friends with Granddad,' I whispered to Bee.

'Gosh, didn't you?' she said in this self-satisfied way that pretty much infuriated me, acting as if she knew everything, even though she was much younger than me and as mad, basically, as a brush.

Quickly, I began to suspect the Misses Allen were having some kind of old-person love affair with Grandfather, from the way they looked at him and how they laughed so loudly at even his not-very-funny jokes, and how much attention they paid to him by rubbing his arm and then kissing him, one cheek each, leaving huge smudges of lipstick on his face. Janine approached him with a tissue to rub it off.

'Goodness no, my dear!' said Granddad, gently evading Janine's best efforts.

'These are marks of romance and glamour!' he said, peering delightedly into the mirror and then spending the rest of the evening declaring, 'I'll never wash my face again!' to the sound of the Misses Allens' uproarious laughter.

'Jemimah? Celia? Is that really what they're called?'

Needless to say, Bee said she'd always known but that it was not polite to call old ladies like the Misses Allen by their first names. 'As a matter of fact,' she said, 'I know loads more other things about them but I don't care to discuss any of it.'

'What do you know?'

She stood in front of me, all grown-up and straight-backed.

'Now is not the time, Gracie. We are celebrating Grandfather's wonderful, everlasting life! Plus we have to hand round nibbles for the guests.'

Granddad insisted on doing his party piece, which was singing a long and tuneless song with Louie, who howled along even more tunelessly beside him.

All through this agonising performance Bee's eyes glistened with pride and love. When he was finished and the applause had trickled out, she said in a huge loud whisper, 'Isn't he simply great? Thank goodness he's never going to die.'

Everyone heard, and everyone laughed.

When Granddad Patrick actually did die, Bee was broken-hearted and sad and lost – along with the rest of us. But most of all she was astonished.

It's not a phenomenon widely discussed, but death in your family feels like the world has kind of been jolted into a parallel universe. Without Granddad, food tasted funny. The house filled up with new, odd sounds and it smelled strange, and there were peculiar empty pockets of space all over the place – in the corners and at the top of the stairs – and unusual little gusts of breeze that seemed to curl in and out of his bookshelves and all those places that he used to linger. It's not only a person who dies. The spaces that he used to fill – it seemed as if they were dead and different too. Everybody felt it, especially Louie, who lay for a whole day pressed up against the part of the sofa where Granddad used to sit and then wandered around the house searching and searching, stopping to sniff Granddad's silver-tipped walking stick.

'So much loss in their young lives,' said the Misses Allen at the funeral. Everyone kept on reminding us about how old he had been as if somehow it was supposed to stop us from being sad.

'I would very much like to do an official speech in honour of him,' said Bee self-importantly to Uncle Freddy, who said if that was what she wanted to do then she must.

I was terrified.

Her head was barely visible above the podium, but her voice was steady and clear.

'Ahem,' she said, reading from a crumpled piece of paper. 'Grandfather Patrick's heart no longer beats. Air does not go in and out of his lungs as once it used to do, and his face is cold. We used to walk on the beach and he told me all his secrets. I will still walk, and I will remember all the secrets, but nothing is ever going to be the same. Everything is changed for ever, and there is nothing to be done but put up with it. Thank you very much.'

Her words were followed by an awkward silence that was only broken by the priest suggesting that we offer each other the sign of peace. Bee went around to every single person in the church, shaking their hands and saying things such as, 'May you find solace in this time of great darkness,' and, 'I think it's possible that we're going to need more sandwiches.'

Luke Morgan

TOUGH STUFF

I can't go beat the shit out of him,
and I certainly can't go beat the shit out of her,
so I decide to go beat the shit out of the ocean
instead.
'Come on so,' it shouts at me,
thumping its chest,
but, as we all know,
the worst kind of person to taunt
is the person who is prepared to die,
and I am,
I'm bloody well prepared to die,
so I kick off my shoes trousers socks
and run into it
and it thumps me
but I thump it back
it grabs my balls and puts me
into a headlock and pulls my hair
until we're both out of breath
and we walk to the shore together
our arms around one another
and it says to me,
'You're made of tough stuff, man –
you're made of tough stuff.'

Gina Moxley

from THE CRUMB TRAIL

HANSEL: We're quite a way from the car.

GRETEL: Surely that's the idea. Can't hear anything. No traffic. Nothing. Just that … fizz.

HANSEL: I don't like unattributable sounds. What is that hiss?

GRETEL: *Sssshhh*. Don't ruin it. It's the world breathing.

HANSEL: Nothing to lie on even. I should go back. There's that blanket in the car.

GRETEL: Yesterday a guy at work touched my wrist there and said: That skin is stolen from the underside of God's leaf.

HANSEL: What's that supposed to mean?

GRETEL: I'm not sure exactly. English isn't his first language.

HANSEL: Or horticulture his field. How could we not have remembered to bring water?

GRETEL: Well, I thought it was a beautiful image.

HANSEL: He was probably trying to say: Where are the tea bags kept?

GRETEL: Fuck you.

HANSEL: What was that noise?

GRETEL: I heard nothing.

HANSEL: Don't move.

GRETEL: You're hurting me.

HANSEL: I'm sure I heard …

GRETEL: Wildlife. What are you afraid of?

HANSEL: I'm not afraid. It's just very fucking foresty is all. Humous. Rotting vegetation. Rent boys. Paedos. Doggers. Axe murderers. Natives fucking. Goats bucking. Deer rutting. God's leaves.

GRETEL: You should get out more.

HANSEL: I feel freaked out without water.

GRETEL: What are you, a supermodel? Will you fucking relax. There's probably a stream.

HANSEL: Full of slurry or pesticides or …

GRETEL: Rapists! If only the world was so exciting. Please.

HANSEL: This place … makes me anxious. It's so claustrophobic.

GRETEL: Don't you have something you could take?

HANSEL: Not with me, no. What are you doing?

GRETEL: Playing. Having my delayed childhood. When I was a kid the other girls used to do this. Strip a chestnut leaf to the ribs. See. That's the fish bone. And put it on a stone, plate, like that. And put a few pebbles next to it. They were the peas. 'Look my husband ate all his dinner. Oh he said, "that was a lovely bit of fish".' And bustle bustle bustle they'd all clean up after their men, scraping plates, delighted with themselves. I bet they're all married now, doing it for real.

HANSEL: Sweet.

GRETEL: Once they roped me in to play the husband. I nearly killed this girl, Julia. I kept hitting her. Went totally ballistic. Screaming 'I told you, you stupid bitch, I don't like fish.' I terrorised her, mouthing the word fish at her in the street.

HANSEL: Yeah?

GRETEL: I loved it. Scaring the shit out of her. Fish. Fish. Fish.

HANSEL: Want a piece of chocolate?

GRETEL: Oh yes. Where did you get that?

HANSEL: Had it in my pocket.

GRETEL: I'd like to have children.

HANSEL: With me?

GRETEL: To have the future inside me. It's so sweet. I love this. Lying here, with nothing. Sing me something.

HANSEL: What? No. It's stupid. Being out here. Pretending.

GRETEL: Sing. Or …

HANSEL: Or?

GRETEL: Sing. Please. Just sing something, will you? It's one tiny thing I'm asking you to do for me.

HANSEL: Ok. Ok. I will. I can't remember all the words so maybe I'll hum it for you. (*He sings/hums a tiny bit of 'The Singing Bird').* I can't really remember it.

GRETEL: That's a funny little song. Where did you hear it?

HANSEL: My dad. Scouts.

GRETEL: You were in Scouts? What did you learn?

HANSEL: How to tie a few knots, to avoid men in shorts. Important things.

GRETEL: Come here, Hansel.

HANSEL: No. Let's go home. I hate this.

GRETEL: Did the brown owl do something bad to you?

HANSEL: That's Girl Guides.

GRETEL: Oh. Can you make fire by rubbing sticks?

HANSEL: No. I can't.

GRETEL: Wait until it gets bright.

HANSEL: No. I'm going now. This place gives me the creeps.

The pyros are detonated. They explode.

WITCH: Something is eating my house and home, all that I've worked for, my very foundations. Oh, what's that smell? Boy. My favourite. Now that'll make a dainty bite. This is my lucky day, my prince has come.

GRETEL: Hello.

WITCH: And he's gay.

HANSEL: I am not.

GRETEL: Well, at eight it's a bit early to say, conclusively.

HANSEL: Give me a break. I'm just afraid.

WITCH: Hello. What's your name little boy?

HANSEL: Hansel.

WITCH: Who led you here? No ill shall befall you. Oh, I like that triple el. Ill shall befall. Sorry I'm not used to talking.

GRETEL: We're lost.

WITCH: Who's that?

HANSEL: My sister. She thinks she's the boss.

GRETEL: Gretel.

WITCH: How unfortunate. Gretel ...

GRETEL: I like my name. It has ... dignity, gravitas, strength.

WITCH: I guess you must be around ten.

HANSEL: How can you tell?

WITCH: She has no smell. Doesn't register at all. Give her a year or two and then ... stinking, leaving a trail like a slug, heralding her virginity.

GRETEL: I've never been so insulted in all my life.

WITCH: The insults will come later. Along with your smell.

GRETEL: I can't wait. Look, can we use your phone? I'm out of credit on mine.

HANSEL: I'm not allowed one. Radiation.

GRETEL: We need to ring our parents. Please. Well, our mother and him.

HANSEL: Arthur.

GRETEL: Well, our mother and him, Arthur. Well our mother and ...

HANSEL: Arthur. They lost us when they went to chop wood.

WITCH: Have you come across metaphors at school?

GRETEL: Eh ... your phone ... can we use it?

HANSEL: I don't think so. Not yet.

WITCH: I can't help you, there's no signal here. I'm operating off grid, relying on the kindness of the wilderness and the occasional stranger. I haven't figured how to manufacture a substitute for company yet, though there have been several trials. They were no use, so I ate them. Oh relax; I'd forgotten children can be so earnest, Fuck's sake. The upside is you can do whatever you like because nobody knows about this place. Yes, you're lost now all right, utterly astray.

Helena Mulkerns

YOU THINK YOU'RE SMART

They were always fighting, but the row that did it this time was when the news came on the radio that a girl called Tess Lavin down the country had had a baby in a grotto and died. And the baby died too. She was fourteen – younger than Ria, even. Nobody knew she was pregnant until they found her there in the morning, right under the statue of the Virgin Mary.

The row was at the tea table, the worst one in a long while. Dad started ranting that it was a disgrace. Usually Mammy shut up and said nothing, not to give him an excuse, like. But she seemed upset about this girl.

'Little slut,' Dad said. 'Deserves what she got. Young ones these days – do they not listen to the nuns any more?'

'Tiarnan! The child died screaming in a field in the middle of the night – in a *field* – with no one to help her. She was afraid to go to the nuns!'

'Well, if either of these two came home in that state, they'd want to be afraid as well.'

'You'd have them die screaming in a field, is it?'

'Look,' Dad said. 'Don't get me started.'

But of course, he did get started. Slow at first, building up to scary. Ria was afraid he was going to have a go at Mammy again, except that he hadn't been across the way yet. Instead he smashed his steak knife down into his plate so hard that it split right in two, and the blood from the meat went running across the white formica table like a warning. Mammy screamed 'Jesus!' and Fiachra and Tom started to giggle so Susan dragged them away upstairs. This was Ria's cue to go into the front room to watch telly.

Susan always took the twins up to the back bedroom and read them stories, as if they couldn't still hear the roaring in the kitchen. And if Susan was the little mammy, then Ria stayed downstairs to make sure he didn't damage the real one. She used to think she would just kill him one day, but he was so much bigger than her, and she was afraid if she tried and didn't manage it, that he'd turn around and just kill her instead, or put Mammy in the hospital again.

Once, she went into a pharmacy in the city centre and asked them what was the fastest way to kill rats. Would it be arsenic, maybe. But all the aul dear had was this stuff that came with big signs you were supposed to put up around your garden saying 'poison'. Feck all good that'd do. Eventually she worked out that threatening him with the guards was fairly effective. Except when he had drink on him – then his ire turned on her: *little bitch, you think you're smart.*

After Da had stormed off to the pub, Ria found herself helping Mammy pack the big battered suitcase that went once a year to Benidorm. They were all off to Nana's again, for jayzus sake.

'I didn't marry *him*, Maria! I married a different man ...'

'Yeah,' Ria mumbled. She didn't know what to say. Susan was the one who could always talk to Mammy, not her. Ria was barely listening, anyway. She was thinking it was time, maybe, to act on her plan. Not maybe – definitely. It was what she'd wanted to do for years, but so far she'd never had the chance.

When the taxi arrived, there was another scene. Ria refused to leave. 'Em. Somebody has to stay to take care of Dad ...'

Mammy exploded. 'You ungrateful little cow!' she shrieked. 'After all the times I've stood up for you! Well, you can stay here and do what you bloody want. On your own head be it.'

The twins started to cry and Susan looked at her as if she'd lost it, but Ria just stood in the porch, feeling like shite. After she closed the door, she ran up to her room. The evening sailing was at half eight. She packed her rucksack, took her money out of the tea caddy under her bed and put on some make-up, stomach churning like a spin dryer. It hardly seemed like an hour and a half since the six o'clock news. She sat on her bed for a minute to catch her breath. After two years of scheming, of saving up working at the shop, this was it. Time to go. She had followed the packing list she kept folded up in the tea caddy, even remembering to put in her inhaler and her *Purple Rain* cassette. As an afterthought, she took Fiachra's stick man drawing of Charlie Haughey down off the wall near her bed, stuffed it in as well.

There was a crash downstairs then, as Dad came in the front door and it slammed back against the hall table. Ria jumped, grabbed her bag and waited until she heard him stagger upstairs and into the loo. Jesus – the actual sound of him back in the house drunk made her stomach heave. She slung the rucksack onto her back, took her bag, glanced at the room and went down the stairs as quietly as she could.

Outside, she hurried down to the main road, running the last twenty yards as she spotted a Number 8 in the distance. She had her student card. That should do for ID. One change at Holyhead; train to Euston Station by morning. As she held her hand out for the bus, she started laughing. She was actually doing this. She was going to London.

On the boat there was a telly in the bar, and the news was going on about that girl in the grotto. Poor Tess Lavin, who'd been afraid of the nuns. She'd probably been afraid of her dad, too, God love her. The volume was up really high, and the entire bar watched as a priest and a social worker were interviewed about the scandal. The archbishop would make no comment, but there were some choice opinions from politicians, the ones Mammy called 'pigs in suits'.

'Them bastards,' said a woman beside her with an English accent. 'What would they know?'

Then a severe-looking woman with short hair was on the screen, talking to a reporter. 'She's a tragic symbol of the oppression of women in this country. All the more tragic because of her absolute innocence.'

Ria wondered if Mammy and Susan were watching it in Nana's.

'Who's that bitch?' barked one of the men sitting at the bar.

'She's the one started up a half-way house for battered wives,' said the barman.

'Jayzus,' snorted the drinker. 'If she was my wife I'd bat'ther her ...'

Laughter echoed down the pints. A lump rose in Ria's throat. She took a drink of her Harp to get rid of it. What did she care – she was leaving. She took a cigarette out of the packet on the table in front of her, trying to look the eighteen that she'd have to be by the time she got to London.

It wasn't that hard.

Val Mulkerns

THE NAMING OF AN IRISH CLASSIC

I first found my way to Jimmy Plunkett's house on Richmond Hill in Rathmines on a warm summer's evening. I had forgotten the number of the house, but as I walked along the road I was led to the right door by what I guessed was a Mozart trio that came through the open windows across the garden hedges to where I stood listening. That was Valerie playing the piano and probably John Beckett on the violin. And who but Jimmy himself on the viola?

It was magic, that summer's evening more than 60 years ago, and I remember thinking at the time that Mozart must have tried his new trio out on friends before presenting it to his patron. However it wasn't music we talked about that evening but the long novel we'd heard so much about – it was almost finished, Jimmy told us, but he couldn't make up his mind about the title. After all these years I've forgotten the three he tried out on us, but I do remember what he said when I suggested *Strumpet City*.

'Do you want to have the thing banned on me, Val, for the title alone?'

This caused fits of laughter but you must remember these were the bad old days of the Censorship of Publications Act, when virtually every Irish writer worth his or her salt had been banned, together with Graham Greene, Aldous Huxley, and many others from across the channel. I had recently read *All For Hecuba*, by Micheál Mac Liammóir, in which he had quoted that whole marvellous passage from *The Old Lady Says 'No!'* by Denis Johnston. Since I'd also reviewed a revival of the play for *The Bell*, it was quite easy to remember:

Strumpet City in the sunset
Suckling the bastard brats of Scot, of Englishry, and Huguenot

Brave sons breaking from the womb
Wild sons fleeing from their mother
Wistful city of savage dreamers
So old, so sick with memories
Old mother
Some they say are damned
But you I think one day shall walk the streets of Paradise
Head high and unashamed.

The talk moved on and Valerie went away to make coffee, and I can't remember any other reference that evening to the new novel for which the right title hadn't yet been decided. However, many years afterwards the postman brought a parcel to my door, which contained a superb new novel for review, called *Strumpet City*.

And Jimmy made no reference to the matter ever again, nor did I – until this evening as I write, half a lifetime after Jimmy's by then legendary big book became an international bestseller, and 14 years after the death of my dear friend himself.

Pete Mullineaux

CHANGING DUBLIN

When yellow hats, hard and shiny – like some
strange summer flower – pop up all over town,
I slip inside a bookshop for solitude:
rail against the march of time – slow lament of
inch by inch, flinch by flinch; grating metal,
splintering block, kerbs and walkways
re-aligned like nouns and verbs of a language
under siege.

Within the cooling pages, fluttering like a fan
I flip through text and images … transported
now to Stephen's Green – an instant leap,
not the surface fix: a different matrix
in the never-mind. And perhaps some genius
will find a way of mimicking this page to
page with stage to stage –
not green to red, but Green to green
through College Green and on and on
into Phoenix scene where the only links are
cycle lanes, daisy chains; golden, soft-headed
buttercups.

E.R. Murray

Storm Witch

On the hill, home stands like a warden watching Jake's every move. Inside the barn, five pokes of light stream through holes in the roof. Five spotlights. Jake ties several knots, secures the penultimate rope from roof beam to ground, readying the gnarly structure for the imminent onslaught. Foolish to worry about a collapsing building, he thinks, especially when there are no longer cattle to care for.

Jake and Thomas tried to take over after their father vanished; the disappearance seared in Jake's mind, still trying to comprehend what he'd witnessed. Ma watching from the hill, hair wild in the wind and cigarette tip glowing, though she still pretends otherwise. The two young brothers had tilled the land, sectioned the fields, moved the cattle, applied tinctures and checked for mites. It had almost seemed possible, their mother's dream of continuing on.

Jake was the first to admit defeat. An act of betrayal Ma refuses to forgive. After they sold the animals, the crops failed. The spirits are angry, Ma warned. She was proud of the land, a remnant of her family's prosperity. So despite the danger, it was Jake's penance to protect the barn from harm.

Three pokes of light now. Then two. Something crawls across Jake's heart; what, he cannot tell. But it is darker than the sky and something to fear.

The storm arrives quick and furious. The heavy purple clouds look close and ripe enough to pluck. Thomas watches for his brother.

His father had always hated the land. Claimed bad spirits lurked. Ancestral witches. Ghouls. Tried to make Ma move just before he disappeared – his superstition deepening as his marriage grew apart. Looking over his shoulder. Always. Thomas felt it too.

In the distant field, rain pelts the rounded barn, fields where maize and barley should stand. Its cold grey mass, gargantuan and eager, races towards Thomas.

'There's no sign yet, Ma,' he says, turning.

He is grateful for the power cut. Candlelight softens his mother's face as the red tip of her cigarette rises and falls with mechanical precision.

'The devil take him,' says Ma. 'For the worry he causes.'

A blanket of white, then violet, illuminates the sky and his mother's facial creases. Her cold eyes toughened by hardship. Failures all: husband, cattle, crops, and now sons. Nothing to show for a lifetime but bitter disappointments and whispered curses.

Twelve seconds pass before thunder rumbles. Twelve miles from harm, but Thomas knows lightning can strike from ten miles away and it's creeping closer.

'Shall I go help?'

'The storm will pass before you make it. You're as useless as your father. Both of you.'

Her words scald and he imagines her dragged into the storm. Sucked away – just like Jake's bedtime stories about their father. Tales meant to soothe but bringing terrors in the night.

The pokes of light disappear, rainwater in their place. Jake squints out at the icy deluge, counts the seconds between lightning and thunder. Only four. He scales the ladder, fingers slippery on the wet rope as he ties. The house is in darkness on the hill but he senses Ma watching.

A storm was raging too when their father disappeared; dead crows had fallen from the sky and he was different that day. Haunted. Pausing in the middle field, he had waved. Then lightning. Then nothing. Just his crumpled and sodden red coat on the ground. When Jake screamed for Ma's help, she discarded her cigarette and calmly returned to the house. Ever since she was changed. Like she had forgotten how to exhale.

A thump sounds as a dead crow lands on the roof, blood fringing its beak. He shudders. There's movement in the field: a figure in red. Eyes playing tricks in the half-light, he thinks. Yet Jake climbs down and retreats into the barn, shaking.

This time, two seconds pass between the flash and thunder. Rain batters the roof tiles and rattles the window, smearing Thomas's view. In the distance, a dot of red. His father's coat that Jake has taken to wearing.

'He's coming.'

'About time.'

Thomas hears the smile on her lips. The red dot grows closer. Behind it, a shadow rises, dark and wayward, a gathering of dust and wind and crows.

'It's getting really bad out there.'

'Stay where you are.'

Ma sighs smoke plumes into the air. His eyes fixed on the storm, Thomas presses his hand to the window, the coolness of the glass offering little comfort.

Jake observes the storm through a roof hole. The bruise of sky. The black feeling loops his heart and squeezes. He brushes straw from his knees, a memory rushing in of his father doing the same. Reaching for his coat, he realises it has gone. Outside, the figure is wearing it.

He chases the thief, calling with each step. Rage builds like wind and fire and earth as he catches up, grabbing the figure's shoulder and spinning it round.

There's a flock of crows where a face should be, his mother's laughter in the wind. Jake glances at the house, sees Ma looming behind his brother, her cigarette a glowing pinprick. He tries to call out as lightning strikes. Feels his flesh scorch as his voice turns to ash.

The rattle of thunder is the loudest Thomas has ever heard. At the same time, lightning. It makes the walls rumble and his heart too. He smells burning flesh and thinks of Jake's bedtime stories. Feeling his mother's breath on his neck, he turns to face her. She grinds her cigarette into her palm. She is smiling.

Back in the field, Jake has gone. Only a red crumpled coat and a heap of dead crows left behind. The storm has changed course.

'What do you see?' asks Ma.

Thomas shakes his head. Seals his lips tight. On the windowpane, the greasy imprint of a wide-open hand, waving goodbye.

odges Figgis o.

Completion of ambitious expansion programme

Irish Independent, 4 December 1973

Gerry Murphy

CANNIBAL
for Seán

The first time
I tasted human flesh,
I was ten years old.
It happened during an argument
with my twelve-year-old brother
in which he dismissed
my beloved Beatles,
as overblown, overplayed
and strictly for cretins.
I lost the plot,
fastened onto him
and took a sizeable chunk
of flesh from his shoulder,
a piece of which
(probably gristle)
got stuck in my teeth.
Howling and gnashing ensued
until my mother intervened.
She was so shocked
at what I had done,
she clean forgot to beat me
and sent me straight to bed
without my supper.
But hey, I had already eaten.

Dairena Ní Chinnéide

AG SNÁMH SA CHUAN CAOL

Craiceann na báistí
ar leicne na fuinneoige
poll sa lá
ceilte cois tine
mar a ndathaíonn
rúnta d'aigne na lasracha
dóite le machnamh
cliathánach ar nós
taobh sléibhe sa cheo
cos nocht mar atá do choinsias
ar urlár gainimhe
mian ionat meilt isteach sa taoide
tonn fhuar ar nós oighearshruth
do chois thar thairseach
bhun na spéire.

Caitríona Ní Chléirchín

IARSMALANN NA GCUMANN BRISTE, SAGRÁB

In iarsmalann na gcumann briste,
tá tua
lenár scrios leannán
troscán uilig leannáin eile
nuair a d'fhág sí í
le himeacht ar saoire
le bean eile

Tá dornasc bándearg
agus clúmhach ann
a d'iarr leannán
ar a iarleannán
a chur air

Tá brógaí *stiletto*
a líoraigh grá geal
dá chéile
is *dildo* dubh ó phósadh
nár éirigh leis

Tá iarann ann
lenár iarnáil bean a gúna bainise
an t-aon iarsma
a fhanann den nasc

Tá gloine formhéadúcháin
a d'fhág bean mar fhéirín
ag a fear a thréig í
leis an dóigh
ar bhraith sí 'beag' ina theannta
a mhíniú dó

Tá cárta poist
eochair
is buidéal fíona
fíon dearg a bhí le hól
le chéile ag leannáin
nuair a d'fhág siad beirt a gcéilí,
fíon nár óladh riamh

In iarsmalann na gcumann briste
tá na mílte mílte
iarsmaí ar an ghrá
tá na mílte
cuimhní

published by Hodges, Smith and Foster in 1868

A CHARGE

DELIVERED

TO THE CLERGY OF THE
UNITED DIOCESES

OF

DUBLIN AND GLANDELAGH, AND KILDARE

AND, WITH SOME ALTERATIONS,

TO THE CLERGY

OF

THE PROVINCES OF DUBLIN AND CASHEL,

AT THE

TRIENNIAL VISITATION, SEPTEMBER, 1868.

BY

RICHARD CHENEVIX,
ARCHBISHOP OF DUBLIN, BISHOP OF GLANDELAGH AND KILDARE,
PRIMATE OF IRELAND, AND METROPOLITAN.

Dublin:
HODGES, SMITH AND FOSTER,
PUBLISHERS TO THE UNIVERSITY.
London and Cambridge:
MACMILLAN AND CO.
1868.

Price Two Shillings.

Eiléan Ní Chuilleanáin

MONSTERS

Now that there's nothing I don't understand,
why do they come to me with their informations?
They come in my dreams with their highlighting pens,
they tell me the roman numerals
on the shelf-end panels in the cathedral library
have all been regilded, someone has worked
with agate and crows' feathers to raise
gold flourishes and leaf script capitals. Show us,
they ask, the book that opens like a curtain;
and I tell them about the day I met
Ovid in the street, and he passed me
without a greeting.
                                        He had just thought
of the words that made the shrouds and tackling
swell with small buds, then looping stems,
then five-pointed leaves of ivy
catching, clutching the oars.

When I read it again myself I can see the oarsmen
frozen at their work, the sleepy drunk youngster
they were planning to sell, that wept
when they tied his hands, all of a sudden in charge,
his forehead ornate with grapes –
he is balanced on delicate sandals,
watching how they change, their spines
curve, they dance in the waves, each man
a monster to his neighbour.

Nuala Ní Dhomhnaill

CEAPACH CHLOCH
baile i gCorca Dhuibhne a chuaigh ar lár i rith an Ghorta Mhóir

N'fheadar ar chuimhníodar riamh,
ins na ceithre bliana nó mar sin
a bhí ceapaithe dóibh ar an saol seo,
ins na háiteanna aduaine
inar scaipeadh iad, –
áiteanna ar nós Lána Drury i Londain
nó Ceantar na gCúig Pointí i Nua-Eabhrac –

n'fheadar ar chuimhíodar riamh
ar an radharc siar ó thuaidh
ar Chnoc Bhréanainn is ar Srón Bhroin
mar a dtéann an cnoc i bhfarraige.

An radharc siar ó thuaidh ó Cheapach Chloch,
– baile nár fágadh dhá chloch os cionn cloiche dó
ná oiread fiú is cloch ar chloch.

Éilís Ní Dhuibhne

MEDIEVAL NEWSTALK

Recently, unpacking the boxes containing my late husband's wide ranging library, I came across a book I hadn't thought about since my days as a student of Medieval Studies in UCD – namely the *Heptameron* of Marguerite of Navarre. We didn't read this in college although it was often referred to. I suspect it was not read because its contents were too racy for the 1970s syllabus.

Margaruite of Navarre was born in 1492 – her mother, Louise, was fifteen years old, and had been married at the age of eleven to Charles, Count of Angeleme. Marguerite herself married twice, the second time to Henry of Navarre. Her brother became king of France. In short, she moved in the best circles. But the most interesting thing about her is that she was a writer, of poetry and fiction.

The *Heptameron* belongs to the same genre as Boccaccio's *Decameron*, which inspired it, or Chaucer's *Canterbury Tales*. It is a collection of stories told by a a group of people who are forced together for a period, and try to amuse themselves. Marguerite's people are stuck because of severe flooding in the Pyrenees, where they are on holiday in September at a spa, Cauterets (near Lourdes). The rivers swell, a bridge breaks, and they can't get home until it is repaired. Someone suggests that they could pass the time in reading the Bible. One of the men thinks he could put in the time happily having sex with his wife, Parlamente. But she points out they need group entertainment, and, although of course nothing would be more fun than scripture reading, suggests that they tell stories. She stipulates that these stories must be true.

So, no orgies, but the stories are mainly about love and sex. Adultery is a common theme. By way of compensation for the titillating contents the narrators adopt a high moral tone, disapproving of the shenanigans they describe. And, although several of the storytellers are women, their tales are generally highly misogynistic.

One story reminded me of the recent controversy about the radio comments suggesting that women can be partly to blame for rape.

Novel 62, on the Seventh Day, is about a beautiful woman who is married to an older man. One of their neighbours falls in love with her. He woos her over some years but she is uninterested and rejects him. So, wild with desire, he decides to take her by force. His chance comes when the husband goes away for a few weeks. When the ladies in waiting are off guard, he breaks into the princess's room. She is asleep. He gets into her bed, in his hurry neglecting to take off his boots and spurs. When she wakes up she is terrified. But he warns her if she screams he will tell her husband and everyone else that she invited him to her bed, so she had better shut up. To this she agrees – apparently her word will be no match for his. He has his pleasure with her. He hears the maids approaching the room and jumps out of bed. But one of his spurs catches in the quilt and pulls it off. He gets away, but the woman is revealed, stark naked, as the maids come into the room.

The story is offered as a comic tale, curiously enough, and like all the stories in the collection it is followed by a spirited discussion among the listeners, a sort of après-match debate. Some are on the woman's side and see her as an innocent victim. But the more pious insist that in succumbing to the man who jumped into her bed and raped her she was to blame. Saying 'no' wasn't enough. 'Think you that a woman can give quittance of her virtue and let it go, when she as two or three times refused? If this were so, many a slut would be esteemed an honest woman,' says Parlamente – the mistress of ceremonies, the chief presenter of the *Heptameron*, one might say.

September, floods, disruption of travel plans, and blaming the woman? Much has changed since the fifteenth century, but sometimes *c'est la même chose, n'est pas?*

published by Allen Figgis in 1973

OPERA
IN DUBLIN
1705~1797

THE SOCIAL
SCENE
T.J.Walsh

ALLEN FIGGIS DUBLIN 1973

Eithne Ní Ghallchobhair

ó GAOL

Ní raibh aon dá thráth a ghéill an mháthair úr don chodladh nár mhúscail an tachrán í lena ghártha géibheannacha. Chaoin sé, scread sé agus scaoil sé amach a racht. Ní raibh na seacht bpunta féin ann ach bhainfeadh a ghlór an díon den tigh. Nuair a chnagfadh taom an aighnis go trom é d'fhosclódh sé a bhéal, theannfadh sé a ghialla agus tharraingeodh sé achan anáil mar a bheadh sí ina hanáil dheireanach dhomhanda aige. Bhí a mháthair cloíte, bhí sí tinn. Bhí súile s'aici nimhneach ag an tsíorchaoineadh, frithir ag an easpa codlata. Cúig lá agus cúig oíche gan néal suain faighte aici: bhí an mháthair bhocht ag feo, ag meath, ag cliseadh. Dá dtiocfadh léi néal maith codlata a fháil shíl an mháthair go mb'fhéidir go dtiocfadh sí slán. Luigh sí ina leabaidh léi féin sa dorchadas agus bhog sí léi ó thaobh go taobh: casadh tuathal, casadh deiseal, rothlú anonn agus anall. Bhí corp s'aici craplaithe ó smior go smúsach. Bhí sí stiallta, stróicthe, sceanta, scríobtha idir réamhbhreith, bhreith agus iarbhreith. Bhí an mháthair i ngéarphian: pian cholainne, pian intinne, ach ba sheacht measa i bhfad an brón.

Bhí an mháthair ag iarraidh éalú ó dhochtachas an mháithreachais. Ní raibh éalú ar bith i ndán di. Thréig neart na mná seolta go luath í. Ní thiocfadh léi díriú ar neach ar bith beo. Ní thiocfadh léi an tsuim a mhúscailt inti féin a thuilleadh chun amharc ar chlár nó leabhar a léamh. Ní thiocfadh léi smaointeamh a choinneáil ina ceann. D'airigh sí féin gur i gcarcair a bhí sí, i gcarcair ina corp agus i gcarcair ina ceann agus níor aithin sí ceachtar acu a thuilleadh. Bhronnfadh an mháthair a beocht ar an mharbh anois agus deis aici. Bhí ball bán ag teacht ar an lá. Lá eile roimpi. Lá eile. Ní raibh ach an t-aon achainí amháin as a béal: saoraigh mé ón daoirse seo ina bhfuil mé.

Bhí sé ag sárú ar an mháthair a leanbh a chothú. Bhí a cíocha ataithe agus trom. Bhí a heití briste, brúite, bolgtha, an craiceann thart orthu breactha le fuil. Ní raibh an tachrán ag glacadh le bainne na máthara agus bhris sin a croí. Bhí sí i ndiaidh achan alt a scríobhadh ariamh faoin nasc idir máthair agus a leanbh a léamh. D'éist sí leis na podchraoltaí, d'amharc sí ar na físeáin. Anois bhí a leanbh féin á diúltú. Thriail an mháthair arís agus arís eile a leanbh a mhealladh chun cíche ach ní raibh gar ar bith ann óir shocraigh seisean gan diúl. In ardealaín an mháithreachais bhí ag teip uirthi. Shil deora na máthara óna súile agus thit siad ar an adhairt faoina ceann. Má thug deor ón tsúil faoiseamh d'aon chréatúr ariamh chan faoiseamh ar bith a fuair an mháthair. Chaoin sí.

Scread an tachrán sa chliabhán ag bun leabaidh a mháthara. Le méid an tormáin músclaíodh an mháthair. Ní raibh sí ach i ndiaidh a cuid súl a dhruidim. D'fhoscail sí iad. Bhí sí folamh. Bhí sí fuar. Líon an tormán an seomra. Caoineadh truacánta, caoineadh truamhéalach, caoineadh taibhsiúil tachráin. A leithéid de ghárthach níor mhothaigh an mháthair ariamh. Ba mhór di a bheith bodhar, chomh bodhar le clár. Bhí intinn na máthara ar seachrán, a croí réabtha, a stuaim ar shiúl. Easpa codlata, easpa cuideachta, easpa cairdis is cothaithe. Bhrúigh sí a cairde agus a clann ar shiúl uaithi a fhad is a bhí sí ag iompar clainne. Rinne sí beag is fiú dá n-iarrachtaí tacaíocht a thabhairt di agus ar deireadh, nuair nach dtiocfadh leo dul chun cainte léi, d'imigh achan duine acu a bhealach féin. Níor bhain a dtréigint cleite den ábhar máthara an uair sin óir bhí sí ar lasadh, lán dóchais. B'fhoscadh croí an dóchas - múchadh bróin. Bhí an mháthair ag dréim leis an leanbh an oiread le haon bhean a mhair roimpi nó lena linn. Ní raibh ceol na hóige ariamh inti agus chreid sí dá mbeadh leanbh aici go mbainfeadh sé an cian di. Chreid sí dá mbeadh leanbh aici go líonfaí an bhearna ina saol. Chuaigh a corp i mbun a chomhráite lena croí chan a ceann agus thug sise cluas le héisteacht. Fuil agus feoil a hoidhreachta, bíodh sin aici. Bhí sí líonta lán d'aigeantacht roimhe. Bhí sí fágtha ar an trá fholamh gan chuideachta, gan chuidiú ina dhiaidh. Mhéadaigh an scairtí, d'ardaigh an screadaíl. Bhí an tachrán ar an daoraí ina dhomhan úr féin. Bhrúigh an mháthair uaithi na héadaí leapa agus leag sí a cosa fúithi ar an urlár.

Dá luaithe agus a sheas an mháthair, chrom sí. Bhí sí réabtha ag piantaí an chothaithe – meáchan na gcíoch á tarraingt anuas, an phian ag géarú achan bhomaite. Ní raibh sa mháthair a thuilleadh ach blaosc de chorpán mná. Bhí sí ar bhealach a bheith stiúgtha leis an ocras agus bhí sí spalptha leis an tart. Bhí an bhreith agus ar tháinig ina diaidh ag cur go cruaidh uirthi. Bhí an mháthair slogtha siar ag dorchadas na hiarbhreithe agus ní raibh a fhios aici cad é an chearn ar cheart di a haghaidh a thabhairt uirthi. Sheas an mháthair cromtha ar thaobh na leapa agus bheir sí greim ar dhá thaobh a hadhairte. Thóg sí an adhairt ón leabaidh agus leag sí a cloigeann isteach inti. Mhothaigh sí anáil s'aici ag séideadh fríd a gaosán. Bhí an codladh ag teacht uirthi agus í ina seasamh, ina seasamh idir dhá cheann na meá. Bhéarfadh an mháthair conradh ach an tsíorscreadaíl a mhaolú. Ba mhór leis an mháthair an tachrán a shú ar ais ina corp, na naoi mí agus na sé lá a mhairstean droim ar ais. Bhronnfadh sí saol agus síol ar an chéad bhean a chasfaí uirthi. Bhronnfadh sí a torthúlacht ar choimhthíoch dhubh an bhealaigh mhóir agus mhairfeadh sí féin ar an uaigneas ... sa chiúnas. Mhair an caoineadh. D'airigh an mháthair go raibh sí faoi ionsaí, go raibh sí beo i bpáirc an áir.

Colette Ní Ghallchóir

Mise Éire

Ní maith liomsa,
Boladh na gcoinneal
Ná an lasóg.
Ní maith liomsa,
Dul isteach
I dteach na gcoinneal
Áit na péine
Áit an áir
Áit múchta an tsaoil,
Áit múchta na beatha
Áit na duáilce
Áit na péine
Pian na nathracha
Pian na máthracha
Na gasúraí crochta
Na gasúraí marbha
Na gasúraí báite
Na gasúraí caillte
Gasúraí na ndrugaí
Gasúraí na dí
Iadsan á d'fhág a saol,
Ar altóir na péine
Nó sa tseomra gléasta
A soineantacht crochta
Ar chrann na páise
Ligeadh saor Barabbas
Ach maraíodh iadsan.
Is ní thig liomsa dul isteach
Is fuath liom boladh na gcoinneal.

Colette Nic Aodha

TRÁ

Íomhá an mhuir doiléir
tríd an fhearthainn seasta is bonnán ceo,
pholl slogaide le taobh na haillte,

bóthar ag éirí níos casta
maraon leis an gCoireán Mara
a sheasann go maorga

i measc na gcloch duirlinge
scaipithe ar fud na háite,

brisim soithí ildaite.

published by Allen Figgis in 1963

Joan Newmann

FALLING IN GLENSTAL ABBEY

Prostrating myself
before the Virgin Mary
in the gloomy vestibule.

She may be smiling.
She may be smirking.
I cannot see her.
She may be indifferent.

I cannot move.
I grasp the corduroy trousers
with my hands
and
the corduroy trousers
of General Gordon Ferguson.
I trail myself
to my knees
moving my hands
one past the other
to his upper thigh.

They look down at me
as if I am surfacing
from the primordial soup –
that I will not speak their tongue.

It was the fault
of the walking stick
I bought in the Dominican Republic.
Its handle, the head of a beast,
came undone. Maybe voodoo.

It's the handle,
the handle of the stick, I say
as if the accident
might have happened to anyone.
It became unglued.
I repeat this, twice,
as if normal conversation
might resume.

Out in the light
'Are you all right?'
My left knee swelling
I keep saying about the stick and voodoo
but nowadays I wonder
if some power pushed me
slammed me on the ground
publicly punished me
for my lack of piety.

Kate Newmann

Peacock on the Stairs

I thought Byron had swum the Bosphorous
and from my room on the sixteenth floor
I was watching that misty shipping lane
separating Asia from Europe, thinking
separating the past from how we imagined it;
our selves from our exotic selves.

It was easier for him
than the short long weak strong
of his club-foot walk iambicking
across a room with his built-up shoe,
to lave his limbs through water,
letting it wash the scandalous scansions.

Easier – in the water – than loving
wholly his half-sister, and loving
abstractly his daughter – he'd already stipulated
stipulated whom she mustn't marry –
abstracted to a convent near Ravenna
where she died, aged five.

And easier – it was, in fact, the Hellespont …
he knew to head north
before the current swept him south,
like a capital J –
in the water his thoughts
the Armenian alphabet and its 38 letters;
… Lord Elgin had no right …
couldn't quite sweep him away.

Those days on dry biscuits and
dry white wine. His centre of gravity
skimmed like metre across the page before

he sank into friendships of the flesh,
those beloved men completing him
between their thighs.

Hiding his halt awkward
among the peacock and the guinea fowl on the stairs,
the goat, the monkey, the Egyptian crane,
in the house. He couldn't bear it
when Boatswain died in his arms
of rabies: his dog, his best, his Newfoundland dog.

When Shelley's reckless body
was recovered from the sea, a volume
of Keats bound in kid leather
drowned with him in his pocket,
they brought that reckless body
to cremate on Viareggia beach

and Byron swam – watching from the waves
the dank smoulder, the inept flames.
With the syncopated stare
of the sea's slapping distraction,
he watched smoke lingering

as if

his own memoir choking in the chimney
of his publisher's office a month
after his death in Messolonghi
(the fever the sepsis
and they drained the life
out of him with blood-letting
and more blood-letting)

as if

his own body lay unclaimed already,

refused by Westminster Abbey,
his marble statue in storage,
he swam deeper from that pyre
swam as if he knew
they wouldn't ever permit him
to come ashore.

published by Hodges Figgis in 1948

THE BRIGHT HILLSIDE

POEMS

BY

RHODA COGHILL

3 Herbert St.,
Dublin

May 8 1957.

10.5.57

(108 cops)

Dear Mr. Figgis,

Thank you for your letter of April 9th — Please excuse delay in replying. I have been thinking over the question of "amending" *The Bright Hillside*, & have decided not to do so. Will you please let me have 50 copies for use as presents, & retain the rest. The 6 copies were possibly faultily over put aside — or soiled only, which I returned to you as unusable.

Yours sincerely
Rhoda S. Coghill

S.E. Figgis Esq.,
Messrs. Hodges Figgis & Co. Ltd

Letter from Rhoda Coghill to Mr Figgis re her poetry collection.
Rhoda Coghill was the accompanist on Radio Éireann (1939–1969)
(Dublin City Public Libraries and Archive)

Liz Nugent

from SKIN DEEP

In ancient times, MacDermod the weaver was famous throughout the length and breadth of the country for the fine garments he could produce from even the roughest wool. But MacDermod had a scold for a wife. She was possessed of the longest red hair that swung down to her ankles, and it was her pride and joy. She would sit outside her cottage on a stool, combing it through with hard fish bones, to be admired by the passing islanders. But she was lazy, it was said, and if her children ran wild and hungry like stray dogs, and brought trouble to the harbour where they'd be hopping boats and pegging stones at fishermen, she would blame her husband and roar at him in the street, bringing shame upon the man.

MacDermod could not help but love her despite all her nagging but the neighbours got fed up of it and one day they held her down and hacked her hair off with knives. Then they ordered MacDermod to weave a sheet from her hair that would sit on the harbour wall, as a warning to all the wives. Daddy always said that the red fronds that covered the wall was the woven hair of MacDermod's wife but I was old enough to know it was seaweed.

MacDermod and his wife and children rarely ventured outside their cottage after that day, except for to collect necessary items for their household. They spoke little, and kept their heads down when at the market.

The wife's hair grew back faster than anyone had imagined possible. When one year had passed her flame-coloured mane reached her knees and she began to look up again, and to hold her head straight and look the world in the eye. But the islanders did not like her arrogance and it was said that the nagging had begun again, that children passing had heard it through the thick walls of the cottage.

One day MacDermod's wife was caught in the act of badgering her husband as she came out of the cottage, complaining that he hadn't built the fire hot enough for her to bake bread. This time, her neighbours were merciless. They dragged her down to the harbour wall and hacked her hair off again, but this time, they forced her to eat it until she choked.

Daddy used to tell me this story while I was curled on his lap, but he'd be staring at Mammy while he told it. Daddy said if a man couldn't keep his woman in order, his neighbours would have to do it for him.

printed in 1809 for Gilbert and Hodges, Figgis etc

EVENINGS AT HOME;

CONSISTING OF

A VARIETY OF MISCELLANEOUS PIECES

FOR THE

INSTRUCTION,

AND

AMUSEMENT,

OF

YOUNG PERSONS:

IN ONE VOLUME.

BY J. AIKIN, M. D.

EIGHTH EDITION.

DUBLIN :

Printed by R. SMITH,

FOR MESSRS. GILBERT AND HODGES, B. DUGDALE, W. WATSON, M. KEENE, J. MARTIN, AND W. FIGGIS.

1809.

519

published by Allen Figgis in 1969

An exciting, authentic novel of Irish U.N. forces ambushed in the Congo at the height of the Katanga affair. This story of the army's first full-scale taste of foreign service is told with wit, sympathy and power.

riverrun

the sunburst
and the dove
Eamon Francis

Micheál Ó Conghaile

ó Sa Teach seo Anocht

Athnuachan. Athghríosadh. Athphósadh beagnach ... Na smiochóideacha a bhí sa ngríosach a bheoú is a fhadú arís ... Níor chreid mise riamh ann nó b'fhéidir gurbh amhlaidh nár theastaigh uaim. Ná an chaint a bhíodh againn air, cé gur lean muid leis. An gá le spás. Deis cheart cainte is machnaimh. Comhrá meáite a bheadh saor ó shíorbhrú an tsaoil. Briseadh lár seachtaine nó saoire athmhuintearais fiú molta ag lánúineacha athaontaithe eile ... an ceann fánach, a deirimse ... Athfhilleadh ar chuid de na hóstáin ar chaith muid deirí seachtainí iontu sul má phós muid. An clog a chur siar ar bhealach. Spiorad pléascach an ama sin a athghabháil, a athbhlaiseadh. An doras a fhágáil oscailte. Doirse nua a aimsiú b'fhéidir. An ghloine leathlán. Agus araile, agus araile.

Is nach féidir an ghloine a líonadh ar aon nós.

Nuair nach féidir aon chlog a chur siar. Nuair atá snáthaidí an chloig briste ar aon nós. Is cliste le fada. Leanbaí a cheapadh gur féidir tosú ag an tús arís. Ní bhíonn ann ach tús amháin. Mar nach féidir dhá thús a chur le aon rud. Cá bhfuil an tús go beacht dá dtiocfadh sé go dtí sin? Cé chomh fada siar is atá siar ann ...

Ligean don nóiméad órga a bhí ann a bheith agus fág mar sin é mar scéal. Úsáid d'fhuinneamh chun slacht éigin a chur ar an nóiméad atá in do thimpeall anois díreach más féidir agus beidh sí sin nó a scáth agat duit féin ar a laghad. Dá easpaí í, ní bheidh ina coinneal mhúchta nach bhfuil ach deatach liath scagach ag éirí as a buacais ... óir is iomaí craiceann a chuireann an duine di.

Agus níl bean eile i gceist. Faoi láthair. Gach seans go mbeidh amach anseo, ach níl faoi láthair. Agus sin mar is fearr liomsa é. Fágáil ar mhaithe le fágáil. Fágáil mar gurb in an rud ceart le déanamh ag an tráth seo. Go bhfágfainn ar aon nós, bean eile nó gan bean eile. Agus nuair nach bhfuil bean eile i gceist anois, beidh sí saor ó aon mhilleán nuair is ann di amach anseo. Ní bheidh a ladar sise mar neascóid ar an gcuid seo den scéal. Admhaím go raibh mná eile ann, bhí. Bhí fir eile ann chomh maith. Tá a fhios agamsa sin. Is tá a fhios aicise go bhfuil a fhios agamsa. Ach sin scéal eile is ní hin é mo ghnósa feasta. A comhairle féin. A chomhairle féin do Mhac Anna. Ach is cinnte nach bean eile an chloch is mó ar mo phaidrín faoi láthair. Cé go ndéanfadh an uair seo níos éasca is níos nádúrtha ar bhealach eile. Ar nós duine nach ndíolfadh a sheancharr gan carr nua a cheannach i dtosach.

Tuigeann Séamas mo chás mar is minic a labhair muid faoi. Agus beidh seomra agam ar iasacht ina theach an t-am seo amárach. Tá na heochracha amuigh sa gcarr. Faoin *dashboard*. Chomh fada agus atá sé uaim, a áitíonn sé. Tabhair do rogha duine ar ais ann agus déan do rogha rud chomh fada agus nach gcuireann tú isteach ná amach ormsa. Agus, dar ndóigh, ní chuirfidh mise isteach ortsa. Ar do shaolsa. Tuigeann Tadhg Taidhgín.

Íocfaidh mé cíos leis má shocraím fanacht ann thar dhá mhí nó trí má bhíonn gach rud ag dul i gceart. Óir is mór idir mo theach cónaithe anseo agus seomra leapan i dteach strainséarach. Tá aithne againn ar a chéile le blianta agus ní fheicim aon deacracht romham ina chomhluadar. Faoi aon díon. Feicim ár spás féin againn araon. Agus is féidir liom gach a dtabharfaidh mé liom ón teach seo a stóráil i seomra amháin go héasca, faoi láthair ar aon nós mar nach cnuasálaí mé. Níorbh ea riamh. Ligim le rudaí. Agus má chaillim rud nó má dhéanaim dearmad ar rud, bím ag súil go mbeidh sé de leas ar shaol duine éigin eile agus ní ceilte ar an saol seo ar fad. Nílim, dar ndóigh, ag déanamh aon chomparáid anois idir rud a chailleadh agus bean a chailleadh. Bean a fhágáil ba chirte dom a rá.

Tá Séamus é féin scartha óna bhean le fada. Agus é níos sásta ná riamh. Ach tá níos mó ná sin i gceist. Tá sé aerach anois, a deireann sé. Níor chóir dom an focal 'anois' a úsáid san abairt sin a dúirt sé nuair a d'inis sé i dtosach dom roinnt mhaith blianta ó shin. É aerach riamh ach nár thuig sé sin nó nár thug aghaidh air. Pósta i bhfad ró-óg mar go raibh a chomhghleacaithe ar fad ag pósadh ina maidhmeanna. Mar a bheadh ina choimhlint eatarthu. Scartha théis dhá bhliain nuair a bhí tuirseach den phósadh. An t-ádh dearg air nach raibh cúram clainne orthu. Gan tada a choinneodh le chéile iad. Iad saor ó ladhar an chasúir. Thuig sé go maith faoin am sin go raibh sé aerach mar go raibh tástáilte go maith ar an gcúlráid aige. Is ba mise, i ngan fhios dom féin, a chuir é féin is a chéad leannán ar chaith sé trí bliana leis in aithne dá chéile ... agus braitheann sé féin faoi chomaoin éigin agam dá bharr aineoinn gur trí dheargsheans a tharla sé ... Sraith leannán agus comrádaithe craicinn aige ó shin. Is iad a choinníonn lasracha ina shaol, a áitíonn sé. A bheith ag dul ó shaol go saol. Féach ar fhormhór na lánúineacha díreach atá ar d'aithne a d'áitíodh sé. Oscail do shúile, a Sheosaimh. Oscail. Féach chomh tuirseach is atá siad dá chéile. Chomh stálaithe is atá a saol. Chomh míshocair ina saol pearsanta is ag síorbhreathnú thar a gcuid ina mbrionglóidí. Ina mbrionglóidí amháin go minic, dar ndóigh. Chomh leadránach atá siad ina saol gnéis – ní hea, ach gan caidreamh gnéis ar bith ag a bhformhór ach cur i gcéill leanúnach. Rud amháin nó rud eile dá gcoinneáil lena chéile. Cuireann suas lena chéile lá i ndiaidh lae, mí i ndiaidh míosa, bliain i ndiaidh bliana nó go dtí nach mbíonn siad in ann tabhairt faoina mhalairt. Nó nach mbíonn sé de mhisneach acu tabhairt faoina mhalairt. Ní drochshaol ar bith é an saol aerach, a Sheosaimh, creid uaimse é. Ná saol an fhéileacáin, dá n-abraínn é. Ní chreidimse sa tseafóid sin níos mó gurb é nádúr an duine – bíodh sé díreach nó casta – a shaol iomlán a chaitheamh i bhfochair duine amháin eile go scarann an bás iad. Ní hé ach a mhalairt. Nílim ag rá go bhfuil tada mícheart leis má oibríonn amach ach, de réir mar a fheicim, is annamh a oibríonn. Agus dá dtabharfadh na daoine daonna cluas dá gcorp scaití, thuigfidís sin go maith. Thuigfidís a nádúr daonna féin níos fearr mar a thuigeann fir aeracha go minic. Fad atá beocht sa tine í a choinneáil coigilte. Má tá sí ar tí múchadh, bíodh. Ní bheadh murach gurb in é a nádúr. Thuas seal thíos seal. Rotha mór an tsaoil, mar a dúirt an té a dúirt. Foc is ea foc i ndeireadh báire agus chomh luath agus a chailleann fear spéis san aicsean sin lena pháirtí, tá leataobh de, nó sciar suntasach de, righin marbh. Tá. Díreach mar a bheadh théis stróc a fháil.

'Seosamh,' is í ag baint ceoil chomh grámhar as gach siolla den fhocal, ag leagan béime ar gach siolla is dá sealbhú go leochaileach di féin. Í dá rá ar bhealach nár chuala mé éinne eile dá rá riamh roimhe sin. Ná ó shin … 'Seosamh,' is í díreach théis filleadh ón leithreas … Gan aithne agam uirthi ach le dhá lá ag an gcomhdháil … Uair roimhe sin, mise in mo sheasamh leataobhach ach os a comhair ag an gcabhantar, ag iompú agus ag casadh ansin arís is arís eile ag súil le go dtabharfadh sí faoi deara an cruas a bhí leathcheilte istigh in mo threabhsar. Moilleadóireacht bheag eile ansin chun an tsinseáil cheart a chomhaireamh amach cent ar cent d'fhreastalaí foighneach an bheáir. Is an fuílleach a shíothlú síos i mbosca St Anthony a bhí faoi m'uillinn ansin. Fios maith agam go raibh sí ag breathnú. Ormsa. Agus níor ghá dúinn labhairt le chéile ina dhiaidh sin. Seosamh ná Sinéad a rá os ard ná os íseal ná i gcogar. Am amú. Ár dteangacha a bhí i mbéal a chéile ag labhairt go slupach ar ár son … ag dearbhú an chéad chéim eile dá chéile an oíche sin ar bhuaicphointe thar bhuaicphointí a bhí ann domsa. I gcompord sábháilte seomra glasáilte an óstáin. Níor thuig mé go dtí sin go bhféadfadh gach féith de mo chorp a bheith chomh beo breabhsach le fuil, go bhféadfadh corp duine eile an bhail is an chóir seo a chur orm. Go raibh mé féin is mo chorp uile ag géilleadh dá smacht, dá riail, go fonnmhar. Go coinsiasach. Le mo mhíle milliún beannacht …

Is ní ba dheireanaí san óstán bhí muid in ann an bháisteach a chloisteáil ag clagarnach taobh amuigh, ag raideadh go fórsúil i gcoinne phána na fuinneoige, rud a mhaisigh ár milseacht allasach tuilleadh. Agus ina dhiaidh sin arís braonacha móra ag titim den díon agus anuas ar leic na fuinneoige ar feadh tamaill fhada … nó gur mhothaigh muid na braillíní tais inár dtimpeall agus buille beag míchompordach ansin ag ár sruthanna allais féin a shil dár gcorp sa teocht …

D'imigh sin is tháinig seo … Dá fhaide dár chónaigh muid le chéile sea ba mhíchompordaí a bhí muid i gcomhluadar seasc a chéile ionas in imeacht ama go n-éiríodh muid fuar scaití nuair a bhíodh muid sa seomra céanna mura mbeadh ann ach an bheirt againn. Dá dtiocfadh Shane isteach sa seomra, shlánódh a theocht muid, más go sealadach féin é. B'eisean bun is barr an scéil.

Simon Ó Faoláin

THÉIS SOISCÉAL MHAITIÚ *LE PASOLINI A FHEISCINT*

Is dúirt an t-aingeal lena shúile grinne
An leanbh is a mháthair a bhailiú chun teite.

Ba mhaith an t-ábhar saighdiúra thú, a Sheosaimh,
Do lean ordú is sos ní thógais

Fiú fada a dhóthain chun aon rabhadh
A thabhairt do thuismitheoirí an bhaile

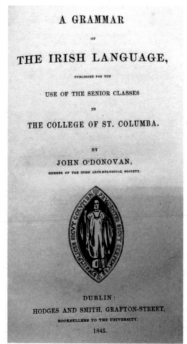

Irish language grammar book published by Hodges and Smith in 1845

Pól Ó Muirí

EARRÁIDÍ KLÓ

Thug sé Scríbhneoir air féin. Bhí a chroí istigh san fhocal scríofa. Thug sé grá do dhúch ar leathanach. Bhain sé pléisiúr as fearann bán an leathanaigh a mhaisiú le sraitheanna focal, as daoine a chur a chónaí i ndúichí nach raibh daoine iontu roimhe, as caint a chumadh nár chualathas roimhe, as focail a chur in ord agus in eagar nach bhfacthas roimhe. Shiúil sé cladach na cruthaitheachta agus thóg éadáil ó thonnta na samhlaíochta. Chreid sé sa scríbhneoireacht. Bhain sé sult as an scríbhneoireacht. Chleacht sé an scríbhneoireacht – más go ciotach féin é de réir lucht a chánta. Scríobh sé gach lá agus gach oíche agus bhí a ainm dílis féin le feiceáil ar a chuid scéalta, dánta agus léirmheasanna. Ghéill sé don litríocht agus chuir an litríocht a geimhleacha troma seasca thart air go dtí go ndearnadh giall gan dóchas de, sclábhaí gan saoirse, cime gan chiall. I gcillín na bhfocal a chónaigh sé de ló agus d'oíche.

Scríobh sé úrscéal mór amháin, úrscéal a bhí chomh tiubh le builín aráin agus chuir ar shiúl chuig na foilsitheoirí é. Chuir an foilsitheoir i gcló é agus sheol an Scríbhneoir roinnt cóipeanna ar aghaidh chuig daoine céimiúla san earnáil, ina measc, an tOllamh. Dá dtabharfadh an tOllamh aird ar an leabhar, b'fhéidir go léifeadh duine nó beirt é, a smaointigh an Scríbhneoir. Nó b'fhéidir dosaen nó b'fhéidir fiche duine?

Bhí bród ar an Scríbhneoir as an leabhar. Bhí sé i lár aonach na healaíne, ag cruthú as an úr. Flatley na bhfocal a bhí ann. Ní raibh an damhsa seo feicthe ag an lucht féachana riamh roimhe, an traidisiún lúbtha ag an tsamhlaíocht, an cor tobann pinn gan choinne, coiscéim chruthaitheach rince – a haon, dó, trí; a haon, dó, trí.

Sea, bhí a chuid féin déanta aige ar son an chultúir. Scríobh sé.

An tOllamh a chuir scairt air sa deireadh. 'Fuair mé do leabhar,' ar seisean.

'Ar thaitin sé leat?' a d'fhiafraigh an Scríbhneoir. Níor bhac sé le mionchaint a dhéanamh leis an Ollamh. Bhí an leabhar róthábhachtach le ham a chur amú ar dhea-bhéasa.

'Thaitin – cé gur trua liom na hearráidí cló.'

'Earráidí cló?' a dúirt an Scríbhneoir agus a chroí ag preabarnach. 'Earráidí cló? Earráidí cló? Cad é atá i gceist agat? Earráidí cló?'

'Tá sé cinn d'earráidí cló ann.'

'Tá 400,000 focal sa leabhar sin.'

'Mar sin féin, sé cinn d'earráidí cló.'

'Ach an téis a bhí agam. An fhealsúnacht? Na tuairimí? Cad é do bharúil faoi sin?'

'Sé cinn d'earráidí cló.'

'Na tagairtí do na fealsúna? Do na scríbhneoirí móra eile ar domhan? An nasc a rinne mé idir seanchultúir na hEorpa agus an cultúr comhaimseartha seo againne? Cad é do bharúil faoi sin? An dóigh ar scríobh mé ar na sean-Ghréagaigh, ar ...'

'Ááááá!' a scairt an tOllamh. 'Ááááá! Ááááá! Ááááá! Ááááá! Ááááá!'

Bhain an scairt preab as an Scríbhneoir. Shíl sé go raibh an bás ag an Ollamh: 'Ááááá! Ááááá! Ááááá! Ááááá! Ááááá! Ááááá! Ááááá! Ááááá! Ááááá! Ááááá! Ááááá! Ááááá! Ááááá! Ááááá! Ááááá!'

'A Ollaimh! A Ollaimh! An bhfuil tú i gceart? An bhfuil pian ort?'

'Seacht gcinn d'earráidí cló! Seacht gcinn d'earráidí cló! Seacht gcinn d'earráidí cló!'

'Cad é?' a dúirt an Scríbhneoir. 'Cad é a dúirt tú, a Ollaimh?'

'Seacht gcinn d'earráidí cló! Seacht gcinn d'earráidí cló! D'aimsigh mé botún eile! Botún eile! Botún eile!

"Greagaigh" atá anseo. Greagaigh! Gréagaigh a ba cheart bheith ann. *Gréagaigh*. Tá "é" ar iarraidh ann. Tá "é" ar iarraidh agat. Fan anois go bhfeice mé an bhfuil "é" ar iarraidh áit ar bith eile. Fan anois. Fan anois. Fan go bhfeice mé. Fan anois. Fan anois go bhfeice mé. Tá peann luaidhe anseo agam. Fan anois an dtig liom ceann eile a aimsiú. Fan anois. Hmmmm. Ní fheicim ceann ar bith eile faoi láthair. Seacht gcinn d'earráidí cló. Anois, cad é sin a dúirt tú faoi chúrsaí fealsúnachta? Ní fear mór fealsúnachta mé.'

Thost an Scríbhneoir. Tháinig tocht air. Tháinig deoir chun súile. Seacht gcinn d'earráidí cló. Seacht gcinn d'earráidí cló ina eipic. Bhí a úrscéal gan mhaith. Níorbh fhiú an braon dúigh é. Ní raibh sé ag damhsa os comhair an tslua. Bhí sé ina chnap truacánta rompu; bhí a chosa i ndiaidh tuisle a bhaint as agus bhí a spága anois sáinnithe ina thóin féin.

Rinne sé iarracht bheag é féin a chosaint: 'Is ag scríobh ar mo chonlán féin a bhím. Níl cuidiú ar bith le fáil agam. Éiríonn na súile tuirseach. Ní i gcónaí a fheicim na meancóga ...'

'Seacht gcinn d'earráidí cló.'

'Ní mórán é i gcomhthéacs an tsaothair ar fad.'

'Is leor é.'

'Seacht gcinn,' a dúirt an Scríbhneoir agus fios aige dá gcuirfeadh sé ceist ar an Ollamh go n-inseodh an tOllamh dó cá raibh siad uilig go léir.

'Sea. Seacht gcinn.'

'Ach tá na focail eile ceart go leor, an bhfuil?'

'Tá. Ceart go leor. Ach níl an saothar foirfe.'

'Go raibh maith agat,' a dúirt an Scríbhneoir agus an leabhar ina luaithreach aige.

Ba mhór an buille don Scríbhneoir go raibh earráidí cló sa leabhar. Thuig sé gur mhó aird a thabharfadh daoine anois ar na hearráidí ná mar a thabharfadh siad ar ábhar an scéil. Chuaigh sé faoi chónaí an oíche sin faoi chroí trom. Tromluí a tháinig air faoi earráidí cló. Bhí siad gach aon áit. Bhí earráidí cló le feiceáil ar bhosca na gcalóg arbhair, ar chinnlínte na nuachta, ar nuachtáin, ar ainmneacha scoile, ar chomharthaí bóthair, ar leacacha uaighe, ar cháipéisí oifigiúla, ar cháipéisí neamhoifigiúla, ar ailt nuachtáin, ar líne, as líne, faoi líne ...

Chlis sé as a chodladh agus an t-allas ag bárcadh leis. Bhí rún aige tabhairt faoi leabhar eile ach cad é mar a thiocfadh leis agus bagairt na n-earráidí cló i gcónaí ann? Ní thuigeann duine ar bith d'earráidí cló, don aigne dhall i láthair an fhocail mhílitrithe. B'fhéidir nár cheart dó an dara húrscéal a scríobh? Cad a dhéanfaidh muid feasta gan eipic, a d'fhiafraigh sé de féin.

Níor mhaith leis cur le líon na n-earráidí cló. I ndeireadh thiar thall, bhí a sáith fadhbanna féin ag an teanga gan eisean a bheith ag cur leo. Bhí an teanga bhocht ag titim as a chéile. Lobhar de theanga a bhí inti; bhí sí ar leathshúil agus ar leathchluais agus ar leathchois. Bhí píosaí craicinn ag titim dá cnámha gach uile lá agus bhí a cuid cuislí ris. Cá hiontas go mbeadh deacrachtaí ag an Scríbhneoir leis an Frankenteanga? Bhí sé ag iarraidh an teanga a fhuáil le chéile lena pheann bearnach féin.

Tháinig ciall chuige sa deireadh. Scríbhneoir a bhí ann. B'éigean dó scríobh. I gcillín na bhfocal a chónaigh sé. Shocraigh sé go scríobhfadh sé an dara húrscéal agus go mbeadh an dara leabhar foirfe, go mbeadh an dara leabhar gan locht, go mbeadh gach aon fhocal litrithe mar ba cheart ann, go mbeadh ciall le gach aon fhocal, go mbeadh gach aon bhriathar ag teacht le chéile, go mbeadh gaois agus dúchas ag siúl le chéile rann ar rann, go bhfíoródh sé an aisling a bhí ina anam istigh, nach mbeadh earráidí cló ann.

Liam Ó Muirthile

GILE NA GILE (*Being Beauteous*)

Gile na Gile i gcoinne sneachta an bhé mós ard.
Feadanna báis, timthriallta múchta ceolta
is í ag éirí, ar crith, ag pléascadh ina gósta
scarlóideach is na créachta dubha sna feolta

i gcolainn seo na hadhartha is í róbhreá. Doirchíonn
dathanna na beatha domhanda, eascraíonn is rinceann
mórthimpeall na haislinge á fíorú ar an ród romhainn.
Crithfhuachta ar tinneall, tormáil is riastradh aoibhinn

blasta na nithe seo uile faoi chrann na bhfeadanna
básmhara, na gceolta grágacha a stealltar ón domhan
i bhfad ar gcúl le máthair na scéimhe a dhruideann uainn,
a sheasann go hard. Ó! ár gcnámha faoi chraiceann colna
   nua an ghrá!

XXX

Ó an dreach ina luaithreach, an sciath armais ina ribí róin,
géaga na lámh smiota ina gcriostail is an chanóin
go gcaithfead mé féin a thuairteáil air trí chlibirt
na gcrann agus éadroime an aeir ar domhan ag imirt!

Mícheál Ó Ruairc

LEATH BEALAIGH

… agus
gan choinne
buaileann taom
obann
doilíosa thú
san ionad siopadóireachta
mar chóras aláraim
ag tuargaint id chloigeann
ag fógairt foghlaí
fánaigh
i lár na hoíche
leath bealaigh
idir an bréagfhuarán
ina gcaitheann leannáin
splanctha
boinn shochair
áidh agus ghrá
éagmaise
agus
O'Brien's Sandwich Bar
ina bhfuil faoiseamh
(dar leat)
ó d'anró
i ndán
duit i g*Cappuccino*
suite i d'aonar
ar stól ard
ag fuinneog
nach fuinneog í
ag éisteacht le ceol
nach gcloiseann tú
ag féachaint ar dhaoine
nach bhfeiceann tú

ag ól caife
nach mblaiseann tú
gafa ag cuimhní
nach mian leat
a choinneáil
i d'intinn
níos mó
agus ...

published by Allen Figgis in 1970

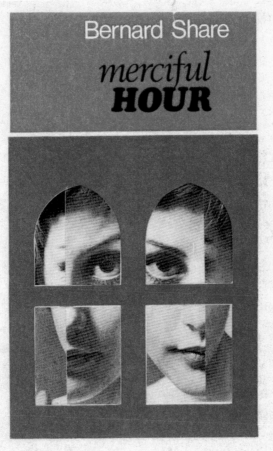

Cathal Ó Searcaigh

BLAKE

Ag gearán i dtaobh an fhile
dúirt bean an Bhlácaigh;
'Crothnaím comhluadar mo chéile,
is minic é i bhfad as
imithe leis go Parthas.'

Nárbh aoibhinn do
eisean a shiúil as an cheo,
a sháraigh na ballaí críche
is a shuigh é féin
sa tsíoraíocht bithbheo.

Is a thug arís, corruair,
blas den tsaol eile, tuar
na nIontas ar fud na hUile.
Is, a bhean Uí Bhlácaigh, bímis
buíoch as tíolacthaí an fhile.

Edna O'Brien

from ON THE BONE

Like a yew tree
You hovered over me,
You hemmed and hawed
You decided the drapes
And how much seasoning in the soup.
A motor ride
Between four and five
On a bit of London heath,
Famished heather
Home to tea
Silent as chapel
In Lent
Bandaged in gloom.
One Christmas you dropped
Cyanide into my sauerkraut
I lapped it up.
You see
I thought I was doing someone
Some good
By being so fervently unhappy

After you
There was Peter
And Paul
And James the Apostle
And Judas
Whose kisses were silver –
All thirty pieces of it.
For whom I would gladly
Loiter in that garden again,
Where the earth perennially short of rain

Says – 'Let's, let's have a massacre
Around here
For a change'.

published by Allen Figgis in 1973

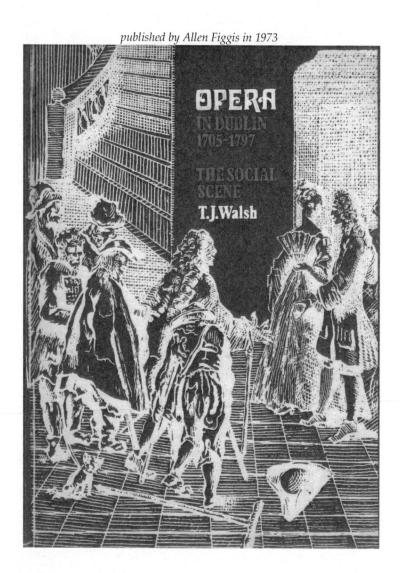

Jean O'Brien

Dear Doctor

Greetings, I am your first patient
and your silent teacher, only you
can make me speak, only you
can breach the rupture between
air and breath. Steady your hand.

Just because I remain cold and still
doesn't mean I don't need you
to make a clean break of it, a neat
cut, tie off my tongue, it has done
with reasoning and talking.

We will communicate through skin, bone,
hair, dried blood and my desiccated organs.
You will use your hands and eyes
and an array of tools. Take a hammer and break open
my chest cavity to get to the heart of things.

The glint of steel from the scalpel reflects
your troubled eyes. My skin is tougher now
than it ever was when I used it to rub up
against the world. You're going to need
a serried saw for my stubborn ribs and sternum.

I will share with you all I know, I am
your first patient. Through my liver, kidneys,
and battered heart you will learn, though not a word
passes between us. I am past hurt, death has no sting.
I have become your silent teacher. Make me sing.

Billy O'Callaghan

from BEGINISH

Towards the end of their first week the weather started to turn. Isabelle was down on the beach – enjoying the sun, as she did for a couple of hours on most afternoons – when she became aware of the shift: something subtle about the glow of the light, and a guttering to the slightest breeze that plucked small peaks into the ocean's surface. She wasn't afraid. Instead of hurrying back to their shelter, she stood for a long time down where the water rolled up onto the sand, feeling the electricity in the day and how it seemed to move against her in walls, not wind yet, not exactly that, but as if the air had gained new heft. Within an hour, the water had turned slow and thick, and she knew without ever having seen this before that the sea was set to roughen and that by the following morning, or maybe even the fall of night, the waves would be rolling in high. When eventually she climbed the path she saw Thomas over on the island's highest edge, also gazing westward. He'd felt the difference, too, he said, when she came to stand beside him, and was trying to read the signs, to make out what mattered and what didn't, because even though whatever was happening hardly bothered the surface of the latening day, and even though the sky remained clear, at least for now, there were more gulls than usual down among the rocks, the light hadn't quite the softness of previous evenings, and out in the water vague, crawling shadow-lines seemed to stripe the distance, as if something huge was rising from the depths.

Dusk was already upon them by the time they got around to preparing supper. The tent had been pitched since the first evening of their arrival but had gone largely unused except as a place of storage because, most nights, they'd chosen to sleep outside, warming themselves against one another in a large shared sleeping bag and lying awake in one another's arms late into the darkness, listening to the sound of the water lapping at the island's edges and gazing up at the stars sprayed with such density across the sky. Thomas checked the tent's ropes and stakes, and further secured any that had begun to slacken. Then he set about building a fire, using dried kelp and dead grass to catch the flame, stoking it in sparing fashion with a few small pieces of the driftwood that he'd salvaged from the rocks their third or fourth day here. Out of habit, he lit the fire behind the stone stumps at the far end of the ruined cottage, so that its light would be largely shielded from both the mainland and the other islands.

Once the flames took hold, Isabelle set down a pot with water to boil for coffee, and a small pan, into which she laid a chunk of butter and four thickly cut strips of bacon. While the bacon was frying, she emptied a tin of baked beans into the pan, and readied two plates.

They ate slowly, contented, sitting cross-legged on the warm grass, the cast of the fire yellowing their faces.

'It's a long time since I remember food tasting this good,' Thomas said, using the pad of his thumb to wipe his plate clean of tomato sauce.

'Bacon and beans,' she smiled. 'Nectar of the gods. I just wish we had a slice of bread and butter to go with it.'

'We better make the most of this, though, because if the weather turns bad on us this'll likely be the last hot food we have for a while. Keeping a fire lit is tough enough at the best of times, but factor in the wind and rain and you can forget it.'

Isabelle looked up, thinking that it was difficult to imagine a more beautiful night. The sky was still clear, apart from a few rags of horizon cloud shining like lit stone beneath the blood-orange stains left behind in the west by the sinking sun. Away in the opposite direction, the empty blueness had already deepened enough for the first stars to have pressed into view. 'We might be spared the rain,' she said, in a small voice. 'We might be lucky.'

They weren't. That night, at Thomas' insistence, they slept in the tent, and it was strange at first, though in no way unpleasant, to be so confined after the recent nights of freedom, but when Isabelle woke shortly before dawn to the torrential drumbeating of the rain against the pitched roof and canvas walls, her first thought, even before clarity weighed their situation, was one of immense relief for this shelter, however limited. She crawled from the sleeping bag without disturbing Thomas, and undid a little of the door flap's upper binding. The waiting darkness was awash, the rain so smothering that no morsel of detail survived.

Soon after, Thomas woke. He sat up and listened.

'How bad is it?'

'Bad,' she said. 'The morning's thick with rain. Visibility is down to nothing. But at least we're protected here from the wind.'

'You can still feel it, though, can't you? And this mightn't even be the worst of it.'

'Or it might blow itself out in an hour or two. We're neither of us experts on storms. For all we know, by mid-morning we could be sunbathing again.'

'Christ,' he said, 'I love your optimism, sweetheart.'

'It's cold, isn't it?' she said, slipping back into the sleeping bag and curling herself against him. 'Any idea what we can do to get ourselves warmed up?'

She lay with her right arm raised and crooked above her head, and she'd shaken her hair loose of its bindings to spill across the pillow. Her eyes were a wide wet shine even in the tent's dark, and her mouth had thickened to the pout she always wore when trying to tease him into some game.

Conor O'Callaghan

outtakes from HIS LAST LEGS

I leave my brothers, our mam, watching telly in the sitting room. *Dallas? Match of the Day?* I leave them and go upstairs. The wardrobe of the middle bedroom is full of clothes left behind. I choose a pair of grey slacks, a diamond Pringle pullover, a sheepskin coat. Under the bathroom's fluorescent shaving light, I fix myself a combover.

Round the rear in darkness, past the coal shed, the garden steps, the passage between hedge and garage wall. The knock I do on the front door is five standard-issue jaunty taps.

There's ructions. Voices, slamming, the telly muted, mam hissing: I'm telling you! I know his knock!

The door from sitting room to hall shuts. The front door's mahogany drags slowly inwards along the carpet's pile. Neil, the youngest of us. When he goes to laugh, I hold one finger upright to my lips.

Neil barks, Well! to play his part and be heard within.

I push my hands halfway into the pockets of my slacks, my shoulders back. I suck sharply in one side of my mouth, the way any businessman does when he's had a couple of jars and still wants to be taken serious.

I bark back: Well kid, how's the form?

He was a great man, wasn't he?

One woman, peering into my father's open casket, asks rhetorically. He fluttered away premiums collected in cash from Cooley farmers. He got casual take-home work from Clarks factory, hand-stitching seventies leather espadrilles, and left us to it. He ran off to Fuengerola with the neighbour's wife. He delivered bananas, badly. When the till of his gentleman's club was short, he steered suspicion towards Harold from Somerset who'd served there donkeys years, and Harold from Somerset was sacked. He keeled over into a ditch, three sheets to the wind, and sued public liability to the tune of twelve grand.

He was, she says. He was a very great man.

It does damage, writing this. I dream him before me in a bikini, brandishing a pot of tea and oven glove, asking me:

Any new anthologies you're working on?

I'm writing about you. It's the only reason you're here.

He laughs his Mutley laugh: Go on out of that!

Where's the bikini from? I don't chase it, but it's somewhere, most probably in the drawer in her bedroom where my mother stores our past, being worn by one of my cousins in hazy Polaroid. A skimpy relic, a blue and yellow floral pattern, crash debris washed ashore.

Two black-and-white photos in one frame.

My father before he was my father. He's with the Barton Cup team, half everyone else's age. He's the gangly suited teenager to the left: short back and sides, quiff on top, hollow cheeks and mouth agape.

My son at his debs in Manchester: black tux, necktie, hands in pockets and jacket unbuttoned. The main cluster is all Max and Harry. He is to the right, with some sidelong wisecrack, belonging by being comical.

So alike! I rest my finger on his face. I know such tenderness.

Eugene O'Connell

Chalk and Cheese or so it was said of
those brothers who lived together one
time in a house. One brother who'd come
in to the hall and knock at the *Glass*, slang
for the gauge that gave out the weather.
Knock Knock though the harvest was done
and he didn't have to know whatever lows
were coming in from the Atlantic. While
the other brother retired to his room would
peck at the button on the mobile, Pip Pip on
the off chance of a high. Knock Knock Pip Pip
as between two lifers tap tapping in their
cells. A rap that sounded in the rooms,
Morse that had to do instead of words.

Jamie O'Connell

from MARIA

'Tie up your lace Maria ... you'll fall. Look where you're going ... Oh, Maria. You nearly walked into ... oh, I do apologise.'

The wind gusts up Eighth Avenue, whipping brown leaves around Maria's face as she bends to her shoe, avoiding the billowing skirts of the women passing by. She watches a single maple leaf quiver in the gutter, its stem caught on the grate and she reaches to pick it up. A car rushes past, its engine loud and close, and she pulls her hand away.

'Maria,' the voice exclaims. 'Jackie. Get your sister.'

Maria feels a hand slip into hers. She glances up. Though the face is unclear, she knows from the high arch of the brow and the way the light hits the cheekbone that it's Jackie. As she stands, her sister's face becomes clear; she can make out the light in Jackie's brown eyes. Beautiful Jackie: the most beautiful sister in the world.

They continue to walk up the avenue; Mother holds Maria's hand and her knuckles feel squashed under Mother's grip.

'How many times have I told you? How many times can you forget? You'll be back in St Elizabeth's, or worse. Oh God, what did I do to deserve this?'

Maria remembers the noisy grey hospital. It's almost a year ago now. She'd sat on a chair next to a man who smelt of burning rubber with a strange bandage on his foot. Father sat on her other side; he was wearing his grey suit; he must've taken his apron off before coming.

Mother was very angry even though the nurse told her a doctor would come. 'It's an emergency. The motorcar was going at such a speed,' she said.

'The doctor will see her soon,' Father replied.

Mother gave him one of her looks. He shifted in his chair.

'Jackie said Maria stood straight up,' he added. 'At Maria's age, you know, they are flexible – they are made to survive a few falls.'

'She was dragged thirty metres.'

'That far? Surely not.'

'Jackie saw the whole thing.'

Maria didn't say a word. Ten minutes ago, Mother had said she was dragged twenty metres but she knew better than to say a word. Mother leaned over her head and Maria smelt lavender. Mother's voice became a whisper.

'You've no love for your children, or for me. In Meligala we would have been first to see the doctor. If she dies, it's all your doing.' Mother's voice grew to a pitch. 'Oh God, why did I ever ...' Her voice trailed off into a sob.

After a little while, Maria asked for something to eat.

'See, she wants food,' Father's voice grew more confident.

'Don't give me that look ... where's that doctor? Do you feel ill, Maria? Do you need water? Yes, I'll get water. These ridiculous Americans.'

Mother stood up and went to the counter.

The doctor did come after some hours. He asked her to look at something shiny, left then right. There was a cold metal disc he put on her chest to see if her heart beated, and it did beat. He put his fingers on her wrist and it was there she felt afterwards the thump thump thump.

'You have nothing to worry about.'

All the way home, Mother complained, 'To wait for so long only to be told to go home. All that fuss for nothing. Why could they not see her straight away? Ah, this city ... nobody cares. Why did we not just stay where we fitted in?'

'Would you rather the doctor told us Maria had broken bones?' Father's voice grew sharp as he opened the front door of their apartment.

'Don't be preposterous.'

Father threw his hat onto the couch. He sighed, stroking his black full moustache.

'Can't a man have five minutes peace in his own home?'

'Look at that. Just throwing your hat aside. Who'll have to pick that up? You never think. You never think of me.'

Jackie came out from her room. She was holding a book, the one Mother had chosen from the library.

'Is Maria well?'

'Yes,' Father said.

'Have you said sorry to your sister?' Mother asked.

'Said sorry?'

'She followed you onto the road. Have you no sense?'

'Maria.' Mother is calling again. Maria runs after Mother and Jackie. Ahead is New York Public Library and she makes a run for the steps, turning as she spots the plinth with a large stone lion, wondering if she can tickle its toes. She bundles past a number of coats. A hand grabs her lower arm. It hurts as the nails dig in.

'Maria,' Mother says, pulling her back. 'Control yourself. You are not a wild animal.'

For a second, Maria thinks about pulling hard, wondering if she can escape. Then she stops knowing there is no point as Mother will send Jackie after her and Jackie is sure to catch her.

'You must walk like a lady. Like a Dimitriadou. Think of who your grandfather is, and your uncles, back in Greece. Do not shame who you are.'

Maria nods, glancing at the lion again. She sees how it holds its head, thinking this is how Mother would like her to be. Proud, gazing forward. Knowing the blood that runs in her veins, that she is more than just a girl. She is someone. She comes from somewhere.

published by Allen Figgis in 1970

In presenting Daniel O'Connell as the epitome of a peculiarly Irish cast of mind—shrewd, hard-edged, self-protecting—Sean O'Faolain illuminates not merely a man, but a national character and the historic period which formed it.

rivarrun

SEAN O'FAOLAIN

King of the Beggars

A LIFE OF DANIEL O'CONNELL

Clairr O'Connor

CAVE-IN

Danger. Do not enter.
I put the sign up
after that submerged resonance,
the rumble underground.
I shovelled out
its insides over years,
sat at the fire-pit kitchen,
admired that curved expanse
of space. In the end
I was the lone digger
hoarse with dusty excitement
behind the mask, as my fingers closed
over the ancient gold headband.

Joseph O'Connor

On Seeing Brendan Kennelly Looking
in the Window of Hodges Figgis

I think of you, Brendan, in hushed Dublin streets,
Walking at dawn past a shuttered store
Or pausing a moment to look at the statues
Of Goldsmith, Grattan, Connolly, Moore.
Grey gulls over Christchurch, the city still sleeping;
The burger bars closed and a rumour of snow.
Little to hear but the dawn alleluia
Of a Garda-car siren on Merrion Row.

Your mind rhyming melody, street-cry and humour,
Passionate memory, heart-aching loss;
Your heroes the ordinary; quiet Dublin widows
Hurrying in for early Mass
Past ghosts outside pubs in the hunger of morning,
Five-o-clock shadowmen, shook by the fates;
Cromwells and Judases, waiting for openings;
The people unnoticed by cold-eyed Yeats.

I think of you, Brendan, walking The Liberties,
Meath Street and Francis Street, down towards The Coombe,
Watching the city in all of her vagaries
Wandering back to her lonely room.
Loving her streelings and early-hour homecomings,
The whip of her wit, and her dirty-faced talk,
You and the spirit of James Clarence Mangan
Sharing a coffee on Bachelors Walk.

I think of you, Brendan, drifting through Trinity,
Cobbles of history moistened by mist,
Head full of stanzas and jostling images,
Lovers you kissed by the rivers of Kerry.
The ferry from Tarbert traversing your memory;

Carrigafoyle in the dawn of the day,
The stream of your poetry flowing in eddies
From Béal Átha Longfoirt to Baile Átha Cliath.

Your shy smile by Bewleys, your handshake on Duke Street
One evening when August had glittered the town
And the windows all shining in mischievous cadence
With your stubble-cheeked grin, and your radiant frown
As you looked at the flower-sellers, told me a story
Told you in boyhood one Christmas night
By an old *seanchaí* with a hatful of characters;
Advent budded on Grafton Street.

Dawn-walker, teacher, lover of Dublin,
Leopold Bloom with the glistening eyes
Of a man who has seen all the ice-floes of folly
Drift down the Liffey and out towards the bay.
You pause on the bridges named for our poets.
I see you there, Brendan. You always knew
That words are a bridge on uncrossable rivers.
Beir bua, my brother. This bridge is for you.

Nuala O'Connor

LONG LIVE THE POPE

I was having sex with David, that last day in Rome, when the pope died. Through my hotel window church bells rang out. We heard them, yes, but we considered their tintinnabulation a fortuitous chime with our own clash and bang.

My phone buzzed and I rolled away from David and sat up in the bed to answer it.

It was my husband. 'So now you've managed to kill the pope,' he said.

'The pope is dead,' I said, 'yes.' I larged my eyes at David and motioned to him not to speak.

When I was on business in London the Queen Mother died. And while I was in Baghdad, Saddam was executed. So my capacity for murder-by-proximity was a thing with my husband and me, something we liked to joke about.

I asked him how the cats were doing and the child. Then I hung up.

'You heard that; the pope is no more, it seems,' I said.

'Wow,' David replied.

My husband's phone-call dimmed our mood and we shared our post-sex chocolate bar in a gloom, listening to more church bells take up the mourning clangour.

'My network will expect a report ASAP,' David said. He got up and frowned over the missed calls on his mobile.

'Go,' I said, 'you should go.'

Later that afternoon David and I held each other in Saint Peter's Square, flanked by rosary-worrying weepers and flocks of nuns, their faces destroyed by grief.

David put his mouth close to my ear. 'I'm someone who always leaves other people behind,' he said. 'You should know that.'

I didn't cry until my aeroplane rose up from Ciampino Airport. I looked down and was stirred to sorrow by the slug-tracks of the city lights stretched below me in blurred, bright strips. I was overtired, I knew; I swabbed away my tears with a tissue, gentle with myself. Death, like love, exhausts me.

Memo from The Irish Citizen *to Hodges Figgis requesting a copy of Thomas MacDonagh's book on the poet Thomas Campion, 4 March 1913 (NLI)*

John O'Donnell

THE TIDE

This morning, a new offering
on the altar of the strand: a young
bull seal, left behind after last night's
acts of war, his wounds carnelian,
still fresh. The others watch him
from the water, their gleaming,
whiskery heads diving and then
popping up, standing off or swerving
close to witness his once-sleek flesh
becoming rock. One of their own.

But when he dies they disappear, leaving
what is left of him alone; no dreams of sunlit
oceans, herring-throngs, since we dream these for him
instead. We put on black, and stand for songs
and weep because we cannot let go, ever,
of our dead, or bear to think that this is all there is,
this foam-frilled beach which tomorrow will be
empty; and the sea, that we can just about
make out from the window of this corridor
where we are gathered, waiting for the tide.

Mary O'Donnell

COMMUNION DAY, 2001

A snail-trail of frost crackles the pavement.
I bolt towards the internet café,
so intent on a writer's junket in Katumba
that I've crossed a hemisphere and missed
her First Communion.
                    So much for silence
and words, the white robe of art. And now,
as photos download in slow slivers on the screen,
the bitter spike of loss: for here is her body shape,
ghostly until images are complete.

I sip my coffee, unnerved
by the full unfolding spectacle, ivory white,
a trembling veil and crown of florets;
they've prepared her well for this rite,
snowdrop fresh, silken purse on wrist.

Her father stands close, smiling,
grandparents widen the wings of her protection.
She's happy. But I am not present,
having forfeited the radiant hour.
I trudge back to the writers' house,
resenting friends who urged me to leave,
hear my mother's truth all the way from Ireland:
You'll regret it for the rest of your days.
Above me, cockatoos fill the dusk whitely,
flocking home to roost.

Roisín O'Donnell

from ZERO TO ONE

This morning your dad slept in, which is to say he woke at 6:30 instead of 5:30. So comforting, to feel the weight of him in bed beside me when I woke. I was so full of warm, fuzzy emotion as I showered, dressed and dried my hair, that I didn't notice you weren't moving. Once I became aware of your stillness, I sat down at the kitchen table, jiggled my belly and gulped down some cold water, but you didn't budge. In the brindled shadows, I lay down on the bed on my left side to increase the blood flow to you, but my belly was a silent mound.

'I'm sorry,' I told you as I drove to work, 'that stuff I said yesterday ... I didn't mean it.'

But there was no movement at all, and I felt my brain lurching towards nightmare scenarios. In vivid snatches of daymare, I saw myself running from work and driving to the hospital. My mind dodged a fusillade of words the doctors might say. I tried not to think about the silence of afterwards, the gaping sense of things stalled, the impossibility of beginning over.

I'd been teaching for about an hour when I finally felt you stir. Your languid roll tripped me into giddiness, and I spent the rest of the morning deliriously enthusing the students through some crap lesson on the present perfect.

Dear God.

The fright you gave me.

My daughter. If I could time-travel thirty-three years into the future and sit opposite you in a Temple Bar café, one of those places that smell of nutmeg and fresh coffee, with garlands of fairy lights in the windows, both of us the same age, what would you advise me?

What would we say to each other if we could talk face to face at the exact same life stage?

By the time you're thirty three, I'll be sixty six, the age your granny is now.

Imagine how it would be if we could meet at the same age. I'd be shy of you, I imagine. I can feel the hush of the café, and see the lights outside. You're wriggling around inside me now, but one day you'll be a woman who will tuck her hair behind her ear and stir her cinnamon latte.

At the end of the antenatal class today, Nora took us to see the delivery ward. My heartbeat started to speed up as soon as we climbed the scuffed staircase and turned into the hushed corridor with the high ceilings. The hospital reminds me of my secondary school back home. It has that old building smell of warm radiators and waxed flooring. Nora led us into a vacant delivery room, and my adrenaline rocketed at the sight of an empty incubator and a trolley full of sterilised equipment. Boxes of powdery gloves and tubes of cerise disinfectant lay in wait. We, the class of expectant parents, crowded elbow-to-elbow. *'Can you see? Sorry am I blocking your view?'* As if there was anything to see, apart from whatever each of us was imagining. Perhaps ten couples, we stood around the bed, its crisp sheets folded back.

'Wait now till I see if I can find a baby for yous,' Nora said, and she bustled off, leaving the assembled couples gawking at the empty bed, which grinned back.

'Here we go,' Nora returned moments later, a young lad in his twenties in tow. He was dressed in a t-shirt and grey jogging bottoms, and to his chest he cradled a tiny new born swaddled in standard hospital-blue blankets.

Collective 'aww's were exhaled around the room as the parents-to-be stared at this totemic bundle. Tiny eyes, dark as a lizard's, blinked stoically under the strip lighting. Coral-like fronds of pink fingers conducted imperceptible air flows. Among the gathered parents-to-be, the baby's sacrosanct presence drew a nervous hush. She was too young to even have been named. Her dad, pinking to the colour of his daughter's fingertips, told us, 'We're thinking about calling her Leila.'

'And the mammy's doing great,' Nora gushed. 'Isn't that right?'

'She is, yeah.'

'Looking fantastic, so she is. She told me it was just like taking a poo.'

There was incredulous laughter, anxious-eyed dads looking grateful at Nora's ability to abrade the fear from the scenario. And that was it. The end of our tutorials on *Bringing an Entirely New Person into the World*, and the end of our time with Nora.

We traipsed out of the delivery room, back down the staircase and out into the cold. A girl from the class who I've been timidly exchanging hellos with for the last five weeks came up to shake my hand, 'Very best of luck Evelyn!'

'You too! Hope everything goes great.'

It's giving birth we're talking about, I thought abstractly. The chaotic mess of birth, and yet we're wishing each other well as if it were an exam we were facing, or an interview. We lack the vocabulary to phrase this any other way, and it would be weird if either of us turned to the other and said: *I HOPE YOU DON'T DIE AND I HOPE YOUR CHILD DOESN'T DIE EITHER*, which is really, let's face it, what we're both thinking.

Traffic charged past Merrion Square and the evening blue deepened.

Casual acquaintances panic me. I felt the need to take this girl's number, to suggest meeting again, knowing it would never happen, but I resisted the urge. I've always found it hard to let people go, and to walk away knowing I will never see someone again. It's a gathering and consolidating instinct. Still, today I found the ability to walk away without any awkward number exchange. The streetlights had just come on, dead leaves skittered against the pavement, and wet paving stones carried a cobalt lustre in the dusk.

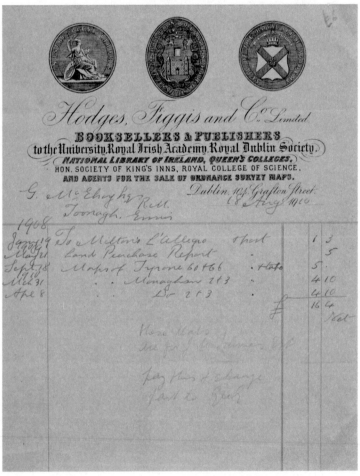

Invoice from Hodges, Figgis and Co. Limited, 104 Grafton Street, Dublin to George McElroy, Toonagh, Ennis, Co. Clare for a number of listed purchases from the period 1908–1910 (handwritten list of products includes a copy of Thomas Milton's pastoral poem L'Allegro, *a land purchase report and maps of Tyrone and Monaghan, with a total sum of purchases on the right-hand side of the sheet) (NLI)*

Bernard O'Donoghue

LEPUS

I thought I heard a car in the early hours,
stealing down the road beneath the window
with its engine cut. But when I came downstairs
to see if it was parked in the front yard,
there was nothing. Puzzled, I trudged back up
towards bed; but when I reached the landing
with its westward view across the fields
towards Glounthane, I saw a blue mountain hare
on the stones behind the house, a visitant
that the earlier dwellers in this house
would see as a messenger or harbinger
of doom. It sensed my presence, and turned
back to the road by which no car had come
past fuchsia, willowherb and clematis.
I got back into bed and dreamed of airports
and ferries and a failed attempt to keep
the taillights of the car ahead in view.

Nessa O'Mahony

A VERTEBRA IN SLOW TIME
for Geraldine Mitchell

It could be
a Henry Moore,
propped by the door
in the sun-bleached glare
of calcium.
Mossed saddle
emerald-bright,
topmost point
of its tricorn
casting shadow
on the plastered wall.
The ovoid gape
where the spinal chord
once ran
a perfect eye
of whatever storm
beached it.
No living memory
recalls who found it,
dragged it up
from the shore,
placed it in lieu
of a boot-scrape
perhaps,
a hiding place
for keys.
Still useful, then,
all these centuries
later, calcified
into art,
unravished
by quietness.

Mary O'Malley

PEREGRINE IN SPIDDAL
for John and Thelma

The mind is reined but
Dreams are riderless. They rut
Run wild, rot. We party on. Behind us
In a long room the hawk sits
Hooded, baronial, silent.

You show me the brown feathers
Tiny chevrons that will moult – *mews*
Comes from this –
And the not yet formed bars
Across his chest. The hood
Has eyes tooled into the leather.

The real eyes can scan heather
An acre at a time but the artifice
Works like hidden faces
Revealed by masks without
The distraction of gesture.

At ease, his pedigree of words
Lure, mantling, and the silver varvel
Are unvoiced jesses
That bind us to him, this still revenant
Of king and vassal
To his hard eyes, serene as gemstones.

Micheal O'Siadhail

EAST 79th

East 79th runs from the River west –
At dawn our bedroom's low-hail-fellow guest,

A lemon slice of sun announces day,
But soon slips south and out of view to play

A game of hide-and-seek on all our streets.
Behind skyscrapers' shadows it retreats

Or casts its shafts of light down avenues,
A harbinger of heaven dropping clues

Of how at dusk East 79th will forge
A canyon of late light, a still lit gorge,

A lesson on perspective down a street
Where high-rise parallels will almost meet

To frame a promising beyond the dark.
A slice of orange glows over Central Park.

So thankful I have loved and been loved twice,
I'm walking westward towards paradise.

Frank Ormsby

THE BLACK KETTLE

Now that the new stove is in place and throwing its heat
the full length of the kitchen,
we have replaced the black kettle.
It no longer hangs over the open fire
on a lethal hook like a piece of dungeon furniture.
I want to angle it at the front door, fill it with clay
and seed it with snowdrops and primroses.

                    Or better still,
we could cultivate something scarlet and spreading,
a nasturtium, say,
with a statement to make about colour.
Saved from a rusty nail in the barn,
its colours doubled, the kettle would bed in
as though it had always been there,
at home and visible and unmistakably ours;
a local fire-god with a tongue of flowers.

Siobhán Parkinson

THE ROSE AND THE NIGHTINGALE
after Oscar Wilde

There once was a Girl who was not in love with a tedious old Student, but, unfortunately for the Girl, the tedious old Student was in love with her. He was not old in years, only in his fuddy-duddy manner and his fussy habits. His shoulders were bent from hunching over books in the university library, his eyebrows met in the middle in a constant frown from picking over semi-colons, and his elbows were worn to the bone from leaning on his desk. He was, in short, a right specimen. Though he had nice hair, so black it had a blue sheen to it. And his eyes were rather beautiful.

Every time the Girl tried to arrange a little fun, the tedious old Student would muscle in. She and her friends hired a boat with an antique gramophone for a river picnic, and the elbowy old Student turned up with a Foxford rug and a plastic box of sandwiches and insisted on joining them. They got tickets to a rock concert, and no sooner had they settled themselves than the Foxford rug was spread out beside them, and there was the fuddy-duddy wearing the wrong kind of jeans and pouring pre-milked tea out of a tartan-patterned old flask. And when they went to the trendiest place in town for the most colourful cocktails, you can guess who was there, sucking on his pink-striped straw and nobbling all the olives and rice crackers.

It was time to call a halt, the Girl said, and her friends agreed that the situation could not be allowed to continue. It was the college ball the following week, and sure as anything he would be there in his father's dinner jacket, trying to get her to dance with him.

'You could promise to dance with him,' said someone, 'on one condition, and then you make the condition impossible. But of course you have to make it *look* possible.'

So the Girl and her friends spent the rest of the evening coming up with impossible conditions.

'Tell him he will have to wear a decent suit,' suggested one friend.

The fuddy-duddy old Student always wore terrible clothes.

'No; he could just hire one,' said the Girl. 'Or borrow one.'

'Tell him he must collect you in a chauffeur-driven vintage Rolls-Royce,' said someone else. 'He'll never be able to afford that.'

'He might be able to borrow one of those too,' said the Girl, 'but anyway I don't want to spend half an hour with him in the back seat of any kind of car.'

'Tell him he must bring you a perfect red rose,' suggested another friend.

'What is so impossible about that?' asked the Girl.

'No matter how beautiful the rose,' said her friend slyly, 'you can always find fault with it.'

'That's clever,' said the Girl.

The fussy old hunch-shouldered Student was ecstatic when the Girl said she would dance with him if he brought her a perfect red rose.

He went first to his mother's garden, but the roses there were all white or yellow or pink.

Then he went to the florist's shop, and the roses there were beautiful but they had no scent.

Then he went to the rose walk in the park, where the fragrance of roses filled the air, but the roses were all overblown and losing their petals.

The Student began to see how difficult a condition had been imposed upon him and he was in despair. He went to the pub to have a long drink and a long think, and there he met an old friend of his who worked in the pub most nights as a cabaret singer. She was nicknamed the Nightingale because she only sang at night. Unaccountably, she had been in love with the fuddy-duddy old Student for many years, and he had never noticed.

The Student told the Nightingale the story, and she really wasn't sure what to do. On the one hand, she didn't want to help the Student to win the heart of the girl of his dreams, because she wanted him for herself. On the other hand, she hated to see him so sad and lovesick and she wanted him to be happy, because she loved him. If she had had a third hand, there would no doubt have been yet another way of looking at the case.

The Student was on his third pint by now and the Nightingale could see that the situation was serious, so she said she would help him, even though it would break her heart. (She did not say the last bit out loud).

'How?' asked the Student tearfully.

'I will write you a song,' said the Nightingale, 'called "The Red, Red Rose", and when you sing it to her, she will know that it is perfect.'

The Student was very doubtful. 'I am sure she meant a real rose,' he said.

'Look,' said the Nightingale, 'anyone at all could bring her a real red rose. Only you will have this perfect song for her.'

And for all he was a fuddy-duddy and a tedious old Student, he did have a beautiful voice.

'Come back tomorrow evening,' said the Nightingale, 'and I will have the song for you.'

The Nightingale sat up all night writing the song. The next evening she gave it to the Student and she taught him the tune and he learnt the words.

'How will she know it is perfect?' asked the Student.

'By the first line,' she said. 'Because it describes herself as perfect, she will think it is perfect.' For the song began with the line 'My love is a perfect red rose'.

So the Nightingale gave the song to the Student and the Student put on his father's dinner jacket and brushed his beautiful blue-black hair and set off with a whistle to the ball.

He found the Girl and he asked her to dance and she said, 'But where is my perfect red rose?' and the Student sang her the song.

She fell for it. She loved the idea that *she* was a perfect red rose, so she put out her hand to the Student. But as soon as the Student saw the glint of vanity in her eyes, he realised his dreadful mistake. He dropped her hand, gave a long, low bow in his father's dinner jacket and turned on his heel and left her standing there at the edge of the dance-floor, all alone.

H.R.H. The Prince of Wales Installed as a Knight of the most illustrious order of St Patrick, in St Patrick's Cathedral, Dublin, now on view, painted by M. Angelo Hayes, Esq., R.H.A. / Hodges, Foster & Co. (NLI)

Julie Parsons

from THE MARINER'S CHILD

When I was little girl I wasn't afraid of the dark. Not the outside dark. Outside dark was standing on tiptoes, my head just sneaking over the sitting room window sill, looking in and seeing Mummy lying on the sofa reading. She's wearing one of her dresses from Cole of California. It has a big skirt and shoulder straps, and it's spread out around her on the sofa, the one with the pink rose pattern cover. Mummy's kicked off her sandals and there is a ring of green around the bottom of her feet from mowing the lawn. A cigarette burns down in an ashtray and there's a glass on the carpet beside the sofa.

It's summer and my skin smells and tastes of salt. I suck my wrist and in the light from the window I can see how the marks of my teeth stand out white against the brown of my skin. I've been wearing my stretchy red swimming togs since I got up this morning and they've been wet and dry all through the day. Now they're stiff with sea water and there's sand caught in my bottom. It's itchy. I hope I don't have worms again. Mummy says the worms come out at night. They're called thread worms, she says. And sighs. We never got things like that in Ireland. Then she puts yellow ointment on the end of her finger and sticks it up. I wriggle and scratch. I sniff my own fingers. They smell of bottom. Not a bad smell, I think. I smell other smells. Cut grass drying in heaps all over the tennis court. Freesias growing among the weeds beside the drive. Cigarette smoke as old Mrs Harvey who lives in our cottage under the giant Macrocarpa tree opens her door. Light spills out as she stands, a great lump of a silhouette, having her after-tea cigarette. Frank Sinatra's voice pours from the radio. 'Saturday night is the loneliest night of the week'. The cigarette end scatters a shower of sparks and Mrs Harvey slams the door shut.

A car grinds up the hill from the beach. The tide is on the turn and the waves slip and slither up and over the rocks tumbled at the foot of the cliffs. My cliffs, I think.

Above, the stars crystallize into the constellations of the Southern hemisphere. I know their names from the *Wonder Book of Do You Know* which I've left lying face down on the lavatory's brown lino. When I tilt my head back, my plaits are nearly as long as my friend Kathleen, who sits next to me at school. Mummy doesn't like Kathleen. She says she's common. But Kathleen stopped the big boys teasing me when I wouldn't let them take my knickers down and have a feel. Kathleen doesn't mind because her brothers are always doing it to her. Boys are like that, Kathleen says.

Look! A star has dropped away from the others and is heading for the ground. For a moment it looks as if it will land right beside me in a puddle of silver.

'Julie. Where are you? Bedtime.' Mummy is standing in the French windows. The glass is in her hand. The ice tinkles as she drinks.

I want to do a wee, but I don't want to go in. I cross my legs, wrapping one calf around the other. Bedtime means the dark inside. Dark inside is lying stiffly in the room that's so pretty in daylight, with its pale pink wallpaper covered with little raised dots that it's fun to pick at, like picking my nose. There's a view through the plum trees to the sea down below. And on the wall just above my head are my favourite horse pictures. Great leaping Chinese stallions, with flying manes and tails.

But they can't keep the scary pictures away. I've seen them in *Life* magazine. My older brother showed me. The most terrifying photographs you'll ever see, he said and threw the magazine at me. There's mounds of bodies, piled high. Piles of bones and people who are just bones too. Crowds pouring out of trains wearing clothes like

Mummy and Daddy wear in the photo albums. There's a parade of black and white which flickers across the inside of my eyelids. Children with shaven heads, eyes opened wide, staring at nothing. Faces stretched on skulls. Women sitting in the snow, their hands reaching out. Huge dogs leaping up, biting. A man with a whip. There's books on the shelf beside the fireplace. Their covers are dark and dreary, faded by the sun. They are all books about the War. The War is important. It's something Mummy and Daddy were in. The books are all about terrible things. There's a woman called Odette. She was French. She was brave. The Germans captured her and put her in prison. They asked her questions. She wouldn't answer. So they pulled out her toe nails. Would I be brave? I wonder. If they asked me questions would I answer? Could I stand the pain or would I give in?

Push the pictures back into the books on the shelf. Think about Daddy. Mummy says he's your Guardian angel and he's sitting on the end of your bed, because that's where guardian angels sit. But they don't believe me in school. They say he's at the bottom of the sea with the crabs and the sharks feeding on him. Sharks like the hammer head I saw hanging up by its tail on the wharf, all the men standing around boasting about the struggle they had to get it into the boat.

But if I can hold Daddy's face right in front of my eyes, the smile that shows his teeth all white. And the black hair falling down into his eyes and his big tummy covered with more black hair that curls into his tummy button. And sometimes when I'm sitting on his knee I can fish out bits of smelly fluff to show him. If I can keep him there, then I'm safe. But sometimes, often, I can't. And then I have to crawl into the other bed beside my little brother, and wrap myself around his skinny body. He's wet the bed. He's soaking wet but he's warm. And Mummy will find us like that in the morning, soaking and stinking and her eyes will smart as she pulls back the bed clothes. The stink of piss and fear that would rise like morning mist as the guards slid back the iron bolts on the cattle trucks that came from Salonika and Budapest and Paris and Amsterdam and revealed their sobbing, moaning, doomed prisoners. That's the dark inside.

MR. W. F. FIGGIS

who was elected honorary secretary of the Irish Branch of the Booksellers Association at its first meeting in 1902. At the Branch's jubilee dinner recently he was presented with this portrait of himself by Sean O'Sullivan, R.H.A., in recognition of his past services. Speakers at the dinner included Mr. F. D. Sanders (for the Publishers Association), Mr. H. H. Sweeten (for the Booksellers Association), Mr. R. A. Nolan (Browne & Nolan), Mr. W. Gill (Gill & Son), Mr. M. F. K. Longman and Mr. R. W. Severn. The chairman of the branch, Mr. A. Hanna, presided and made the presentation

The Bookseller, undated

Paul Perry

LEONORA'S VIOLIN

It is a tomato
If you say so or a flamingo
Or a whatnot
It is the laughter you gather at dusk
It is the talk talk
Guffaw and shush of the wind
It is the rain in a glass jar
Ha or the sun pooling at your feet
It is the sound of love
It is love too

Louise Phillips

THE OTHER TRUTH

The water wraps you like a new skin, easing the hurt that still lingers in your bones. You wonder if you could hide there; perhaps forever, allow the steaming shower door to be your veil. You will of course revisit it again, examine each minute detail, question everything that led to that moment, and everything within it. Remembering has become ritualistic now, but it is all that you have left.

You see his body as it was, not as it finally came to be, visualising the tightening of his limbs and muscles before penetration. He was extraordinary in his way, that dangerous mix of fulfilment and disaster, beauty, and ugliness, so close, they sparkled.

What was it about him that first day? Was it the stillness of his gaze? Or was it because he saw what no one else could see?

You can go back to the beginning, ghostlike, as if you were never in that room at all, but somehow looking down on a different version of yourself. If truth and memory are victims of each other, the truth is you remember him even before he opened that door. You quite definitely watched him walking in.

He touched you that afternoon, an innocent touch, but his hand lingered long enough for you to sense it. Then you did the strangest thing, you picked a hair off his shoulder with a familiarity not yet gained, and you looked at each other. In the looking, you both knew.

Was it then that you decided you were mad, when the prospect of love revealed how strange you were, and having reached the edge of madness, there was no more going back.

When he kissed you, you got the feeling that what was happening, was happening to someone else, even though you knew that in the kissing you were testing him. He was gentle initially, nervous, then his kiss became stronger, his tongue pushing, playful, more powerful. A part of you thought this was all imagined. You bit him hard on the lips. They bled, and you tasted him. When his hand went between your legs, there was no asking, he felt entitled. You had half-pretended it wasn't there, as if to acknowledge it might break the spell.

It was he who suggested the cutting. At the start, you rejected it, and he did that thing with his head, that flip back, raised chin, fuck you anyway kind of thing. Why didn't you see it then, his badness?

The first time you cut yourself, the joy moved in waves, a chemical release to counter balance an inner pain. You felt the rush, but it was more than that. It was the feeling of control, surprising you initially. But, we all do similar things, clenching our fists when darted with pain, or scratching, cutting the skin during lovemaking.

The cutting was like sex.

He saw the pleasure it gave you. You remember him smirking, as if something else had fallen into place. That was the strange thing about him, the way he was so connected to your thoughts, as if he stole them for himself. Was that what enraged you the most, the night you found him with someone else?

They lay naked, but it was he who devoured you with his gaze, angry, as if you had done something wrong, asking, did you think you were the only one? Did you think he really cared?

You couldn't speak, and he said, '*fuck you*'. A part of you died, right there. So, you turned, and in the turning, you had one question. Did he even care enough to keep looking until the moment you closed that door?

And that was why you did what you did, why fate dealt you this cruel hand, because a part of you no one else had touched, could not bear to know the answer.

The night of his death, you remember arriving at the party. The beam of the car lights shone across the pebbled drive. Your husband was driving. You wore a simple black dress with steely pearls and earrings that dangled and glistened like fairy lights. Your hair was worn up off your neck. A long fringe slid sideways across your face. To the outside world you gave the impression of sophisticated togetherness, but inside you were that same jigsaw of broken pieces. You can still see the look of eagerness in your husband's eyes. That party was going to get him up close and personal with those that mattered. He turned and looked at you. His smile said he approved. The trophy wife. All part of the persona, but then you were both playing that particular game.

When he opened the car door, you thought about not moving, that somehow you could control what fate had in store. The lights and sounds of the party spilled onto the drive. You heard your feet crunch on the pebbles, your body moving, feeling it belonged to someone else.

At times, you question if any of it really happened. How could you have done such a thing? You felt lost within your own mind, although you were absolutely conscious of the knife in your bag. Part of you wondered why no one else knew the knife was there. How can people not know these things? How can you be the only one to know?

The recollections come in waves, him naked with someone else, the anger from him, not you, the pendulum in your head swinging back and forth, slicing pieces of you. The calmness of your final decision, knowing life would be inextricably changed, then the realisation, it already was.

Leaving the party, you did so without a word. Silence is a great friend to secrecy. Your breath dispelled into the night-air in sideway puffs of smoke. The moon followed your drive to him; watching. When you turned the key into the darkness, everything, even the walls retracted.

You counted inside your head, knowing things would happen in good time.

Slash.

The first cut across his neck while he was sleeping – blood gulping from his throat.

Slash.

The second cut deeper, his back arching in spasms.

You kept counting while he clenched his throat and you stabbed him hard in the stomach – his body folded, recoiled. The bed, red with blood. You felt that rush despite the blood not being your own. The acceptance later, that that part at least was over, and without planning to or knowing why for sure, you waited like a common thief and stole his last breath in your kiss. In retrospect; it was all inevitable, but you felt weary nonetheless that it was done.

But what about the other truth? The one that even now causes you to shiver, the one you never said, the one you have always known, and now when all is done, you know it still, that you loved him like you loved no other, and in his death, the heartbreak brought the pain, and in the pain, you loved him more.

published by Allen Figgis in 1969

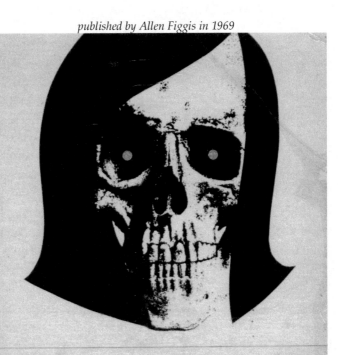

These startling accounts of unexplained happenings were supplied by people all over Ireland following an appeal made in the national press for evidence of paranormal experiences. The compilers offer no explanations or interpretations—you are left to draw your own chilling conclusions!

riverrun

Seymour & Neligan

True Irish
Ghost Stories

Nicola Pierce

from CHASING GHOSTS

It was Sarah who saw her first although she was not the least bit surprised since two-year olds hardly understand what is real anyway. Laura, our maid, was polishing the staircase, the morning after papa left, when she was interrupted by Sarah clapping her hands and exclaiming, 'Weesy! Weesy!' It was one of the few words she could say properly. The others were 'me' and 'no' and my name 'Ann'. Used to being trailed by Sarah as she tended to her morning duties, Laura took her time to turn around and see that Sarah was beaming at the wall as if it had made a joke. Laura, wanting to be clear but gentle, put down her cloth and, kneeling in front of Sarah, told her, 'No, darling, Weesy is asleep in Heaven' while pointing at the ceiling. However, she soon saw she was wasting her time as Sarah was too absorbed in her mysterious game. Giving up, Laura returned to her polishing.

A couple of days later, on hearing a thud from the landing and William's howl, Harriet and I dashed up the staircase to find him sprawled on the floor, a perfect dot of blood winking at us from his grazed forehead. Harriet flung herself upon him, 'Oh, my goodness, what happened to you? Did you fall?'

Instead of answering our aunt's questions, William appeared to be looking for something. Harriet cupped his face in her hands, 'William, are you alright? Do you know where you are? Do you know who I am?'

It took a moment before he finally focussed on her and he certainly amazed me with his answer, 'I saw Weesy. She was standing just there, by the wall. I ran to hug her but ...'

The bell went for dinner. Harriet pulled her handkerchief from her sleeve, wiped the blood away and told us to go wash our hands. We watched her straighten her skirt and head back downstairs.

Waiting until Harriet had reached the lowest step, William asked me, 'Do you believe me? I really saw her. Honest!'

Unwilling to give in straight away, I gave a curt, 'Yes'.

Next, he exhaled in relief, 'Oh, she's back again! Where did you go to, Weesy? Harriet was here.'

Realising that we were staring at the exact same spot, he whispered, 'You see her too, don't you?'

I don't know why but I suddenly felt annoyed, 'Of course I can. Stop asking me stupid questions!'

I wasn't scared, I mean it was my little sister – at least I assumed it was. It looked like her alright … mostly. There was the white ribbon in her hair and she was still wearing her princess dress but it was different from seeing her normally. There was a light around her, bluish and glowing like the flames of a fire. I had never seen anything like this before and yet, at the same time, it was only Weesy. I needed to think. Unfortunately, William still had questions, 'Why isn't she in Heaven? You said that's where she was going.'

'Don't blame me, William Coppin!' I snapped, 'This is not my fault!'

William bowed his head and mumbled, 'Why aren't you happy she's back?'

All the while, Weesy never said a word, just smiled at us as if she was glad to be home again. Goodness knows how long we stood there before we were surprised by Laura who had been sent to fetch us, 'C'mon you pair, you're keeping everyone waiting!'

She grabbed us by the hands and Weesy disappeared just like that. In the dining room Mama asked what had kept us. She was seated in her usual place with Harriet to her left and Grandfather at the head of the table and they were not alone. Before I could stop him, William blurted out, 'How did you get here so fast?'

Harriet laughed, 'Because I came down ahead of you, remember?'

Peering at his forehead, Mother asked, 'Is your poor head alright, dear?'

'No', said William, not hearing her, 'I wasn't talking to you, Aunt Harriet.'

He stopped short and everyone stared at him. Mother shrugged and said, 'Ah, you were talking to me then, were you? Well, I was already down here waiting for you and Ann.'

William looked at me as he shook his head.

I became the centre of attention as each adult, including Laura, who still held our hands, waited for me to explain my brother's strange behaviour. It was Weesy who let me feel that it would be alright to tell. So, I just said it straight out as I didn't know how else to, 'Weesy is here.'

Laura gasped and dropped my hand. The others made no immediate reaction except that Harriet and Mother exchanged glances before Mother asked, 'Where, darling?'

'There!' said William, pointing at Weesy's chair which wasn't even pulled out from the table.

Harriet tried to persuade us otherwise, 'Children, we all miss her and it is perfectly acceptable to want to see her so badly that you almost think you do ...'

William broke in, 'I saw her upstairs just now. I told you. I ran to hug her and that's how I hit my head against the wall.'

'Well, yes, pet', Harriet assured him, 'Because she wasn't actually there.'

'I saw her too', I added, 'she looks the same except she's not sick anymore. She's happy now.'

'Is she?'

Mother's eyes filled with tears while Harriet and Grandfather seemed unsure what to say next. Then, to everyone's surprise, Laura ventured, 'Beggin your pardon, Missus, but I think little Sarah sees her most mornings … that is, ever since Captain Poppin left. She chats away and acts likes she's listening to Weesy talking to her. I … well, I just didn't like to say before.'

Mother gave her a watery smile as Laura suddenly choked up, covering her hand with her mouth as if in shock that she had spoken at all.

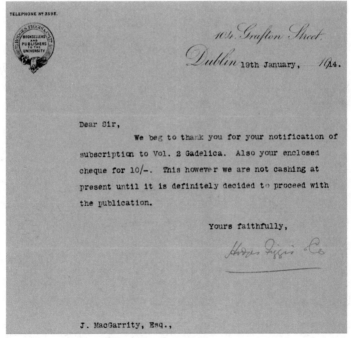

Letter from Hodges Figgis regarding Joseph McGarrity's subscription to Gadelica, *9 January 1914* (NLI)

Kevin Power

The Nihilists

Night fell. This was Spain: olive groves, frangipani, cliffs of notched brown rock. A slew of teetering whitewashed villas. Cicadas stridulating – stridulating, I believe, is the word. The seafront of Alicante, a strip of incendiary light along the near horizon. The south coast of Spain, where, once you get outside the urban centres, life has a post-historical feel – as if nothing will ever happen here again.

We were single, in our thirties, on holiday. Life had taken strange turnings for us, into remunerative professions, beautiful apartments, a mysterious absence of love. We rented expensive villas for weeks in the summer and consumed enormous amounts of drugs. We mixed coke and MDMA and felt sick; we brought ourselves down with Xanax, vodka, weed. Everyone else we knew was getting married, having babies. We curled our lips and arrived at a consensus: babies made us all feel sick.

This year we were imparadised in a Moorish villa with its own steamroom and heated pool. Every evening the sky above the hills was a dreamy shade of pearl. I had fallen in love with Danni, or decided, at least, that we should probably fuck. We had known each other for fifteen years. She was an expert in software deployment, scalability for remote sites.

'I have no idea what that means,' I said. We were shoulder-to-shoulder on the terrace, watching the Mediterranean night descend.

'Neither do I,' Danni said. She clamped a cigarette between her teeth, like a 1940s wiseguy. She was wearing a hoodie patterned with pictures of cartoon cakes.

With a grandiloquent gesture I said, 'People make these deals. If neither of us is married by a certain age, yadda yadda yadda.'

I had just hoofed back a sturdy line of coke and I felt an overwhelming urge to talk about my feelings.

'Are you proposing to me?' Danni said.

'My feelings about marriage are best describable as extremely mixed,' I said.

Danni pushed me with her shoulder and made a sour face. I had been going for debonair; I had ended up at dickhead. But that's cocaine for you, I thought, lighting a cigarette of my own and chalking it up to experience.

In the sunken living room with its professional-grade sound system Alex was carding up another chunky rail and Peter was blasting dubstep, already half a baggie deep.

'I saw these guys at EP last year,' Peter said, nodding violently and tapping ash onto the shagpile rug. In Dublin he was a professor of legal ethics.

'I'm thinking of buying a house,' Danni said, sitting on my lap.

'I really do love you, you know,' I said.

'You're high,' she said.

'When is that not true,' I said.

On the first night of the holiday we had eaten mushrooms and gone for a midnight swim. The lit water all around us exhaled bright wisps of sapphire-tinted gas. In the depths of the trip I had found myself staring at Danni as if for the very first time, a real dawn-of-creation moment. Her ass in black bikini bottoms revealed itself as a thing of unsurpassable perfection. Of course I was a psilocybin eunuch, unfit for coitus until the shrooms wore off. But there was always tomorrow, and tomorrow, and tomorrow. I held out hope that I might at last be succoured in the misery of my success.

I was a risk analyst for an international firm of auditors. I read copies of *Foreign Affairs* in airports. I masturbated to online porn in 5-star hotel suites, once I had obtained the wifi password. I seemed to have forgotten how to talk to women.

'Snortski,' Alex said, and applied his nostrils to the heaped coke on the coffee table. We draped ourselves across the furniture, or across each other. Our heartbeats neared arrhythmia. We had a long and rancorous debate about the films of Krzysztof Kieślowski. Peter Spotified a chill-out playlist of his own devising.

The venue shifted to a bathroom. Danni was sitting, fully clothed, on the toilet seat. I was lounging, also fully clothed, in a room-sized empty tub. I felt like Tiberius at Capri, but also my jaw was clamped shut and my head was throbbing and there seemed to be a swelling in the vicinity of my liver.

'It must be tough,' I said, 'being the only girl in the group.'

'You're not my only friends,' Danni said.

'But we're your best friends,' I said.

'You don't really love me,' Danni said.

'You can't possibly know that,' I said.

We kissed.

'I'm going to bed,' Danni said.

'I'll join you in a minute,' I said. 'I just have to figure out how to climb out of the bathtub.'

'I don't want you to join me,' Danni said. 'I mean it. This is hopeless.'

'You just kissed me,' I said. I felt I had an airtight case.

'Goodnight,' Danni said.

The expression on her face left no room to manoeuvre.

At 5am I walked alone down a long series of concrete steps to the beach and watched the sand turn grey in the early light. I had managed to lose my jacket somewhere in the warren of the villa but I didn't seem to mind, I was doing ok in my t-shirt and shorts, and my body temperature was off the charts in any case. The sand was still warm from yesterday's sun and the loose light streamed along the world's bright edges – it was the light of a gentle comedown. Beyond the initial wavelets of surf two bronzed Adonises with boogie boards were cresting the breakers, waving their arms in windmilling gestures as they mowed against the tide. I lit a cigarette and observed in silence as the dawn broke beyond them in successive waves of heliotrope, mulberry, violet, indigo, ash. For whole minutes at a time there was no doubt in my mind. I was one hundred per cent right about everything. I felt saturated in love. I knew exactly what I was doing.

published by Hodges Figgis in 1959

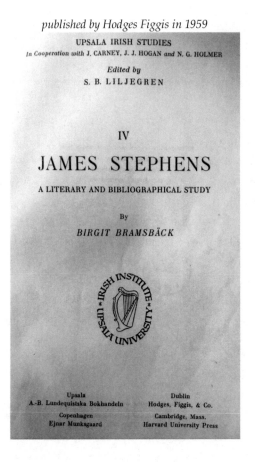

UPSALA IRISH STUDIES
In Cooperation with J. CARNEY, J. J. HOGAN *and* N. G. HOLMER

Edited by
S. B. LILJEGREN

IV

JAMES STEPHENS

A LITERARY AND BIBLIOGRAPHICAL STUDY

By

BIRGIT BRAMSBÄCK

Upsala	Dublin
A.-B. Lundequistska Bokhandeln	Hodges, Figgis, & Co.
Copenhagen	Cambridge, Mass.
Ejnar Munksgaard	Harvard University Press

Elske Rahill

from A WILL

Nowadays people have babies in their forties, but back then thirty-six was old enough to be called barren.

After they had taken the last one out of her, the word clung; whispering in her skin and glaring out from the great sanitary napkins they sent her home with – huge long, fat things, sterile white – it was the word on her dry palms and tremble-tender belly; barren. She was barren now.

She had lost pregnancies before but that last time was different – no spotting; no cramps. The morning of the ultrasound she had vomited four times. Everyone said that was a good sign; she had been so sure of herself that she had even told Aoife about it. Once, resting on her back in bed, she had felt it ripple under her skin – could that be true? Or was it a lie that had come into its own?

Truth or trick, she remembered how it felt; soft, petals fanning out, tiny fleshlet skimming quick as light beneath the surface of her.

It was the first time she'd made it to the twelve-week mark, but at the hospital they said it had been dead since week nine. They said it was her head keeping it in. Now that she knew it was over, it would start to come out.

But a week later her belly was so swollen she couldn't wear trousers, and even on the way to the appointment Terence had to pull over three times so that she could vomit onto the road. She felt sure they had made a mistake. Mistakes happened. When they went in with their metal tools and scooped it out of her, one of the nurses would spot a tiny fairy-child, wriggling there in the bright bucket, and they would know they had made a mistake but it would be too late. That's not the kind of thing they'd ever tell you, of course; they would never say sorry.

'They've made a mistake,' she said, 'Terence they're wrong; they've made a mistake.'

That must have been hard on Terence. It must have frightened him to see her eyes wild like that, the frothy yellow bile coming up out of her lips. He said it was just because she was fasting – she always felt sick when she fasted – and the hormones could be making her paranoid.

He was right, of course, he was right. She had seen it herself there on the screen, a little black shadow, no bigger than the last one. The girl pushed and pushed with the scanner on her belly, but the shadow was stubbornly still, stubbornly dark; engrained like a stain into the fabric of her. The girl switched on the sound, searching for a heartbeat; it sounded like being under water; the whoosh of her own body, nothing more.

'Have you had any bleeding?'

Sinéad shook her head; and when they asked again – 'Sure? No bleeding?' – she knew she was foiled. 'No bleeding, no,' she said, and – as though it might make them change their minds – 'I've been really very sick. Vomiting.'

Who did she think she was fooling? Inside her it sounded like an empty sea. There was nothing in her that could emerge to a new thing. *Me*, she thought. *I am full only of me.*

The girl switched off the sound. Terence touched her hand but she flinched to a fist.

She'd had a dilation and curation before – 'a D and C' is what it was called – and lots of women had them. It would give her the best chance, said the doctor, of conceiving again.

In the pre-op room, the nurse tied a strip tight around her upper arm. She watched her skin crepe together; dry and yielding, no muscle left in her, and she thought *no*. No, there would be no more. She would not conceive again. On the back of her hand a vein bulged to a petrol-coloured glob, and the nurse pushed a thick plastic tube into it. She was a young nurse, pretty, and she avoided Sinéad's eyes, because Sinéad kept gathering up big tearful sighs, and whispering to herself in a soothing tone, 'Ok, it's ok. Shhhh.' The nurse stuck a film of clear plastic over her hand to keep the tube in place.

For the previous D and C, they had put her to sleep while they did it, but she was vomiting all morning she told them – what if she vomited when she was under? This was her way of telling them, but they didn't hear, that she was pregnant, still pregnant.

The anaesthetist said they could give her an epidural instead, and she nodded. She liked that idea.

She had to curl over herself; the foetal position, and an elderly nurse with a Donegal accent stroked her arm, 'Think of something nice darlin.' All the nice she could think of, though, was the small swelling in her belly, the little baby booties she had allowed herself to crochet, the tiny tumble of creation; a whole flower-fish world unfurling inside her.

'Now they've numbed the spot. That's just the needle going in now … Oh I know darlin. I know it's hard. There now.'

It didn't hurt. The numbness then, billowing down from her buttocks. She felt terribly large and they asked her to shift down on the table.

'Further, can you move down a little further for us?'

The anaesthetist was a young man. He took some cotton wool in cold water and moved it down her body.

'Can you feel the cold?'

'Yes.'

'Now.'

'Yes.'

E.M. Reapy

from KINGDOM OF GOLD

The river narrows and swells. On turning bends, we can never predict if we'll be plunged into falls or crash into boulders that surround us. The natives do the rowing and one of them uses an animal horn to warn other tribes of our arrival, to appease them before we trespass into their lands. These warning sounds vary from hoots to long, mournful blows which pulsate through us. I have to wonder, Mary, if a lot more is being communicated to these tree people than we request.

The natives are rather well-natured and seem to enjoy the adventuring. I've tried to maintain a professional distance but there is a certain warmth in their characters that is magnetic. I would never call them friends, they can barely speak English and you would be horrified to see how little they wear – their modesty is barely restrained underneath leather pouches. The women go barebreasted and unashamed. They laugh and try to show us things, explain us things. Depending on my anxiety, I will sometimes offer attention though it can be very testing.

I am hot here. Outlandishly hot. Even after a cooling dip, my clothes stick to my skin with dampness. My pores leak constantly in the humidity. Sweat stalks my face, dripping into my eyes and mouth. It is a curious thing too, you can see the white of the salt on the trails the sweat follows. I wonder what we are made up of at all.

The birds scream and dart in the branches overhead. Their giant black bead eyes rotate off their large heads as they scan us. Their beaks are pointed and yellow and their feathers are in vibrant shades. Deep amber. Molten red. I think of the miserable hooded crows outside our door in the mornings, begging for scraps of loaf, how utterly inferior they are in size and spectacle to their tropical cousins.

The flies too, furrier and noisier than at home. They bumble slowly and their plump blue rear ends seem to be full of juice – blood. I dread to think of the land animals when I see the insects and birds here. I won't allow myself to consider them at camp because it is intense enough to attempt sleeping in the jungle without wondering about the natural predators.

I dare not complain about the fish though. They are so aplenty in the waters that the natives just reach over the canoe and drag them on board. They beat them in a frenzied way and chant over them after to make a spiritual treaty with their creator. We are able to cook the fish when we are ashore, by the banks of the river. The natives make fire from rocks and they gather herbs from the plants around us. Primitive as it may sound, the food is better than anything I've tasted in the finest dining establishments in the city.

At night, I miss you, Mary. You, the children and the fuggy noise of carriages, the blue-white flame from the streetlamps.

I've not seen any evidence that there is a kingdom of gold here, or even a city of gold, or even any acknowledgement of the value of gold. The natives live a simple life and seem more interested in sunrise and sunsets, in petals and leaves, in the phases of the moon – they know nothing of the riches that they may possess. We shall continue on with our search, but sometimes, Mary, I dread to think there's nothing of worth to be found here at all.

John Redmond

SEAWEED CUTTING

To read *Wide Sargasso Sea* for hours
underwater – just the title.
To wait with our knives
until the tide was out,
then reaching down to cut
the slippery throats of past, present, future.
To pull sometimes and feel it give.

For the rocks beneath to be as they have been:
baby-smooth. Your feet
almost at your face, to rotate clockwise
towards the tumbledown
jetty, the whole bay at eye-level
dragging currents away.
Thigh-deep in water, to put

your foot down in the same space
every year – both my aunts
claiming, as they would, to be able
to float but not to swim, never going
out of their depths. My father
perpetually out of his.
My mother to turn over, doing brief
doggy-paddles this way. That.

To look at things from far enough away –
they are waves.

All along the coast, to gather it by hand – a few
pounds a bag. To watch
long islands of the stuff pulled by currachs
between us and the actual islands.

To cut the seaweed in your head,
Jean Rhys, because you need to breathe.

Everyone is beginning to stand up
in the middle of my nostalgia.

Thomas MacDonagh, 1916 leader, published 2 books with Hodges Figgis

Lucille Redmond

from EXTINCT

– We're all extinct, the old fellow shouted, we are already extinct, we are walking around in a state of extinction without knowing it.

Ann-Marie stopped to watch as she stepped up on to the pavement, swinging her Penney's bag. He looked familiar, but she couldn't think where she'd seen him.

– We're letting the rich make our choices for us and they're making their fortunes and they're spewing carbon into the air. We've only got a few months to stop it and reverse it or we're into climate change that will kill our planet as a home for humanity. And they're not going to do it! No way!

There was spit on the corner of his mouth, and a bunch of people standing around laughing at him. Where the hell did she know him from?

She went off and got herself a Flame-Grilled Whopper in Burger King and sat up in the window seat, watching the people sauntering by the O'Connell statue.

Were we, though? Extinct. There certainly weren't as many butterflies as she remembered. Birds either. Flowers. She remembered the time they got away from the orphanage, the mountain meadow, the wild donkeys … What age was he, that shouting man? She leaned down to see if she could see him, and she thought she saw a gesticulating arm appear at the corner.

– There you are, blue-eyes!

Susie Green plonked down the tray and slid in. She hadn't changed a day. Ann-Marie could see her smile hidden by the flowers in that meadow: buttercups, cowslips, harebells, bee orchids – she learned the names later in a Fetac course. Maybe she was misremembering the flowers.

– I got the letter.

– You got the what? Ann-Marie stole a chip.

Susie Green took the envelope out of her bag, shut the bag with a snick. Official. Brown envelope, with a harp on it.

– I didn't open it yet.

The two of them gripped on to the edge of the table, looking down at it.

– Well, go on!

– Not till I have my chips. Strengthen myself. I'm extinct with the day. Had the pair of them up with me all morning, I tell you, I don't know how their parents do it, they never stop. I don't remember yours and mine being like that.

– They were! I got up on top of a cupboard once I was so desperate for a bit of time without them dragging out of me. Of course, I didn't have any training for it.

– How d'you mean, training?

– Well, you know the way they say you shouldn't get a pup that hasn't been raised by its mother, it won't be socialised? After all, we weren't socialised, with only the orphanage. We didn't know how mammies and kids worked.

The man was packing up, down there.

– What are you gawking at?

– That preaching fellow down there, reminds me of someone, can't think. Anyway … but they say you should adopt, you shouldn't buy off some fellow in a car park.

– What? Susie Green stared at her. Who buys kids in a car park?

– No, no, not kids, pups! But if you're adopting, you know, if you adopt, get a pup from a pound, sure someone probably might have put it in there because it wasn't –

– Socialised. Yeah. Now that you say it.

– You think we shouldn't have had kids?

– Ah, stop, now, said Susie Green. She put out her hand to the envelope, drew it back.

– You want me to read it for you?

– No! She snatched it up, ripped it open but then put it down again quick. I'll just get a, a milkshake. D'you want anything?

She came back with two Fantas.

– D'you remember when these were Irish?

– Were they? I don't think they were.

Ann-Marie was holding the straps of her bag together in her hands. I can't remember. She turned her face away. The old fellow had folded up the stool thing he'd been standing on, and was involved in a rousing discussion at the corner with a group of men and women around him.

– Are you sure you want to know, Susie?

Susie sat down hard, put her hand out to the envelope, put one finger on it.

– I mean, if they left you in there, maybe it's better for you to leave them where they are now.

– In the orphanage?

– And the foster homes and all. If they'd wanted us back, couldn't they have found out where we were, all of us? Did you never think about that?

– All my life. Every time the door bell rang I thought it would be my mammy and my daddy, and my heart would be racing. Maybe if we'd got educated we could have letters after our name for the discovery, Ann-Marie, Orphan Racing Heart Syndrome.

– Yeah, must be why orphans die so young, they wear their hearts out beating too fast waiting.

– Ah hell, she said, I'm opening it, and she grasped the envelope fully in her speckled hands and pulled the letter out. She flattened it out on the table. Ann-Marie turned away, looked at the road so she wouldn't be in on Susie Green's private moment as she found out what the nuns had agreed to say.

– Nothing. Her voice was flat. They've no records.

– Nothing? They must have something!

– There was a fire and the records were destroyed.

– That's convenient.

They sat there in silence drinking their Fantas.

– Did you think about DNA? People sometimes find a son or a mother or a sister that way. I've heard stories –

– Maybe.

But she knew Susie Green wasn't going to go down that road. She reached out and gripped her friend's hand.

– Susie, we have each other and we – she stopped, then she said it, we love each other.

– Yeah, we socialised each other. Susie Green laughed, and closed her teeth on the laugh. Ann-Marie, did you ever think of looking for your own self, looking for your own people?

Down below there was a bang, and screams, faint through the glass.

– Oh Jesus, the poor man! Ann-Marie was up and out of the seat and running, and didn't hear if Susie Green followed her. She half-slipped down the terrazzo steps, ran across between the blare of traffic, got to the man, pushed her way through, knelt beside him. His leaflets were all around him, gluey and bubbling with blood. She knelt in the blood. Her hand was in it. She put her hand on his face and he took a deep, gasping breath and opened his eyes, blue eyes. What did he say? She leaned to hear what he said, to hear what he whispered, his hoarse whisper: It's like looking in a mirror.

BOOKSELLERS
AND
PUBLISHERS
TO THE
UNIVERSITY

104, Grafton Street.

Dublin 25th April, 1913

Dear Mr. MacDonagh,

        I have pleasure in sending you a memorandum
of the printing expenses of your "THOMAS CAMPION", which
I hope you will find satisfactory.

                Yours faithfully,

                William F. Figgis

                H. F. & Co

*Letter from William Figgis, of HF, informing Thomas MacDonagh he has
enclosed a memo with the expenses of* Thomas Campion, *with enclosed
statement for the price of £52 1 shilling and 6 pence, 25 April 1913* (NLI)

Nell Regan

LIKE A SLEEVE OR A BOOK
for Theresa

Like a sleeve the years have turned
inside out and fit, as we sit in the café

under the railway bridge, or more –
like a book, a simple origami book

I want to make; take one sheet of paper –
on which two teenagers walk
(they only stop speaking
as they pass under the dank and dreep

of this line,
                    before sky flickers ahead
to meet horizon). Now, double it thrice

and cut along a single crease.
Unfold. Plicate so each page is a plane

that accordions out like a vowel
or a palm emerging from that sleeve
so the lit stories of twenty five years
flitter from its weave to settle on their lines.

Ger Reidy

The Tool Box

I gape out their window towards the foothills
where cloud whispers waft up within a corrie
like revelations from behind an altar.
Late sunshine scanning between storms finds a shack
where once we gathered black faced sheep.
Suddenly I hear a cello faintly oozing from a wireless
and see him floating towards me across the years
then dancing with her in that wartime photo
to 'In the Mood' before evaporating before me.

In this scullery flooded with urgent light
I open his tool box of obsolete wrenches
mixed with her jewellery and rusting brooches.
It vibrates fused with a menagerie of memories
and jolts a compulsion to sprinkle their grave
with this kaleidoscope of refractions,
to forgive him for the sins he never committed.
The way she flung up her bones to adorn his coffin
after everything he had done and not done.

Maurice Riordan

THE SWAP
for Hugo

Someone snuck over the back wall
last night and pinched my ladder.
Then I found a bronze BMX
leaning outside the front door.

Was this like some ancient barter?
Oats for alcohol, salt for a new wife.
Or a neighbour's test, some version
of the Good versus the Bad Thief?

Did that man need to top leylandii?
This day take rag and bucket
to his high windows, or climb
into the dusty heat of an attic?

While I took to the roads,
blinking between the oaks
along the towpath, knowing
I was chosen for such latitude.

Moya Roddy

MIRACLE

You spent most afternoons
on the living-room couch
buried beneath a mound of coats.
Home from school I'd sit
on the matching chair,
watch your breath push
against my father's Crombie,
his old sports jacket –
buttons rising and falling
rising and falling
while I prayed for you to
open your eyes.

Around five you'd surface,
unwind the long scarf
worn to protect your hair,
bring wan lips to life
with a dab of lipstick –
then sally forth
to get something for tea
– eggs or cheese –
waving and smiling
waving and smiling
as if you'd just risen from the dead.

Ethel Rohan

from THE OTHER SIDE OF THE WORLD

Belfast Harbour, 1935: Roche made horrible noises, as if his lungs were caught in his throat. Deirdre patted his hollow back and immediately wanted to pull her hand away. Just standing this close made her cringe. The need to flee filled her again.

An officer spoke through the *Gigantic's* loudspeakers, ordering everyone to board. Deirdre dropped her hand from Roche and wiped her palm and fingers on her coat. She readied to run.

The woman with the black scarf slapped at her head with both hands. 'We'll all be drowned.'

Deirdre looked from her to the ship, its gangplank like a fantastic beast's enormous tongue, impatient to swallow them. The man in the sad-looking brown suit squawked about getting his money back. Others spoke up, also wanting to postpone their voyage.

A young crewman in navy uniform and a ginger moustache moved amongst the passengers, ordering them to board in an orderly fashion. 'Everyone stay calm,' the crewman repeated. 'No one's going to drown. The *Gigantic* is the White Star's finest. You'll never sail the likes of her again, trust me.'

'That's what we're afraid of,' a man quipped.

A ripple of nervous laughter spread through the group. Deirdre wanted to be back home, warm in her bed with her sisters, her stomach full of her mother's stew and her head full of images of herself in a flowing dress, dancing over the stone kitchen floor, her long frame lit by sunshine.

The frightened woman wouldn't be calmed. 'Pope Pius himself couldn't get me on that ship and the rest of you are fools if you go. You'll perish, mark my words.'

Shouts and fists went up, and then cries from the children. Deirdre consoled the little girl next to her, her blond ringlets long and shiny.

Roche's limp hand slapped at the air as if patting the heads of invisible children. 'Whist, people. That's enough now.'

The young crewman's voice turned to a bark. 'Order! Order, I say! Everyone needs to board immediately or the Captain will leave without you. No refunds, either!'

'No one's going to drown,' Roche said, louder.

'What do you know?' the terrified woman shouted.

Roche waved his handkerchief through the air like a white bird. 'Ladies and Gentlemen –'

Deirdre's face softened in surprise. Roche's voice had taken on deep, rich tones and he seemed younger and stronger. The group pressed around him. With a flick of his right wrist, he threw his handkerchief overhead. The square of white cotton arced in the night and sailed into his left hand. His free hand jumped to his coat pocket, removing an object with a flourish.

Deirdre stretched onto tiptoe, peered around the waist of the broad man blocking her view and teetered, her shoulder hitting the man. He swung around, snapping. 'Watch what you're at, child.' She was always getting confused for a child, until people took a closer look. Then came their inevitable, unsettled surprise.

Roche raised his right hand, revealing a glass globe. 'I have,' he boomed in his theatrical voice, 'the gift of seeing the past and the future!'

Onlookers cackled. Some turned away, but most remained in place, their eyes fastened to the globe balanced on Roche's palm.

'What are you blathering about?' the woman in the headscarf asked.

Roche beckoned and asked if he could touch the cuff of her coat sleeve.

'Are you mad?' she said.

Roche coaxed the woman. 'Just the barest brush of your sleeve.'

Deirdre could feel her heartbeat in her face and palms. The woman reached out, letting Roche's fingers glance her sleeve. Roche closed his eyes. Deirdre raked his face for some sign of fakery. When he spoke, he sounded ghostly. 'You're a Kildare woman, the fifth in a long line of children. You're sailing to meet your husband in Chicago. The man went ahead of you two years back, trying to make a go. You're afraid you won't want him anymore.'

The woman clutched at her coat. 'How could you know?'

The man with the fingernail of eggy wax scoffed. 'Sure didn't we all hear you going on about yourself. It's you has a diesel motor, never mind the ship.' The group chuckled.

'I never said all of that. And most certainly not that last part.' Her voice quavered. 'I hardly told myself that.'

Deirdre grasped at plausible ways Roche could have hit on the woman's deepest worry.

'Are you really a seer?' a young mother asked, her baby held tight to her chest. 'Is she safe to sail? Will we make it to the New World?'

'We will, of course,' Roche said. 'I'll stake my life on it,' he added dryly, drawing more chortles.

The young man in the brown suit pulled his cigarette from his mouth. 'And I suppose you want us to grease your palm for this foretelling of good fortune?'

'Our gifts are God given, Sir, to be shared freely where most needed. This one's on me.' Roche flew his handkerchief through the air once more and again bowed low. His right hand remained raised, the glass globe like a miniature moon on his palm. Deirdre's pulse quickened.

Maybe Roche was for real. Maybe his vision was real, too. *Together we'll be big.* Her eyes jumped to the sea. The water appeared calmer now, silvery and shimmering. She cut to the ship's name. Maybe it wasn't mocking. Maybe it was a promise.

'Show's over,' the crewman said. 'All aboard now.'

Roche returned his handkerchief and the baby moon to his coat pocket. The passengers moved toward the ship, as meek now as babes on the teat. The Kildare woman hooked her fingers to the knot of scarf at her throat and stepped onto the gangplank with a haunted look. Deirdre forced herself forward, refusing to look back at her divided country or to think of things split in two. Instead, she faced the bigness of the ocean and allowed the ship to take her in.

T. C. D.

FOUNDED
1894

A COLLEGE
MISCELLANY
VOLUME LXV
NUMBER 1142

NOVEMBER 14th, 1958 (Copyright) **Price : SIXPENCE**

TCD, unnamed, 1958

Sally Rooney

from NEW MESSAGE

One morning in October I saw you on Leicester Square. It was raining and you were coming out of the station looking at your phone. Although we haven't seen each other in 10 years I was immediately certain that it was you, because you haven't changed at all and your hairline is distinctive. I'll tell you why I didn't say hello. I had just come out of the bathroom of a fast food restaurant nearby, where I had taken a pregnancy test for the first time in my life and discovered I was pregnant. Literally seconds later, I saw you coming out of the station. I didn't feel in any condition to say hello to anyone. My face was red and I had leftover make-up on my eyes from the night before. I stood under the awning of the coffee shop opposite the station entrance and watched you walk along on the other side of the road, still studying your phone.

When you were about to leave my eyeline I was overwhelmed by a sense of catastrophe. I knew that I could only repress this feeling by continuing to hold you in my eyeline, and that is the reason I followed you down the street, actually crossing the street at one point to follow you more closely. Jesus, I was murmuring to myself audibly. Oh my god. I think maybe you received or made a phone call during this time. You stopped at traffic lights certainly, at which juncture I hid in a bookshop doorway, and when I emerged you were gone. That's when I started to cry. I wept very openly. I have never been big into crying, as you might remember, or maybe you don't. Allowing you to slip out of my field of vision felt like losing something physical from inside my own body. Perfect strangers expressed concern for me. How long had I been following you? I wasn't conscious of time while we travelled together ('together') but I know that when I lost you I was standing on Whitcomb Street.

Afterwards I went very quietly into a small cafe, ordered a cappuccino, visited the bathroom and looked at my face in the mirror. It was the same face, so it seemed to me, but would it seem that way to you? I no longer had any idea. My face was like a letter in an alphabet, loaded with potential significance but also signifying nothing. Calmly I dabbed a square of tissue under my eyes, where my tears had irrigated little freckles of black make-up. Then I went out to the counter, collected my coffee, sat at a blue flatpack table and called Louisa.

Does it surprise you to learn that I am still on spontaneous calling terms with Louisa? I do find myself wondering who you still speak to, whether it would be the same people I might expect. Louisa and I are always talking, the way babies are always talking, without communicating anything except the assuring desire to speak.

Hello gorgeous, Louisa said on the phone.

I have a school question for you, I said. What is Aidan doing with himself these days? I'm 90% sure I just saw him on Leicester Square.

I want to tell you how completely calm, how practically regal, I felt while conducting this phone call. I picked up my coffee cup and set it down again intermittently but did not drink from it, feeling like an Audrey Hepburn character in a heist film.

How out of the loop are you? said Louisa. You're hilarious. He lives in London, he's a professional footballer. He plays for some second or third division team, I don't know who. How did you not know that?

He's a professional footballer? I didn't even know that was a real thing.

Oh, it's very real. They make buckets of money, so Brian says.

Is he any good? I said. Is he married?

I assume you have to be at a certain level to be doing it professionally.

Yeah. Is he married?

This is a funny conversation we're having, said Louisa. You're the only one who's married. I don't think I've ever met anyone who's more married than you.

I did drink from the coffee then. I swallowed it right down although it burned the inside of my mouth. Burn to me has a particular taste of its own, a bitter and swollen quality.

Anyway, I said. You're not going to believe this. Something crazy happened.

What? said Louisa. Are you and Aidan having an affair together?

No, this is moving on from that topic. I didn't even talk to Aidan, I just saw him.

Why not say hello? she said.

You know like in a dream. You don't want to wake yourself up by doing the wrong thing. But as I was saying.

Did you just glimpse him? Maybe it was someone else.

Why would it be someone else? I said. I saw him clearly, I know for a fact it was him. I do remember his face strikingly well.

Oh, I completely forgot. About your thing with him. Isn't it weird I forgot about that?

It wasn't really a thing. Anyway listen, I'm pregnant.

Louisa went quiet on the phone. I swallowed an irresponsibly huge mouthful of coffee and some of it came out of my lips and down my chin. No one in the cafe was looking. I just wiped my jaw with a napkin and waited for Louisa to speak again.

Gabriel Rosenstock

CRÉ
Ich am of Irlonde
and of the holy londe
of Irlonde ...

Ní d'Éirinn mé níos mó
ná de náisiúnstát ar bith
más aon ní mé
is féar mé i bhforaois
ar shatail eilifintí air
foraois chomh fairsing sin
nach eol don mhoncaí féin 'bhfuil teorainn léi
áit a nglacfaidh saoithe scíth
sula gcumfaidh siad na hÚpainiseaidí

Orna Ross

from Dancing in the Wind

Souer Therese, a simple Auvergnat only seven years older than Iseult, has a trio of afflictions: a squint, a short leg and a permanent scowl. This might seem to make her a poor choice to play rounders with a child … but in the convent, the mothers and sisters superior like the kitchen and helper nuns to do what they're least fitted for. Mortification is deemed good for the soul. The lower class soul, anyhow.

So poor little Sr Therese has to limp through the motions, and take it right slowly. Not that slowly bothers Iseult. She's got used to convent life now, where nobody ever rushes around wondering where on earth the time has gone, as Moura always did. In the convent, each morning, afternoon and evening has its allotted allocation of hours.

Sr Therese bats the ball. Instead of giving chase, Iseult decides to do a dance. At breakfast, Sr Suzanne told her that Moura was coming today.

Moura's arrivals are always sudden as spring showers. Up she appears, wherever Iseult happens to be, at lunch or lessons, with Iseult's name overflowing from her lips, as if she has to repeat it over and over for for all the times she's not been around to say it. 'Iseult! Iseult darling girl! Beautiful Iseult, *ma belle animale*! Oh my Iseult, how I have missed you!'

'Run!' shouts Sr Therese. 'What are you doing? You're supposed to *run*.'

Iseult dances Moura's coming into the grass, how Moura will bend from her great height and swoop her up into her arms and swaddle her in kisses, then give her a gift: a scarf or pen or book. Once, from America she brought a pet alligator called Ali. He now lives in the convent pond, where he swims and smiles his tough-toothed alligator smile with a ribbon round his neck. Sister Therese helped her put it on him another day.

Sr Therese retrieves the ball, comes across, presses bat and ball into Iseult's hands.

'All right then, you do the hitting.'

The little nun blows on her nails. Her fingers are red, blue at the tips. Yes, it's cold, another reason why Iseult keeps dancing.

In the garden, the roses and lilies are a brown, dry tangle of stalks. They left so gradually Iseult hardly noticed and now she's forgotten they were ever there, and has no thought that they might come back. She's too young to think about seeds and blooms and pods. Time, for her, is still each open moment, not yet a line through years.

'You don't want to play, do you?'

Iseult shakes her head, hands back bat and ball.

'All right then, go talk to the grass or whatever it is you do.' Sr Therese whacks the ball as far as she can towards the far end of the pitch and sets off limping after it.

On a blade of grass near her right foot, Iseult notices the shell of a ladybird. She bends down. 'Moura is coming,' she whispers to the ladybird. 'Crack your shell-body open, flutter out your wings ...'

It doesn't move.

A sound jangles from the building. The bell: two rings, short and sharp. Sr Conciliata is waving from the steps. Iseult jumps up, ladybird forgotten. Sr Therese, rounders game, dancing: forgotten. Only running, oh yes, running now. Past the Virgin Mary smiling her blank smile down from her pedestal, past the big trees, past the fountain, all the way to the door, where she knows she must stop and walk ... but she doesn't.

In the parlour, Mother Suzanne has embraced her dear, dear friend, Madame Gonne, and Canon Dissard has arrived too, just as Sr Jeanne was wheeling in the tea trolley.

How serene and peaceful it is here, thinks Maud, settling back into the cushions plumped by Sr Maria-Angeles. How ordered and comfortable. It is women who have the truest sense of life. Look at the shining silver pots, the precious china cups, the immaculate cleanliness. If you want your drawing room beautified, or indeed your birthday remembered, your clothes appreciated, your emotions soothed, it's to a woman you must turn.

The door bursts open. Two huge eyes cast themselves around the room and almost before they have even landed on Maud, a fierce little body is flinging itself in her direction.

'Iseult!' says Sr Suzanne. 'Is this how a young lady enters a room?' The other nuns are tut-tutting too, fearing the Canon or Maud might think Iseult's behaviour reflects badly on them. Iseult doesn't care, she has Moura's dress in her hands, Moura's smell in her nostrils.

But she doesn't like the laugh Moura is laughing. That tinkling noise that's not for her but for the grown-ups.

'Iseult, darling Iseult!' She is taken by the shoulder's held at arm's length. 'Let me see you, my beloved angel. How tall you've grown.'

'Moura,' she whispers, though she knows her mother will not listen properly with the others about. 'You must wish to see Ali?'

'Not just now, *cherie.*'

'We tied a ribbon round his neck. I think you *would* like to see him.'

'Yes, yes. After tea. First, Iseult.' Moura pauses, looks round the room. 'First, Moura has something to tell you.'

'Sr Therese thought he might eat the fish. But he's too small. All he does is smile.'

'Iseult!' Sr Suzanne's says her name soft and hard, both together, like the body of a snake. 'Listen to your mother.

Today is a day for great rejoicing. Madame is to join our Catholic faith.'

'And something else too, darling.' Moura puts a cupcake into her hand. 'Do you remember my new friend the major, Iseult? Come now, don't make that face, of course you do.'

Moura bends until her face is level with Iseult. She is asking for something with her eyes. They glint like wet pebbles after rain. 'Major MacBride, remember? Remember all I told you, all about what a brave soldier he was, a real Irish hero? Well, I have the most wonderful news for you. The Major and I are to marry.'

'Why?'

'Why? My dear, what a strange question.'

'No, Moura, I do not like him. I hate him.'

Moura laughs, her terrible tinkly laugh, looking all round. Without moving, the nuns seem to press in closer. They stare like gulls stare at the sea. 'Dearest, you barely know him.'

'I believe we shall have a banquet, Iseult, here in the convent, on the wedding day,' says Sr Suzanne. 'And you shall be princess of the feast. Wouldn't you like that?'

'Oh darling, you'll make such a lovely princess. And we are going to Spain for our honeymoon and I shall bring you back something very beautiful. The Spanish know what is beautiful.'

Iseult drops the cupcake, holds her fury in her fingers as she grips Moura's skirt. The fabric of the blue dress is scratchy but she burrows in. If she does not hold hard, she knows she shall start to fling the teacakes and sandwiches. She is supposed to be learning to control her temper.

'He has the eyes of an assassin.'

'Iseult!' Moura pulls her close, whispers in her ear: 'It is for you, darling, I am doing this for you.'

Dave Rudden

from THE ENDLESS KING

The door opened.

The chamber beyond was as bright as the surface of the sun, the air hot and arid. Looking at the floor provided no escape from the light, and Denizen realised through watering eyes and the sudden hollow clang of his steps that the floor was polished metal.

Spoken steel – forged by a Knight's fire to burn away a Tenebrous' real form like a cobweb touched by a flame. Grey propelled him forward, the heat palpable even through the exposed iron of his hands, before he was unceremoniously shoved into a knot of other robed teenagers.

He wanted to turn, but the hand on his back had disappeared and so instead Denizen ducked his head down, shuffling through the group, listening for –

'I'm just saying – it's nice to finally get black robes. Magical organisations should have black robes.'

'You look like a tent with half its poles missing.'

'Hi guys,' Denizen whispered.

They both jumped.

'You found us!' Abigail whispered. 'I tried to go back for you, but they wouldn't let us.'

'You missed all the fun,' Simon said. 'Abigail has a boyfriend.'

'Simon, I will punch your neck out the back of your head.'

'That isn't possible. Right, Denizen?'

'I don't know,' Denizen said, half because he didn't and half because the relief at seeing them was a physical pain. 'But I'd bet on her every time.'

Denizen knew without lifting his head when Greaves swept into the chamber, those powerful, confident footsteps driving a hush before them. The footsteps stopped, and his rich voice rang out, no longer warm, no longer pleasant. Denizen had always thought Greaves … not soft exactly, but able to hide his sharp corners when needed.

Now he was the Palatine.

'There are many tests you will endure before you become a Knight,' he intoned. Emotions made Knights run hot, even without whatever was giving off that painful light, and the air was full of the smell of nervous sweat.

'Your bravery. Your will to fight, and your will to walk away. You will be tested by pain. By loss. By loneliness. Children will recoil from you in the street. Those you love will choose easier lives than loving you. You will live in candlelight, in shadow, in fire.'

'And there will never be victory. I say this as it was said to me, and I didn't believe it either. There will a prophecy. Some secret trinket. Some holdout that will allow us to snatch triumph from the dark. No such thing exists. You must understand the work that we do.'

Denizen's stomach turned. Not from nervousness. Not from the constant baseline of strange that came from having so many Knights together. No – he *knew* that feeling. It shook the strings of his heart and, one hand on the hem of his hood to keep it steady, he slowly raised his head.

The chamber was a hexagon, and six great lamps glared from the walls. There were Knights, two in each corner, all armed, all robed in black.

And above … something squirmed.

The light from the lamps was so bright it was almost solid, but where the beams met it took on a different hue –

sickly, colourless … tainted. That, even before his iron eye began to ache, told Denizen what it was.

He'd never seen a Breach like the one outside Adumbral's walls yesterday. He'd likely never see one like it again. They were unique as paper cuts, unique as the thing they birthed. Sometimes you saw the hole in the air, sometimes you merely felt its effects, sometimes the Tenebrous was just *there*, like the sudden appearance of a spider.

But this one just … hung there, a rippling, bubbling gap.

'A wound that will never heal. The reason for this fortress. A Glimpse into our eternal crusade.'

It ached to look at. It ached to be around. It was an affront to everything the Order stood for, and it languished here like a prisoner of war.

'This too is sacred ground.'

The Palatine's eyes were stony. He raised a hand, and with a spike of fear Denizen thought Greaves was pointing at *him* before the hand swung left.

'Can Miriam Bell please step forward.'

A Neophyte stepped forward, pushing her hood back to reveal blonde curls and delicate features. The Knight behind Greaves stepped forward as well, a harness and cord in his hand.

Denizen stared at it a moment without comprehending. It looked like … *A bungee cord?* Bungee jumping had always seemed like madness to Denizen – surely it was bad enough falling off something without still being around to remember it – and it was doubly confusing to see it here.

The cord was dark with etchings. *More spoken steel.* Knights didn't go for show – like its wielder, the favoured metal of the Knights looked no different until battle began.

With swift, sure motions, Greaves and the other Knight attached the harness to her slim shoulders. Each buckle was tugged on, each strap checked, Greaves even lifting her by it for a moment before clicking the cord into place, just as another Knight wheeled forward a set of steps. The whole process had taken just long enough for the Neophytes to realise its purpose.

Miriam's eyes were fixed on the Breach. She had gone very, very pale.

'Miriam Bell,' Greaves said. 'Do you want to be a Knight?'

'Yes,' she said, and her voice did not waver.

Greaves nodded. 'You will take fourteen steps. No more. No less. Then tilt your head upwards … and open your eyes.'

Murmurs rippled around the Neophytes before a look from Greaves quelled them. *Open your eyes.* The one rule of being in the Tenebrae, on the rare occasions the Order braved its depths. You never, ever opened your eyes. Knights could see in the dark, but that didn't always mean that they should.

'You will never speak of what you see there, do you understand?'

She nodded.

Then go, Miriam Bell,' said Greaves. 'And then I will ask you that question a second time.'

Catherine Ryan Howard

The Liar's Girl

It's 4.17 a.m. on Saturday morning when Jen comes to on a battered couch in a house somewhere in Rathmines, one of those redbrick terraces that's been divided into flats, let out to students and left to rot.

He watches as her face betrays her confusion, but she's quick to cover it up. How much does she remember? Maybe her friend Michelle clutching some guy's arm, turning back, calling out to her. Saying they were moving onto some guy's party, that they could walk there.

'*Whose* party?' he'd heard her ask.

'Jack's!' came the shouted answer.

Now, Jen is sitting – slumped – on a sofa in a room filled with faces she probably doesn't recognise. The thin straps of her shimmery black dress stand out against her pale, freckled skin and the make-up around her eyes is smudged and messy. Her lids look heavy. Her head lolls slightly to one side.

A single bare, dusty bulb hangs from the ceiling. The carpet is old and stained. There are broken bits of crisps, hairs and cigarette ash nestled deep in its pile. It hasn't been laid. Instead, the floor is covered with large, loose sections of carpet, ragged and frayed at the edges, with patches of dusty bare floor showing in between. The couch faces a fireplace that's been blocked off with chipboard, while an area of green paint on the otherwise magnolia chimney breast marks where a mantelpiece once stood. Mismatched chairs – white patio, folding camping accessory, ripped beanbag – are arranged in front of it. Three guys sit in them, passing around a joint.

Another, smaller couch is to Jen's left. That's where he sits.

The air is thick with smoke and the only window has no curtains or blinds. The bare glass is dripping with tributaries of condensation.

He can't wait to leave.

Jen is growing uncomfortable. Her brow is furrowed. He watches as she clasps her hands between her thighs and hunches her shoulders. She shifts her weight on the couch. Her gaze fixes on each of the three smokers in turn, studying their faces. Does she know any of them? She turns her head to take in the rest of the room –

And stops.

She's seen them.

To the right of the fireplace, too big to fit fully into the depression between the chimney breast and the room's side wall, stands an American-style fridge/freezer, gone yellow-white and stuck haphazardly with a collection of garish magnets.

Jen blinks at it.

A fridge in a living room can't be that unusual to her. As any student looking for an affordable place to rent in Dublin quickly discovers, fridges free-standing in the middle of living rooms adjacent to tiny kitchens are, apparently, all the rage. But if Jen can find a clearing in the fog in her head, she'll realise there's something *very* familiar about this one.

She pushes her palms down flat on the couch, scrambling into an upright position. Stares at the fridge.

This is it.

Her mouth falls open slightly and then the can in her hand drops to the floor, falls over and rolls underneath the couch. Its contents spill out, spread out, making a *glug-glug-glug* sound as they do. She makes no move to pick it up. She doesn't seem to realise it's fallen.

Unsteadily, Jen gets to her feet, pausing for a second to catch her balance on towering heels. She takes a step, two, three forward, until she's within touching distance of the fridge door. There, she stops and shakes her head, as if she can't believe what she's seeing.

And who could blame her?

Those are *her* magnets.

The ones her airline pilot mother has been bringing home for her since she was a little girl. A pink Eiffel Tower. A relief of the Grand Canyon. The Sydney Opera House. The Colosseum in Rome. A Hollywood Boulevard star with her name on it.

The magnets that should be clinging to the microwave back in her apartment in Halls, in the kitchen she shares with Michelle. That were there when she left it earlier this evening.

Jen mumbles something incoherent and then she's moving, stumbling back from the fridge, turning towards the door, hurrying out of the room, leaving behind her coat and bag, which had been underneath her on the couch all this time.

No one pays any attention to her odd departure. The party-goers are all too drunk or too stoned or both, and it is too dark, too late, too early. If anyone notices, they don't care enough to be interested. He wonders how guilty they'll feel about this when, in the days to come, they are forced to admit to the Gardaí what little they know.

He counts to ten as slowly as he can stand to before he rises from his seat, collects Jen's coat and bag and follows her out of the house.

She'll be headed home. A thirty-minute walk because she'll never flag down a taxi around here. On deserted, dark streets because this is the quietest hour, that strange one after most of the pub and club patrons have fallen asleep in their beds but before the city's early-risers have woken up in theirs. And her journey will take her alongside the Grand Canal, where the black water can look level with the street and where there isn't always a barrier to prevent you from falling in and where the street lights can be few and far between.

He can't let her go by herself. And he won't, because he's a gentleman. A gentleman who doesn't let young girls walk home alone from parties when they've been drinking enough to forget their coat, bag and – he lifts the flap on the little velvet envelope, checks inside – keys, college ID and phone too.

And he wants to make sure Jen knows that.

Mr Nice Guy, he calls himself.

He hopes she will too.

published by Hodges Figgis in 1904

THE

LANDLORDS' AND TENANTS'

HANDY GUIDE TO LAND PURCHASE,

INCLUDING

THE IRISH LAND ACTS, 1903 & 1904,

And Sections of Acts incorporated therewith;

THE LAND PURCHASE RULES AND FORMS;

WITH

An Introduction and Explanation

OF THE PROVISIONS OF THE ACTS AND OF THE PROCEDURE OF SALES; A SCHEDULE OF FEES AND ABSTRACT OF DECISIONS UNDER THE ACTS.

BY

JOHN ROBERT O'CONNELL, M.A., LL.D. (Univ. Dub.), SOLICITOR AND NOTARY.

DUBLIN:

HODGES, FIGGIS & CO., Ltd., BOOKSELLERS TO THE HON. SOCIETY OF KING'S INNS, 104 GRAFTON STREET.

———

Price One Shilling net.

Donal Ryan

from FROM A LOW AND QUIET SEA

The crucified boy swung the argument. He'd been resisting until then, saying, Let's just see what the next month brings, whether this will pass. No one would dare touch us, and the fighting still is mostly far away; the front may even be retreating, not coming closer. Then the pooled blood in the crucified boy's bare feet, purplish and distended as though they might at any second burst like berries swollen on the vine, the plastic cable ties pulled to the last of their tolerance above his ankles; his curiously pale hands. Perhaps, he thought, the blood had drained from them, as they were raised above the line of his shoulders, and he'd been dead an hour or more when he'd come upon the scene. The dust of the marketplace was settled that day, the crowd was thin and mostly still, people stepped softly where they stepped at all, and no man raised his voice or looked too long at the creature on the cross, the hooded boy who'd been a spy, it seemed, who'd spoken out of turn or sent a message from his phone or emailed someone, or transgressed in some way. He wasn't even sure it was a boy, just something in the way his knees were scabbed, and his shorts were belted low, spoke of childhood or the time just past it, when it's nearly impossible to keep the rules of men, to think of the world in terms of given things, to stop oneself from laughing out of turn, from acting on the impulses that flame and boil beneath the skin. A man stood at the cross's foot with a rifle cradled in his meaty arms, his feet planted in the dust, a black scarf tied around his lower face and one around his head, so all that was visible of his features were his eyes, and they were fathomless, and lightless, and dead.

Farouk, his wife said now. And then nothing. This was a thing she often did, as though to reinforce her own sense of his presence, of his realness to her. Always he used to say, Yes? Or, What is it? But he had learned with the years to stay silent when he sensed a certain mood of hers, a certain type of heavy quietness. Worry was passed now, discarded like a garment worn too long: they knew the ins and outs of the plan, of each stage of the journey, the rendezvous and routes and the vehicles that would be used. There was only a kind of cold tension left, a brittleness, as they each intently regarded the other, trying to hear the things unspoken. He'd left instructions in a letter for his closest friend, a doctor with no wife, whom he'd known since childhood, who'd shared a room with him at the university, who'd toasted him at his wedding, who'd smiled at his newborn daughter, his eyes filled with tears. His house could be used by the hospital, and anything in it, and his car, and he was sorry it had come to this. He'd measured the weights of his conflicting duties carefully, he told his friend in the letter, and he'd measured and measured again, and he'd mourned the time when such duties weren't in conflict one against the other but were all part of a good life and all given to the same end, but this now was how the world was, and he was left with no choice but to get his daughter and his wife to safety.

His wife's family had crowded into their house the previous evening, and her sisters, one a year older and one a year younger, had covered Martha's face with kisses as they clung to her, and they'd cried so loudly that he'd feared a passerby would hear and think it strange that such sounds were coming from a house where no one had been lost, and deduce that they were leaving. Amira asked why her aunts were crying and her grandmother said they were crying for joy, because they were so happy that their sister and their niece were going to have such an adventure. And she took Amira on her knee and said, When I see you again, my love, you might be a scientist, like your mother, or a doctor, like your father, or a baker, like your grandfather and me. Be happy, whatever you are, and remember how precious you are, and how much I love you. And Amira had smiled at her grandmother's words, and had lain in her lap awhile like a baby, and Martha's father had stood close beside Farouk, and they had watched the women's leave-taking in silence, until the old man whispered, Go with God, my son, and live long, and he had taken Farouk's hand in his, and the old man's hand was shaking hard.

published by Hodges Figgis in 1905

Little Red
Riding=Hood:

Told in Verse by
MAURICE C. HIME, M.A., LL.D.

LONDON: SIMPKIN, MARSHALL & CO.
HODGES, FIGGIS & CO., LTD.
104 GRAFTON STREET, DUBLIN

Price One Shilling, net.

Séamus Scanlon

from THE BLOOD FLOW GAME

WOMAN: (*Very surprised, stuck for words*). Sor ... Sorry. I thought you didn't care. You never said. You never said stay. You never said, don't go. You never said one thing that was real.

VICTOR: Sure. Why would I say it? It's a free country – well once the Brits leave. Everyone has free will. You can go and come. I do not own you. It's my thing – take it or leave it.

WOMAN: (*Sadly*). I left it, sure.

VICTOR: (*Angrily*). Yes – you are great. Well, why are you back so?

WOMAN: (*Beat. Dispirited*). I don't know.

VICTOR: Some things should not have to be said. You should just know.

WOMAN: (*Perplexed*). Victor – people can't mind read – especially yours. (*Long beat. Upset*). I suppose I should be going.

VICTOR: Yes. That would be best.

WOMAN: (*Sarcastically*). Would it?

WOMAN slowly walks to door and looks back. She looks away. VICTOR stares at table. She reaches for the door handle.

VICTOR: Hold up!

WOMAN: (*Expectantly, turns back*). Yes?

VICTOR says nothing. Is thinking.

VICTOR: Nothing. Forget it. (*Beat*). Sorry.

WOMAN: Ok.

WOMAN slowly begins to open door. Bell over door rings.

VICTOR: Hold up!

WOMAN: (*Trying to be lighthearted*). Your favourite. It's a hold up. (*Long beat*). Yes, Victor?

VICTOR: You know yourself!

WOMAN: No, I don't. Don't forget the fucking mind reading thing I just said.

VICTOR: What? (*Beat*). Oh yeah. (*Not annoyed*). Fuck – forget it. (*WOMAN turns back as if to leave*). Hold up!

WOMAN: (*Turning back abruptly again to face VICTOR*). For fuck sake, Victor, what is it? (*Kindly*). Victor – it's ok – say it.

VICTOR: (*With difficulty. Long beat*). I am sorry. (*Beat*). You know?

WOMAN: No. What about?

VICTOR: Fuck – you know – the thing. (*Annoyed. Embarrassed*). The things!

WOMAN: (*Bewildered*). What things?

VICTOR: (*Annoyed*). Fuck – You know the '*you make me feel mighty fucking real*' thing. For not being real. For the real cruelty thing. For the gun thing. (*Takes it from his jacket*). For the white Albino black coelacanth thing. For the Dettol thing. For the ineffectual affection thing. For the no smiling thing. For the blood flow thing. For the lost in thought far ceiling thing. For the killing thing. For the random error thought thing.

WOMAN: (*Sadly*). That's a lot of things there, Victor.

VICTOR: Yeah. (*Exhausted, sits down, still has gun*). Yes. Too many. It's hard to keep count. *Tá me tréachta.*

WOMAN: (*Cries*). Thanks for saying all that. (*WOMAN moves one step away from door towards VICTOR*). You can still stop. (*Kindly*).

VICTOR: No. It is too late. (*Beat*). I am too far gone now. (*Touches gun against temple*). All the strands of the killing thing are fused in here. They can't be separated out anymore.

WOMAN: (*Sadly*). 'We' are separate now though, Victor.

VICTOR: Yes. (*Thinking, comes to decision, long beat*). Look, you can visit Ma if you like. Best day is Thursday – it is my busy day – I am never there that day. Errands and the like.

WOMAN: Ok. (*Beat*). If you are sure? I would like that. Thanks.

VICTOR: (*Bit calmer*). Ok. She used to say – 'You have a great wee girl there. She would look dynamite in black carrying an armalite!'

WOMAN: (*Amused*). No! You never said. Why am I not surprised? She had some weird ideas.

VICTOR: I suppose.

WOMAN: I know where you got it so.

VICTOR: How do you mean?

WOMAN: The weirdness!

VICTOR: Oh, ok I suppose. I see. I got you.

WOMAN: You are mellowing in your old age! The chronological one! (*Beat*). We can talk about armalites!

VICTOR: Ok. (*Beat*). And Blitzkrieg.

WOMAN: What?

VICTOR: (*Mildly*). Nothing. Don't mind me.

WOMAN: (*Long beat*). Victor?

VICTOR: Yeah?

WOMAN: (*Emotional*). Nothing. (*Long beat. Hurriedly, upset*). I love you. Sorry. I mean I loved you. You were the real thing. For me. For such a long time. Goodbye. Sorry about things. Sorry about everything.

WOMAN comes over from door. Bends down and kisses VICTOR on the cheek and then leaves abruptly. She does not look back. Bell on door rings as she leaves. Beat (20 seconds). VICTOR stands up suddenly and sweeps everything off the table in a rage using the gun hand. He then upends table, stomps on plates and radio and other crockery until everything is in bits.

VICTOR: Fuck!

A WESTERN WAKENING

BY

BLIGH TALBOT-CROSBIE

SECOND EDITION

DUBLIN
HODGES, FIGGIS & CO., LTD.
104 GRAFTON STREET
1912

Order form for A Western Wakening: *by Bligh Talbot Crosbie* (NLI)

ORDER FORM

Messrs. HODGES, FIGGIS & CO., Ltd.
    104 Grafton Street, DUBLIN.

Please forward me .... cop...... of " A WESTERN WAKENING,"
by BLIGH TALBOT-CROSBIE. Crown 8vo, 176 pages. Price 2s. 6d. net,
per post 2s. 9d., for which I enclose £   s.   d.

Date.

Mike Scott

HOW SHE MADE IRELAND

Early in the procession of illusions known as time, the being which some call Goddess, and some Great Mystery, dreamed the Earth into existence, creating its blue globe as an expression of her vast mind.

If we had been born then and had watched through the ages that are but minutes in the life span of worlds, and had we eyes to bear the splendour, we would have witnessed Her as a storm of energy contained in human shape, miles tall, as She stood ankle-deep in the great sea that covered the earth.

She bent and scooped from the ocean bed a mass of clay and stone. With the heat from Her hands, clumsily She fashioned this mass into scarped and cracked shapes, and as Her fingers worked they infused Her creation with life. And when it made a shape that pleased Her She placed it in the sea.

Her sculpture splashed into the ocean with a mighty hiss and its top stuck out over the waves and under the sky. It was a crude barren thing but it formed an island that would one day be called Inishmore, most ancient of all lands, and largest of the scattering of rocks known as the Aran Isles.

The Goddess looked on what She'd made and the image of a more elaborate creation touched Her mind. She drew a double handful of earth from the ocean bed. Again She shaped it, this time with more skill, and threw it back down. And once more the top rose from the sea, this time forming a mountainous peak. She repeated the motion, creating another peak, then another, then a high ridge, then a plateau, then another peak, and so on, honing Her skills, creating with each piece greater harmony of form, greater coherency.

Rising from the foaming seas, these shapes fused and formed Connacht, from the Twelve Bens of Connemara north to the drumlin hills of Leitrim and Sligo, south to the ragged stonelands of Mayo and Galway, and a rough wild beautiful thing it was.

And as She beheld Her handiwork, understandings of shape, structure and form arose in Her mind. And this understanding was embodied in the creation itself, dwelling thereafter in the soil, rocks and air of Connacht as the essence of Knowledge.

She turned north and looking on the waters envisioned in their place the province of Ulster, grander than Connacht, strewn with green hills, rich flatlands and long sparkling sea lochs.

As before, She gathered clay from the seabed, shaped it and set it in place. But though the cliffs and mountainlands of Donegal were swiftly made in similar fashion to Connacht, when She sought to create low, fertile lands stretching far from ocean's edge the work grew difficult. She had not yet mastered the principles of breadth and distance, or those of flow and rigidity, and Her attempts resulted in the tangled lakelands of Fermanagh, Cavan and Monaghan. What She cast with Her hands failed to embody what She saw in Her mind; vision outstripped skill.

Driven, she gathered Her will into a focussed storm and persevered until She grasped how to make a body of land from the interlocking of small pieces, though She achieved this only by the creation of Lough Neagh as an inland sea around which to cluster them.

Impatience rose like a tempest in Her mind and raged against the limits of Her skill and understanding. Inflamed by the warring powers within Her, in a passion of creative fever She forged the coastal rim of Ulster, casting the bewildering Giant's Causeway, dramatic Antrim Coast and wild, cliff-strewn Rathlin Island. Yet even as She worked the fever abated and mastery grew until, at last satisfying Herself, She laid the islands of Strangford Lough like green jewels in the foam and clove the sloping, graceful Mountains of Mourne.

Yet because of the process of its creation Ulster would ever after bear the imprint of Conflict.

Next, and with increasing precision, She fashioned Leinster, its green pastures and noble coastline sweeping southward. Here the work flowed with grace. Skill matched vision, vision took account of skill, and a quality of ease was woven into the landscape as a hallmark; a quality of the efficient and flowing movement of energy which, in time to come, humans would call Prosperity.

And between Leinster in the east and Connacht in the west She gouged out with one of Her great fingers a lordly river, the Shannon.

And now, inspired by the beauty of Her work, She made her masterpiece: Munster to the south, its bejewelled lakes and valleys, chains of tumbling mountains, its sweet mazy coastline, and in the far west – glory upon glory – a series of wild peninsulas, each more beautiful than the last, stretching like arms into the great ocean. And yet, even beyond these, in the ecstasy of her creation She flung strange final islands that scattered like buckshot; islands with backs like cockscombs and high torn peaks.

And the essence of Munster, imbued by the eloquence of its making, was Poetry.

And when the last rock of the last crag of the last island off the last peninsula of Munster had been cast on the ocean, She found some pale lumps of earth left in Her hands. Taking the best of these, and in a spirit of play that followed the intensity of Munster's creation like a gentle coda might follow the final movement of a symphony, She fashioned the exquisite county of Clare between Munster to the south and Connacht to the north.

And the essence of Clare was Music.

All She had left was a thumb-and-fingerful of cracked limestone, yet from this, with playful masterstrokes, She made the queer, beautiful Burren with its scarped hills and corkscrew valleys.

Her creation was complete, and She loved it.

But looking at Her hands, She saw one last piece of limestone. Tenderly She placed it in the ocean, its tip forming the perfectly-shaped island of Inisheer, west of the Burren, east of the isle of Inishmore where She had begun.

She turned southward, new lands to make. But as She did, a scrap of clay tumbled from beneath Her fingernail. Falling between Inisheer and Inishmore, it became the accidental island of Inishmaan, which lay low in the water like a dark serpent head, brooding over the sleepless waves.

published by Hodges Figgis in 1916

THE

SINN FEIN RISING:

A Narrative, and Some Reflections

By FREDERIC W. PIM.

PRICE THREEPENCE.

DUBLIN:
Hodges, Figgis & Co., Limited, 104, Grafton Street.
1916.

Frank Sewell

CLOSE ENCOUNTERS

'Runaround Sue' my cousins called you
though all the boys ran after you.
Remember that night in the dinette,
cards on the table, footsie under it?
Us caught wild-haired on the settee
by my aunt who still slegs me ...?

Your school-grey mini-skirt clings
to my mind. 'I'm wearing stockings,'
you teased. '*Don't* let your hands wander!'
We tackled behind the leisure centre
like athletes trying to win a place
in the *Guinness Book of Records* for kisses.

Sue, you were Champions' League.
Fog came fumbling over the field,
then torches, voices and armed men
in camouflage, their accents foreign:
'Wot's a noice young Caff'lick whore
loike you out 'ere wiv 'im for?'

'It's none of your bloody business'
– I turned to the bigmouth, my size.
'Oh yeah? I'll 'ave you.' He raised his gun.
'They're kids,' the commander said. 'Move on.'
He could have killed me, and I knew.
That cowboy had it in for you.

Lorna Shaughnessy

LOOP

I cannot face the bog today
nor the windmills on the hill,
their arms waving in persistent distress,
reminders of the loop that carries us
from the first and hardest thing we do
                              to the last.

I cannot bear to hear the green creak
of new growth, or the lark's frantic song,
spectacular denial of its quickening ebb
and I dread the razor-edge of tooth and claw,
the sight of another fledgling
                    in the cat's maw.

I need to walk in a peopled place,
take comfort in venial commerce
in shops whose shining surfaces reveal nothing
of the creeping truth beneath our clothes:
that we are all survivors, for now,
                    of the body's last assault.

Eithne Shortall

from GRACE AFTER HENRY

'Ah feck!'

The cyclist at the bike rail beside him looked up.

'Forgot something,' Henry told the stranger, before redoing his bike lock and jogging back to his office building. He bounded up the steps, taking two at a time, using the handrail to propel himself onward.

'Forget something else?'

'Helmet. She'll kill me if I'm not wearing it.'

Henry went to the cloakroom, grabbed the green armour from his cubbyhole and waved it at the receptionist. 'That's the last time I'll be back. I swear.'

'Until tomorrow anyway,' she called out the door after him. 'Best of luck with the house!'

But Henry was already on the staircase, winding the scarf tighter around his neck as he hotfooted it down the steps. He was dressed in a near homage to Grace. The bright red scarf she'd knit him, and which he adored, and the helmet she insisted he start wearing. If he died, or suffered a terrible brain injury, what about her? It wasn't just about him anymore.

Henry had never felt so half of something as the day he bought that helmet. It was scary to love someone so much that the end of one life could mean the end of two. He had never found the words to describe how much he loved Grace but he tried to show it in his actions; in wearing a helmet, in being her biggest champion, in not being late for this house viewing.

He looked at his watch. 5.35pm. Ok. If he put his meddle to the pedal and didn't hit any red lights he would make it for 5.50. He only needed ten minutes to look around. Less, usually. And unless this house was significantly better than the shamelessly wide-angled photographs online suggested, his heart was still set on Aberdeen Street.

Henry unlocked his bike for the second time and stuffed *A Christmas Carol* into his bag. That was what he had gone back to the office for the first time. He and Grace were reading it. Again. Even though it was February. Henry had brought it to work for a project they were working on – the book was just the right size for a poster mock-up – but he needed to have it back before bedtime. It was his turn to read tonight. Though Grace could sing for him doing the voices.

Henry pushed off, pulling the scarf into position again. The sky was grey but he reckoned he could make it to East Wall before the heavens opened. He got stuck behind a group of tourists cycling two abreast down Dame Street and had to dismount his bike because of roadworks at College Green. The clock at O'Connell Bridge said 5.44. Shit. He'd take the quays. Less traffic lights and less cyclists. He looked right, left, threw the boisterous scarf over his shoulder and pushed right in unison with an articulated truck.

The quays were always jammed with industrial vehicles at this hour but at least they were moving, their massive wheels turning, the bolts the size of Henry's head. The cycle lane was empty. He picked up speed, recalculating his arrival time. 5.55, probably. 5.53, if he stepped on it. It didn't really matter; he just had to get there. He pushed down harder, feeling the strain in his thighs. If Henry made Grace a promise, he kept it. He loved her. He *fucking* loved her! Three years together and he hadn't grown tired of this same startling realisation that boomed outwards from his heart, reverberating in every part of him. He'd tell her when he got there. He was always telling her, but he'd tell her again. He grinned to himself. They'd get that Aberdeen Street house and properly, really properly, begin their life together. His heart swelled, driving him forward, faster. He loved this feeling; he was cycling towards her.

A splash on his wrist, Henry looked up. He didn't feel his scarf coming loose, didn't register the pull around his neck as the wind that had been holding it in the air finally dropped and it looped its way through the spokes. A second splash, and another. In the spokes, wrapping round and round, and now the breaks. A sudden halt. Fuck.

Rain keeping time on his handlebars as they fell to the right. Wheels skidding, his feet down to balance but too late, too fast, too determined not to be late for Grace. Grace. Bike toppled, big wheel, as big as him, bolt the size of his head. The suction. Suck! And under. Oh god Grace. Crunch, crun – Black.

All gone. In the flutter of an eye. Her eyes. Grace.

Peter Sirr

READING TO THE WOLVES

Remember how they cursed you,
the movers in Milan, sweating
the four steep flights to my flat?
Not only you, who were many,
but someone else's entire *Larousse*.

You came from Holland, marked *Poppen*,
so that the administrator, embarrassed,
called me aside:
'I've had a call from Customs,
it's about your *dolls* …'

Now you're on the move again
stacked in boxes
from floor to ceiling, wall to wall.
Only the dog is unencumbered:
no books, no music, no subscriptions
to unread mounds of *Gramophone*
or the *Times Literary Spaniel*.

Simplify. Purify. No one loves a hoarder.
I should throw you to the wolves,
let you dance in ghostly libraries
where angels sway to mix tapes
and someone plans to send me back
as an ear forever hesitating
between Finnish tango and Norwegian jazz,
a nose glued to a shelf
in Books Upstairs or Hodges Figgis.

A baton falls
through the dust of my skull
and here come the movers now,

groaning under the weight of you
and cursing again
the *bastardo* with the *libri*.

If only I could hold out my empty hands
and point at the clean, wordless air.
Your breath at my shoulder, your tunes in my bones:
you lighten my load but make me heavy.

So check the inventory and keep us quiet,
find some wolves and play them Bach
or Nusrat or Cooley or Björk,
read to them all night so they forget to howl
and remember, sometimes,
heaviness is all.

Advert from the late 1970s

Undated, no source

Stephen James Smith

I'VE HAD LOVERS AND I'VE HAD LOVES ...

But when I love again,
I will love like Michael Furey.
Is it unrealistic to love
like a fictional character?

That's been conjured up
in the mind of Jimmy.
A young Traveller who serenaded
his love in the dead of winter.

His lungs frozen
with a snowy song of ache.
Unable to rest with the yearning,
to proclaim.

I want to proclaim
all my love with fury.
I'm done with
tepid encounters.

Sparks and dying embers
only warm the souls in passing.
Flames can only extinguish lost
feelings burning me up.

Let's not insult each other
with kind kisses.
Let's tear out our hearts
or nothing at all!

Cherry Smyth

GIANT PEOPLE

We are living ourselves again,
as children, hypothetical,
as if we were never there.
We try to peer through three year old
eyes at giant people making us put
on our socks and have to admire
the feral fury of the baby banshee
in a mermaid suit stamping his feet,
leaving us stranded

on an island of rational persuasion
and gentle leverage that back off
from bribes and a good shake.
It's hard to be right and good. It's hard
to undo the cruelties this world requires.
They've run amok in us for so long.

But there is a line beginning with 'no'
that we must speak for the animal tyranny
of his 'yes' will hurt more.

And we are living our parents again,
as ourselves, hypothetical,
as if we were there in their warm arms,
the difficult rain, picnics spent looking for
the best spot, the perfect family
to sit on it. It's true: the refusals, the subterfuge
that are asked of even the kindest love.

And when we ask this boy
if he knows a new thing, he never
says 'no' or lies with 'yes',

he widens his eyes and says what
none of us ever said,
'Tell me,' he says.

published by Hodges Figgis in 1903

ISLĀM

𝔄 Prelection

DELIVERED BEFORE THE UNIVERSITY OF DUBLIN

MARCH 10, 1903

BY

STANLEY LANE-POOLE, M.A., Litt.D.

PROFESSOR OF ARABIC

DUBLIN

HODGES, FIGGIS, & CO., Ltd.

BOOKSELLERS TO THE UNIVERSITY

104, GRAFTON STREET

MCMIII

Price One Shilling

Damian Smyth

FRANCIS SHEEHY SKEFFINGTON IN DOWNPATRICK

There used to be a way to get into the old gaol
Though it was foreign lands: Victorian,
Oddly English but equally oddly our own. It's '75;
A back door on a shocking hinge; an eye skinned
Across a gravel yard where convicts certainly trod
A surface so rattly even a ghost's foot would register
In a tiny subsidence, absolute certainties giving way.
Then inside to the cool of everything secret and confined:
Pigeon shit and their throaty purring overhead.
Then there were the discards from Hayes's Hotel
– Tall bottles of Guinness like a procession of rectors;
With the hare's lip of a bottle opener, shiny
And as coveted as a key. Such transfiguration.
Such living among the forbidden dead; a crossing over;
Acts of stealth in a stone maze, an empire's bone house.
Half a mile off, in Skeffington's Butchers (or *Skivvitons*
As our own English had it), they were wheeling carcasses out
Like bony cages the animals themselves had been held in.
Who was to know then what unfinished business was?
Not that corpse of his stretched out in Portobello Barracks
A lifetime before, the bullet that killed him stuck in a brick;
Or that of the dead President, his gaunt beak right then
Rising in Dublin Castle above borders of satin and oak;
Any more than those kids climbing into ruins, in the months
The summer was hot, and the truce just about holding.

Gerard Smyth

CINEMA ON THE GREEN

At the late show in our tattered
parterre seats, in the back row or close to it
we kissed, caressed, held hands – whatever
love-lust demanded by way of words and deeds.

The late show was one with screams,
a script by Edgar Allan Poe.
Once it was *The Brides of Dracula*,
their pale complexions paler still in the Gothic dark.

We waited for the moment when the first
streak of light or a stake put through the heart
revealed that beneath his cloak
the vampire was only dust.

There were nights of London fog,
moon-clouds, ravens. We heard the first cries
of *Rosemary's Baby*, saw *The Wicker Man* burning
and the last Hitchcockian murder.

The late show was our nocturnal escape
into occult stories, tales from the crypt,
into the long shadow of Christopher Lee
in his many guises of metamorphosis.

Dolores Stewart

GO DEIREADH NA SCRÍBE
a haithle C.P. Cavafy

Roimh sheoladh duit ar mhuir mhór do thurais
iarr achainí ar Dhia go mba fada slán do bhealach.
Agus iarr achainí ar Dhia nach gcaillfear le faitíos thú:

ní baol duit déithe bréige na spéire
ní mó ná deamhain faoi thoinn.

'Fad is atá lóchrann os do chomhair, ní bheadh a leithéid
faoi scáth romhat: déithe bréige nó deamhain aeir

muna bhfuil an dubh ina sheasamh ionat,
muna bhfuil sé i bhfolach i do chroí.

Go mba fada slán do bhóthar,
go mba mhéanar duit do léim in áiteanna diamhra do-eolais
is go dté oscailt na bhflaitheas romhat –

éascaíocht rí i do ghlac agus tuilleadh
as iothlainn na gréine,
ómra na céadmhaidine ag taitneamh i do ghleannta.

Go mba mhéanar duit do bhealach,
ach bíodh an trá thall i gcónaí i do cheann
mar is ann atá do thriall.

Agus ná bíodh síneadh ar bith ort –
más folamh do dháil faoi dheireadh
ná fág ar cheann do riain é

murach an turas, ní bheadh fáilte abhaile romhat
nó do líonta lán de sheoda cuimhne

Go dtí deireadh na scríbe, ní fheicfidh tú snáth geal na slí
ag dealramh i do dhiaidh.

published by Hodges Figgis in 1905

" LITTLE MARY'S " UP-TO-DATE

DISHES EASILY COOKED.

" A perfect woman, nobly planned,
To warn, to comfort, and command."

DUBLIN : HODGES, FIGGIS, & CO., LTD.

LONDON : SIMPKIN, MARSHALL, HAMILTON,

KENT, & CO., LTD.   MCMV.

Deirdre Sullivan

THE WORD THAT MEANS A WITCH

The hot breath of a robber bridegroom on the nape of your pale neck inside the night. The slice of a long fingered hand through the air. The shadow that it casts. Images collect here, gathering like birds in trees, on poles.

Familiar thoughts to have in foreign places.

You have vocabulary for the things there are. But it is strange to be a stranger here. The tongue you know is foreign to them and you. You'd love to be a polyglot. To have that skill. An easy tongue encoding and decoding. But even so, and even with their kindness, the awkward shape of you lurks strange in rooms. Too wide in places and too small in others. You tell yourself that it will all be fine. And search for hidden beauty out the window.

The figure eight would be a shape to be. But you like sevens, elevens. The number thirteen too. You find it here. You count the trees, the small bumps in the road. The cracks in plaster, window-panes. Creases on your skin when you awake. You would always pick seven first. When you were small. Between the one and ten. And if you couldn't grab that seven, four. There is a comfort. Things that you prefer can be around you, if you work to find them. They warned you, a lady by herself. In every hostel someone calls you brave. So brave to be alone, without a person. You smile at them and shrug. You had no choice. There are places that call girls like you. Your eyes were crusty, dry with want to see them. Here you feel them welling up with colour. Every day. And in the night, you wear a decade of the rosary around your wrist. Your digits shape the soft round painted beads.

The joyful.

The luminous.

The sorrowful.

The glorious.

You have to travel roads to go a place. It's what you know. You murmur what you know inside the night. The words that live in you since you were small. In fourth class, your teacher was an old, kind woman with a lined face. She wore a thick gold band on the fourth finger of her small right hand. You thought, until Maria pointed out, that she was married. You didn't know that there were sides to put things on. To say things. You didn't grow up knowing things like that. Shapes and rules. Directions. You liked to count. You liked to repeat words. To build a comfort structure in your brain. Warp the world into a shape that makes a sort of sense. To dull the sharp of it. To tick it off.

The night is long. The shapes that shadows cast upon the walls as breath collects. Twelve people or fifteen or even more inside a room, the stench of them together. Food and sleep. A mist of food and sleep that coils and curves. You almost see it making shapes in air, paprika clouds. They like their spices here, to warm their stomachs. Spices and potatoes and sweet wine. You finger at your bracelet and feel the cheap sheets on your tight, dry skin. You've only packed essentials. It's not like you will be away forever. What you told them.

'Not like it's forever. Just for now.'

The Agony in the Garden.

You learned them like nursery rhymes. Recited them in loud, hard chants together. It was a bit old-fashioned, even then, but there was comfort. It felt like Harry Potter. Casting spells. Protect us from all harm. That would be lovely.

You school was in a large, old convent building. High ceilings for the patients there had been. They'd had TB. You once passed by a classroom and heard the rattle of a hacking cough. The whirr of phlegm beneath. You peered inside the thin rectangled glass inside the door. You remember it was covered, tiny squares, like copies for your sums. The room was empty. There is more to here than you can say. And sometimes broken things are left behind. You know what that can feel like.

They betrayed him with a kiss. A kiss. A soft thing turning into something else. Warped to something hard. The day that you decided what to do. Where you would go. There was a trigger there. There was no safety. You remember that he took you shooting. Once. As a 'fun' date. His words. He loved that stuff. Go-Karting. Paint-balling. Things that veered toward a little dangerous. You like to look at things inside the world. But doing is a lot. He pulled you to that. Made you do the things. And afterwards he'd ask you what you thought. And you would say 'I loved it. It was class.'

A faithful little parrot.

When things are broken, memories can err. Can warp and shape. And there are always, say, at least two stories. At least two stories. Whoever makes them. Actors in the tales. They shape it and they see it with their eyes in different ways. The light hits details differently. But still. Your version is too close to you to change. You carry it. You hold it in your womb, as though a child. A sharp-toothed, hungry baby. The weight of it is growing, pulsing, swelling. It gnaws at you. And it will worm its way inside you more and hollow you to be a puppet-shade.

You are a person.

You can be a person if you like.

And hurt won't stop you.

You wanted to go somewhere cheap and wild. You gave your notice, and you bought a ticket. Put your things back in your parents' house. It's not where you grew up. It's smaller, manageable. They wanted somewhere grand for them to clean. To have a tidy house, a tidy life. The space to be together. Go on cruises with the profit made. They like to travel too, your Mam and Dad. They smile together bright in front of places, and behind orange, yellow, red and purple drinks. They love a fancy cocktail. 'Ice-Pop drinks' your father calls them. There's something of the child about them now. You see it. Name it. Put your finger on it. Trace the shape.

Your things will be safe there. But they take up space. And make a little mess. Ungainly boxes. When you get back. They said. When you get back. You'll move them out. Of course.

Of course you will.

The things are only temporary.

Stationed.

The dreams you have are strange and heavy here. Dogs howling in the night. A broken chorus, too harsh to be music. Lips upon a beard. A weight against your stomach thighs and breasts. A climbing thing, like ivy. Like a vine. The thirst. The thirst. The whirring cough. The clockwork tick of mucus in the throat. There are so many hollows in our skull. So many places for the green, the grey, the yellow stuff to hide. It isn't weight loss. Blood upon a handkerchief.

Three little drops. Like rubies from a mouth. Pale skin. Blue eyes. A perfect woman with a perfect death. And is that what you want? You are not sure. There are different matters to consider. You do not want to think. You want to look. You want to sit beside the window in a mini-bus, rattling up mountain slopes. You want to see the bloom of trees. Cherry-blossom, apple, pear and plum. The bright of sun against the slopes. The colours that they turn. The bright, the dark, and, higher up, the cold.

You want to look at it.

You want to look.

You want to reach a slender finger out across the slopes, as long as an aerial, picking signals up, and tracing, touching. Till you reach a point.

Where you can name it.

You can say it out.

What happened.

What it was.

The shape.

Your story.

Matthew Sweeney

MY MOTHER'S WINE

In my mother's late years she liked her wine,
her *red* wine. She never touched white,
just as earlier she'd avoided all alcohol, and
objected to anyone drinking it near her.
My father was the same, wearing a Pioneer
Pin to every public event. One evening, over
dinner, I slid in the fact that in France and Italy
wine was considered part of a meal. I see,
he said, and began trying small sups of wine.
My mother followed suit, of course, and soon
was outdoing him, sliding her glass down
to be refilled. Soon the empties began to
accumulate beneath her bed, although the
supplier remained a mystery. Was this after
the Alzheimer's had started to take over?
It was round about then that my brother
began substituting alcohol-free wine,
claiming she wouldn't notice the difference.
Yet, one evening, shortly before she died,
we ate together, and when my brother left,
she pushed her glass away, asking me to pour
some of *my* wine, saying she preferred that,
but my brother trumped my recounting of this
by telling me that in a video viewed after mother
had died, she could be clearly seen swapping
her offering for his real dose of wine, so I
raise this humble glass of a passible Bordeaux
to my mother, wishing she was here to join me.

Rosita Sweetman

An Ode to Dublin

My Dublin is black and white, grey and sepia.
It's Georgian buildings dark with rain, and ruin,
it's seagulls, whippet thin young lads from the flats
diving into the canal in the choppy sunshine,
a green Morris Minor proceeding down the empty road.

My Dublin is 1965. It's The Beatles and The Rolling Stones
crowds of girls screaming damply; 'an atmosphere hot and
sharp; full of powder and perfume and a frightening
excitement'. It's big navy policemen from the country
looking on astounded: what *is* it about them English boyos
that's driving our young ones crazy?

My Dublin is artisan cottages in Portobello for sale
at £6,000; another £4,000 to do one up; it's a slaughterhouse
on Synge Street, a Family Planning Clinic beside it; pigs
screaming in the summer afternoon. An abattoir stench.

My Dublin is Bewley's coffee and sticky buns
on Saturday mornings. The Bailey, Davy Byrne's, McDaids
later; Patrick Kavanagh, Tony Cronin, Eddie Maguire
ruled. It's 'Broadsheet', with contributions from John
Behan, Seamus Heaney, Michael Kane, John Heath Stubbs,
Michael Hartnett, Paul Durcan, Yevgeny Yevtushenko,
Leland Bardwell. *Me!*

My Dublin is the Pope's visit, walking to the Phoenix Park
with Hattie (daughter of Evelyn), Adrian Kenny, Mum.
Adrian waving a white handkerchief
as the helicopter circles steeply.
My Dublin is mini skirts, *hurrah!* boots,
massive mirror shades. – Eh, Is that a pelmet you're
wearing, asks Dad – or a skirt?

My Dublin is Bloody Sunday
– *THIRTEEN DEAD IN DERRY!*
It's being crushed in Merrion Square two days later as the
British Embassy is burnt to toast amidst roars and cheers.

It's Mrs Gaj's restaurant and the Irish Women's Liberation
Movement. Fuck you Patriarchy – secular and religious.
Yeah! It's consciousness raising, making friends
with our vaginas in hand-held mirrors. *Jesu!*

It's the contraception train to Belfast. It's marching for
freedom of choice. It's invading Neary's snug.
Invading Sandycove's MEN ONLY! premier
swimming hole, the old fellas running for cover
as twenty somethings demand equal access. *Oh* yeah;
it's a young activist spray painting Gloria Steinem's battle
cry on the plinth of the (hideous) Papal Cross:
If men got pregnant abortion would be a sacrament.
The powers-that-be marshaled every JCB in Ireland
and earthed it up prontissimo.
A metaphor for their general approach to cries for change;
hence the terrible revelations to come.

In my Dublin Alfred is on the bridge at O'Connell Street
offering polaroids, it's pre-celebrity, pre global capitalism,
pre the super rich, pre the Dart, pre the Luas,
pre duvets, pre the internet, pre mobile phones,
pre Facebook. Weirdly, it's (mostly) pre-drugs,
apart, of course, from sensational amounts of alcohol,
the smell of hops all over the city,
the Guinness barges with their tilt down funnels
sliding under the Liffey bridges,
the pubs rammed to the rafters,
everyone penniless,
smoking their heads off.

Anne Tannam

CYCLING IN CHENNAI

Srilata lends me her bicycle –
its faded purple frame, rusty gears,
threadbare tyres begging me to love it,
begging me to sit astride its bum-sore saddle
and take to the highways of the college campus;

follow the road flanked with trees, trees
sundrenched trees, and deer, deer
searching for food in overflowing bins,
birds riding the waves of their dappled backs;

follow, follow, follow the curve, faster
faster into the breeze, past students
cycling in twos and threes,
and as we pass each other by
give them the secret nod that says:

hail universal tribe of pedal pushers;
hail kings and queens of forward motion;
hail the triumph of our journey.

Alice Taylor

KINDNESS

The goodness of your kindness
kept me in my mind.
Its worth could not be measured.
It had goodness undefined.
You held out a caring hand
when I was full of pain.
You thawed my frozen being
and made me live again.

Debbie Thomas

from BREATHTAKING

If my grandparents had got their way, I wouldn't be here at all.

Don't get me wrong. Nando and Gramps adore me. I'm not just their only grandchild, I'm also a huge relief. When I was born with everything in order, they must have felt like ... well, like they'd found a toilet after nine months of bursting. They'd been dead against Mum having a baby, which is why they'd been dead against her marrying Dad. Again don't get me wrong. They liked him a lot, at least at first. What they didn't like – what they hated, in fact – was the thought of Mum passing on her genes.

So did Dad, as it turned out. He must have been in love with Mum to start with because, when he found out about her *thinginess* (as he apparently called it), he promised (so she says) to protect her forever from the big, wide, shockable world. And when she got pregnant, he jumped (she tells me) for joy and said he'd love me just the same if I had *thingy* parts or not.

Yeah right. What's that saying again? If you can't stand the heat, get out of the kitchen. Well Dad couldn't so he did, literally, one morning when Mum was six months pregnant. And he didn't stop there but carried on down the hall, opened the front door, went along the pavement, turned left at the Spar, met Someone Else, got divorced and emigrated to New Zealand. The way Mum tells it, you'd think it all happened in one day.

Thanks for nothing, Dad – except your ordinary genes.

Back to those extraordinary ones. As I said, Nando and Gramps didn't want Mum to pass them on. Pretty rich, I know, when they'd given them to her in the first place. But they didn't know that until she was born. Like me, they don't have a trace of *thinginess*, at least not on the outside.

I started wondering about that a couple of years ago. Why was she the only one? I Googled stuff on genes and learned that they can hide in families for generations then reappear, apparently out of the blue. There have been dark-skinned babies born to light-skinned parents, and the other way round, because two people of different skin colour got together generations ago. And – take a deep breath – some babies are born with tails. Now take a deeper one, because we all had one once. Me, the postman, Ronaldo: every human embryo has a tiny tail that's absorbed by the body as it grows. Even after birth, our tail bone sits at the bottom of our spine, like a Post-It note reminding us of our animal ancestors. In Mum's case, though, it wasn't just tails or skin colour. It was more than different race or even species. It was different worlds. When she was born, fact and fiction collided.

Nando and Gramps didn't know that at first. What they *did* know was that their baby was deformed. That's not my word. But I can't blame Nando for thinking it when she saw the scales that covered Mum's hands and feet like polished bruises, and the bone-white claws in place of fingers and toes. I can understand why she needed to have a little scream while the no-nonsense midwife did the usual checks for breathing and reflexes. Then Nurse Shauna McHale wrapped Mum up, popped her into Nando's arms and waddled out to tell Gramps that his brand-new daughter was *exceptionally* beautiful.

'Meringue,' Nando told me. 'That's the colour he went when he saw your mum's hands and feet.'

Nurse Shauna agreed not to tell the doctors until Nando and Gramps had adjusted to the *particular* beauty of their child. 'She's passed all the tests,' she said. 'So there's nothing wrong. You tell me when you're ready to show her to a doctor.'

Not in an hour. Not in four. When it was time to go home, Ready still hadn't tapped them on the shoulder.

'Grand,' said Nurse Shauna. 'I'll come and visit you, make sure the baby stays healthy. Beyond that, she's none of my business. And no one else's either,' she said, patting Nando's arm, 'if that's the way you want it.'

Nando cried and hugged her. And it was the nurse's turn to cry when Nando named the baby Shauna. Then Nurse McHale waddled away from the most fabulous delivery of her life.

Mini-mum was gorgeous. The photos are all squashy smiles, not a scale or claw in sight. Nando and Gramps hid them under babygros and blankets. They considered taking her to a doctor. But Nando told me that Mum was so happy they couldn't bear the thought of worried frowns and millions of tests. I have another theory. It was really her 'deformity' that my grandparents couldn't bear. By hiding it they could escape their embarrassment and shame.

It's only when Mum turned two that they had a spark, so to speak, of understanding. And *that* was only thanks to one of those amazing coincidences that tell reason to pack its bags and leave by the back door, because wonder is knocking at the front. Mum's back teeth had come through. She was chewing on a rattle and looking at a book with Nando. They *happened* to turn to a picture of a dragon just as Mum *happened* to chomp extra hard on her rattle. A spark flew from the side of her mouth.

After much shrieking (grown-up) and forced drinking of water (toddler), Nando phoned Gramps and ordered him home from the bank. 'Now, George. Right NOW.'

She sat him on the sofa with the dragon picture, and Mum on the floor with a rattle. After a minute, another spark shot from Mum's mouth. This one burst into a tiny flame at the edge of her lips. While Nando poured more water down her throat, Gramps picked up the rattle from the floor. He gasped at the dent where the plastic had melted.

It was five days before they could say the word 'dragon'.

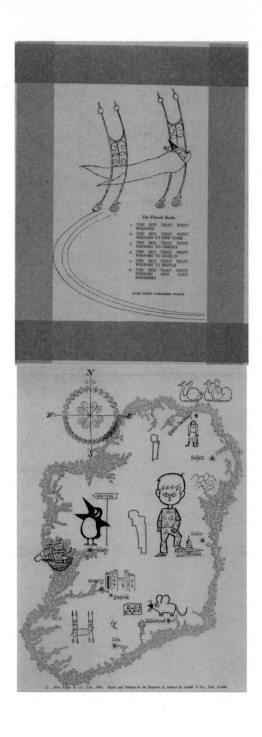

Gráinne Tobin

HEAVY RAIN, LOW LIGHT

This murky morning needs the lamp turned on,
but what's to stop me sitting up in bed
watching wet leaves sparkle beyond glass,
with three pillows at my back, my feet stuck out
to the hot-water bottle's remaining heat
in my padded envelope of quilt and mattress?

I've been saving myself for a dark and rainy day,
my bright hoard concealed by branches,
a hedge against the theft of time,
saved-up daylight, my trunk of minutes
to be spent, whatever I do, by nightfall.

The rain collects its light in millions,
floods river valleys, fills the newspapers,
draws a shining beaded veil
across the window of my lamp-lit hide.

Nobody expected, nothing to be done,
food in the fridge and oil in the tank.
The power lines are still ok.
I hear the boiler singing below stairs.

Colm Tóibín

from WORK IN PROGRESS

From his teenage years until his early twenties, he had had a problem with sex. It began in his parents' apartment on a Saturday evening when he took advantage of their absence and asked a girl from his school to come and watch a video with him. Soon, he found, as they lay on the sofa that he had, after a small amount of encouragement from the girl, ejaculated prematurely, thus causing her to depart in disgust. He had left a sticky stain not only on his own trousers but on the sofa itself. He got rid of his underpants by putting them at the bottom of the garbage can. Having changed into another pair, he used soap and a nailbrush on his trousers.

Although his efforts to remove any sign of the stain on the sofa seemed to make it worse, he was relieved when his parents did not notice it.

No matter what he did after that, as soon as he touched a girl he came all over himself. Eventually, since every weekend a pair of freshly laundered trousers had to be put into the laundry basket and another pair of underpants made their way into the garbage, he realized that he would have to tell his mother.

'Oh darling,' she said, 'that is so normal. You must not worry about it.'

He explained, however, that he did worry about it because girls were beginning to avoid him.

'I know a wonderful doctor,' she said, 'whom you must see. Now let me make an appointment with him.'

Thus after school one day he found himself in an empty doctor's waiting room in a shady side street in Schwabing. The receptionist looked at him strangely when he arrived. He wondered if she knew why he was here or if she imagined, in fact, that he had some worse problem than premature ejaculation.

As he leafed through some very old magazines, he could hear the doctor's voice faintly coming from the adjoining room. He wondered were he to move closer if he would actually be able to hear what was being said. When the receptionist came and peered at him for no apparent reason, he was tempted to run out into the street. Soon, an elderly couple came and sat near the door to the surgery. They both, he saw, were leaning forward, listening eagerly to the doctor's voice. Soon, he knew, once he went in, they would know all about him. He wondered if it would be too rude to ask the doctor to keep his voice down.

As a middle-aged man slinked out of the surgery and Heinrich waited for the doctor to call him, the elderly couple was joined by a mother and her teenage daughter who also placed themselves suspiciously close to the door that led to the doctor's surgery.

When the doctor, whom Heinrich thought must be in his sixties, invited him to sit on the other side of his large and archaic desk, he asked him to describe in detail what had occurred between him and the several girls who would no longer go on dates with him, and then he began to question him about his own feelings of panic as he ejaculated and the guilt and shame once he had done so. Heinrich, as he tried to reply, kept his voice down, hoping that the doctor would take the hint and follow suit.

But the doctor, he saw, liked the sound of his own voice. As he began to explain to Heinrich that his problem could be best solved by regular masturbation, Heinrich knew that the elderly couple in the waiting room plus the woman and her daughter would definitely be able to hear every word.

'As often as you can,' the doctor said, 'morning and night, and if you get a chance in the middle of the day. Just go at it. Get it all out. And then the girls of Munich will be panting mad for you, and maybe some of the boys too. Now, have you had many homosexual experiences yet?'

Heinrich almost ran at the doctor, waiting to put a hand over his mouth, as he denied hotly that he had any such experiences.

'Well, you are old enough to know your own mind,' the doctor said. 'But masturbation is the best way to discover where your real interests lie. Maybe when you are trying to come for the third or fourth time you will have the strangest thoughts, but don't worry about them, we all have them. Our sexual desires come in all shapes and sizes.'

As he saw that the doctor was merely beginning his diagnosis and was sitting back in his chair so he could further ruminate, Heinrich stood up and said that he had urgent homework to do. And his mother expected him home soon.

'I think you'll be over this problem in no time,' the doctor continued. 'It is a terrible end to an evening and girls don't like it. That is one thing we can be sure of. They like you to be able to wait your turn.'

Heinrich was standing at the door when the doctor indicated that he should hang on for a moment.

'Now, I suppose we had better make sure that you know the most efficient way to masturbate,' he said. He leaned forward and stood up from his chair.

'No, I do know, I definitely do,' Heinrich said as the doctor seemed actually to be preparing to show him how to masturbate.

'And, you know, a good porn magazine is often a great help,' the doctor went on. 'A great stimulation.'

'I really have to go,' Heinrich said.

'I suppose the younger generation nowadays knows more than we imagine,' the doctor said.

'I have to go,' Heinrich repeated.

'Give your mother my regards,' the doctor said. 'And remind your father from me that *cogito ergo sum.*'

Outside, Heinrich was sure, as he passed the mother who gave him a small nod of recognition and a sly smile, that they had all, including the daughter, heard every word.

At home, when his own mother asked him how the appointment had gone, he told her it had been fine.

'I knew that it would go well,' she said. 'He is such a clever man. When we were married first, your father had exactly the same problem and Dr Mannheim sorted it out in no time. I was at my wit's end and your father was a nervous wreck, and then suddenly it was all cured. And we have never looked back.'

The idea of his father suffering from premature ejaculation made Heinrich go to the bathroom and lock the door. He had to keep both taps running so that he could not be heard laughing. He laughed so much that he almost vomited. In his room, he could not stop picturing his father's lower body jerking uncontrollably as he came all over himself, and then having to take his underpants off and throw them away. And even when Heinrich tried not to think about it, he would find himself shaking in fits of laughter again before becoming almost sad. He wondered how he would ever look at his father again.

His father was out that evening. In the morning, on his way to the bathroom, however, Heinrich had briefly forgotten about his visit to the doctor when he encountered his father on the corridor.

Carrying a newspaper and a cup of coffee, his father leaned over and put the cup on a shelf so that his right hand was free. He stood in front of Heinrich, who was still in his pajamas, blocking his way, and began to mimic a man masturbating. He nodded then in satisfaction as he took the cup in his hand again and shuffled by.

'I am glad you are following the doctor's orders,' he muttered as he went towards the living room.

5 Dawson Street, c 1968

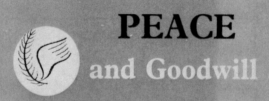

PEACE
and Goodwill ...

Whether from motives of fear
or because mankind has reached an age
of greater reason, it is certain that
the peoples of the world have never before
been so united in their desire for peace. . . .

Peace, however, is an experience of
the heart and world peace can
only come when individuals have
understood the true meaning of
Christmas for their own lives. . . .

We hope that the Season
may bring you
this joy in full measure.

HODGES FIGGIS & Co., Ltd.

back cover, Hodges Figgis catalogue, undated

LEAVES
for the turning

booksellers **HODGES FIGGIS & Co. Ltd. 6 Dawson Street DUBLIN**

front cover, Hodges Figgis catalogue, undated

Jessica Traynor

LULLABY

In the small hours you ask me:
where does sleep go?
It hangs in the trees
on the North Circular Road,
it clings to the streetlamps,
flits like bats or night birds
from window to window.
It does not settle.

You might catch it
in the cage of your eyelashes
before it springs to hide again
among grey-scale swirls
on wallpaper,
or in the wardrobe
with its creaking spirits.

But some night you will clasp
its matted fur, hitch your legs
to its sides and fly with it
above the moon.

And on that night
when you are lost to it
and I am left alone,
I will wonder where you go.

Mary Turley-McGrath

The Lost Café

One shot or two? she asks, her eyes dark as Polish forests;
eyes like yours, just like yours

and I remember that winter café years ago
where we escaped from frozen crowded streets

you were always late from study in the Berkeley
so I waited, immersed in coffee aromas

then you'd arrive, full of new ideas and connections
that exploded like summer cocktails between us

those evenings I forgot to savour the Arabica from
high Columbian plantations where pickers harvested
cherries, two coffee beans in each; wild parrot cries
and calls of meandering geese split their silent work.

One shot or two? she asks again.
Two, I say, not knowing why.

Breda Wall Ryan

NOW THAT THE WHITE BEAR IS GONE

There will be no polar ice by 2060. Somewhere along that path,
the polar bear drops out – Larry Schweiger

Now that the white bear is gone,
the Witch of the North
clears a window in the ozone.

She expands the oceans.
Amphibious, they bask on low lands,
offer cold blood to the Fire King,

invade the nomad's campground
in the Territories of the Whale.

We have worshipped the ISEQ, traded
people and country for black gold
invested for Scorching Day.

We dole coffee-spoons of melt-water
to infants and parched elders.

Lovers pledge undying love
in high-carat ice chips,
raise snowcones in terrible toast.

We have eaten the salmon of knowledge,
sacrificed a puny glacial calf.

The flames of our oil wells mock us,
the waters rise up against us,
our own creations destroy us.

Splinters from the One True Icecap
are relics we pay diamonds to touch.

Lightkeepers hold vigils
for a glimpse of the rumoured saviour
fingernailed to a passing floe.

published by Hodges Figgis in 1913

IRISH
WITCHCRAFT AND
DEMONOLOGY

BY

S^T JOHN D. SEYMOUR, B.D.

AUTHOR OF
'' THE DIOCESE OF EMLY,''
ETC.

DUBLIN
HODGES, FIGGIS & CO. L<small>TD</small>.
104 GRAFTON STREET
LONDON
HUMPHREY MILFORD
AMEN CORNER, E.C.
1913

Eamonn Wall

I AM SPRONG

Borne in hands coarse as boot gravel
rank spittle to my own wood handle
rubbed. By harsh Wexford labourers
I am beaten banged cursed ten times
flung at wall and drain like fish bone.
Dinner-time call, I am cast off to loiter
with motor, crow, skeagh, wellington
where sunlight is harshly cast on foul
bog water, men uproarious at table.
No bonny sprong is bounced on virgin
lap or oiled back from labour into art!

In Limerick, Cork, and far off Donegal,
I go by pitchfork though it is as sprong
I am known in Co. Wexford, our corner
confluence of Flemish, Old Norse, Irish,
Cant, gibberish, many hard consonants
deep vowels lodged in wood and stone
on paths lining narrow waterways all
cleansed by estuary sediment and gull.

A visitor who crosses the River Barrow
at New Ross is dumbstruck by English
as it is spoken here: Dixons, Kavanaghs,
Doyles and Quirkes our holy offerings
affixed to yew and larch and elm. I am
sprong, the strangest of them all: when
my name is called, the tourist thinks
of weapons raised in *Fahrenheit 451*;
my word heralds arrival in another space.
Our *meitheal* has gathered in the yard,
as dust from a beaten rug spreads to air
like an old psalm, on foot men to work.

From ditch my handle soon meets force:
but it is the sun that lures me back to life.

published by Hodges Figgis

Hermathena

A DUBLIN UNIVERSITY REVIEW

No CXVII. Summer 1974

DUBLIN: HODGES FIGGIS AND CO. LTD

LONDON: THE ACADEMIC PRESS LTD

Hermathena: A Dublin University Review (this issue from 1974 contains the 1st essay on Anna Parnell and the Ladies Land League)

William Wall

from SUZY SUZY

Someone will kill my mother. It could be me. There is something wrong with me I know, but I see my Dad thinking about it too. Only my brother loves her and she loves him idk it must be a mother son thing like you see. She thinks she is so hot. She comes home from work full of testosterone or whatever, and if someone didn't already cook the dinner, do the washing, hoover everything including the underside of the cushions Where Dust Collects and take The Dog for a walk, it's the end of the world and there will be Shouting and Insults and People Will End Up Crying, usually me. She works for a computer company, you can't even get into her office without a retina scan, it terrifies me so I never go in. What if they can read something in your eyes? You can tell a lot from a person's eyes, like the secrets of their heart, or so I believe. Eyes can lie too, everybody knows that, but not mine. I don't think I have the brains to hide anything from anybody, I always get caught. And I have secrets. I feel like getting a retina scanner for my bedroom. Access denied, Mam. I've asked them to give me a flat. Like they have so many flats and houses. They're always evicting someone. My Dad does evictions like Terminator Three For Tenants In Arrears. He is a Property Addict. He can't stop buying houses because the Housing Market Crashed and Everything Is SO Cheap. It's like a hobby, it's disgusting, and we keep reading about people who don't have homes to go to. We even debated The Housing Crisis in Religion class. My Mam Never Tires of Telling Me our religion teacher is a commie, which is ironic when you come to think of it, and she says nobody would have houses if it wasn't for people like Dad. And I think maybe my Dad is causing it. Like single-handedly causing the shortage because he owns like everything almost. My Dad says nothing, he just goes to the solicitors and comes home with another three-bed semi in a desirable area. He has the property gene bad. I heard someone on the radio talking about it. It goes back to the Great Famine apparently, but I don't know why my Dad got it because he was never hungry a day in his life.

You just have to look at him to know that.

Like my Dad has baby bellies where he should have love handles.

My Mam says I'm useless and I know she's right but in school I get A1 in everything, I hardly even need to look at a book, I remember everything, absolutely everything I read. My English teacher says I remind him of a story by some South American writer, I can't pronounce the name never mind spell it, about someone who was able to remember every single thing he ever saw or heard or smelled idk I'm not that bad. Ask me to recite *Macbeth* which we are studying and I can do all the voices up to Act Three where we stopped before Christmas, I can do poetry until it's Coming Out My Ears, poetry is easy. My Mam says poetry is useless which is another reason I might kill her. She's only the boss's PA but she acts like she runs Computing Solutions herself. I don't even know what they make in there, some kind of software, maybe a game for mobiles, or parts of a game idk like what's so great about that? There must be a billion software companies in the world, most of them probably have retina scanners too. I couldn't care less. I am For History and I'm For Poetry. I'm against Technology.

She comes home with a takeaway from KFC.

I don't eat that shit.

I said I would cook some boil-in-the-bag rice and do a stir fry with whatever was in the fridge but she said no cooking two dinners, I should eat what's put in front of me. So like I didn't eat.

So now I'm anorexic.

You're going to die, she goes, you're going to die a horrible awful way, anorexia is a terrible way to go. You'll turn into a stick and every bone in your body will hurt.

This went on all through dinner. I ate four chips. They disgust me. They are not even potato but some potato simulacrum, like a virtual potato, a Playstation Potato. When you eat it you don't feel like you've eaten except for the salt.

My Dad said that Ballyshane was for sale. They were selling the house with a couple of acres and the farm separately. That took the heat off me. My Dad has wanted to buy Ballyshane House as long as I can remember. He even got me to do a project on it for History once. He said: The local company of The Irish Volunteers was formed up there, Captain Corry was head and tail of it, and the Black and Tans raided it so often, I remember my own father telling me about the Crossley tenders going up full of men with rifles and Glengarry caps. Right Dad. Dad and History don't go together. I am staring at him with my mouth open. But I should have known. He knows the history of houses all right.

Holly and me say politics is just coloured stickers now. We don't have big causes to fight for like The Freedom of Ireland or Revenge For Skibbereen. We have a Blue Party, a Green Party and a Pink Party. My Dad is Blue Party. Instead of elections people should just be asked what's their favourite colour. And they should wear coloured shirts or track-suits or something. And my Dad is in well with the blues and the greens because of property. Blues and Greens are for Property, Pink is for The Working Man except it turns out they're for property too lol just not saying. Like the motto for this country should be The Builders Will Save Us. I don't know what the actual motto is if we have one idk.

Hodges Figgis & Co. Ltd.

STEPHEN COURT, ST. STEPHEN'S GREEN, DUBLIN 2.
Telephones: Stephen Court 760461, Donnybrook 695236,
Dun Laoghaire 809917, Belfield 691750.

Hodges Figgis dates back to the eighteenth century through two distinct bookselling businesses, the firm of Hodges Smith & Co., with origins in the 1750's and John Milliken who started a bookshop in Skinner Row in 1768. The two came together in the 1840's when the former bought out Milliken's grandson and established the present firm. Pentos Ltd., the English public company which owns Hudsons Bookshops in Birmingham, Dillons University Bookshop in London, and Sissons and Parker in Nottingham, took over the company from the Figgis family in 1978.

The business now operates from a number of branches. Fine premises at Stephen Court, St. Stephen's Green accomodate general and educational books together with paperbacks. A new service for libraries commenced recently and this operates from Stephen Court also. The offices and warehouse are at The Mall, Donnybrook, together with a general bookshop, which also handles the bulk of the schoolbook business. A substantial mail order service is also carried on from these premises. A new general bookshop was opened in the Dun Laoghaire Shopping Centre which offers an excellent selection of all types of books. A campus bookshop is operated at Belfield which caters extensively for the Students there.

Directors: John Davey [Managing], Allen Figgis, Jonathan Goodbody, George Hodgins, William Hornby, Lindsay Scott, Robert Twigg.

 Designed by The O'Brien Press (Publishers).
Printed by E. & T. O'Brien Ltd., 11 Clare Street, Dublin 2.

Advert from the late 1970s

Sarah Webb

Once Upon a Time
A Bookseller's Tale

I was the first born in my family. The eldest of four. Three girls, one boy. My mother, a primary school teacher and, to this day, an avid recorder and documenter of our family history, arrived at the house recently with two large boxes and a padded envelope. One box was full of my old toys: Panda Ted, Bunny One Ear, Sindy dolls with strange haircuts, a red Fisher Price bus, complete with its wooden-bodied little passengers.

The second was full of my old children's books, ragged and torn from use: *Richard Scarry's Busy Busy World*, *But Where Is the Green Parrot?*, *The Elephant and the Bad Baby*, and a Tomi Ungurer book called *Zeralda's Ogre* in which a young girl is abducted by an ogre and forced to cook feasts for him. For someone who is obsessed with children's books, it was quite the treasure.

The padded envelope held another prize, my baby book. The first two years of my life are chronicled in stunning detail as my siblings hadn't yet arrived. After that it gets patchier. Most interesting and telling are my first two sentences. The first words I patched together were: 'I do it'. Anyone who knows me won't find that in the least bit surprising. The second was 'Read me uuk.' Or book in non-baby speak.

Read me a book.

Luckily my parents, grandparents, uncles and aunts did just that. To paraphrase the remarkable Wanda Gag: 'Hundreds of books, thousands of books, millions and billions and trillions of books.' Those early stories coloured my world; they taught me how to be a little human.

I slept with books under my pillow, refused to get into my pram without a book, and going to bed without a story was simply out of the question.

Twenty years later, is it any wonder I ended up working in a bookshop?

Bookshops have always been my happy places. When I left college in the early nineties Ireland was still crawling out of a bleak recession. My closest friends had all left Ireland to work abroad and I felt very alone.

However I had a plan. Rather a simple plan. Books made me happy and I wanted to work surrounded by them. I sent out CVs to every bookshop in Dublin and the store that gave me that vital first chance was Hodges Figgis.

I was taken on as a very junior part-time bookseller, working on the academic floor. I remember working a lot of evenings from 5pm to 7pm and also every weekend. At first I wasn't a particularly good bookseller. I must admit that sometimes if it was quiet I'd lie down on the floor behind the till and take a quick nap.

But quickly it grew on me. I enjoyed talking to the customers and trying to find the right books for them. Occasionally I was allowed work in the children's department and it was here I came into my own. I knew exactly what to recommend to a 'nine-year-old who loves animals', *Charlotte's Web*. Or a 'clever eight-year-old who loves adventure', the Famous Five.

Most people grow out of children's books. They put Anne with an e and Fern and Wilbur and Aslan behind them. But I've stayed loyal to Tom Waits and Abba all my life and I've never, ever stopped reading children's books. When feeling different and out of whack with my friends as a teenager, I'd read *Are You There God? It's Me, Margaret* by Judy Blume, one of the finest books on the teenage condition ever written. In college I'd curl up with *The Lion, the Witch and the Wardrobe* when I needed some comfort.

I've always read like a child. I step into another world and, as Anne Fadiman once described, have 'to be woken out of a book'. It still happens now. If I'm reading a good novel and someone talks to me I simply do not hear them.

I'm also a diary keeper, have been since I was a teenager. Another thing I've never grown out of. Hence I know exactly when I started working in Hodges Figgis – 7 August 1991. What was Hodges Figgis like in those days? Much like it is now. Big but never too big, calm, soothing. The booksellers (my colleagues) were kind and funny and always had time to talk about the new books they were reading or old favourites they had discovered.

After Hodges Figgis, I moved to a full-time bookselling role in Hughes and Hughes and then on to Waterstones, where I was the children's buyer for many years, a job I adored. From there I moved to Eason's head office where I was the children's buyer and marketing manager before leaving to write full time. However I've never fully left bookselling – I still work for Dubray Books as a consultant.

Working in bookshops gave me the courage to try writing a book of my own. I started off modestly, with a cookery book for children, but I've now published over thirty novels and non-fiction books for all ages, some published internationally, others published for the Irish market.

In *Breakfast at Tiffany's*, Holly Golightly says of Tiffany's: 'It calms me down right away, the quietness and the proud look of it; nothing very bad could happen to you there.' That's how I feel about Hodges Figgis. It's an oasis for thinkers and dreamers and one of my favourite places in the world.

Thank you for giving me my first 'real' job, Hodges Figgis, and for starting me on my book journey.

David Wheatley

BRUSH

Assisted
first steps on
the mountain

feet brushing it
sideways like smooth
jazz drumming

carry you never-
theless to
the threshold of

our grip
beyond which for
the moment

there is nothing
you understand
nothing

Vol. XI No. 42　　　　　　　　　SEPTEMBER 1958

IRISH
HISTORICAL
STUDIES

The joint journal of the IRISH HISTORICAL SOCIETY
and the ULSTER SOCIETY FOR IRISH HISTORICAL STUDIES

Joint editors; T. W. MOODY & T. D. WILLIAMS

CONTENTS

DUBLIN
HODGES, FIGGIS & CO., LTD

Sheena Wilkinson

from THE GREATER MALADY

By now the room looked like a murder scene.

Rosalind's body slumped sideways, fronds of dark hair spread across the bloodstained pillows, lips and cheeks still hectic purple. Would that remain in death, Alice wondered, or would her skin fade back to its usual clear pallor? Well, no, it would be the pallor of death, wouldn't it? She took Rosalind by the shoulders and heaved her up so that she lay more naturally, and drew the sheet up over the stained nightie as if she were tucking up a child for the night. Her hand rested for a moment on the slight swell of Rosalind's belly. She pulled at a tendril of hair stuck to Rosalind's cheek, but blood held it fast. Alice licked her thumb and used it to prise the hair away. She thought, briefly, about infection. Too late now. She combed her fingers through the long tangled locks and bunched them in a rough tail over Rosalind's shoulder. When she laid her out, she would give her a simple plait, such as Rosalind always wore for bed. The hair would take some brushing – it was matted in places into what Alice's mother called a bee's wisp.

Alice had often wondered how it might feel to brush or even stroke Rosalind's dark, glossy hair.

I'll have to clean up, she thought. Jessie will be in from school, and she mustn't see the place like this; it would give her nightmares. The sheets would have to be burned. She would do it herself; she wouldn't ask Mrs Donnelly, though Mrs Donnelly would know much better than she what would take stains out of the bedside rug, the wall – how had the blood spattered even the pale-blue wall? – the counterpane – perhaps that too, should be burned. After all, they would be a small household now, no shortage of bedclothes.

What *was* a bee's wisp? And why was she thinking such futile, random things? She had never been present at a death, never seen a corpse, except for Eddie's twin who had died in infancy, and it was the photo she remembered, not her actual dead baby brother; she had been only two. She probably ought to pray, but had never felt less like doing so. What she wanted was to hold Rosalind in her arms and scream and howl, like Heathcliff, except that wasn't what people did in Cyclamen Park, Belfast, however they might have carried on in Yorkshire.

Anyway, that was only a book.

From below she heard the front door slam. Jessie never could learn to shut it gently. 'Sorry!' Jessie called up. 'It was the wind! Hello, Ros! Are you better?' Her voice got nearer; the stairs creaked under her clumping school boots. 'I got into awful trouble over my French. Mademoiselle wouldn't excuse it, mean pig. But Miss Morgan was decent about me not doing hockey. She said –'

'Jessie.' Alice came out and stood at the bedroom door, pulling it closed behind her. The air in the landing was fresh and Jessie, windblown and panting, had brought something of outdoors in with her. 'I'm so sorry ...'

Jessie stared at her, her face, always pale since the flu, whitening further. She looked down at Alice's skirt, smudged with blood. 'What do you mean? Ros was better. She was getting up today.'

'I know. But this morning – she – well, she took a turn for the worse.' How often had she heard her father use this phrase? 'She was struggling for breath. And then she had a massive haemorrhage. She died very quickly.' She emphasised the word *died*: Jessie was rather stupid; there must be no fudging or euphemism, no possibility of doubt.

Even if there was some doubt about the cause of death.

It hadn't seemed quick: Rosalind twisting in the bed, the frantic choking; the frothy blood spurting from her purple lips. Alice had telephoned for a doctor, despite her misgivings, but Dr Bolton was out, rushed off his feet, his housekeeper said, night, noon and morning, and Dr Smyth was down with the flu himself, and she didn't know of any others. Except her father, and much good he was, away down in Newcastle. Anyway, there wasn't much a doctor could do; that's what everyone said. It was nursing that counted. And luck. Mostly luck. Rosalind had been unlucky.

'You made me go to school!' Jessie wailed. 'I could have stayed and helped!'

'There wasn't anything you could have –'

'I could have said goodbye!' Jessie's satchel slipped from her shoulder; she shook back her dark plaits and tried to push past Alice. 'Let me see her!'

'No! Jessie – wait until I've cleaned up. It's – it isn't very – Jessie!' But Jessie's shock seemed to make her strong – she was taller than Alice for all she was so skinny – and she yanked at the doorhandle before Alice could stop her. Alice spun round, her hand on Jessie's shaking shoulder. 'Don't! It's too ups –'

She saw the room as Jessie must see it – Rosalind so obviously dead; the blood-spattered bed – and, noticing it now after the freshness of the landing – the mousey, fusty stench of disease. She thought Jessie would scream, or burst into tears, but at first she just stood, trembling all over, her breath coming in little huffs; then she gave a shuddering gulp and collapsed to her knees, retching. A bowl, Alice thought, I must fetch a bowl, but all the bowls in the house were full of stained handkerchiefs and bloody phlegm.

An excessive reaction, she thought wearily, as she put the girl to bed in her attic room afterwards. Typical of Jessie not only to get out of having to do anything practical, but to add to the mess and worry.

She heaved herself back downstairs to do all that was needed in Rosalind's room. Rosalind's body lay as she had left it, mouth gaping. She looked helplessly round the room, wondering what to start cleaning up first.

It still looked like a murder had taken place. And in a way it had.

published by Hodges Figgis in 1944

THE STORY

OF

IRISH ORIENTALISM

M. MANSOOR, Ph.D.

FOREWORD BY

PROFESSOR R. M. GWYNN, S.F.T.C.D.

Joseph Woods

SUNDAYS IN RANGOON
And books give off more nastier dust than any other class of objects
invented, and the top of a book is where every bluebottle prefers to die.
— George Orwell, *Bookshop Memories*
for Shane Brady

The crushing sadness of Rangoon on a Sunday afternoon
when the city flags under monsoon and an all day
darkness and deluge, broken gutters expectorating,

balconies weep and walls and gables all mapped in patinas
of black mould where every drain has overflowed to river
the streets and your feet. And it's your nose that brings

you to a bookshop where mildew almost suffocates,
as if every book will soon bind into one lumpen mass,
having absorbed the shelves, sponged up the damp

surrounds and the very air, all bearing witness to nothing
ever lasting here. An hour in and little of interest,
Successful Poultry Management among the ubiquitous

manuals for the merchant navy, once the only way out
of this country's isolation. No surprises, until *another*
edition of Du Fu, which my elsewhere shelves are full of,

but drawn to the cover of colourful murals
from the Tonhuaung Caves and where the book falls open,
Travel in the Middle Years, 'the scent of the orchid fades

away … the wicked have not yet been brought to justice'
and *Melancholy in the Autumn Rain,* 'we have not seen
the sun, when will mother earth became dry again.'

Difficult to resist and made more so because
of the bookmarks; a 1979 ticket to a vanished cinema,
a tiny printed recipe which could pass for a prayer,

two worthless five Kyat notes and a folded page
of yellowed paper with an inked handprint on either side,
one male and the other female? Both hands etched ghostly,

skiagram of their union and beneath and written
in Burmese, *5am Thursday 21st of October in the Burmese
year of 1315.* So sixty years since they separated,

while Du Fu presided across twelve centuries,
since that morning perhaps, when one walked out
into the empty streets, each returned to themselves,

the monsoon tailing and like Du Fu's lone wild goose,
replying to cries that were its own echoes.

SOME

Oriental Bindings

IN THE

Chester Beatty
Library

BY BERTHE VAN REGEMORTER

with 71 plates, 21 in colour

DUBLIN
HODGES FIGGIS & CO LTD
1961

Macdara Woods

RETURN REMONT REHEARSED REPEATED
for Tasha

Welcome back
Said the mercury lake
In the park – too long
You have been away:
Wait wait wait
Urgently trilled the bird
But which bird it was
I cannot say

Lost in silhouettes
Of indoor plants
Sharp and long like
The seven swords
Of the Mother of Sorrows
I carried home:
Outlined by snow
Against the onion domes

Of Moscow – improbable
Snow in May
Takes nothing from
Adds nothing to
The silence
Of knowing where you are
And that you have
Arrived almost too late

And out of sync:
Time and snow
Themselves are engineers
Of silence – melting
Battlements like hot

Camembert and covering
Up the marvellous
Remembered Squares:

I span two worlds
Today – from
The wide Atlantic Ocean
To Sarinskiy Proezd:
Among ducks
On a mercury lake
The icons I recall
Of what is always there
The truth in cobwebbed
Streets of words

published by Hodges Figgis in 1914

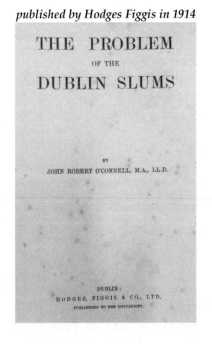

Adam Wyeth

UNTITLED

The woman who runs the charity shop
says she feels she's given birth to me.
All those years in my country I was
a gestating egg amorphous as the night.
Now here I am limbs and head
a recently arrived émigré.
I lock the shop and watch it
grow small and dark.
I feel like a drone circling above
as someone thumbs the controls.

My whole life
          could fall
                    through their fingers
          in a matter
of seconds.

I am plunging towards the city lights
the tall buildings rise up like sharp teeth.
I don't know if I'm at the beginning
or coming to an end.
An unbroken stream of people
rush past. Am I a stone
in the middle of the river
or a river constantly
in contact with the stone?
There is a book in the shop
yet to be picked up
it stands on the shelf waiting
for eyes to give it sight
and tongue to give it breath.

Enda Wyley

LEDGER
for Peter Sirr

In the attic dark the red box
that's waited for years to be
hauled down into the light again.

Standard Feint, yellow notebooks
of your past, all dusty – your ancient longing
made real with the swipe of cloth

and those poems you wrote still there
from when you'd first imagined them,
rushed words into life. Frantic ink of desire.

How you ran through the snow to lose her,
unlearning her name to find her again in days
of bed and feasts of wine, nights of Callas –

unending light, unending splendour
that I later reached for on the bookshop shelf,
knelt to read in the hush of the poetry corner.

Her alabaster breasts, his querulous stare
and poised quill, her gentle hand on his
velvet blue jacket – that cover, your book

trembling in the palms of my hands,
this ledger of lost love I'd never read before
that thrilled, made me stand up in Hodges Figgis

then make for the door, our future racing out onto
Dawson Street and into the wideness of the city,
Larkin raising his hands to me, the gulls cawing

encouragement as I sought you out, your face staring
from a high window over Parnell Square, waiting for me,
the life you'd described becoming ours, the door unlatched.

published by Hodges Figgis in 1885

THE

PRICE OF PEACE

IN

IRELAND.

𝔄 𝔏etter

TO

HIS EXCELLENCY THE EARL OF CARNARVON.

BY

SIR CHARLES GAVAN DUFFY, K.C.M.G.

WITH SOME EXTRACTS FROM

"𝔄n 𝔄ppeal to the Conserbatibe Party,"

BY THE SAME WRITER.

PRICE SIXPENCE.

DUBLIN :
HODGES AND FIGGIS, Grafton Street,
JAMES DUFFY AND SONS, 15 Wellington Quay.
LONDON :
RIDGEWAY, Piccadilly,
JAMES DUFFY AND SONS, 1 Paternoster Row.

Hermathena

A DUBLIN UNIVERSITY REVIEW

No. CX. 1970

DUBLIN: HODGES FIGGIS AND CO. LTD

LONDON: THE ACADEMIC PRESS LTD

Liam Donnelly and Tony Hayes

HODGES FIGGIS: A BRIEF HISTORY

Darkness is in our souls, do you not think? Flutier. Our souls, shamewounded by our sins, cling to us yet more, a woman to her lover clinging, the more the more.

She trusts me, her hand gentle, the long lashed eyes. Now where the blue hell am I bringing her beyond the veil? Into the ineluctable modality of the ineluctable visuality. She, she, she. What she? The virgin at Hodges Figgis' window on Monday looking in for one of the alphabet books you wre going to write. Keen glance you gave her. Wrist through the braided jesse of her sunshade. She lives in Leeson park, with a grief and kickshaws, a lady of letters. Talk that to some one else, Stevie: a pickmeup. Bet she wears those curse of God stays suspenders and yellow stockings, darned with lumpy wool. Talk about apple dumplings, *piuttosto*. Where are your wits?

Touch me. Soft eyes. Soft soft soft hand. I am lonely here. O, touch me soon, now. What is that word known to all men? I am quiet here alone. Sad too. Touch, touch me.

– James Joyce, *Ulysses*, 1922

Hodges Figgis, one of the oldest bookshops in the world and the oldest in Ireland has been an icon of Dublin retailing for the last 250 years, celebrated in prose and poetry. Writers from James Joyce to Sally Rooney and Paul Durcan have mentioned it. Our journey to this point has been full of ups and downs, success and failure but through it all a passion for books and bookselling has been ever present.

Hodges Figgis traces its history back to 1768 when John Milliken opened a bookshop at 10 Skinners Row, near Christ Church Cathedral. John Milliken was the son of William Milliken who in the mid-eighteenth century owned a considerable amount of property in the Grafton Street area, which was then considered to be part of the suburbs of the city. In 1797 John Milliken moved his bookshop to 32 Grafton Street, which due to the rapid expansion of the city had become a centre for business. From there John, whose loyalties were strongly on the side of the Crown, published and sold a great quantity of books and pamphlets in support of the Union of the Irish and English Parliaments. When the Act of Union was passed in 1800 he must have jumped for joy – and he must also have made a tidy profit out of his activities as a pamphleteer who supported the successful cause.

Like his father, who he succeeded, Richard Milliken was an ultra-loyalist. He was also the sire of an enormous family. An old Dublin tradition pictures him standing on the balcony of his Grafton Street premises, surrounded by his twenty two daughters all dressed in white to welcome George IV when he visited Dublin in 1825. As a bookseller he was successful and in 1819 he moved his business down the street to 104 Grafton Street where he established a bookshop which was to be one of the great centres of learning in Dublin for more than a century.

Richard Milliken died in 1834 and his son Andrew took command. Andrew appears to have invested unwisely in some very rare and expensive books and the firm ran into difficulties, eventually being taken over lock stock and barrel by Hodges and Smith who had previously been successful booksellers in College Green. They could trace their history back to William Gilbert, a bookbinder who had opened a bookshop in South Great Georges Street seventy years earlier. Among the signatures on the Deed of Assignment, two are worth mentioning; that of Michael Henry Gill, then of the Dublin University Press, and that of William Foster, nephew of Andrew Milliken, who had been apprenticed to his uncle, and who by continuing in the firm after the change of hands, helped to preserve the sense of continuity.

With the arrival of Hodges and Smith and their established clientele a new wind swept through 104 Grafton Street, which brought a far more liberal outlook towards the history of Ireland and her religious divisions. Thus the shop became a great centre for books relating to Ireland. George Smith was largely responsible for this. That he was a bookman of great ability and much vision can be seen from the many important works published during his long period of leadership. This is perhaps best evidenced by the firm's magnum opus, O'Donovan's edition of the *Annals of the Four Masters* in 1848 which seems to have been financed from his own private purse. John Hodges, on the other hand, though his name is still retained to the present day in the firm's title, seems to have withdrawn into the background soon after the move to Grafton Street.

John Hodges died in 1853 and George Smith soon took a new partner – William Foster, the firm becoming Hodges Foster & Co. Eleven years later Smith retired and Samuel Figgis who had been with the firm for some time was taken on as an additional partner. The name of the firm was once again changed after William Foster's retirement. In 1892 Samuel Figgis turned the business into a limited company and for the first time it bore its current title. The following year Samuel was joined by his second son William Fernsley who gave the firm more than sixty years of dedication, and with not a little courage he saved it in 1920 when all seemed lost.

William's early years in the book trade were happy ones and 104 Grafton Street was an excellent place to learn bookselling, since a large stock was maintained and a steady stream of customers passed through the doors. After Samuel Figgis' death in 1899 Thomas Brown who had already been with the firm for almost thirty years became Managing Director and in the early years of the twentieth century the firm prospered under the leadership of this genial Scotsman. Darker days were to come however and when in 1911 the old lease expired and it became necessary to rebuild, the firm incurred an expense which was to prove a crippling burden. The new building was designed to follow the plan of the old as closely as possible, and trade was maintained, but now the outgoings were greatly increased by the large interest due on the building loan and the profits dwindled. In 1914 war broke out and a year later William Figgis volunteered for the army, resulting in his absence from the firm for almost four years. Shortly after his return an agent of the Provincial Bank made a very tempting offer for the premises, and at an extraordinary meeting of the company on 9 February 1920 it was agreed that this should be accepted. The building loan was now redeemed and the Company's capital paid up in full, but it was a sad day when after more than a century 104 Grafton Street bade goodbye to bookselling. William Figgis agreed with the rest of the company to take the firm's stock-in-hand and goodwill in lieu of cash, and with these he set up shop once more at 20 Nassau Street. With him went Thomas Brown who after so many years in 104 Grafton Street still felt that he could be of service to the firm in its new abode.

For a quarter of a century the firm remained in Nassau Street and though there were lean as well as good years it was generally a successful period of re-building and remodeling, by the end of which William Figgis alone survived from the Grafton Street staff and a new generation led by J.F. Murray had arisen to assist him. Outside the shop, however, it was an eventful era during which, among other things, Ireland established her independence and a Second World War was fought. In the early 1940s however the ownership of the building changed hands and William Figgis found the new landlord incompatible. So he looked for other premises and in May 1945 the firm moved to 6 Dawson Street where it enjoyed many happy years.

After William Figgis's death in 1956, he was succeeded by his son, Allen and the firm continued to expand under his leadership. In 1963 the firm was fortunate to acquire the extensive adjoining premises at 5 Dawson Street which was converted into a fine modern shop.

The shop remained on Dawson Street until 1974 when the company underwent a dramatic change, moving to St Stephen's Green, opening a shop and warehouse in Donnybrook, and a shop in Dún Laoghaire, alongside campus shops in Belfield, Cork and Galway. Further shops were opened in Kilkenny and Cork City Centre.

The Figgis family sold the business to Pentos in 1978 and it moved to 56 Dawson Street. The business was then restructured leaving No 56 as the last remaining shop in 1981. In 1989 Hodges Figgis moved to 57–58 Dawson Street and in 1992 reintegrated the old No 56 premises. In 1995 EMI acquired Pentos and three years later was merged with Waterstones as part of the HMV group. The company prospered and underwent many years of growth and in 2011, Alexander Mamut bought Waterstones and Hodges Figgis from HMV and they were formed into a new company.

The company continued publishing books until the 1970s, but the core business has always been bookselling and Irish published books in particular have been the basis of its success. The shop retails over four floors now, and has a strong focus on books of Irish interest, fiction, history and academic texts. In recent years the children's department has expanded and flourished. Challenges remain, competition both locally and from internet retailers has changed the way books are sold. But throughout the last 250 years the shop has weathered a lot of changes. We look forward to the next 250 years of this great institution.

published by Allen Figgis in 1965

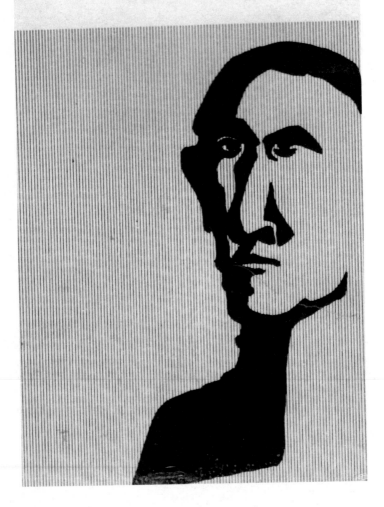

Introduction by Padraic Colum

The
Weaver's Grave

Seumas O'Kelly

Alan Hayes

RECOMMENDED READING BY *Reading the Future* CONTRIBUTORS

Here are some titles published by contributors to *Reading the Future: New Writing from Ireland* which we recommend you check out, either in your favourite bookshop, or your local library:

Chris Agee, *Next to Nothing, Irish Pages, First Light, Scar on the Stone*

John Banville, *Mrs Osmond, The Blue Guitar, The Sea, Time Pieces: A Dublin Memoir*

Kevin Barry, *Beatlebone, City of Bohane, Winter Papers, There Are Little Kingdoms*

Eileen Battersby, *Teethmarks on My Tongue, Ordinary Dogs, Second Readings*

Claire-Louise Bennett, *Pond*

Pauline Bewick, *80: A Memoir, The Yellow Man, Pauline Bewick's Seven Ages, The South Seas and a Box of Paints*

Maeve Binchy, *Minding Frankie, Light a Penny Candle, Circle of Friends, Deeply Regretted By …*

Sam Blake, *In Deep Water, Little Bones*

Gerry Boland, *The Far Side of Happiness, In the Space Between, Marco Moves In, Marco: Moonwalker*

Rosita Boland, *Dissecting the Heart, A Secret Map of Ireland, Muscle Creek, Sea Legs*

Pat Boran, *A Man Is Only As Good, The Next Life, The Invisible Prison, If Ever You Go*

Eva Bourke, *Piano, Spring in Henry Street, Landing Places, Fermata*

Conor Bowman, *Horace Winter Says Goodbye, The Last Estate/The Redemption of George Baxter Henry, Wasting by Degrees, Life and Death and In Between*

Niamh Boyce, *The Herbalist*

Maureen Boyle, *The Work of a Winter*

John Boyne, *A History of Loneliness, The Heart's Invisible Furies, Mutiny on the Bounty, The Boy in the Striped Pyjamas*

Deirdre Brennan, *Staying Thin for Daddy, Cuislí Allta : Wild Pulses, Ag Mealladh Réalta, Hidden Places : Scáthán Eile*

Olive Broderick, *Night Divers, Darkhaired*

Ken Bruen, *The Ghosts of Galway, The Guards, London Boulevard, Priest*

Declan Burke, *Crime Always Pays, Absolute Zero Cool, The Big O, The Lost and the Blind*

Paddy Bushe, *On a Turning Wing, Gile na Gile, My Lord Buddha of Carraig Eanna, Voices at the World's Edge*

David Butler, *City of Dis, All the Barbaric Glass, No Greater Love, The Judas Kiss*

June Caldwell, *Room Little Darker*

Siobhán Campbell, *Heat Signature, Cross-Talk, That Water Speaks in Tongues, Eavan Boland: Inside History*

Moya Cannon, *Keats Lives, Carrying the Songs, Hands, Oar*

Ruth Carr, *Feather and Bone, The Airing Cupboard, There is a House, The Female Line*

Alvy Carragher, *Falling in Love with Broken Things*

Jan Carson, *Children's Children, Malcolm Orange Disappears, Postcard Stories*

Andrea Carter, *Death at Whitewater Church, The Well of Ice, Treacherous Strand*

Deirdre Cartmill, *The Return of the Buffalo, Midnight Solo*

Eileen Casey, *Snow Shoes, Drinking the Colour Blue, A Fascination with Fabric, Circle and Square*

Paul Casey, *Virtual Tides, Home More or Less*

Patrick Chapman, *Slow Clocks of Decay, The Negative Cutter, A Promiscuity of Spines, Breaking Hearts and Traffic Lights*

Sarah Clancy, *The Truth and Other Stories, Thanks for Nothing, Hippies, Stacey and the Mechanical Bull*

Jane Clarke, *The River*

Harry Clifton, *Portobello Sonnets, The Winter Sleep of Captain Lemass, Berkeley's Telephone and Other Fictions, Ireland and its Elsewheres*

Michael Coady, *Given Light, One Another, Going by Water, All Souls*

Mary Coll, *Silver, All Things Considered, Faithful Companions*

Evelyn Conlon, *Not the Same Sky, Telling, A Glassful of Letters, Cutting the Night in Two*

Stephanie Conn, *The Woman on the Other Side, Copeland's Daughter, Island*

John Connolly, *he, A Game of Ghosts, The Book of Lost Things, A Time of Torment*

Gavin Corbett, *This Is The Way, Green Glowing Skull, Innocence*

Patrick Cotter, *Perplexed Skin, Making Music, A Socialist's Dozen, The Misogynist's Blue Nightmare*

Enda Coyle-Greene, *Map of the Last, Snow Negatives*

Catherine Ann Cullen, *The Other Now, Strange Familiar, A Bone in My Throat*

Peter Cunningham, *Acts of Allegiance, The Trout, Capital Sins, Consequences of the Heart*

Judi Curtin, *Stand By Me, Time After Time, Alice to the Rescue, Eva's Holiday*

Tony Curtis, *Approximately in the Key of C, Folk, Pony, Three Songs of Home*

Gerald Dawe, *Mickey Finn's Air, In Another World, Earth Voices Whispering, Catching the Light*

Celia de Fréine, *Blood Debts, Imram : Odyssey, Scarecrows at Newtownards, The Midnight Court*

Kit de Waal, *My Name is Leon*

John F. Deane, *Give Dust a Tongue, Semibreve, Snow Falling on Chestnut Hill, The Instruments of Art*

Patrick Deeley, *The Hurley Maker's Son, Groundswell, The Bones of Creation, Snobby Cat*

Kate Dempsey, *The Space Between*

Anne Devlin, *Ourselves Alone, After Easter, The Way-Paver, Titanic Town*

Martina Devlin, *The House Where it Happened, About Sisterland, Three Wise Men, Ship of Dreams*

Moyra Donaldson, *The Goose Tree, Miracle Fruit, The Horse's Nest, Kissing Ghosts*

JP Donleavy, *The Ginger Man, The Beastly Beatitudes of Balthazar B, The Lady Who Liked Clean Restrooms, A Fairy Tale of New York*

Neil Donnelly, *Tullamore Train, Upstarts, The Plays of Neil Donnelly*

Katie Donovan, *Off Duty, Rootling, Day of the Dead, Entering the Mare*

Mary Dorcey, *To Air the Soul, Throw All the Windows Wide, Like Joy in Season, Like Sorrow, Biography of Desire, Moving into the Space Cleared by Our Mothers*

Theo Dorgan, *Nine Bright Shiners, Making Way, Sailing for Home, Greek*

Garbhan Downey, *Once Upon a Time in the North West, Across the Line, The American Envoy, War of the Blue Roses*

Rob Doyle, *This is the Ritual, Here are the Young Men*

Roddy Doyle, *Smile, A Star Called Henry, A Greyhound of a Girl, Paddy Clarke Ha Ha Ha*

Catherine Dunne, *The Years that Followed, The Things We Know Now, A Name for Himself, Another Kind of Life*

Christine Dwyer Hickey, *The Lives of Women, Last Train from Liguria, Tatty, The House on Parkgate Street*

Martin Dyar, *Maiden Names*

Alan Early, *Arthur Quinn and Hell's Keeper, Arthur Quinn and the Fenris Wolf, Arthur Quinn and the World Serpent*

Martina Evans, *The Windows of Graceland, Petrol, Facing the Public, Burnfort, Las Vegas*

Bernard Farrell, *Bookworms, Many Happy Returns, Canaries, All the Way Back*

Tanya Farrelly, *When Black Dogs Sing, The Girl Behind the Lens*

Elaine Feeney, *Rise, The Radio was Gospel, Where's Katie?*

John Fitzgerald, *First Cut*

Gabriel Fitzmaurice, *The Lonesome Road, Poems of Faith and Doubt, Twenty One Sonnets, Do Teachers Go to the Toilet?*

Patricia Forde, *The Wordsmith, Queen Maebh's Raging Return to Galway, Witches Do Not Like Bicycles, Hedgehogs Do Not Like Heights*

Órfhlaith Foyle, *Clemency Browne Dreams of Gin, Belios, Red Riding Hood's Dilemma, Somewhere in Minnesota*

Mia Gallagher, *Beautiful Pictures of the Lost Homeland, Hellfire, You First*

Carlo Gébler, *The Innocent of Falkland Road, The Wing Orderly's Tales, The Dead Eight, How to Murder a Man*

Patricia Gibney, *The Lost Child, The Missing Ones, The Stolen Girls*

Karen Gillece, *Seven Nights in Zaragoza, Longshore Drift, My Glass Heart, The Absent Wife*

Shauna Gilligan, *Happiness Comes from Nowhere*

Anthony Glavin, *Colours Other Than Blue, Nighthawk Alley, The Draughtsman and the Unicorn, One for Sorrow*

Sinéad Gleeson, *Constellations, The Long Gaze Back, The Glass Shore, Silver Threads of Hope*

Julian Gough, *Jude in London, Juno and Juliet, Free Sex Chocolate, Rabbit and Bear: The Pest in the Nest*

Eamon Grennan, *There Now, Still Life with Waterfall, But the Body, Out of Breath*

Sarah Maria Griffin, *Spare and Found Parts, Not Lost: A Story About Leaving Home*

Kerry Hardie, *The Zebra Stood in the Night, The Ash and the Oak and the Wild Cherry, Only This Room, The Bird Woman*

Lisa Harding, *Harvesting*

James Harpur, *Angels and Harvesters, The Dark Age, Oracle Bones, The Monk's Dream*

Jack Harte, *Rehabilitating the Serpent, Language of the Mute, Reflections in a Tar-Barrel, Homage*

Anne Haverty, *The Free and Easy, One Day as a Tiger, The Beauty of the Moon, Constance Markievicz*

Claire Hennessy, *Like Other Girls, Nothing Tastes as Good, Big Picture, Afterwards*

Aideen Henry, *Hugging Thistles, Slow Bruise, Hands Moving at the Speed of Falling Snow*

Phyl Herbert, *The Price of Desire, After Desire*

Michael D Higgins, *New and Selected Poems, An Arid Season, When Ideas Matter, Renewing the Republic*

Rita Ann Higgins, *Tongulish, Ireland is Changing Mother, Hurting God, Goddess on the Mervue Bus*

Sophia Hillan, *The Friday Tree, The Way We Danced, May, Lou and Cass, Silken Twine*

Desmond Hogan, *The History of Magpies, Old Swords and Other Stories, A Farewell to Prague, The Ikon Maker*

Declan Hughes, *All the Things You Are, City of Lost Girls, All the Dead Voices, The Price of Blood*

Rosemary Jenkinson, *Contemporary Problems Nos 53 & 54, The Bonefire, Aphrodite's Kiss and Further Stories, Catholic Boy*

Jennifer Johnston, *Naming the Stars, A Sixpenny Song, The Captains and the Kings, How Many Miles to Babylon?*

Neil Jordan, *Carnivalesque, The Drowned Detective, Mistaken, Sunrise with Sea Monster*

Ann Joyce, *Watching for Signs, Threads from Maeve's Mantle*

Joe Joyce, *Echoland, Echowave, Echobeat*

Colm Keegan, *Don't Go There*

John Kelly, *From Out of the City, Grace Notes & Bad Thoughts, The Little Hammer, Cool About the Ankles*

Brian Kennedy, *The Arrival of Fergal Flynn, Roman Song*

Victoria Kennefick, *White Whale*

Brendan Kennelly, *Guff, Reservoir Voices, Familiar Strangers, Now*

Adrian Kenny, *Before the Wax Hardened, Portobello Notebook, Istanbul Diary, Arcady and Other Stories*

Des Kenny, *Kenny's Choice: 101 Irish Books You Must Read*

Kate Kerrigan, *It was Only Ever You, The Dress, City of Hope, Land of Dreams*

Marian Keyes, *The Break, Anybody Out There, Rachel's Holiday, The Woman who Stole My Life*

Jess Kidd, *Himself, The Hoarder*

Claire Kilroy, *The Devil I Know, All Names have Been Changed, All Summer, Tenderwire*

Thomas Kilroy, *Blake, The Big Chapel, My Scandalous Life, Christ Deliver Us!*

Deirdre Kinahan, *Melody, Halcyon Days, Moment*

Susan Knight, *Out of Order, Letting Rip and Other Stories, Gomorrah, The Invisible Woman*

Conor Kostick, *Epic, Saga, Edda, Strongbow: The Norman Invasion of Ireland*

Nick Laird, *Modern Gods, Go Giants, Utterly Monkey, Glover's Mistake*

Caitriona Lally, *Eggshells*

Brian Leyden, *Sweet Old World: New and Selected Stories, The Home Place: A Memoir, Death and Plenty, Departures*

Paula Leyden, *Keepsake, The Sleeping Baobab Tree, The Butterfly Heart*

Simon Lewis, *Jewtown*

Michael Longley, *Angel Hill, The Stairwell, A Hundred Doors, One Wide Expanse*

Paul Lynch, *Grace, The Black Snow, Red Sky in Morning*

Aifric Mac Aodha, *Gabháil Syrinx, Foreign News*

Gearóid Mac Lochlainn, *Sruth Teangacha, Na Scéalaithe, Babylon Gaeilgeoir, Rakish Paddy Blues*

John McAuliffe, *The Way In, Of All Places, Next Door, A Better Life*

Niamh McBrannan, *The Devil Looks After His Own*

Joan McBreen, *Map and Atlas, Heather Island, Winter in the Eye, The White Page : An Bhileog Bhán*

Eugene McCabe, *The Love of Sisters, Death and Nightingales, Tales from the Poorhouse, Roma*

Patrick McCabe, *Mondo Desperado, The Holy City, Breakfast on Pluto, The Butcher Boy*

Colum McCann, *Thirteen Ways of Looking, This Side of Brightness, TransAtlantic, Let the Great World Spin*

Thomas McCarthy, *Pandemonium, The Last Geraldine Officer, Merchant Prince, Mr Dineen's Careful Parade*

Mike McCormack, *Solar Bones, Forensic Songs, Getting it in the Head, Notes from a Coma*

Barry McCrea, *The First Verse, Languages of the Night, In the Company of Strangers*

Rosaleen McDonagh, *Mainstream*

Bernie McGill, *The Watch House, The Butterfly Cabinet, Sleepwalkers*

Afric McGlinchey, *Ghost of the Fisher Cat, The Lucky Star of Hidden Things*

Iggy McGovern, *The Eyes of Isaac Newton, Safe House, A Mystic Dream of 4, The King of Suburbia*

Claire McGowan, *The Killing House, A Savage Hunger, The Lost, The Dead Ground*

Medbh McGuckian, *Love, the Magician, Blaris Moor, The Unfixed Horizon, Captain Lavender*

Lisa McInerney, *The Blood Miracles, The Glorious Heresies*

Danielle McLaughlin, *Dinosaurs on Other Planets*

Maria McManus, *Available Light, We Are Bone, Reading the Dog, The Cello Suites*

Alan McMonagle, *Ithaca, Psychotic Episodes, Liar, Liar*

Eoin McNamee, *Blue is the Night, Resurrection Man, Orchid Blue, 12:23*

Paul McVeigh, *The Good Son*

Paul Maddern, *The Beachcomber's Report, Kelpdings*

Mary Madec, *Demeter Does Not Remember, In Other Words*

Emer Martin, *Baby Zero, More Bread Or I'll Appear, Breakfast in Babylon*

Máighréad Medbh, *Parvit of Agelast, Pagan to the Core, Twelve Beds for the Dreamer, When the Air Inhales You*

Mary Melvin Geoghegan, *Say It Like a Paragraph, The Bright Unknown, When They Come Home, Abbeycartron Epiphanies*

Geraldine Mills, *Gold, Hellkite, The Weight of Feathers, An Urgency of Stars*

Lia Mills, *Fallen, Nothing Simple, Another Alice, In Your Face*

Geraldine Mitchell, *Mountains for Breakfast, Of Birds and Bones, World Without Maps, Deeds Not Words*

Noel Monahan, *Where the Wind Sleeps, Curve of the Moon, The Funeral Game, Curse of the Birds*

Mary Montague, *Tribe, Black Wolf on a White Plain*

Sarah Moore Fitzgerald, *A Very Good Chance, The Apple Tart of Hope, Back to Blackbrick*

Luke Morgan, *Honest Walls*

Gina Moxley, *Dog House*

Helena Mulkerns, *Ferenji, Turbulence: Corrib Voices, Red Lamp, Black Piano*

Val Mulkerns, *Memory and Desire, The Summer House, Very Like a Whale, Antiquities*

Pete Mullineaux, *How to Bake a Planet, Session, A Father's Day, Zen Traffic Lights*

E.R. Murray, *The Book of Shadows, The Book of Learning, Caramel Hearts*

Gerry Murphy, *Muse, My Flirtation with International Socialism, End of Part One, Torso of an Ex-Girlfriend*

Dairena Ní Chinnéide, *Fé Gheasa : Spellbound, Cloithear, Labhraíonn Fungie : Fungie Speaks, An Trodaí agus Dánta Eile*

Caitríona Ní Chléirchín, *An Bhrídeach Sí, Crithloinnir*

Eiléan Ní Chuilleanáin, *The Boys of Bluehill, The Sun-Fish, The Girl Who Married the Reindeer, Legend of the Walled-Up Wife*

Nuala Ní Dhomhnaill, *An Dealg sa bhFéar, Feis & Cead Aighnis, The Fifty Minute Mermaid, The Askrakhan Cloak*

Éilís Ní Dhuibhne, *Selected Stories, The Shelter of Neighbours, Aisling Nó Iníon A, The Dancers Dancing*

Eithne Ní Ghallchobhair, *Loingseoireacht, Dhá Chluas Capaill ar Labhraí Loingseach, Cóisir sa Choill, Tomás na hOrdóige*

Colette Ní Ghallchóir, *An tAmharc Deireannach : The Last Look, Na Sióga i Lag na hAltóra, Idir Dhá Ghleann*

Colette Nic Aodha, *Bainne Géar : Spoilt Milk, Oíche Nollag na mBan sa bhFasach, In Castlewood : An Ghaoth Aduaidh, Scéal ón Oirthear*

Joan Newmann, *Prone, Coming of Age, Thin Ice, Circumcision Party*

Kate Newmann, *Grim, I Am a Horse, Belongings, The Blind Woman in the Blue House*

Liz Nugent, *Unravelling Oliver, Lying in Wait*

Micheál Ó Conghaile, *Diabhlaíocht Dé, Sna Fir, The Connemara Five, An Fear Nach nDéanann Gáire*

Simon Ó Faoláin, *Fé Sholas Luaineach, As Gaineamh, Anam Mhadra*

Pól Ó Muirí, *Srapnal, Acht, Milltown: A Belfast Novella, Seosamh Mac Grianna: Mireanna Saoil*

Liam Ó Muirthile, *Sceon na Mara, Sanas, Sister Elizabeth ag Eitilt, Walking Time*

Mícheál Ó Ruairc, *Dambatheanga : Damlanguage, Toraiocht Taisce, Caisleán Ghriaire, Na Luacha ag Rince*

Cathal Ó Searcaigh, *An Fear Glas : The Green Man, An Bhé Ghlas, An tAm Marfach ina Mairimid, Light on Distant Hills: A Memoir*

Edna O'Brien, *The Little Red Chairs, Saints and Sinners, Byron in Love, The Country Girls Trilogy*

Jean O'Brien, *Fish on a Bicycle, Merman, Lovely Legs, Dangerous Dresses*

Billy O'Callaghan, *The Dead House, The Things We Lose, The Things We Leave Behind, In Too Deep, In Exile*

Conor O'Callaghan, *Live Streaming, Nothing on Earth, The Sun King, Red Mist*

Eugene O'Connell, *In the Deep Heart's Core, Diviner, One Clear Call, Chapters of Little Times*

Jamie O'Connell, *Some Sort of Beauty, Best-Loved Joyce*

Clairr O'Connor, *So Far, Breast, Love in Another Room, Belonging*

Joseph O'Connor, *The Thrill of It All, Ghost Light, Star of the Sea, Where Have You Been?*

Nuala O'Connor, *Miss Emily, You, To the World of Men, Welcome, Tattoo : Tatú*

John O'Donnell, *On Water, Icarus Sees his Father Fly, Some Other Country*

Mary O'Donnell, *The Light-Makers, Those April Fevers, Where They Lie, The Ark Builders*

Roisín O'Donnell, *Wild Quiet*

Bernard O'Donoghue, *Farmers Cross, Outliving, Gunpowder, Poaching Rights*

Nessa O'Mahony, *Her Father's Daughter, In Sight of Home, Trapping a Ghost, Bar Talk*

Mary O'Malley, *Playing the Octopus, Valparaiso, A Perfect V, The Boning Hall*

Micheal O'Siadhail, *Tongues, The Gossamer Wall, Globe, Love Life*

Frank Ormsby, *The Darkness of Snow, Goat's Milk, Fireflies, The Ghost Train*

Siobhán Parkinson, *Miraculous Miranda, No Peace for Amelia, Painted Ladies, The World's Worst Mothers*

Julie Parsons, *The Therapy House, The Hourglass, The Courtship Gift, Mary, Mary*

Paul Perry, *Gunpowder Valentine, The Last Falcon and Small Ordinance, The Orchid Keeper, The Drowning of the Saints*

Louise Phillips, *The Game Changer, The Doll's House, Red Ribbons, Last Kiss*

Nicola Pierce, *Kings of the Boyne, Spirit of the Titanic, City of Fate, Behind the Walls*

Kevin Power, *Bad Day in Blackrock*

Elske Rahill, *Between Dog and Wolf, In White Ink*

E.M. Reapy, *Red Dirt*

John Redmond, *The Alexandra Sequence, MUDe, Thumb's Width, Poetry and Privacy*

Lucille Redmond, *Love and Other Stories, Who Breaks Up The Old Moons To Make New Stars*

Nell Regan, *One Still Thing, Preparing for Spring, Bound for Home, Helena Molony: A Radical Life*

Ger Reidy, *Jobs for a Wet Day, Before Rain, Drifting Under the Moon, Pictures from a Reservation*

Maurice Riordan, *The Water Stealer, The Holy Land, Floods, A Word from the Loki*

Moya Roddy, *Other People, The Long Way Home*

Ethel Rohan, *The Weight of Him, Cut Through the Bone*

Sally Rooney, *Conversations with Friends*

Gabriel Rosenstock, *Rogha Dánta, Orpheus in the Underpass, Sasquatch, The Partisan and Other Stories*

Orna Ross, *Her Secret Rose, After the Rising, Lovers' Hollow, A Dance in Time*

Dave Rudden, *Knights of the Borrowed Dark, The Forever Court, The Endless King*

Catherine Ryan Howard, *Distress Signals, Mousetrapped, Self-Printed*

Donal Ryan, *All We Shall Know, A Slanting of the Sun, The Thing About December, The Spinning Heart*

Séamus Scanlon, *Afterburn, The McGowan Trilogy, Irlanda en el Corazón, As Close as You'll Ever Be*

Mike Scott, *Adventures of a Waterboy*

Frank Sewell, *Modern Irish Poetry: A New Alhambra, Outside the Walls, Breaking the Skin, On the Side of Light: The Poetry of Cathal Ó Searcaigh*

Lorna Shaughnessy, *Anchored, Witness Trees, Mother Tongue, If We Have Lost Our Oldest Tales*

Eithne Shortall, *Love in Row 27*

Peter Sirr, *Sway, The Rooms, The Thing Is, Nonetheless*

Stephen James Smith, *Fear Not, Three Men Talking about Things they Kinda Know About*

Cherry Smyth, *Hold Still, One Wanted Thing, Test, Orange, When the Lights Go Up*

Damian Smyth, *Mesopotamia, Lamentations, Market Street, The Down Recorder*

Gerard Smyth, *The Yellow River, A Song of Elsewhere, The Fullness of Time, The Mirror Tent*

Dolores Stewart, *Presence of Mind, In Out of the Rain, An Cosán Dearg, 'Sé Sin le Rá*

Deirdre Sullivan, *Tangleweed and Brine, Needlework, Primperfect, Prim Improper*

Matthew Sweeney, *Inquisition Lane, Horse Music, The Night Post, Black Moon*

Rosita Sweetman, *Fathers Come First, On Our Backs, On Our Knees: Ireland 1972*

Anne Tannam, *Tides Shifting Across My Sitting Room Floor, Take This Life*

Alice Taylor, *Home for Christmas, Tea and Talk, The Woman of the House, To School Through the Fields*

Debbie Thomas, *Class Act, Monkie Business, Jungle Tangle, Dead Hairy*

Gráinne Tobin, *Banjaxed, The Nervous Flyer's Companion*

Colm Tóibín, *House of Names, The Master, Brooklyn, Nora Webster*

Jessica Traynor, *Liffey Swim*

Mary Turley-McGrath, *Other Routes, Forget the Lake, New Grass under Snow*

Breda Wall Ryan, *In a Hare's Eye*

Eamonn Wall, *Junction City, A Tour of Your Country, Sailing Lake Mareotis, Writing the Irish West*

William Wall, *The Yellow House, Hearing Voices Seeing Things, This is the Country, Ghost Estate*

Sarah Webb, *Aurora and the Popcorn Dolphin, The Shoestring Club, The Loving Kind, A Sailor Went to Sea, Sea, Sea*

David Wheatley, *The President of Planet Earth, A Nest on the Waves, Mocker, Misery Hill*

Sheena Wilkinson, *Name Upon Name, Too Many Ponies, Grounded, Taking Flight*

Joseph Woods, *Ocean Letters, Cargo, Bearings, Our Shared Japan*

Macdara Woods, *Music from the Big Tent, The Cotard Dimension, Artichoke Wine, Knowledge in the Blood*

Adam Wyeth, *The Art of Dying, Silent Music, The Hidden World of Poetry*

Enda Wyley, *Borrowed Space, Socrates in the Garden, The Silver Notebook, Boo and Bear*

THE EDITOR

Alan Hayes, *Washing Windows? Irish Women Write Poetry, The Irish Women's History Reader, A Century of Progress? Irish Women Reflect, Pauline Bewick at 75: A Photo Biography*